TELOS

A Quarterly Journal of Critical Thought
Number 62   Winter 1984-85

Special Issue on
Debates in Contemporary Culture

Table of Contents

Note on Contributors

A *Telos* editor, **RICHARD WOLIN** teaches history at Rice University in Houston, Texas. Another *Telos* editor, **RUSSELL A. BERMAN** teaches German literature at Stanford University in California. Yet another *Telos* editor, **JOAN ROELOFS** teaches political science in Keene College in New Hampshire. A frequent *Telos* contributor, **ALBRECHT WELLMER** will be teaching social theory in the New School for Social Research in New York. **PETER BÜRGER**'s book on *The Theory of the Avant-Garde* has just been translated into English by Minnesota University Press. He teaches French and comparative literature at the University of Bremen in West Germany. Presently on leave in Paris, **MARTIN JAY** normally teaches history at the University of California at Berkeley. Although now teaching philosophy in LaTrobe University in Melbourne, Australia, **AGNES HELLER** will be coming to teach philosophy in the New School for Social Research in New York next year. Presently working on a book in Rome, Italy, **VICTOR ZASLAVSKY** normally teaches sociology at Memorial University in St. John's, Newfoundland in Canada. **KENNETH ASHER** teaches English in Georgia Institute of Technology in Atlanta, Georgia. **JAMES D. HERBERT** is a graduate student in the Department of History of Art in Yale University. **DIANE GHIRARDO** teaches in the School of Architecture in the University of Southern California in Los Angeles, California. **DOUGLAS KELLNER** teaches philosophy in the University of Texas in Austin, Texas. **MOISHE GONZALES** teaches astrology in Oral Roberts University in Oklahoma. **CASEY BLAKE** teaches history in Reed College in Portland, Oregon. **MICHAEL S. ROTH** teaches history in Scripps College in Claremont, California. **ROBERT EHRLICH** teaches sociology at the University of California at Berkeley. **MICHAEL BERNHARD** and **JOSEPH MCCAHERY** are graduate students in political science and philosophy in Columbia University in New York City.

INTRODUCTION

It has been almost half a century since Horkheimer and Adorno formulated their analysis of mass culture in the "Culture Industry: Enlightenment as Mass Deception" chapter of *Dialectic of Enlightenment*. This special issue on "Debates in Contemporary Culture" is an attempt to evaluate the relevance of this legacy in the mid-eighties. It has become part of the left conventional wisdom that the critical theory analysis of late capitalism, focusing on concepts such as the "totally administered world" (Adorno) or "one-dimensional society" (Marcuse), was overly resigned and it remained unable to identify inchoate oppositional tendencies within the 'iron cage' of capitalist totalization. Since *culture* played such a leading role in their analysis, they claimed that in an era in which religion had dissolved as the primary means of social integration, mass culture had stepped in to fill the void — a new theory of culture is allegedly needed to account for new developments. After all, the repressive atmosphere of the cold war years gave way in the 1960s to a plethora of apparently non-conformist tendencies. And whereas the meaning of the short-lived era of anti-war protest, the New Left, and the counter-culture remains a debated issue, clearly the naive faith in 'the American way' suffered a setback and — the Reagan Revolution notwithstanding — many of the critical motifs from this period have become integrated in the contemporary cultural scene.

Consequently, there have been constant calls for an updating of the classical critical theory critique of mass culture. Yet, there seems to be little agreement as to precisely what form this updated cultural criticism should take. For example, in *Theory of Communicative Action*, Habermas browbeats his former Frankfurt School mentors for having remained indebted to a "philosophy of consciousness" which takes individually acting and speaking subjects as its point of departure. Instead, his *communicative* theory of action emphasizes the primacy of an *intersubjective* basis for the understanding of human action; and this changed perspective purports to have significant repercussions for cultural theory. The fallacy of Adorno et al., argues Habermas, was to believe that the culture industry represents a one-way, monolithic medium of communication. Instead, he emphasizes the fact that the messages of the culture industry are in the last analysis dependent on the way in which they are assimilated by the viewer, who can react either passively or critically. But even if one were to accept Habermas' claim that the culture industry falls short of monolithic status, a reified consciousness comfortably adjusted to its alienation does not dissipate overnight. The fact remains that 1) control of the mass media is far from democratic but still bureaucratically administered; and 2) most viewers' reactions to the culture industry's products remain quietistic and affirmative. Critical cultural awareness requires an autonomous subjectivity which cannot merely be philosophically postulated or deduced from

3

communication theory. Rather, it presupposes drastic transformations in both current processes of socialization and patterns of cultural consumption; both of which, regrettably, have remained formidably constant.

In a similar vein, recently there has been extensive praise for the allegedly untapped emancipatory potentials of mass culture. Here, the bad conscience of cultural privilege engages in a masochistic exercise in self-flagellation: merely because it is indulged in by 'masses' does not make mass culture an authentic expression of popular sentiments, longings, and hopes (something one could say more easily of popular culture in the past). A familiar process is at work. The lack of an existing "revolutionary subject" leads to a false projection whereby the masses in their sheer immediacy are endowed with a capacity for critical consciousness which could only result from a long and painstaking process of enlightenment.

Wolin's essay "Modernism vs. Postmodernism" attempts to trace the genesis of the contemporary cultural climate with particular emphasis on postmodernism. If the modern can be identified with the rationalist legacy of the Enlightenment, postmodernism emerges as a cynical detractor of modernity, turning its back on the illusions of progress and rational coherence. The dilemma lies in the fact that in the brave new world of postmodernism, the cure is more frightening than the disease. In the work of Derrida and Foucault, the critical theory theme of the 'end of the individual' is perversely turned into a praise, as the death of "man" and of the "subject" become the new desiderata for postmodern philosophy. In the cultural sphere, the postmodern sensibility tends to fetishize and promote a collapse of the boundaries between art and life to the detriment of both spheres. The net result is a flat and affirmative universe of aesthetic discourse, in which the critical capacities of autonomous art have been relinquished in favor of a pseudo-democratic, ephemeral emphasis on the sheer immediacy of aesthetic experience. As a general phenomenon, postmodernism is viewed as an unconscious expression of a broader socio-historical trend toward a cybernetic society, in which the glib postmodernist thesis concerning the 'end of man' threatens to become an accomplished fact.

The essays by Wellmer and Bürger attempt in similar ways to break through the aesthetic *cul-de-sac* of Adorno's critical theory, where the last bastion of negativity is said to reside in a select number of critical autonomous works of art which simultaneously stand as fragile images of "reconciliation." Wellmer's account is clearly indebted to Habermas. He faults Adorno for remaining too exclusively on the level of *intra-aesthetic* analysis and therefore neglecting the communicative potentials of art, which can only be fully appreciated from an approach that takes reception theory seriously. If works of art can be said to have a real relation to "reconciliation," this cannot merely transpire at the level of "aesthetic appearance," but requires that art play a role in the recipients' attitude toward themselves and life. According to Wellmer, however, while it would be unwise to recommend (as Bürger does at times) an immediate *sublation* of art in the domain of life, it is imperative that in the future greater links be forged between these two spheres so that the communicative potentials of art have an impact on consciousness and cognition. Ultimately, however, Wellmer's concrete proposals to bridge this gap, e.g., his emphasis on rock music as a possible manifestation of an "industrial folk culture," remain unsatisfying, at least in an era where rock appears to be largely an effective means of adolescent socialization.

Similarly, Bürger expresses impatience with Adorno's understanding of the avant-garde movement. Once modernism has been recuperated and its formerly radical techniques become the norm, it loses the potential for critique Adorno assigned to it. Hence the progressive artistic tendencies Adorno detects in Schoenberg's compositions no longer hold today: where artistic developments have become irreversibly pluralistic, a *single* canon will no longer suffice. This is the dilemma of postmodernism. Yet, in the last analysis, for Bürger the breach between the avant-garde and the postmodern might not be so total. Instead, the relevant works of postmodernism will both utilize the formal innovations achieved by the avant-garde and continue to question the "autonomy" of art in bourgeois society. Brecht's work thus tends to become a model for these new tendencies.

While Wolin draws attention to the theoretical inadequacy of the postmodernist discourse and Bürger insists on the historical prematurity of the corollary announcement of an epochal break, both take as their starting point the contemporary fascination with cultural practices that have allegedly displaced the forms of historical modernism and the avant-garde movements of the early twentieth century. However one evaluates the pretenses of postmodernism (Wellmer and Berman provide alternative accounts), there can no longer be any doubt that the enthusiasm which formerly accompanied the project of a supersession of life and art has disappeared; the avant-garde's attack on the bourgeois institution of art, which envisioned a radical social transformation on the basis of aesthetic innovation, has left behind a repeatedly broken *promesse de bonheur*. The trajectory of dadaist vanguardism mirrors its Leninist cousin: the revolution guarantees heteronomy in Western culture and Soviet society. This parallel is less abstract than it may seem, as Herbert's archaeology of the origins of modernist art criticism in the United States demonstrates. The orthodox revolutionism of Greenberg and Rosenberg in their Marxist phase turns into the elitist defense of abstract expressionism, the prototype of an American modernism. It is however less a matter of an intellectual history of Marxist aesthetics than a chapter in the recuperative institutionalization of the avant-garde. The anti-bourgeois art of the erstwhile bohemia surrenders its critical edge and becomes the ornamental decoration of established society. Abstract art has done away with wallpaper in banks, and the "great works" of literary modernism, considered scandalous half a century ago, have become standard fare in university English departments. This is no mere shift in taste. A critical theory of culture is challenged to explain how cultural institutions like art criticism or the universities function as both instigators and neutralizers of cultural innovation. Roelofs' description of the role of foundations — motors of social change in order to preserve the status quo — is particularly suggestive and needs to be expanded into an inquiry into the specific management of the aesthetic discussion.

If Herbert shows the demise of the critical import of institutionalized modernism, Ghirardo demonstrates the fallacy of attributing an emancipatory potential to post-modernism in architecture, where it has achieved its most salient prominence. Classical modernist architecture, i.e., the international style of Bauhaus, was historically subject to a variety of attacks: a conservative historicism attacked its "soulless" abstraction, while a social conservatism resented its association with social-democratic public housing projects, especially in Weimar Germany. Transported to the United States in the Thirties, the international style soon lost its political content and provided the blueprints for the urban renewal of downtown centers and the urban removal of working-class communities, which generated a new political critique from the left. The advocates of post-modernist building renew the aesthetic critique and therefore return to a neo-historicism, characterized by a radical eclecticism and an extreme fashion consciousness. In their consistent disregard for the social implications of construction (the need for low-income housing), they follow in the footsteps of the international-style building during its commodified phase; despite all the polemics, the difference between modernist and post-modernist architecture tends to boil down to more color, cute facades and, of course, lots of business.

The post-modernist claim that the abstraction of modernist architecture disoriented the public echoes the neo-conservative critique that modern art fosters an atomizing hedonism and undermines authority. "Legible" buildings, i.e. neo-historicism, consequently converge with the imposition of neo-humanist "Western Culture" requirements in university curricula, both corollaries to the conservative political shift. As Asher shows, a similar tendency is evident in the spread of deconstructive precepts in the literary critical establishment. Despite its occasional radical claims and its attention to breaks and ruptures (rather than the organic unity perpetually found by the old New Critics), deconstruction repeats the critical practice of New Criticism by restricting its attention to the canonic literary texts. The canon of course shifts from the modernism of Joyce and Proust, favored by the older generation, to the purported post-modernism of Beckett, Borges and Pynchon, but both critical schools recoil in horror at the thought of reflecting on the interaction of text and social context. In addition, Asher points out the highly selective reading of Nietzsche on which this literary critical strategy is based; the substance of his attacks on historical liberalism, Christianity and bourgeois society are dropped, and only the rejection of an objectivist understanding of truth remains. The academy reassures itself once again that its speech is at best self-referential.

Post-modernism is hardly an answer to the failings of modernism, but it may well be, as Berman suggests, a consequence of the modernist success in delegitimizing the traditional organic work of art *and* in carrying out an aestheticization of everyday life. This dual project of the historical avant-garde bears fruit in the second half of the twentieth century but without any of the promised emancipatory consequences. Contemporary aesthetic production loses the critical edge of earlier artistic innovation and is constantly recuperated by a feverish art-market. Even the distinction between high culture and popular forms, a central tenet of Adorno's aesthetics, has dwindled thanks to the commuter shuttle between Soho and the South Bronx: grafitti and break-dance have made it to the galleries. Conversely, everyday life undergoes a massive invasion by artistic form: Muzak, life-styles and the aestheticization of politics in the grand spectacles of the party conventions. The ubiquity of the culture industry explodes the version provided in the *Dialectic of the Enlightenment* which still referred largely only to specific products like films. The universalization of art leads in fact to a revised instinctual economy — not, however, as the neo-conservatives claim, to a plummeting work ethic but rather to an exacerbated aggressiveness and a recrudescent nationalism. The *Gesamtkunstwerk* of the post-modern age is the invasion of Grenada.

The expansion of the culture industry as the legacy of the avant-garde may perhaps generate new political contradictions and potentials: traditional signs of authority lose their credibility and, once culture becomes the ineluctable medium of domination, it could also become a terrain for opposition. However the indications of an effective counter-hegemonic cultural practice are few and far between, and the claims of left-wing post-modernists and others regarding the emancipatory potential of so-called "popular" culture — does it really belong to the populace or to CBS? — are hardly credible. Kellner does his best to find an example of a progressive culture industry in the "Holocaust" series, but a half a decade after the allegedly profound responses in West Germany, the left is flirting with neo-nationalism. Hollywood liberalism may occasionally play around with ideological expressions that liberals may care to interpret as progressive, but the impact of this or that film or rock star remains embedded in the commercial structure and the overall organization of culture. An emancipatory response to the culture industry still can only mean rejection. As Gonzales points out, only by covertly deploying long-since discredited Marxist-Leninist illusions about realism, competitive capitalism and the irrepressibly progressive character of history can Kellner "transcend" the old culture industry thesis. But in so doing he only ends up with a Panglossian theoretical regression.

On a different topic, Zaslavsky criticizes the ethnocentric imposition of unsuitable Western criteria to analyze Soviet society, Jay criticizes some recent attacks on hierarchy, and Heller points out how, in light of recent developments Lukács, Adorno, Bloch and others of that generation shared much more than they may have been willing to admit.

Russell A. Berman   Paul Piccone   Richard Wolin

MODERNISM VS. POSTMODERNISM

by Richard Wolin

It is well known that in his "Author's Introduction" (1920) to the "Collected Essays on the Sociology of World Religions"[1] Max Weber grapples with the problem of the cultural specificity of the West. He phrases his inquiry in the following way: Why is it "that in Western civilization, and in Western civilization only, cultural phenomena have appeared which (as we like to think) lie in a line of development having universal significance and value"?[2] He continues to cite a wealth of cultural phenomena — systematic theology, the rational concept, standardized methods of scientific experimentation, rational harmonious music, extensive utilization of perspective in painting, bureaucratic conduct of the organizational sphere, and the systematic rational pursuit of economic affairs — that are unique to the West and illustrative of its self-avowed universality.

Yet, the historical emergence of these various cultural developments by no means occurred simultaneously. It is to Judaism that we owe the advent of systematic, monotheistic theology, to ancient Greece the birth of the rational concept, to the Renaissance the emergence of the principles of scientific experimentation and perspective in the arts, and to the Reformation the appearance of the 'this-worldly asceticism' of the Protestant ethic which becomes the hallmark and sine qua non for the extraordinary rationalization of life conduct characteristic of the capitalist spirit. Only when all of the aforementioned variables have been allowed to establish themselves and combine into a single comprehensive ethos — usually designated by Weber by the category of 'rationalization' — does 'modernity' in the full sense of the term emerge. Its emergence corresponds to a world-historical process of crystallization that transpires over the course of the 15th, 16th, and 17th centuries or the 'early modern' period. However, its definitive form is not achieved until the 18th century, with the transition from the absolutist to democratic eras. As Jürgen Habermas has pointed out,[3] it is during this period that the

---

1. In English the "Author's Introduction" appears in *The Protestant Ethic and the Spirit of Capitalism,* trans. by Talcott Parsons (New York, 1958), pp. 13-31.

2. Here, attention should be called to the important parenthetic qualification "as we like to think." This phrase reminds us that what strikes us as 'universal' only takes on this character from within the perspective of our own received value-orientation, and hence can not fully lay claim to a more transcendent value-universality. Ultimately Weber's own (scientific) standpoint is *ethically relativistic* — ultimate ends cannot be rationally adjudicated — therefore even with regards to the West.

3. *Theorie des Kommunikativen Handelns* (Frankfurt am Main, 1981), 2 vols. See especially the Weber interpretation, pp. 225-365.

absolute breach between traditional and modern societies is instituted. This is the age which witnesses the irrevocable transition from societies based on *cosmological* world-views to those based on *de-centered* or *differentiated* world-views. Consequently, society is no longer characterized by the predominance of a single, monolithic value-system which pervades and structures its various partial subsystems. Instead, the latter are henceforth allowed to pursue their own inherent 'inner logics.' These developments allow for a hitherto unprecedented proliferation of individually functioning 'value-spheres' which becomes the signature of the modern age. The primary value-spheres which are relaesed in this process are those of science, morality, and art.[4] Concretely, this means that each of these spheres is 'rationalized' in that they no longer need a priori invoke the authority of an antecedent and determinative cosmological standpoint to legitimate themselves, but instead become self-validating, i.e., they gain their right to exist in terms of a set of *internally developed criteria*. While in principle Weber acknowledged the validity of all three spheres, in his scientific work he concentrated above all on the first form of rationality, scientific or rational-purposive active, whose predominance he viewed as the defining feature of modern culture.[5] Ultimately, he contravenes his own conception of the significance of modernity by judging the other two value spheres — morality and art — in terms of criteria taken over from the scientific sphere, and then branding these as formally irrational.[6]

Today it would be an understatement to claim that the legacy of modernity has fallen under suspicion — in truth, it has fallen victim to a frontal assault from all quarters. The writings of the utopian socialists in the early nineteenth century,[7] still exuded the optimism characteristic of Enlightenment philosophies of history. By the end of the century such ebullient expectations, still a driving motif in Marx's work, had succumbed to a host of disillusioned anti-rationalist trends associated with the names 'decadence,' 'vitalism,' and 'nihilism.' This intellectual mood, so pervasive in the final two decades of the last century, signals a decisive historical rejection of the entire heritage of modernity; and its most formidable exponent, Nietzsche, is often celebrated as the spiritual godfather of contemporary attempts to escape from the modernist-rationalist legacy[8] — attempts which, by virture of this much heralded breach, are associated with the banner of the 'post-modern' or 'post-modernism.'[9]

---

4.   One can see that the fundamental achievements of this era receive their philosophical authentication in the three *Critiques* of Kantian philosophy, to which the aforementioned value spheres correspond.

5.   Cf. Max Weber, *Economy and Society* Vol. I, Guenther Roth and Claus Wittich, eds. (Berkeley, 1978), pp. 3-62.

6.   Habermas's own reconstruction of Weber's system revolves around the attempt to re-establish the independent validity of the two neglected value spheres of morality and art, and in this way overcome Weber's self-professed ethical relativism.

7.   For the best survey of their writings, see Frank E. Manuel, *The Prophets of Paris* (Cambridge, Mass., 1962).

8.   Prototypical in this respect is Gilles Deleuze, *Nietzsche and Philosophy* (New York, 1983).

9.   For a representative illustration of this perspective, see Jean-François Lyotard, *La Condition Postmoderne* (Paris, 1979).

That the attacks on the principle of modernity have come from variegated and diverse sources makes it at times difficult to pinpoint its ideological tenor with precision. Some have attempted to lump the authors of *Dialectic of Enlightenment* among the post-modernist set.[10] However, despite Adorno's avowed preference for non-discursive modes of rationality,[11] he and Horkheimer always emphasized the *dialectical* character of enlightenment reason; hence, ratiocination is in no way condemned *tout court*, only its dogmatic, inflexible, 'recidivist' side. In addition, the trenchant critique of Nietzsche in the aforementioned work should serve as a sober reminder to all such precipitate attempts at classification.[12]

For the sake of greater precision in defining the nature of this controversy, the present essay will focus on the third of the aforementioned three value-spheres — the sphere of aesthetic rationality — in order to gauge its significance in the 'modernism vs. postmodernism' debate.

When we speak of art in terms of its import for the paradigm of modernity, we refer to the unfettered right of the artist to independent self-expression. We moderns assume this right to be self-evident, whereas in fact it is essentially an achievement of recent origin, post-dating centuries in which art was fully implicated in the legitimation of what Weber termed 'traditional authority' — be it in the form of myth (Homer's *Iliad*), religion (medieval Christian painting), or the divine right of kings (courtly art). This embeddedness of art in traditional world-views is what Walter Benjamin has described as its 'cultic function';[13] the latter stands in contrast to the 'exhibition value' of art, that is, the fully secularized status art achieves in the eighteenth century, when it comes to play a constitutive communicative role in the formation of the bourgeois public sphere.

It is Habermas who has analyzed the essential role played by art as a vehicle for generating what might be described as post-conventional subjective identities in his work *Strukturwandel der Öffentlichkeit (Structural Transformation of the Public Sphere).* Here he demonstrates, with special reference to the eighteenth century epistolary novel, the indispensable role played by this new art form in the public conveyance of subjective experiences, and thus in the process of identity-formation, for the rising bourgeois class. While Habermas recognizes, on the one hand, the truncated character of the humanitarian values flaunted in works such as *Pamela, La Nouvelle Heloise,* and *Werther* — above all, the values of love, education, and freedom, which remain confined to the

10.   See, e.g., Fred Dallmayr, *The Twilight of Subjectivity* (Amherst, 1981); Habermas has suggested a similar classification in a recent essay, "The Entwinement of Myth and Enlightenment," *New German Critique* 26 (Summer 1982), pp. 13-30.

11.   Cf. both *Negative Dialectics* (New York, 1973) and *Aesthetic Theory* (London, 1984). Despite this preference, let it be said that even Adorno's apparent partiality for aesthetic over discursive rationality is based on his conception of aesthetics as embodying a higher principle of *rationality.* In the last analysis, he falls in line with an eminently Hegelian, rationalist aesthetics of content in his conviction that works of art are ultimately "sensuous embodiments of the idea."

12.   Max Horkheimer and Theodor Adorno, *Dialectic of Enlightenment* (New York, 1973), "Juliette or Enlightenment and Morality," pp. 81-119.

13.   Cf. Walter Benjamin, "The Work of Art in the Age of Mechanical Reproduction," in *Illuminations* (New York, 1969), pp. 217-252.

bourgeois (private) sphere of *Innerlichkeit* or inwardness — he deems these values themselves authentically universalistic.[14] However, he is wholly without cynicism with regard to the late eighteenth century bourgeois public sphere as an ideal model of communicative praxis, whose original universalistic promise is revoked once the newly victorious bourgeoisie turns conservative with reference to the threatening prospect of the extension of these values beyond the borders of its own class interests. Hence, in Habermas' account, the original promise of bourgeois publicity itself ultimately turns into a 'novel of disillusionment' as this promise is progressively revoked through a process of increasing commercialization, culminating (like Horkheimer and Adorno before him) apocalyptically in the 'culture industry' of late capitalism.[15]

Habermas' depiction of the genesis of classical bourgeois publicity is relevant in the present context insofar as it convincingly demonstrates the impressive *communication potential* possessed by bourgeois post-conventional or autonomous art; a potential which serves as an instructive contrast to the subsequent line of development of bourgeois autonomous art — expressed in a word, its subsequent progressive *esotericization*. Esotericization is the corollary on the 'autonomous' side of the ledger for bourgeois art which, having undergone bifurcation, on the other side regressed to 'cult' in the form of *entertainment literature* (music, cinema, etc.). Such is the fate of art in the bourgeois era: it undergoes a process of dichotomization between 'high' and 'low' forms; and whereas the former maintain allegiance to the original principle of aesthetic autonomy — the process of authentic subjective self-expression — it only succeeds in this task at the expense of the moment of *generalizability*; the moment which then attaches to the 'low sphere.'[16]

It is in large measure the tension generated between these two spheres that accounts for the *dynamism* that becomes the distinguishing feature of aesthetic modernism. That is, the increasing commodification of what was once 'popular culture,' the vast proliferation of entertainment media, compels autonomous art to undergo a series of successive, ever-more radical self-transformations in order to remain abreast of the tide threatening to engulf it from below and thereby remain faithful to the newly established principle of aesthetic autonomy. The developmental history of bourgeois culture is itself a story of disillusionment or abandoned ideals. This process can be traced, in

---

14.   Cf. Habermas, *Strukturwandel der Offentlichkeit* (Neuweid, 1976), pp. 60-69.

15.   Although at this early point (1962) Habermas seemed in accord with Horkheimer and Adorno's view of the culture industry, in his most recent work he definitely is not. In *Theorie des Kommunakativen Handelns* he is of the opinion that rather than being a 'one-way street,' the mass media are at least as dependent on the way in which their communications are received by the community of recipients.

16.   These are of course the chief lines of controversy in the Adorno-Benjamin dispute of the 1930s. For more on this debate, see Richard Wolin, *Walter Benjamin: An Aesthetic of Redemption* (New York, 1982), pp. 163-212. For more on the dichotomy between 'high' and 'low' art, see C. Burger, P. Büger, J. Schulte-Sasse, eds., *Zur Dichotomisierung von hoher und niederer Literatur* (Frankfurt am Main, 1982). See also, Sandor Radnoti, "Mass Culture," *Telos* 48 (Summer, 1981), pp. 27-47. And for a classical discussion of these themes, Leo Löwenthal, *Literature, Populas Culture, and Society* (Palo Alto, 1961).

the literary domain, from the *Bildungsroman* of the late eighteenth and early nineteenth century (a classical example thereof being Goethe's *Wilhelm Meister*), where the prospect of a reconciliation with reality remains intact, to the novel of disillusionment (e.g., Stendahl's *The Red and the Black*), in which the hopes of the *Bildungsroman* are disconsolately abandoned, to the modern 'novel of consciousness' (Proust, Joyce), where all truck with an empirical world perceived as inherently inimical to spirit is relinquished and the novelist thrown back on the resources of his or her own private 'memoire involuntaire.' From the foregoing, it is easy to see that this process entails a progressive artistic renunciation of the bourgeois world of 'objective spirit' and concomitant subjectivization of narrative orientation and structure (the wholesale shift from the third person singular to first person singular narrative voice), resulting in the forfeiture of the domain of 'generalizable experiences' of the original literary public sphere. Certainly, it is not the artist him or herself who is to blame for this state of affairs — as cultural conservatives are wont to claim — but rather developments in the domain of objective spirit itself (e.g., the growing subordination of hiterto autonomous realms of social action — family, school, leisure time — to the media of formal rationality and exchange value). It is the dénouement or culmination of this developmental tendency that is associated with the birth of *literary modernism*. Its defining characteristics, in addition to subjectivization of narrative structure, are an increased self-referentiality, autonomy of literary 'signifiers,' disruption of chronological temporality, and rejection of the classical ideal of the rounded, holistic, integrated work.

At the same time, in recent years an important debate has arisen over the periodization of literary modernism in relation to the twentieth century or historical avant-garde: a debate spurred by Peter Bürger's 1974 study *The Theory of the Avant-garde.*[17] According to Bürger, at issue is a transformation from quantity to quality within the value-sphere of bourgeois autonomous art. Whereas one of the signal features of aesthetic modernism was a concerted assault on any and everything traditional — in the well known words of Rimbaud, "Il faut être absolument moderne" — these attacks, for all their vehemence, ultimately fell short of challenging the bourgeois 'institution of art' as it was originally constituted in the eighteenth century. That is, no matter how far their radicalism went, these works in the last instance remained fully consistent with the ideal of aesthetic autonomy; ultimately, their values were thoroughly *aestheticist*. According to Bürger, this ceases to be the case with the twentieth century avant-garde, an artistic trend synonymous with the proliferation of aesthetic 'isms' in the first two decades of this century: futurism, constructivism, dadaism, and, most importantly, surrealism. For the avant-garde is distinguished not so much by an attack on traditional works of art as by an attack on the ideal of works of art per se as something *separated from life-praxis* — i.e., as defined by the value of aesthetic autonomy as established by

---

17. P. Bürger, *Theorie der Avantgarde* (Frankfurt am Main, 1974); an English translation of this work has recently appeared with University of Minnesota Press.

the bourgeois institution of art. In no uncertain terms, it is the principle of aesthetic autonomy itself that becomes insupportable to the historical avant-garde, that is, the bourgeois affirmative ideal of culture as a sphere of beautiful illusion in which the values denied in the realm of (workaday) material life can be safely enjoyed.[18] To be sure, bourgeois aestheticism, most commonly associated with the mid-nineteenth century doctrine of *l'art pour l'art* or art for art's sake, was always a phenomenon laced with ambivalence. As 'affirmative' as it may have been, it retained an indefeasible critical moment inasmuch as the images of reconciled life it projected always served as a potential indict-ment of the prosaic material world in which these ideals were repulsed. Nevertheless, in Bürger's view, the avant-garde perceived such aestheticist modes of negation as ultimately ineffectual and thus adopted as its program the reintegration *(Aufhebung)* of art in the domain of life-praxis, the transposi-tion of the beautiful illusion from the realm of art to the sphere of empirical reality itself. In this sense, the avant-garde no longer produces 'works of art,' but rather 'demonstrations' *(Manifestationen* — here Bürger is thinking above all of the dadaist fondness for displaying *objets trouvés*).[19]

A few critical remarks concerning Bürger's useful classification, which has elsewhere been subjected to thoroughgoing criticism,[20] are in order. It is undoubtedly the case that it is necessary and fruitful to distinguish between literary modernism and the twentieth century avant-garde; a distinction often wanting in Anglo-American critical discourse where the two are usually dealt with synonymously under the rubric of 'modernism.' Indeed, the aesthetic objectifications of the avant-garde contain at times a radical attack on the traditional concept of the integral work of art that even modernism would find difficult to countenance. Conversely, it is easy to see that literary modernism, for all its iconoclasm and railing against the constraints of tradition, remains committed to several key pillars of the aestheticist program — above all, to the principle of the completed work of art as an end in itself. In this respect, one would have to deem modernism consistent with the aesthetic line of develop-ment initiated with 'art for art's sake.'

However, Bürger's characterization of the avant-garde in terms of the slogan 'the overcoming of art in the realm of life-praxis' remains precipitate and overly simplistic. This standpoint retains some plausibility in the cases of Russian constructivism — which is committed to turning art into a comrade-in-arms in the process of social modernization and industrialization — and Italian futurism — for which art should serve as an apocalyptical summons to martial virtue.[21] It is clear that for both of these movements, their links to determinate historical programs of social transformation have endowed

---

18.   For more on this point, cf. Herbert Marcuse's essay "The Affirmative Character of Cul-ture," *Negations* (Boston, 1968), pp. 88-133, in which he too argues for the overcoming of art in the domain of life-praxis.

19.   *Theorie der Avantgarde, op. cit.,* pp. 68 ff.

20.   See the volume edited by W.M. Lüdke, *'Theorie der Avantgarde': Antworten auf Peter Bürgers Bestimmung von Kunst und Burgerlieher Gesellschaft* (Frankfurt, 1976).

21.   Cf. *Marinetti: Selected Writings,* R.W. Flint, ed. (New York, 1971).

them with a certain ephemeral quality. The same might well be said of dadaist 'provocations' and 'ready-mades'; once the attitude of 'épater le bourgeois' is turned into an aesthetic program, its products soon cease to shock, and to the undoubted dismay of its original proponents, it too soon finds its 'ready-made' niche in museums and courses in modern art history. (Is this perhaps the reason that Duchamp, whose "Urinoir" remains the best known dadaist object, feigned the renunciation of artistic endeavor for the last 45 years of his life in favor of chess?)

Yet, in the case of surrealism, undoubtedly the most charismatic and pro-lific of the twentieth century avant-garde movements, Bürger's classificatory scheme would stand in drastic need of revision. As suggested by the preceding account of avant-garde movements, the aesthetic program for the merging of art and life praxis stands under the sign of *ephemerality*. Or, as Adorno once remarked with reference to the Brechtian/Sartrean aesthetics of 'engage-ment,' such "works of art merely assimilate themselves sedulously to the brute existence against which they protest, in forms so ephemeral that from the very first day they belong to the seminars in which they inevitably end."[22] Ephemerality is the result of the renunciation of the concept of the integral work of art for the sake of extra-aesthetic *effect*. This is not the sign under which surrealism stands; and for this reason its works retain their status to this day as avant-garde exemplars. Bürger fails to take cognizance of the fact that for all the notoriety André Breton's injunction, "pratiquer le poésie," has received, surrealism very much maintains allegiance to the principles of aesthetic autonomy. From the standpoint of the history of the movement, this alle-giance was affirmed by Breton's decision in 1929 to preserve the sovereign powers of the aesthetic imagination over against Aragon's willingness to place them at the beck and call of Stalin.[23] At the same time, when the achievement of the movement is viewed from a work-immanent standpoint, it is clear that whether one takes a poem by Eluard, a 'romance' by Breton or (the pre-1929) Aragon, or a painting by Dali, one is considering aesthetic products at an infinite remove from dadaist 'objets trouvés.' The latter possess a shock-effect which dissipates after the initial act of reception; the former are aesthetic enigmas which invite decipherment. One need only recall the fact that in his seminal "Surrealism" essay of 1929, Walter Benjamin, a precocious observer of the French avant-garde scene in the 1920s, feared above all that the move-ment would remain incapable of transcending its autonomous phase (in which it was still beholden to a series of 'pernicious romantic prejudices' con-cerning the role of art) and thus unable to accommodate itself to the "con-structive, dictatorial side of revolution" (sic).[24]

22. Theodor Adorno, "Commitment," in *The Essential Frankfurt School Reader,* A. Arato and E. Gebhardt, eds. (New York, 1978), p. 301.

23. For a superb discussion of this episode in the history of the movement, see Maurice Nadeau, *The History of Surrealism* (New York, 1973), pp. 169-188. Bürger might also take note of the title of the chapter of Nadeau's survey which covers the years 1930-39: "The Period of *Autonomy*" (italics mine), pp. 191-229.

24. Benjamin, "Surrealism," in *Reflections* (New York, 1978), p. 189.

In order to conceptualize adequately the status of surrealism both in relation to conventional bourgeois aestheticism (*l'art pour l'art*) and the more 'engaged' wings of the avant-garde, Bürger's theoretical framework would be in need of a third term: de-aestheticized autonomous art. This category signifies that surrealism's uniqueness consists in its having simultaneously negated the aura of affirmation characteristic of art for art's sake while remaining consistent with the 'modern' requirement of aesthetic autonomy. The latter feature ensures that the truth-content of surrealism will not merely evaporate immediately in the moment of reception, as tends to be the case for *l'art engagé*. As such, the essence of surrealism is most accurately grasped when it is viewed as an *intra-aesthetic attack on bourgeois aestheticism.* This means that surrealism self-consciously divests itself of the beautiful illusion, the aura of reconciliation, projected by art for art's sake, while at the same time refusing to overstep the boundaries of aesthetic autonomy, beyond which art degenerates to the status of merely a 'thing among things.' Even Bürger, basing himself on Benjamin's theory of allegory, ultimately recognizes the means surrealism employs to distinguish itself from auratic art: a renunciation of the aestheticist ideal of the rounded, integral work of art in favor of the notion of the *fragmentary work.* Surrealism proffers fragmentary works of art, which are nonetheless *still works.* In this respect, it remains, in spirit and actuality, much closer to the domain of literary modernism than to its immediate historical precursor, dada.

From a contemporary standpoint it has become an undeniable fact that the efforts of the historical avant-garde have entered into a state of profound crisis. The dilemma to which it has fallen victim displays the following traits. So dependent were these movements upon elements of shock, provocation, scandal, and (most notably in the case of dada) sheer outrage that, once these artistic tactics become familiar, predictable, and routinized, they too become conventional. Put simply, *newness itself has become traditional,* it has become the new aesthetic canon and achieved a type of bourgeois respectability that would have been anathema to its originators. It is no longer unusual (nor has it been for quite some time) to see non-figurative paintings of all varieties adorning the offices of bank presidents. One of the first to note the phenomenon of the 'recuperation of modernism' was Lionel Trilling, who for that reason refused to teach Joyce, Kafka, Proust, etc. in his Columbia University seminars rather than aid and abet the universal domestication of these authors and their radical impulses.[25] Compounding the identity crisis of the avant-garde is the fact that what is perhaps its central principle of construction — the principle of montage — has by now become the standard modus operandi of the advertising industry, which is interested in 'shocking' the viewer into appreciating the uniqueness of its wares.[26] Hence, the historical avant-garde seems

25.   Lionel Trilling, "On the Modern Element in Modern Literature," in *Literary Modernism,* Irving Howe, ed. (New York, 1967), pp. 59-82.

26.   For more on the technique of montage, which is of course originally derived from film, and which may be defined in terms of the anti-organicist ideal of the independence of the parts *vis-à-vis* the whole, see Bürger, *Theorie der Avantgarde,* pp. 98-111.

threatened with 'normalization' from both above and below.[27] For all of these reasons, the Hegelian thesis concerning the 'end of art' would seem extremely topical.[28]

Of course, Hegel formulated his verdict with respect to the transition from neo-classicism to romanticism in the latter years of the eighteenth century, when it had become evident to him that the extremely subjective and idiosyncratic character of romanticism had made the monumentalism of classical Greek art forever a thing of the past. Yet, art persevered and continues, despite its present crisis, to persevere. The question thus arises: what is the status of the avant-garde legacy in relationship to contemporary art?

The answer to this question hinges on an appraisal of the diverse postwar artistic currents associated with the term *postmodernism*. Perhaps the most basic point of reference for the phenomenon of 'postmodernism' is the American reception of the historical avant-garde following the Second World War, although certainly it is a trend that has made itself felt across the Atlantic as well (where it was perhaps best represented by the *nouveau roman* of Robbe-Grillet and Sarraute). Initially, its best known exponents were the abstract expressionists of the 'New York School' of painting, a generation of American artists that was influenced decisively by the surrealist community-in-exile during the war years.[29] The abstract expressionists were later noted for the techniques of 'tachism' or 'action painting,' methods of composition distinguished by arbitrariness, randomness, and spontaneity. In this respect, their method seems to be the logical painterly corollary to the surrealist technique of automatic writing. All emphasis on artistic foresight and construction was renounced; and the idea of non-figurative painting is carried to an extreme, insofar as the last vestiges of 'representation' or 'subject matter' are extirpated, in keeping with the assault, dating back to cubism, on the inherent illusoriness of the striving for three-dimensionality (perspective) on a two-dimensional surface. The aural complement to these developments was the aleatory music of John Cage, with its analogous penchant for compositional contingency.

The New York School of the 1950s remained sufficiently indebted to its immediate historical antecedent, surrealism, such that it qualifies as a *transitional stage* on the path leading form the historical avant-garde to postmodernism. It keeps one foot in each camp, as it were. What is especially noticeable

27. For one of the earliest proclamations of the crisis of the avant-garde, see H.M. Enzensberger, "The Aporias of the Avant-Garde," in *The Consciousness Industry* (New York, 1974).

28. Cf. *Hegel's Aesthetics,* trans. by I.M. Knox (London, 1975), p. 11: "In all these respects art, considered in its highest vocation, remains for us a thing of the past. Therefore it has lost for us genuine truth and life, and has rather been transferred into our *ideal* instead of maintaining its earlier necessity in reality and occupying its higher place . . . The *philosophy* of art is therefore a greater need in our day than it was in days when art by itself as art yielded full satisfaction. Art invites us to intellectual consideration, and that not for the purpose of creating art again, but for knowing philosophically what art is."

29. For a recent examination of the relationship between the European avant-garde and the New York School, see Serge Guilbaut, *How New York Stole the Idea of Modern Art* (New York, 1983). See the excellent review of this book by Casey Blake in this issue of *Telos*.

about this school is the abandonment of a concern for the relationship between art and everyday life, and the concomitant political implications of this program — a problematic central for so many of the historical avant-garde movements. Yet, this alienation from everyday life lends it distinct affinities with the more aestheticist qualities of surrealist painting. In the case of abstract expressionism, this alienation from everyday life has its sociological origins in the 'one-dimensionality' of the cold war years.

The other noteworthy feature of abstract expressionism is the fact that it carries the avant-garde attack on the romanticist aesthetics of genius to an extreme in its attempted wholesale renunciation of the form-giving capacities of the artist (tachism, aleatory music). For this reason it stands under the regressive sign of the *eclipse of the subject* (cf. the comparable tendency in the *nouveau roman*), a phenomenon which will become increasingly characteristic of the postmodernist sensibility.

It is not, however, until the 1960s that the phenomenon of postmodernism appears full-blown on the American cultural scene. Leading the charge is, once again, the field of painting — riding the crest of momentum provided by the international acclaim accorded the New York School. In this decade it is almost impossible to keep up with the breakneck pace of seasonal changes in artistic fashion: here we have pop, op, conceptual, and body art, minimalism, happenings, etc. A final breach with the absorption and concentration demanded of the viewer by modernist works of art is effected. No conceptual demands whatsoever are placed on the recipient. The effect conveyed by these works of art is one of *unadulterated immediacy*; they possess the immediacy of dadaist aesthetic experience, minus the shock, which has become institutionalized and domesticated. The avant-garde program of the reintegration of art and life-praxis is stood on its head. This program aimed at the reconciliation of culture and material life once the latter itself had been transformed through the forces of aesthetic intoxication. Postmodernist art, conversely, assumes a benign ethic of adjustment. The radical oppositional stance adopted by the historical avant-garde *vis-à-vis* the aura of reconciliation projected by traditional bourgeois aestheticism is wholly relinquished in favor of a new semblance of harmony and affirmation. In essence, a new reconciliation between art and reality is proclaimed; in this sense postmodernism behaves as if the radical transformation of material life had already been achieved. Since this is in fact not the case, what results is merely the *false sublation of autonomous art*. The new marriage between art and a 'bad facticity' can be seen in the choice of artistic subject matter for pop: the detritus of everyday life re-emerges, transfigured, glorified (literally: larger than life), in Warhol's silk-screens, which become indistinguishable from an 'ad campaign.' The throwback to representation in pop fully reveals art's new regressive being-at-home-in-the-world.

The regressive tendencies of pop have been enumerated by one critic as follows: "Pop art denies the autonomy and immanence of the individual work. The picture of a girl in a swimming costume by Roy Lichtenstein shows

no more individual traits than Andy Warhol's cans. Their simple une-
quivocality and formulaic nature, their sharp outlines and monotones, their
schematic drawing and compositions — which lacks any tension — everything about them contradicts the individuality of the work of art in general and
points to its reproducibility in this particular case. . . . Every one of these
works is . . . conceivable in an infinite number of examples and antithetical to
what is individual and unique. . . . Pop painting thus is not only commercial
in spirit like the other forms of pop art, but also uses techniques of the commercial media, placards, magazine illustrations, and newspaper advertisements. . . . It does not depend upon the impressing of actual articles but on
their schematized representation in media of commercial advertising. . . . Instead of immediate reproductions, it consists of quotations from a text which
already represents the material of reality as translated into artifacts. We can see
in this second-hand retreat from the original data just as many signs of fear of
coming into contact with natural reality as of the expression of the perception
that nothing is left for us of the originality and immediacy of nature. . . . Pop
painting denies the mechanized and standardized character of bourgeois
civilization, just as decisively as dada, but without letting the political point of
the movement come to the forefront and, falling into a total nihilism in the
face of the products of the system, excites suspicion. It accepts its forms as the
elements of a milieu in which we do not necessarily take delight, but which
must be accepted because there is no alternative.''[30]

In this passage, Hauser captures three decisive elements of pop as a manifestation of the postmodernist mentality: (1) the renunciation of constitutive
subjectivity and concomitant 'individuality' of works (infinite reproducibility); (2) the reconciliation made with the world of commodity fetishism (commercialism); (3) a pronounced sense of politico-cultural resignation (no alternatives — no *sur*reality — to the existing order). At the same time these works,
in their extreme proximity to mass culture — i.e., their ready consumability
— exude a pseudo-populist ethos which suggests that the gap between (high)
art and life has been definitively bridged, and that aesthetic cultural democracy has been realized in the here and now. Yet, beneath such Panglossian
illusions lies the following unexpressed credo: the frivolity of life in a *societé de
consommation* should be matched by the frivolity of art. The result is mimesis
unto death — of art.

Though the initial influence of postmodernism was felt most keenly in the
sphere of the visual arts, it by no means remained confined to this sphere.
Instead there was scarcely an artistic domain untouched by this new cult of
aesthetic immediacy. One thinks of the neo-dadist sculptures of Rauschen-
berg, poetic 'word salads' of 'beat' inspiration, 'living theater,' the 'new jour-
nalism' of Tom Wolfe, the novels of William Burroughs and Donald
Barthelme, the fusion of classical and pop styles in the music of Philip Glass,
and, more recently, the a-historical architectural eclecticism of Michael
Graves and Philip Johnson. Another critic has perceptively characterized the

---

30. Arnold Hauser, *The Sociology of Art* (Chicago, 1982), pp. 651-653.

anti-intellectualism, a-historicism, and avowed irrationalism of the post-modernist trend in the following passage: "We are confronting, then, a new phase in our culture, which in motive and spring represents a wish to shake off the bleeding heritage of modernism. . . . The new sensibility is impatient with ideas. It is impatient with literary structure of complexity and coherence, only yesterday the catchwords of our criticism. It wants instead works of literature — though literature may be the wrong word — that will be as absolute as the sun, as unarguable as orgasm, as delicious as a lollipop. . . . It has no taste for that ethical nail-biting of those writers of the left who suffered defeat and would never accept the narcotic of certainty. It is sick of those magnifications of irony that Mann gave us, sick of those visions of entrapment to which Kafka led us, sick of those shufflings of daily horror and grace that Joyce left us. It breathes contempt for rationality, impatience with mind. . . . It is bored with the past: for the past is a fink."[31]

The postmodernist devaluation of classical modernism has simultaneously resulted in the valorization of mass culture, especially among eager left-wing critics uncomfortable with the possible elitist implications of modernist high culture — a position strikingly at odds with the Frankfurt School's path-breaking exposé of the "culture industry" back in the 1940s. In part, this seemingly Oedipal rejection of the standpoint of the founders of modern left-wing *Kulturkritik* stems from the correct perception of a genuinely new socio-historical era, an era which to be sure no longer corresponds to the age of 'one-dimensionality' or 'totally administered world' of the first generation of critical theorists.[32] Instead, the quietistic 'end of reason' prognosis of critical theory is dramatically burst asunder in the 1960s as a result of the vigorous protest movements associated with the counter-culture and the student new left. Of course, there is no dearth of historical irony in this turn of events. For it was precisely the critique generated by Adorno, Marcuse, et al. — who had proclaimed that there was 'no exit' from the contemporary socio-historical impasse — which fueled the imagination of the political radicals of the era; this to the great dismay of the critical theorists themselves — with the notable exceptions of Lowenthal and Marcuse.

---

31.   Irving Howe, "The New York Intellectuals," cited in Malei Calinescu, *Faces of Modernity* (Bloomington, 1977) pp. 137-138. Calinescu's book contains many useful observations on the modernism/postmodernism dichotomy. See especially pp. 120-144. For an incisive introduction to the thematic of postmodernism, see Fredric Jameson, "Postmodernism and Consumer Security," in *The Anti-Aesthetic*, Hal Foster, ed. (Port Townsend, 1983). The literature on the postmodernist controversy has become quite voluminous in recent years. For a useful introduction, see the special issue of *New German Critique* 22 (Winter 1981), especially the contributions by Habermas, "Modernity and Postmodernity," pp. 3-14, and Andreas Huyssen, "The Search for Tradition: Avant-Garde and Postmodernism in the 1970s," pp. 23-40. For a critique of post-modernism from a more traditional perspective, see Gerald Graff, "The Myth of the Postmodern-ist Breakthrough," *Triquarterly* 26 (Winter 1973), pp. 383-417, where Graff concludes: "A radical movement in art and culture forfeits its radicalism and impoverishes itself to the degree that it turns its back on what is valid and potentially living in the critical and moral traditions of humanism. In a society increasingly irrational and barbaric, to regard the attack on reason and objectivity as the basis of our radicalism is to perpetuate the nightmare we want to escape."

32.   For a perceptive account of the generational shift in critical theory (i.e., from the first generation to Habermas), see Agnes Heller, "The Positivist Dispute as a Turning Point in German Post-war Theory," *New German Critique* 15 (Fall 1978), pp. 49-56.

The devaluation of classical modernism and resultant emphasis on the projected emancipatory potentials of so-called mass culture derive in part from an awareness of the patent unserviceability of modernism with reference to immediate political, revolutionary ends. In this connection two points bear emphasizing: (1) in keeping with the socio-evolutionary perspective developed at the outset of the present essay, it is a matter of considerable doubt whether the role of art in post-traditional societies should be conceptualized along lines underscoring 'immediate political, revolutionary ends,' especially insofar as this prescription entails the *functionalization* of the aesthetic dimension along affirmative lines more suitable for premodern cultures, where value-spheres remain as yet undifferentiated (and it is of interest to note that precisely such a forced reintegration of art and politics characterizes the relation between the two spheres in bureaucratic socialist regimes, with results that are unquestionably regressive from both an aesthetic and cultural standpoint); (2) the *Zeitdiagnose* characteristic of this perspective draws an illegitimate conclusion in assuming that the obsolescence of the Frankfurt School theory of 'one-dimensionality' *also* entails the negation of its approach to *Kulturkritik*, e.g., that the distinction between 'high' and 'mass' culture no longer holds, or that (in extreme versions of this revisionist thesis) mass culture has become superior in emancipatory potential to the inaccessible high culture of classical modernism. A remark by Adorno is instructive in this respect: "Once the life of spirit renounces the duty and liberty of its own pure objectification, it has abdicated."[33]

This second point bears elucidation. It is an incontestable fact that the nature of late capitalism — and late capitalist culture — has undergone a significant shift since the 'one-dimensionality' of the cold war era. This was an era of well-nigh stifling conformism, adjustment, and — aside from occasional rumblings on the fringes — cultural accommodation. From this standpoint the political (anti-war movement), social (civil rights movement), and cultural (counter-culture) turbulence of the next decade would seem virtually unimaginable. That the social movements of this era seriously challenged the political-cultural hegemony of the inherited social system in many constructive respects remains indubitable. So is the fact that these movements are irreducible to the pejorative status of system-stabilizing 'feedback loops.' Their legacy represents a historical watershed which, despite recent attempts ("The Empire Strikes Back") at a remobilization of traditional conservative values (cold war politics, religious fundamentalism, supply-side economics, cultural anti-modernism), it is impossible simply to efface or roll back. The healthy cynicism raised about traditional bureaucratic party politics and an imperialist foreign policy; the new universal thematization of issues relating to the oppression of minorities, the rights of women, the ruination of the environment, all remain an indispensable, salutary, and relevant part of this legacy. The new awareness stimulated by these at times 'primitive' socio-cultural revolts has been inherited by the so-called 'new social movements' of

---

33. Theodor Adorno, "Commitment," *The Essential Frankfurt School Reader, op. cit.,* p. 301.

the 1970s and 1980s — the women's, anti-nuclear, ecology, and alternative movements.

The point is, however (and now I return to a discussion of the cultural sphere in the more narrow aesthetic sense), that one must be careful at the same time not to overestimate whatever advances have been made and be prepared to aopraise realistically the extreme fragility of these advances. In the cultural domain the balance remains extraordinarily precarious. The inchoate breakthrough of the tenuous, oppositional public spheres that emerged in the 1960s precipitates the thematization of a host of previously repressed social concerns (even in the case of the most conventional of the mass media, film and television) and as such resulted in an unprecedented removal of a set of debilitating cultural taboos. At the same time, what has resulted in fact has been *the proliferation of a cultural pseudo-democracy, with the substance of democracy remaining withheld.* That is, we have witnessed the dissemination of the *semblance* of cultural difference, polyvalence, and otherness, at the expense of the realization of the values feigned by the cultural sphere in the sphere of material life itself. The net result of the institutionalization of the counter-culture and its values (the music industry representing the apotheosis of this phenomenon) is the omnipresent illusion of emancipation ("ours is a culture in which anything is permitted!") only in order to deny more effectively the possibility of its immanent realization.

Let me express this point even more bluntly: in the present context the Frankfurt School critique of the culture industry not only retains its original relevance, but does so in redoubled fashion. For the new myth propagated by the culture industry pertains to an invigorating pluralism of its products, now that the old taboos of a 'one-dimensional' universe have been lifted and everything is permitted, no theme too risqué — clearly, there is nothing totalitarian about a society with such vast parameters of cultural leeway, such infinite tolerance! The question, therefore, arises whether contemporary mass culture remains the phantasmagoria of changing fashions, the perennial repetition of the always-the-same (*das Immergleiche*) under the guise of the 'new,' as unmasked by Walter Benjamin in connection with the *dawn* of the era of the society of consumption — *viz.,* the glittering world of the mid-nineteenth century Paris arcades[34] — or whether it has evolved to a point where we need only tap into the veins of utopian promise that lie in wait beneath the encrusted surface. The latter standpoint is that of the new enthusiasts of mass culture, for whom, in the immortal words of one of its partisans, modernism "is a distinctly male way of seeing. The ruptured narratives of Kafka, Joyce, and Beckett, cannot be taken as the universal discourse of the fractured subject, since women are occluded from the discourse of this subjectivity and are made into an other, the pure alterity of the male ego."[35]

---

34.   Walter Benjamin, *Passagenwerk,* Rolf Tiedemann, ed. (Frankfurt am Main, 1982).
35.   A fact that would come as a great surprise to Virginia Woolf, Gertrude Stein, Doris Lessing, and a host of other twentieth century woman writers with a significant attachment to modernism. These meditations on modernism flow from the pen of Stanley Aronowitz, *The Crisis in Historical Materialism* (South Hadley, Mass., 1981), p. 278.

Two conclusions must be emphasized simultaneously with inference to the contrasting estimations of the worth of mass culture just expressed: (1) after the cultural awakening of the sixties, as a result of which late capitalist societies lose their one-dimensional character, one can no longer proclaim à la Adorno, out of hand and a priori, that whatever emerges from the sphere of mass culture is inherently retrograde and affirmative. To be sure, there exist significant moments of alterity amid the vast desert of cultural conformism, in the fields of film (Woody Allen), literature (the South American novel), and even popular music (Talking Heads, Brian Eno), which point beyond the usual repetition-compulsion and standardization inherent in culture industry products; (2) at the same time, the fact remains that the predominant tendency to have taken root in the last decade and a half has been the *recuperation* (reintegration) of the oppositional impulses of the counter-culture; i.e., the contentious claims of the latter have largely been neutered and transformed into the cultural chic of middle-class narcissistic 'life-styles': its values have merely become grist for the mill of a society of consumption. These are the circumstances that compel the conclusion that the immediate historical upshot of the counter-culture's assault on the sphere of decaying traditional values has been a new period of stabilization, in which rather than having been suppressed outright, the radical imagery of the counter-culture has been readily incorporated *within* the value-system it sought to overthrow, leading to, as stated earlier, the *semblance* of democratization (pseudo-cultural pluralism) without the *substance* (the *actual* transformation of material life itself as originally demanded by the new cultural radicalism). Hence, the net result of this scenario, at least for the time being, seems to have been the *false sublation* (reconciliation) of the antagonism between culture and material life.

The foregoing conclusion then suggests a serious skepticism with reference to what has become of late the extremely fashionable tendency to proclaim the latently emancipatory character of the sphere of mass culture. This is not of course a tendency solely of recent vintage. As far back as the early sixties the critic Leslie Fiedler was sounding the death-knell of classical modernism and singing the praises of hitherto neglected genres of mass culture — 'B' movies, science fiction, detective novels — in essays such as "Cross the Border — Close the Gap" and "The New Mutants."[36] A *Journal of Popular Culture* has emerged, imploring us to take the manifestations of consumer culture as seriously as critics once took works of high culture. Indeed, these products should be taken seriously, but for reasons opposite those suggested by the journal's contributors. Even critics with former critical theory allegiances, such as Fredric Jameson, have come round to according the products of the culture industry a degree of utopian potential on a par with the great works of modernism. For Jameson, mass culture must be grasped "not as an empty distraction or 'mere' false consciousness, but rather as a transformational work on social and political anxieties and fantasies which then must have some effective presence in the mass cultural text in order subsequently to be

36.   Leslie Fiedler, *A Fiedler Reader* (New York, 1977).

'managed' or repressed."[37] He then concludes that mass culture contains a "Utopian or transcendent potential — that dimension of even the most degraded type of mass culture which remains implicitly, and no matter how faintly, negative and critical of the societal order from which, as a product and a commodity, it springs."[38]

Making a virtue of a necessity with regard to the omnipresence of cultural reification cannot help, however, but strike one as an extremely hollow solution. The fact that the products of mass culture serve to channelize and depotentiate mass 'anxieties and fantasies' that in any event can by no means be simply lauded in their pristine original state, but which themselves are thoroughgoing results of pre-existing mechanisms of socialization, would cast considerable doubt on the program of treating these products as 'ciphers of Utopia' — the precipitate upon decipherment, 'unsocialized desire,' is by no means a reliable one. This program is reminiscent of the traditional socialist faith in the immediate spontaneity of the 'masses'; yet, even Brecht, who often enough fell victim to this logic, realized that it was only by way of the modernist techniques of *Verfremdung* and *Unterbrechung* (alienation and interruption) that standardized patterns of perception could be broken down — and the homilies of epic theater thus conveyed.

What must be kept foremost in mind in any discussion concerning the relative merits of 'high' and 'low' art is the social evolutionary mandate accorded the realm of culture as a result of the transition from 'traditional' to 'modern' societies; in a word, this mandate can be expressed through the category of *autonomy*. This category signifies that at a certain point in its historical development the domain of art attains the right to independent self-objectification, a self-objectification unfettered by heteronomous, instrumental considerations. This level of independence permits an inner unfolding of the concept and possibilities of the realm of aesthetic expression. It results in a historically unprecedented extension of the boundaries and varieties of meaningful aesthetic experience. The emancipation and democratization of aesthetic production in the eighteenth century goes hand in hand with the general societal emancipation and democratization of the same period. Both are accomplishments whose preservation remains an essential part of the democratic legacy. Hasty proclamations of the demise of modernist autonomous art and uncritical acclaim of the pseudo-populist character of mass culture run grave risks of feeding the forces of historical regression. Moreover, it downplays the essential fact that contemporary mass culture, in its guise of 'culture-qua-commodity,' in its wholesale indebtedness to forces of industry, remains a thoroughly manipulative and administered phenomenon; in general, whatever elements of value survive the necessary mechanisms of authorial self-censorship are so withered and enfeebled as to be valueless. Before the advent of its commodification, a certain legitimacy attached to discussions of the 'populist' character of popular culture, since such culture

---

37.   Fredric Jameson, "Reification and Utopia in Mass Culture," *Social Text* 1 (Winter 1979), p. 141.

38.   *Ibid.*, p. 144.

remained the only available vehicle for the expression of the sentiments and longings of those segments of society denied access to socially certified cultural forms. In the present cultural context, such talk provokes suspicions of bad faith.

Today, the abolition of the distinction between autonomous culture and the culture industry is accelerated by the ahistorical, anti-humanist mentality of poststructuralism. In these doctrines, two of the essential results of the Enlightenment legacy, historicism and a sense of the infinite worth of the individual human person, are glibly brushed aside as temporary historical fictions from which the contemporary era of post-history has joyously emancipated itself. "As the archaeology of our thought easily shows," Foucault observes, "man is an invention of recent date. And one perhaps nearing an end." If an alteration in the "fundamental arrangements in our knowledge" which produced 'man' at the end of the classical age (1800) were to occur, Foucault continues, "then one can certainly wager that man would be erased, like a face drawn in the sand at the edge of the sea."[39] Yet, as Foucault makes clear in another passage, the end of man is an eventuality to be heartily welcomed rather than dreaded: "It is no longer possible to think in our day other than in the void left by man's disappearance. For this void does not create a deficiency; it does not constitute a lacuna that must be filled. It is nothing more, and nothing less, than the unfolding of a space in which it is once more possible to think. . . . To all those who still wish to talk about man, about his reign or his liberation, to all those who still ask themselves about what man is in his essence, to all those who wish to take him as their starting point in their attempts to reach the truth . . . to all those warped and twisted forms of reflection, we can answer only with a philosophical laugh. . . ."[40]

Simililarly, in his essay "The Ends of Man," Jacques Derrida laments the anthropocentric interpretation Heidegger's category of *Dasein* received among French existentialists — where it was misleadingly translated as "human reality" (a "monstrous mistranslation," Derrida remarks). "The example of the Sartrean project," Derrida observes, "remarkably verifies Heidegger's proposition according to which 'every humanism is metaphysical,' metaphysics being the other name of ontotheology."[41] He goes on to suggest in a programmatic vein: "What is difficult to think today is an end of man which would not be organized by a dialectics of truth and negativity, an end of man which would not be a teleology in the first person plural" (such as Hegel's phenomenological 'we').[42] There is, however, no doubt about the fact that the discovery of a perspective through which the 'end of man' could be thought would be wholly desirable. The shared philosophical inspiration for both Derrida and Foucault in this respect is Heidegger's "Letter on Humanism."[43]

In these texts, the elective affinities between poststructuralism and post-

39. Michel Foucault, *The Order of Things* (London, 1970), p. 387.
40. *Ibid.,* p. 343.
41. Jacques Derrida, "The Ends of Man," in *Margins of Philosophy* (Chicago, 1982), p. 116.
42. *Ibid.,* p. 121.
43. Martin Heidegger, *Basic Writings,* David F. Krell, ed. (New York, 197), pp. 189-242.

modernism are betrayed by a common desire to be free of the burdens of a 'centered' subjectivity, of responsible, autonomous individuality, and a kindred celebration of the 'end of history,' which is conceived of as merely a 'drag' on the activities of the new decentered, amorphous, libidinal self,[44] Is this movement the emancipatory scourge it proclaims itself to be or merely an instance of regression, a Nietzschean-inspired neo-irrationalist attempt to escape from the rigors of Kantian *Mündigkeit* (which contains the connotations of autonomy, maturity, and responsibility in one)? Is it the illusionless force of radical demystification it gives out or a destructive effort on the part of 'discontents' to undo the rigors imposed by the rational ego as part of the logic of civilization/individuation? Is it the new historical embodiment of Freud's primitive 'oceanic feeling,' the narcissistic desire (so prominent in recent years) for immediate and unceasing gratification? Is it, in a more constructive vein, a sign of the periodic return of the forces repressed and marginalized by a repressive civilization, forces — in the tradition of anti-bourgeois *Kulturkritik* (Rousseau, the romantics, Nietzsche, etc.) — whose warnings we would do well to heed, even were we not to take the nihilistic implications of their critique fully to heart? Is it merely a symptom of decline, a desperate cry for release from the omnipotent mechanisms of socialization which leave increasingly fewer domains of social life untouched in the wake of their expansion? Or is it, finally, a perverse instance of 'identifying with the oppressor,' the expression of a feeling of sheer impotence in face of an impending social cataclysm — variously defined as the 'end of history' or the 'end of man' — which is then transformed into a masochistic desire to embrace the catastrophe?

The standpoints of postmodernism and poststructuralism coincide insofar as both currents suggest that the 'modern era' is rapidly becoming a thing of the past, that the values of this era were essentially metaphysical and homocentric illusions, and that the new age of postmodernity will be free from such illusions; or rather it will in a Nietzschean vein become *an age of sheer illusion*, since the inhibiting, hypocritical metaphysical dualisms of 'truth' and 'falsehood,' 'good' and 'evil,' 'reality' and 'illusion' will have been vanquished and the pure play of 'difference' will come into its own. We must be liberated from history and historical thinking in general, since history, as the pernicious realm of 'referentiality,' represents an insupportable condition or limitation placed on the present. Historical thinking, thinking in terms of continuity, contains overt identitarian biases which prove inimical to the proliferation of difference.[45] The new ideal is that of the reign of 'free-floating signifiers,' signifiers fully emancipated from the tyranny of the 'referent,' signifiers that are unconditioned. In short, this is the ideal of the postmodernist 'text' (e.g.,

44.   For the anti-psychoanalytic complement to such tendencies — schizophrenia as liberation — see G. Deleuze and F. Guattari, *Anti-Oedipus* (New York, 1977).

45.   For a good example of the way in which poststructuralist theory has affected the discipline of history itself, see *Modern European Intellectual History: The Appraisals and New Perspectives*, D. Lacapra and S. Kaplan, ed., (Ithaca, 1982), especailly the contribution by Lacapra, "Rethinking Intellectual History and Reading Texts," pp. 47-85.

Philippe Sollers' *Paradis*). We must also be liberated from the humanist legacy of Descartes and (in part) Freud, both of whom are partisans of the ideal of a coherent self, a rational ego, which exists only at the expense of the 'other' which it suppresses. Yet, whereas a critique of humanism becomes a salutary phenomenon in the context of a culture which opportunistically invokes the values of this tradition as a hypocritical diversion from the suffering and injustice that lie at its core, the fashionable chatter about the outright *abolition* of this legacy provokes the suspicion of being ultimately in league with the forces of impending barbarism (the latter is the real truth hidden behind Nietzsche's idea of 'eternal recurrence'). In no uncertain terms, the demise of the individual, the end of history, rather than being causes for rejoicing, are imminent prospects which must be combatted at all cost.

What does it mean to speak of impending barbarism in a purportedly postmodern era? An answer to this question will go far toward clarifying the socio-historical etiology of the postmodernist phenomenon.

The dangers threaten primarily from two sides. On the one hand, there exists the threat of a wholesale regression behind the differentiation of value-spheres characteristic of Enlightenment, as a result of which the various subsystems of social action would stand in danger of being subsumed under a single, totalizing world-view. This is a tendency one can already see operative in the recent resurgence of religious fundamentalism.

On the other hand, there is the increasingly likely prospect of a *cybernetic society*, in which the moral principle of democratic societies — individual autonomy — becomes more and more anachronistic and is replaced by *technical imperatives* handed down from the administrative-economic spheres, which increasingly emerge as the dominant social subsystem. Rather than a regression, this development merely represents an extrapolation of the scientistic turn assumed by Enlightenment rationality in the nineteenth century, as a result of which all claims to knowledge which fail to meet formal-scientific standards of rationality are anathematized as 'irrational.' Habermas has referred to this trend toward 'scientization' in recent years as the bureaucratic-administrative *colonization of the life-world*.[46] According to this view, in the pre-scientific sphere of the 'life-world' (Husserl, Schutz) norms are decided upon through intersubjective processes of communication that are essentially linguistic in nature; whereas the penetration of rational-purpose, functional imperatives (stemming from the social subsystems of state and economy) into the sphere of the life-world results in the latter's *instrumentalization*: under late capitalism, its communicative inner logic (*Eigensinn*) is increasingly violated by a set of heteronomous bureaucratic imperatives.

Partisans of the technocratic approach to managing problems of 'overcomplexity' hail from the camp of systems theory. Dallmayr has characterized the perspective of its leading contemporary exponent, Niklas Luhmann, as follows: " 'The term system,' he [Luhmann] writes, 'is not designed as a synonym for subjectivity, or for a subjective construction, or for an aggregate of indiv-

---

46. Cf. Habermas, *Theorie des Kommunikativen Handelns*, Volume 2, *op. cit.*, pp. 489-547.

idual subjects.' At least since Talcott Parsons, he adds, 'the irreversible aim of systems theory consists in its ability to derive the need of system formation no longer from the vantage point of the (intentional) actor, but rather from the situated character of action' — in other words, from the network of social interaction. The basic thesis connected with this insight is that interaction is possible and conceivable only 'as a system,' and 'to go one step further,' that the actor himself must be construed in systemic terms or as a 'system in interaction.' Far from being a constitutive agent, the individual in Luhmann's view is 'constituted' by social interaction as a 'contingent actor,' that is, a system engaged in the reduction of complexity through selection. In his words: 'The individual subject must be seen first of all as a process of contingent selectivity.' "[47]

In Luhmann's reformulation of Parsonian structural-functionalism, the structuralist side of the equation acquires a new prominence. His is a *post-individualist* systems theory in which the individual social actor is degraded to the status of an expendable locus of a mass of supervening system variables, input factors or 'interactions.' The old liberal myth, inherited by Parsons from Weber, of the intentional, goal-oriented — read: autonomous — actor must be dispelled in order that his or her suffocation at the hands of large-scale organizations and agencies might receive its theoretical due. According to the outlook of the new systems theory, the concept of the 'subject' is as much of a *metaphysical atavism* as it is for poststructuralist thought, in which the subject is the ephemeral phantasm of a particular, moribund nineteenth century 'discursive practice' (Foucault). The problem with such prognoses of the fate of the individual in the postmodern era is that they are not merely idle chatter: instead, they attain an especial, nightmarish plausibility in the context of an objective social situation which meets them halfway.

Hence, at the present stage of social evolution problems of social reproduction can no longer be solved in terms of the rational decisions of individual actors; the inordinate level of complexity endemic to contemporary social systems rules out this idealistic participatory-democratic model. Instead, problems of rational decision-making (in Luhmann's terms, 'selectivity') have been transposed under these conditions of evolutionary complexity to the subsystem of science, which has attained primacy. As a result, all truth-dependent normative questions which were formerly immanent to the life-world are today scientifically *"reinterpreted as the imperative of corresponding complexity of theoretical structures and methods of behavioral research."*[48]

In addition, this social evolutionary turn toward complexity and the scientization of decision-making has, if correctly perceived, extremely retrograde consequences for traditional questions of social justice often associated with the banner of humanism or 'human rights.' According to Luhmann, the

47.   Dallmayr, *The Twilight of Subjectivity,* pp. 22-23.
48.   N. Luhmann, "Systemstheoretische Argumentationen: Eine Entgegnung mit Jürgen Habermas," in J. Habermas, N. Luhmann, *Theorie der Gesellschaft oder Sozialtechnologie* (Frankfurt am Main, 1971), pp. 397-398. Italics in the original.

modern European preoccupation with considerations of social emancipation has become obsolescent, insofar as the Hegelian paradigm of master-slave has itself become inoperative: since social questions have allegedly become strictly neutral matters of 'objective' technocratic management — i.e., questions of efficiency — the 'masters' too have lost their authority. In Luhmann's estimation, egalitarian babble about autonomous and responsible 'subjects' merely presents itself as an anachronistic, irrational interference with contemporary imperatives of social selectivity and system maintenance: since the master's loss of authority has become self-evident "one must ask whether it is necessary and meaningful to relate the traditional claim to reason of Western humanity to a concept of the subject which immediately leads to difficulties of this variety"[49] — i.e., a concept of the subject which still stakes traditional humanist claims to social justice.

The image of a postmodern order heralded by both poststructuralism and systems theory consequently betrays a numbler of pronounced similarities. Foremost among these is the thesis concerning the eclipse of subjectivity. Yet, in the poststructuralist version, with its allergy to diachrony, the underlying socio-historical transformations which account for the seeming obsolescence of 'humanism' as a metaphysical excrescence remain obscured through a type of 'hermeneutic-linguistic idealism': the autonomy of 'signifying practices' is grossly over-estimated, the demise of the subject (which for Foucault becomes a source of bemusement) is conceived of as a virtually *intra-textual event*, and the fact that essential changes in the material reproduction of social life (such as the shift from entrepreneurial to monopolistic stage-managed capitalism) have an *objective compulsion* which remains irreducible to the sphere of discursive signification is something which goes entirely unheeded. In sum, the poststructuralist discussion of the death of the subject remains essentially an act of ideological mystification when it is not tied to the objective sociological determinants of this demise. Only when this connection is made explicit will the eclipse cease to take on the character of an arbitrary and merely relativistic 'archaeological shift' in discursive frames of reference and become capable of being identified as the diabolical turn of events it represents in fact. All of which drives one to the conclusion that the hidden truth of postmodernist glorification of the 'end of man' is to be found in the brave new world of systems theory cybernetics.

---

49. *Ibid.*, p. 328.

MODERN ART AND DESUBLIMATION

by Russell A. Berman

Close to the beginning of *Death in Venice,* Thomas Mann sets up a relationship between aesthetic production and social context that bears strongly on the parameters of twentieth-century cultural life. After introducing his central figure, the fictive writer Aschenbach, Mann goes on to offer some exposition which, as always with Mann, is much more than exposition, since it draws attention to one of the central philosophical questions of the text: "It was a spring afternoon in that year of grace 19--, when Europe sat upon the anxious seat beneath a menace that hung over its head for months. Aschenbach had sought the open soon after tea. He was overwrought by a morning of hard, nerve-taxing work, work which had not ceased to exact his uttermost in the way of sustained concentration, conscientiousness, and tact [. . .]."[1] In the age of high imperialism, international tensions threaten to explode into war, and in the context of this political crisis, an aesthetic crisis ensues. To be sure, Aschenbach's writing problems are in no way an immediate reflection of international disputes, but the juxtaposition of the two crises in the opening lines of the text is significant, especially because when "Aschenbach sought the open soon after tea," he set out on a journey that leads eventually to Venice and the plague, "where horrid death" stalked the streets and "it seemed to him as though the moral law were fallen in ruins [. . .]."[2] Aschenbach's narrative is embedded in the experience of social catastrophe, not the one intimated at first, but one equally devastating. Do Aschenbach's path and the specific character of his crisis as a writer derive in some way from the collective crisis? Or might it even be that the vicissitudes of art, the radical transformation in the character of aesthetic production recorded in the novella, contribute to the social catastrophe?

The ostensible argument sets up a parallel between the immanent contradictions of bourgeois-Prussian society and its representative form of aesthetic production, both predicated on the viability of a Protestant ethic of repression and labor: Aschenbach's flight from work anticipates the crisis of the notion of aesthetic "work," while the shift of scene from German order, established by the force of friderician arms, to Venetian lassitude emancipates previously subliminal forces that are quickly identified as a newly assertive death instinct. Because of this correlation between the social landscape and aesthetic form, the text can describe the etiology of modernism (in the limited

---

1. Thomas Mann, *Death in Venice and Seven Other Stories* (New York, 1963), p. 3.
2. *Ibid.,* p. 65.

31

sense of the innovative literary production of the early twentieth century) by positing three aesthetic models: 1) Aschenbach's epigonic classicism, 2) the dionysian imagination of the desublimated collective, and 3) the text itself carried by the tension between the fictive writer and the foregrounded narrator. The conventional work, dependent on the autonomous writer in whom repression and individuation coexist in a fragile balance, becomes obsolete in the face of the ecstatic crowd of the dream; Mann's modernism characteristically occupies the space between the two poles, dividing its loyalties and subjecting its own voice, the narrator, to parodic techniques. Yet the problem of the narrator is of less interest here than the description of the historical process; a dialectic emerges between the desublimation of art, no longer capable of effecting a repression of its own romantic-sensuous motor, its expressive content, and, on the other hand, an aestheticization of life. The writer who ceases to work on works engages in the ruses of real seduction, the self-debasing cosmetic escapades, and the pederastic pursuit of beauty *in vivo.*

The decline of the individuated artist, the cipher of the formative principle and self-possession, corresponds to the aestheticization of life-practice. In this sense, the account of *Death in Venice* corroborates Peter Bürger's model of the avant-garde project. The sublation of life and art takes on the form of the renunciation of autonomous aesthetic production in order to realize beauty in sensual fulfillment. Of course Mann's pre-World War I evaluation of this project is characteristically pessimistic. By attempting to carry the sequestered values of traditional aesthetics outside the pale of the work, Aschenbach transgresses against the authenticity of aesthetic form, engendering a decay that forebodes the collapse of the moral order, i.e., the aesthetic crisis articulates and antedates the social catastrophe. Mann's own later accounts of a specifically modernist project beyond the precepts of inherited autonomy are less pejorative, just as his earlier conservative pessimism could be contrasted readily with other versions of the aestheticization of life, apotheosized by major figures of European modernism as the guarantor of epiphanic pleasure: "And she saw a long Roman candle going up over the trees up, up, and, in the tense hush, they were all breathless with excitement as it went higher and higher and she had to lean back more and more to look up after it, high, high, almost out of sight, and her face was suffused with a devine, an entrancing blush from straining back [. . .]. And then a rocket spring and bang shot blind and O! then the Roman candle burst and it was like a sigh of O! and everyone cried O! O! in raptures and it gushed out of it a stream of rain gold hair threads and they shed and ah! they were all greeny dewy stars falling with golden, O so lively! O so soft, sweet, soft!"[3] For Joyce, the aesthetic impulse is not imprisoned in the work but becomes a constituent moment of erotic beauty in lived experience. For Mann in 1911, the aestheticization of life engenders a social collapse. Despite these antithetical judgments, in both cases, the project of the historical avant-garde appears as the decoupling of utopian aesthetic ideals

---

3.   James Joyce, *Ulysses* (New York, 1961), pp. 366-367.

(beauty, sensuousness, freedom) from inherited poetological categories (the work, formal constraint) in order to transfer those ideals into social practice: social revolution *via* aesthetic innovation.[4]

Yet the apparently conservative judgment in *Death in Venice* regarding the revolt against form and convention ought not be shrugged off too quickly. It is not adequate merely to relegate it to an early phase in Mann's career or to relativize it with reference to other proponents of the avant-garde project. For this essayistic novella poses foremost a question of contemporary relevance that can provide the discussion of post-modernism with a setting that extends beyond the limits of aesthetic debate: does there exist a subterranean relationship between the rejection of the aesthetic work, the desublimation of art, and the "menace" that now hangs over the head of more than just Europe? Does the historical demise of autonomous art contribute to the virulence of social aggression, especially to recrudescent nationalism? Has the aestheticization of everyday life, the intended corollary to the avant-gardist attack on the institution of art, perhaps succeeded in transforming the life-world, while setting off an unforeseen process leading less to collective utopias of beautiful harmony than to a barbarization no longer counteracted or harnessed by the values of a secure aesthetic institution? If modernism and the historical avant-garde have run their course, as the advocates of post-modernism claim, then it may be more productive to consider how the disappearance of traditional cultural forms contributes to the character of contemporary social life than to argue for this or that artistic ism as the heir to the canonic throne.

In order to clarify the sociological ramifications of the avant-gardist dual project of desublimation and aestheticization, it is crucial to point out a fundamental assumption in the current debate on modernism, shared by both the post-modernist and the critical theoretical camps. Both positions assert that the concepts of modernity and modernism which are at stake correspond to the cultural formations of humanism that have prevailed in the West since the Renaissance or at least the eighteenth century. Hence the apparent similarity of contemporary polemics to the confrontations between the enlightenment and its romantic opposition, so often repeated during the past two

---

4. The reference to Mann and Joyce as representatives of an avant-gardist project diverges from current terminological distinctions between the avant-garde per se and modernism. One version, advocated above all by Matei Calinescu, differentiates among the avant-garde with its confluence of aesthetic revolt and political revolutionism (dada), the modernists committed to major literary production (especially the Pound-Eliot group), and post-modernism as a third and privileged mode of contemporary aesthetic innovation. Peter Bürger separates modernism as a radicalized insistence on autonomy (Valéry) from the avant-garde and its attack on the bourgeois institution of art, while he remains sensitive to the limitations of this conceptual separation. Both Calinescu and Bürger distinguish between the avant-garde and modernism in order to circumscribe strictly the significance of modernism and consequently legitimate aesthetic innovation in the wake of modernism's alleged obsolescence, i.e. a "post-modernism." The tendency to denigrate modernism can lead to a periodization identifying the modernists as largely nineteenth-century figures. The break with the liberal bourgeois culture of the nineteenth century thereby dwindles in signficance. It is precisely this break however which is of concern in this essay; "modernism" and "avant-garde" are therefore used interchangeably to refer to the full range of tendencies commonly identified as "modern" art and literature. Cf. Matei Calinescu, *Faces of Modernity* (Bloomington, 1977) and Peter Bürger, "The Aging of the Modern," in this issue.

centuries. The consequence of this epochal definition of modernity is the relative denigration of the aesthetic revolution at the end of the nineteenth and beginning of the twentieth century and the emergence of what is commonly known as "modern art" or "modernist literature" in contrast to the traditional and conventional forms of the preceding decades. On the one hand, Habermas incorporates this modern art into the larger notion of modernity by treating it as a consequence of the differentiation of an aesthetic sphere within a version of Western specificity derived from Weber.[5] On the other hand, postmodernists like Jameson and Sussman push modernism back into the nineteenth century, either by identifying its purported values (subjectivity, individualism) or its rhetorical forms (bifurcation, sublation) with an inherited cultural legacy.[6] The two strategies pursue diametrically opposite goals: critical theory insists on the continuity of the epoch in order to demonstrate the relevance of the emancipatory contents of the enlightenment, while the postmodernists subsume modernism in a Victorian (or Wilhelmine, etc.) past in order to ground their decisionistic announcement of a new epistemic structure after "the end of man."[7] Given this implicit periodization, the radical aesthetic innovation of the early twentieth century tends to disappear. The lines that separate Joyce and Brecht from Dickens and Schiller, Picasso and Ernst from Ingres and Friedrich, Schoenberg and Stravinsky from Mozart and Schubert pale in significance once the specificity of twentieth-century modernism is reduced to a mere phase within the larger notion of modernity.

For critical theory, this shift in attention from twentieth-century modernism to post-medieval modernity represents a profound discursive break with its own origin in the early phase of Western Marxism, during which aesthetic discussion concentrated on the relationship between avant-gardist innovation and radical social transformation. The revolutionary optimism of Benjamin and Brecht hoped to harness the avant-garde immediately to political progress, while Horkheimer and Adorno viewed authentic art as the placeholder of a potential opposition to monopoly capitalism and the culture industry, i.e., in both cases, the contemporary aesthetic revolution was located within the terms of a profound social reorganization. This crucial particularity of the historical avant-garde, which has disappeared from Habermas' account, is maintained primarily within the work of Christa and Peter Bürger.[8] The avant-garde is presented as a frontal assault on the bourgeois institution of art established in the age of German idealism and classic-romantic aesthetics; the inherited dichotomy of "life and art" was to undergo a sublation whereby the post-auratic work would lose its formal cohesion and work character through the incorporation of elements of life (collage), while social

5.   Jürgen Habermas, *Theorie des kommunikativen Handelns* (Frankfurt, 1982), pp. 205-366.

6.   Cf. Fredric Jameson, *Fables of Aggression: Wyndham Lewis*, (Berkeley, 1979) and Henry Sussman, *The Hegelian Aftermath* (Baltimore, 1982).

7.   Michel Foucault, *The Order of Things* (London, 1970), p. 387.

8.   Christa Bürger, *Der Ursprung der bürgerlichen Institution Kunst* (Frankfurt, 1977), and Peter Bürger, *Theory of the Avant-Garde* (Minneapolis, 1984).

life would be transformed by an infusion of aesthetic values (a tendency apparent not only in the avant-garde movements per se but, with evident consequences, in the craft and industrial products of William Morris, Josef Hoffmann and, especially Bauhaus). This is the dual project alluded to above: desublimation and aestheticization, Aschenbach's renunciation of discipline and the pursuit of a genuine sensuous apparation of truth.

While the Bürgers provide an extremely convincing account of the transformed character of artistic objects in the wake of the historical avant-garde movements, i.e., the specificity of twentieth-century "modernism," their argumentation remains locked within the immanence of high cultural production. Neither is the emergence of the avant-garde related to extra-aesthetic developments (urbanization, industrialization, the First World War, or, more generally, the transition to monopoly capitalism and the transformation of the public sphere), nor are the social consequences of the avant-garde in the realm of "life" examined, despite the pronounced revolutionary claims of the avant-gardists and modernists themselves. It will be helpful to recall these claims; three literary examples ought to suffice to demonstrate the pathos and ambivalence of the modernist project and to provide the foundation for an evaluation of the contemporary legacy of the aestheticization of everyday life.

Hermann Hesse was certainly not one of the most radical or sophisticated modernists, and his problematic reception during the sixties has compounded these shortcomings, but, for those who can stomach it, his *Steppenwolf* in fact provides an illuminating insight into the modernist project. The emphatic scrutinization of a paradigmatic psychological structure makes it clear that the aesthetic innovation of modernism is inextricably tied to a transformation of the individual within a social revolution. This revolution, furthermore, conjoins with the hostility to the liberal nineteenth century, a feature of all versions of modernism with their privileging of the new and the young as the carrier of a *nuda veritas* against the *Lebenslüge* of the old world.[9] For Hesse this means a dual escape from the structures of inherited culture: an escape from a dichotomous individuality, oscillating between bourgeois and the bohemian spheres, in the name of a decentered polyvalence as well as an escape from the reified forms of bourgeois art, where the great figures (Goethe and Mozart) are ensconced as marmoreated heroes, while their authentic significance is obliterated. This critique of the past is, however, merely prologue to the project of an aestheticization of life and the production of a post-individuated community: ". . . the mysterious merging of the personality in the mass, the mystic union of joy. I had often heard it spoken of. It was known, I knew, to every servant girl. . . . A hundred times in my life I had seen examples of those whom rapture had intoxicated and released from the self, of that smile, that half-crazed absorption, of those whose heads have been turned by a common enthusiasm. I had seen it in drunken recruits and sailors, and also

9. Maurizio Calvesi, "Arte e Arti: Attualità e Storia," in *XLI Esposizione Internazionale d'Arte: La Biennale di Venezia* (Venice, 1984), n.p. [p. 13].

in great artists in the enthusiasm, perhaps, of a musical festival; and not less in young soldiers going to war. . . . I myself swam in this deep and childlike happiness of a fairy tale. I myself breathed the sweet intoxication of a common dream and of music and rhythm and wine and women — I, who had in other days so often listened with amusement, or dismal superiority, to its panegyric in the ballroom chatter of some student. I was myself no longer. My personality was dissolved in the intoxication of the festivity like salt in water. I danced with this woman or that, but it was not only the one I had in my arms and whose hair brushed my face that belonged to me. All the other women who were dancing in the same room and the same dance and to the same music, and whose radiant faces floated past me like fantastic flowers, belonged to me, and I to them. All of us had a part in one another. And the men too. I was with them also. They, too, were no strangers to me. Their smile was mine, and mine their wooing and theirs mine."[10] After the attack on established bourgeois culture which is discussed in the initial sections of the novel, Hesse presents this account of the aestheticization of life, located, characteristically enough, at an artists' ball. It represents at least one version of the avant-gardist project, and its features point to some at least potential sociological consequences. First of all, the community is characterized by the obliteration of the distinction between high and low culture (great artists and servant girls), a theme carried out in the novel as the reconciliation of alternative musical forms, jazz and Mozart. Yet the legitimation of popular culture is apparently only possible through its elevation to a religious experience, i.e., the dance cannot be mere fun or entertainment, it must, on the contrary, fulfill all the emphatic requirements of bourgeois art. Hesse's utopian redefinition of low culture therefore anticipates the left post-modernist position that claims to discover emancipatory yearnings in the latest products of the culture industry. Secondly, the community permits no individuality and certainly no privacy; all differences disappear in an ineluctable transparency that belies the claim to a mystery. The dionysian revolt suddenly displays a totalitarian propensity which, in the case of Hesse's narrator, formerly an articulate anti-militarist, forces an identification with fanatic recruits. Not only must his personal history be denied, it is overpowered by a death instinct, hostile to all particularity and intimately tied to the process of desublimation. This leads, thirdly, to a universal eroticization, the apparent ubiquity of pleasure beyond all taboos, in which, however, pleasure is perpetually denied because of the non-specificity of any union. The corollary to the attack on the traditional aesthetic form is a duplicitous instinctual emancipation which in fact subjugates eros to the capitalist logic of serial commodities; the partners are thrust on the narrator, one after another, by a force beyond his comprehension, let alone under his control. This is the secret of the supposed mystery, the capitulation of the individual during the transition to monopoly capitalism.[11]

---

10.   Hermann Hesse, *Steppenwolf* (New York, 1957), pp. 168-169.
11.   Cf. Lucien Goldmann, "Interdependences between Industrial Society and New Forms of Literary Creation," in: *Cultural Creation* (St. Louis, 1976), pp. 76-88.

The social consequences intended by Hesse's modernist desublimation of art are clearly problematic, to say the least. Yet just as Mann's conservative appraisal could be balanced by Joyce's enthusiasm, the regression inherent in the dionysian crowd has to be contrasted with an alternative version of the post-individual community inspired by a leftist project. Benjamin's argument in "The Work of Art in the Age of Mechanical Reproduction" is by now well known: the deauraticization of art carried out by technological innovation and social modernization potentially replaces the fragmented and passively contemplative recipient with a critical audience. It is important to point out that this account of the democratizing function of the cinema postdates a similar defense of a modernist literary project: a new way of writing, which breaks with the inherited forms of bourgeois aesthetics, produces a new, post-bourgeois public. Like Lukács, Benjamin uses the term "epic" to designate the literature of a non-individuated community, but while Lukács ascribes the epic to the "integrated civilization" of the distant past in Homeric Greece, Benjamin identifies an epic potential in contemporary culture.[12] Consider, for example, the following passage from his 1930 review of Döblin's *Berlin Alexanderplatz:* "For the epic, being is an ocean. There is nothing more epic than the ocean. One can of course treat the ocean in very different ways. For example, lie on the beach, listen to the surf and collect the shells it washes ashore. That is what the epic author does. One can also travel the ocean. With many goals and none at all. One can take an ocean voyage, and then, out there, with no land in sight, only sea and sky, wander aimlessly. That is what the author of the novel does. He is truly lonely and mute. Epic man is only at rest. In the epic, the people rest after the day's labor; they listen, dream and collect. The novelist has separated himself from the people and its activity. The birth chamber of the novel is the isolated individual who can no longer discuss his most important concerns in an exemplary manner, who is confused and oblivious to advice. In the presentation of human existence, the novel pushes incommensurability to an extreme. One can feel the difference between the novel and the true epic by thinking of the works of Homer and Dante. Oral tradition, the material of the epic, has a make-up different from the substance of a novel. The novel differs from all other forms of prose — the fairy tale, the legend, the saying, the funny story — in that it neither derives from nor enters into an oral tradition. It differs most clearly however from the narration of epic prose. Nothing contributes more to the dangerous silencing of the human spirit, nothing stifles the soul of narration more thoroughly than the shameless expansion that the reading of novels has undergone in all of our lives."[13] In his literary criticism from the end of the Weimar Republic, Benjamin develops a modernist program that can be designated as "epic leftism" which puts him at odds with the representatives of various forms of tendentious literature and the emerging socialist realism. For Benjamin, epic litera-

12. Georg Lukács, *The Theory of the Novel* (Cambridge, 1971), pp. 29-39.
13. Walter Benjamin, "Krisis des Romans," in *Gesammelte Schriften*, vol. III (Frankfurt, 1972), , pp. 230-231.

ture operates less through the advocacy of any particular message than through a reception process that overcomes individuation in order to invoke a democratic collective: "It is a matter of life or death for the new epic to liquidate this privacy from which the novel derives its legitimacy."[14]

One need not belabor the startling conjunction of a program to liquidate privacy and the Stalinization of European Communism. Benjamin's program converges with Hesse's rejection of individuality as the corollary to the deautonomization of art. It evidently lacks, however, the romantic, instinctual coloration of the dionysian crowd. Benjamin's community is linked instead to the possibility of knowledge; it can learn and listen, the epic is its own speech, and while the individual of the novel remains hopelessly lost in incommensurable particularity, the epic collective can reflect on its experiences "in an exemplary manner." This cogitational character of epic leftism corresponds to the familiar intention of Brecht's epic theater: criticism and ratiocination rather than emotional identification and catharsis. Yet despite this critical characterization of the community intended by the modernist project of epic leftism, the rhetorical designations employed by Benjamin indicate other, highly ambivalent features as well. It is an image of sedentary indolence, an archaic and organic collective that is not only democratic but also national: both epithets are legitimate corollaries to the German term *Volk*. While Hesse links modernist deautonomization to an imitation of military groupings, Benjamin's epic stands in an apparent relationship to a national identity. It would be premature to argue that the critique of bourgeois aesthetics necessarily instigates a nationalist mobilization, but this process seems to be at least a potential tendency within even the leftist version of modernism. This is not the place to enter into an examination of those dubious arguments regarding the progressive potential of a leftist nationalism in the twentieth century nor can one impute an intentional nationalism to Benjamin and his allies; on the contrary their work is marked by an unmistakably internationalist allegiance.[15] The point is rather this: while epic leftism presents a modernist program with certain emancipatory claims regarding the invocation of a critical audience, the realization of those claims is extraordinarily difficult to demonstrate, and the real historical result of the leftist attack on bourgeois forms may have been to amplify the general modernist dismantling of traditional culture with unintended consequences. Given the continuity of a heteronomous social organization, the public produced by a post-auratic art form (despite the claims of Benjamin and Brecht) may end up more a national folk than a democratic folk.

The ramifications of deautonomization, which generated Hesse's dance crowd and Benjamin's nation-folk, take a related but different turn in the fascist version of the critique of bourgeois aesthetics formulated by Ernst Jünger. Despite his own high-brow predilections, a central theme in his writings from the twenties and thirties addresses the alleged obsolescence of the forms

---

14.   Walter Benjamin, "Oskar Maria Graf als Erzähler," *ibid.,*, p. 310.
15.   Peter Brandt and Herbert Ammon, *Die Linke und die nationale Frage* (Reinbek, 1981).

of bourgeois culture, key categories of which, however, are projected onto the battlefield or the organization of the totalitarian state. While the autonomous work of art, for example, is rejected as part of an anachronistic pre-war bourgeoisie, its features recur as the beauty of the battlefield or the perfection of the military machinery: "Today we are writing poems of steel, and we are fighting for power in battles that unfold with the precision of machines. There is a beauty in it which we can already sense: in these battles on land, on sea and in the air in which the hot will of our blood controls itself and finds expression in the mastery of the technical miracle-machines of power."[16] This is what Benjamin would later call the "aestheticization of politics," with reference to a quotation from Marinetti, and Jünger's proximity to the Italian model of a fascist futurism is evident.[17] Yet war does not only replace the art work by usurping its categories; it also transforms them radically, for the aesthetic experience, an erstwhile constituent of the bourgeois public sphere, now no longer permits any individuation. The hostility to differentiation that marked Hesse's serial eroticism becomes a heroic denigration of individual suffering: "All goals are transitory, flux alone is eternal, and it constantly produces wonderful and pitiless spectacles. Only few are granted the opportunity to lose themselves in their sublime purposelessness, as with artworks or the starry heaven. But whoever perceives in this war solely the negation, solely his own suffering, and not the affirmation, the greater movement, has experienced it all as a slave. He has had not an inner, but only an outer experience."[18] The continuity with traditional bourgeois culture is unmistakable: the purposelessness of art, reception as contemplation, the beauty of nature, the dichotomy of outer and inner (body and soul), and especially the elitist class distinctions as the underpinnings of cultural activity. Yet now differentiation, the imperative expression of "individual suffering," which had always been denied to the "slave," is withheld from the members of the elite as well. The passage marks a revolutionary transformation in bourgeois culture where the invocation of interiority, an "inner experience" of the battle, is mobilized against atavistic claims to a privacy that is liquidated in the heroic collective.

Jünger's account describes a process that is fundamentally homologous to the transformations outlined by Hesse and Benjamin: the modernist rejection of inherited bourgeois aesthetic forms is implicated in a deconstruction of bourgeois subjectivity and the corollary production of a charismatic community that breaks radically with the individualism and legal rationality of the liberal period. This shared paradigm holds despite obvious differences among the political intentions: Hesse's romantic pacifism, Benjamin's maverick communism, and Jünger's emphatic militarism. Similar differences can be located in the competing aesthetic programs. Yet despite the relevance of Hesse's insistence on the convergence of high and low culture and Benjamin's attention to the cinema, one finds in Jünger's reflections particularly tren-

---

16.   Ernst Jünger, "Der Kampf als inneres Erlebnis," in *Werke* (Stuttgart, n.d.), Vol. V, p.107.
17.   Walter Benjamin, *Illuminations* (New York, 1969), pp. 241-242.
18.   Jünger, "Der Kampf . . . ," pp. 107-108.

chant observations for our contemporary situation. After linking the art of the bourgeois era to the cult of genius in which the work ultimately represents an "autobiographical document" of the great figure, he underscores the contemporary "decline of the individual and his inherited values not only on the battlefield, not only in politics, but in art as well."[19] The "worker," who is never individuated, replaces the soldier as his point of reference in the early thirties.[20] Art consequently no longer expresses subjectivity, demonstrating instead the exigencies of total planning and the absence of any separate spheres for private endeavors: "For the same power that the art of politics represents in authority is revealed by art in its formative activity. Art must demonstrate how, from a lofty vantage point, life is understood as totality. [Art] is nothing separate, nothing that possesses validity in itself or because of itself. There is on the contrary no realm of life that could not be regarded as material for art."[21] For two centuries innovative aesthetic production had claimed for itself the right to treat previously proscribed material, e.g., the

---

19.   Ernst Jünger, *Der Arbeiter: Herrschaft und Gestalt,* in *Werke* (Stuttgart, n.d.), Vol. VI, p. 228.

20.   On the vicissitudes of the individual in the Weimar period, see Leo Lowenthal, "Die biographische Mode," in: *Sociologica I* (Frankfurt, 1955), pp. 363-86; on Jünger's "heroic realism" see: Herbert Marcuse, "Ker Kampf gegen den Liberalismus in der totalitären Staatsauffassung," in: *Kultur und Gesellschaft I* (Frankfurt, 1965), pp. 17-55. The ease with which Jünger moves from the aristocratic image of the soldierly elite to the proletarian virtue of the "worker" indicates that the seemingly antithetical figures are engendered by the same social substance. Both of course are anti-subjective terms (a feature which explains the current renaissance of Jünger in France who can easily appeal to post-structuralist taste). Both moreover are produced by the same self-destructive logic of bourgeois individuality. The pre-subjective elite and the post-subjective proletarian are less external challenges to bourgeois identity than the externalized personae that it chooses when, experiencing itself as an alienated other, it assumes the masks of its historical competitors: Nietzsche's aristocratic gestures or the mimicry of the proletariat, popular in the bourgeois intelligentsia at least since naturalism (cf. Walter Benjamin, "Bücher, die übersetzt werden sollten" in: *Gesammelte Schriften* III, p. 175). In either case, the imitation of the deadly antagonist represents the culmination of a fundamentally self-destructive urge that was present from the start — vide the paradigmatic suicide of Werther and Emilia Galotti's sacrifice — as a constant companion of bourgeois emancipation, trapped in its own guilt. Because it buries traditional society beneath the tabula rasa of its ego (the reign of terror) and occludes concrete exploitation with the categories of exchange (Manchester), it attempts an atonement in the form of a perpetual reenactment of its own death. After the prototypically bourgeois revolt, Brutus reveals the proximity of violence and freedom:

> And let us bathe our hands in Caesar's blood
> Up to the elbows, and besmear our swords:
> Then walk we forth, even to the market-place,
> And weaving our red weapons o'er our heads,
> Let's all cry, "Peace, freedom, and liberty!"

Cassius' reply indicates a compulsion to repeat, an eternal return, that in fact belies the claim that a substantive freedom has been attained:

> Stoop then, and wash. How many ages hence
> Shall this our lofty scene by acted over,
> In states unborn, and accents yet unknown!

> *Julius Caesar* III.i.106-13.

Crime and exculpation converge in the same ritual of washing because their difference disappears in the ideological structures of a revolt in the name of freedom but designated to preserve hierarchy. The real suffering however cannot be simply denied, so the penance takes the form of theatrical repetition. The bourgeois subject stages this "lofty scene" in its own demontage, from Brutus' suicide to Jünger's worker.

21.   Jünger, *Der Arbeiter,* p. 232.

breakdown of class barriers in the drama of the eighteenth century and later on the naturalist stage, as well as the appearance of quotidian motifs in nineteenth century painting, both tendencies generally considered to be progressive attacks on academic classicism. Jünger appropriates this movement and radicalizes it: because art can address everything, nothing can escape the universal process of aestheticization. The modernist attack on autonomous art and individual privacy consequently points toward two familiar phenomena. First, a generic shift toward types of aesthetic products which were disprivileged within liberal culture because of their essential incompatibility with prevailing notions of privacy: Jünger mentions sculpture, drama and architecture, all public forms (unlike the reading of novels disdained by Benjamin). Their corollaries in contemporary culture are the installation, performance art, and the central importance of architectural post-modernism. Secondly, once the aesthetic principle escapes the strictures of the autonomous work, it invades the previously extra-aesthetic life-world and becomes a formative force that transforms the contemporary individual into a constant recipient, not only in museums or at concerts but in all spheres of daily activity.

If one can speak today of a post-modernist situation, then only in terms of the vicissitudes of the modernist project. Modernism has aged, the avant-garde has become obsolete, to the extent that the early twentieth century faith in the revolutionary power of the artist and the work has dissolved, in part because the utopian social transformation promised by so many avant-gardists has not taken place. The broken *promesse de bonheur* has undermined its own credibility. On the other hand, modernism has succeeded, albeit in an unforeseen manner, in its dual program of dismantling the autonomous work and the aestheticization of everyday life, and this success defines the substance of the post-modernist situation. The avant-garde derived its pathos of protest from its critique of the still very present bourgeois aesthetic assumptions; the same tradition which was under attack provided the anti-traditionalists with their strength. Today that tradition has disappeared, thanks in part to the historical labor of the avant-garde, and there is no longer a foil against which an authentic protest can define itself. No longer committed to traditional aesthetic forms, today's public will no longer be outraged, and it is this obsolescence of shock, a central category of the avant-garde, that explains the resounding insignificance of contemporary aesthetic production.

Given the waning of the avant-garde in the wake of its own success, important changes in the character of art works take place. This distance from the legacy of the historical avant-garde can be discussed in terms of formal technique, the objectivity of works, and their relationship to history. One predominant strand of modernism moved along a trajectory of rationalization toward an increasing abstraction fundamentally hostile to the representational arts of the nineteenth century: cubism, de stijl, constructivism, leading eventually to minimalism, conceptual art and superrealist painting, concerned less with its putative content than with an analysis of the relationship between painting and its ubiquitous technical competitor, photography. Parallel developments include the abstract descriptions in Kafka, the language crisis in Musil, and the self-reflectivity of literature (James, the post-war Vienna group) and film (Godard, Costard). If an aesthetics of abstraction thrived on a critique of a retreating representationalism, more recent works display a sudden revival of figurative painting (neo-expressionism) and referential literature (new subjectivity). The return to representation implies a devaluation of formal-technical matters, i.e., the medial self-reflection that was a hallmark of modernism. This explains the frequently found technical incompetence that characterizes this painting (a feature which is of course also a consequence of the heightened commodification of aesthetic production in the context of a vigorous art market). Representationalism and the denigration of form set the stage for the new popularity of native painters and the rediscovery of figures such as Frida Kahlo and Grant Wood. While neo-figurative painting and new subjectivist literature present their disdain for formal considerations as a protest against an academic modernism (and therefore in fact continue to participate in a discourse of formal reflection), the content of the expression regularly limits itself to a nebulous emotional rage. The public display of the purportedly personal denies any distance between the two spheres through a decisionistic declaration of a universal libidinal impulse, as in the sexual projections of Christian Attersee's paintings. Neo-expressionism as the unmediated revelation of instinctual force can therefore be viewed as the uncritical mirroring of the repressive desublimation of everyday life under the aegis of aestheticization.[22] This conservative authoritarian implication of the anti-modernist return to figurativism corresponds to the historical conjunction of the post-modernist discourse and the politics of the late seventies in which ideologues of both post-modernism and neo-conservatism railed against abstraction and called for the reinstitution of legible, i.e., representational, systems.

While the avant-garde defined itself through the attack on the autonomous work, it still maintained for its own works a claim to objectivity and enclosure, at least as a negative moment. Adorno captures this contradictory, i.e., transitional, stage in the paradoxical formulation that "today the only works which really count are those which are no longer works at all.[23] In Picasso's collages or the political photomontages of Heartfield, elements of everyday life are integrated directly into the work, implicitly exploding its autonomy, while the objectivity guaranteed by the frame retains a labile legitimacy, derived from the object of attack, the pre-modernist organic totality. This receding totality finally disappears in the hegemonic forms of contemporary aesthetic production: the negative space of video art and the ephemerality of performances. Installations similarly radicalize the avant-gardist critique of self-enclosed objectivity and tend toward a multidimensional aestheticization of the environment, as in Thomas Lanigan-Schmidt's "Childhood Memories," while

---

22.   On "repressive desublimation," see: Herbert Marcuse, *One-Dimensional Man* (Boston, 1964).
23.   Theodor W. Adorno, *Philosophy of Modern Music,* New York, 1973), p. 30.

others still operate within a late abstractionist discourse of formal coherence, e.g., Bruce Naumann's "Dream Passage."

The success of the avant-gardist critique of self-enclosed objectivity implies an obsolescence of the critique; what follows is not necessarily a return to the traditional work form (parallel to the return to representation) but rather a transformed function of the open work which ceases to carry a protest potential vis-à-vis a traditional standard of closure. This leads first to a decided enervation, particularly evident if one considers the history of the poster, a popular form related to the avant-garde, that leads from the fin-de-siècle through the revolutionary twenties to a late renaissance in 1968. The decline of the poster as an artistic genre in recent years is perhaps the clearest indication of depoliticization and a new transformation of the public sphere. It has been replaced by the non-self-enclosed form par excellence, mail art (correspondence art) as graphic epistolary communication among the members of a marginalized neo-bohemia. A similar weakening is evident in the transition from the political drama of the avant-garde, epic theater and even its latter-day offspring, the living theater, forms which interlocked with political subcultures and demonstrations, to contemporary performances; this post-modernist popular theater oscillates between its relegation to the same marginalization and a breathtaking commercialization (Laurie Anderson).

In addition to this diminutive character of the non-objective work, an expansive tendency is equally characteristic of recent cultural life. In place of individual aesthetic objects, major events with aesthetic claims or aestheticizing intentions increasingly occupy the place reserved for art in traditional bourgeois culture. These range from equally archaic as hypertrophic forms of drama (Hermann Nitzsch's orgone-mystery theater in Prinzendorf) and state-sponsored spectacle (Andre Heller's fireworks in Lisbon and Berlin), to the imperiousness of the grand museum shows (King Tut, China, Alexander, the Vatican); their grandeur tends to dwarf the significance of any individual work, which in turn corresponds to their ultimate goal. For they are designed less as vehicles to display particular aesthetic objects than, through their very size and substance, to celebrate power. This celebration can provide the mediation for specific political programs (e.g., in Sino-American relations); in general, however, the international character of the exhibitions indicates a universal function in the relegitimation of authority through aesthetic representation. The range of aestheticizing productions can be traced further through media events like the Olympics (conservative insofar as it still pretended to sequester aesthetics in the accompanying arts festival) and the political spectacles of the party conventions. The false sublation of art and life culminates when, in the age of mechanical reproduction, the most advanced technical means available are employed to aestheticize political discourse fully, while exposing the inherent mendacity of bourgeois politics through the nomination of an actor as best suited to carry on the bluff. The deautonomization of art and the aestheticization of life become indistinguishable.[24]

24.   The aestheticization of politics is not only evident in the spectacular character of political

In addition to the questions of formal technique and objectivity, the relationship to history in recent artistic works is indicative of the transition from modernist protest to post-modernist ornamentalism. The modernist work locates itself along a diachronic axis through an immanent critique of tradition, thereby describing an emphatic present counterposed to a rejected past: *vide* the versions of the Mona Lisa by Duchamps and Dali. The modernist present continues history by producing the new while simultaneously rejecting history as the nineteenth-century narrative of development. This contradiction, which echoes the self-contradictory character of the avant-gardist work, is played out in *The Trial* as the tension between the rationalized time of the office world and the organic time is the single year of Josef K.'s life in which the events unroll.This temporal structure applies equally to the non-reconciliation between the developmental narrative and the statis of montage in *Doctor Faustus*, a corollary to the dialectic of myth and history in Adorno's essay on natural history.[25]

The historicity of the modernist work disappears in post-modernism which, no longer defining its present against a rejected past, exists in a temporal void in which any notion of historico-philosophical progress, any promise of hope, becomes meaningless. In contrast to the prototypes by the avant-gardists Duchamps and Dali, Warhol's "Twelve White Mona Lisas" has no critical edge because of the obsolescence of the diachronic tension. With the end of history, the aesethetic category of the new loses its relevance; instead the aesthetic debris of the past (which is no longer a past opposed to the present) reappears as immediately accessible in the historicist eclecticism of post-modernist architectural referentiality. A similar tendency is evident in the proliferation of references to traditional works and, more generally, the allegorical and mythological languages of earlier eras: e.g., Vettor Pisani's "Oedipus and the Sphinx," Michelangelo Pistoletto's "Venus in Rags," Ger-

conventions (from Nürnberg to Dallas) but in the increasing contamination of political discourse with cultural material. "Of all the phenomena of Mr. Reagan on the stump, none are so fascinating as his ability to generate emotional effects from the distinct areas of fact and fiction. In addressing the American Legion convention in Salt Lake City, the President created a patriotic surge in the hall by alternating between such reference points as the joyous homecoming of the Iranian hostages ('that unforgettable moment') and the commercialism of television military fiction ('Maybe you've seen the television show "Call to Glory" that celebrates Air Force officers serving in "the twilight struggle" of the cold war?')" *New York Times*, Sept. 8, 1984, p. 9. The infusion of the categories of the culture industry into politics is purused consciously, with strategic precision. Appearing in Nashville at the Grand Old Opry, Reagan claimed the Bayreuth of Country Music for himself and Republican nationalism: "The event in the packed Opry theater was one of the more spectacular efforts from the Reagan campaign engineers, ending in a storm of confetti and a mass rendition of 'God Bless the U.S.A.,' the red-white-and-blue song used on Reagan television commercials." From within the staged unanimity of the love-feast, the orator produces the pejorative image of an outsider by mixing political characterization and racial slur with a musicological category: "Mr. Reagan, who sang along with his partisans, earlier and said the Opry was no place for his opponents. 'They'll just sing the blues,' he said as the crowd laughed and applauded" (*New York Times*, Sept. 14, 1984, p. 12). The antagonists are associated with an aesthetic form suggesting both black culture (as opposed to the white country music) and pessimistic critique (as opposed to the upbeat optimism of the festival).

25.   Theodor W. Adorno, "The Idea of Natural History" in: *Telos*, No. 60 (Summer 1984), pp. 111-24.

ard Garouste's "Orion et Céladon," Sandro Chia's "Satyrs," and Arnulf Rainer's "Grünwald Variations." The exceptional force of the last example is undoubtedly due to the continued comprehensibility of the christological reference in the "overpainting" of images from the Isenheim altar. In the other examples, however, the mythic lexemes are addressed to a public no longer familiar with the encompassing narratives, nor is such familiarity even expected. The striking tendency for neo-figurativism to turn quickly to myth despite the absence of a correspondingly literate public indicates that the communicative character of art works is not at all the real issue. Instead, neo-classical mythic images are recognizable simply as contentless signs of culture and can be displayed as such by a public eager to distinguish itself through the possession of an art that leaves no doubt as to its artistic character. This instrumentalization of artworks in a semiotic display of class identity was certainly a pronounced tendency in the late nineteenth century as well, when however it was still relativized by the claims of autonomous aesthetics; the philistine misappropriation of art could be condemned in terms of the hegemonic aesthetic values. Today those values have been eroded, and philistinism can flourish without fear of condemnation, hence the epidemic of neo-classical imagery, a style which has repeatedly been used for the conservative representation of power.

While contemporary aesthetic production has finally escaped the limitations demanded by the formal sublimation of the traditional work (and its avant-gardist counterpart), the bourgeois separation of life and art too gives way to a massive aestheticization of everyday life. The aesthetic impulse, which has marched out of the museums and into the streets, casts an inescapable spell, transfiguring both slum and suburb. This encompassing universality still echoes the universal-human claims of classical aesthetics, but while the older notion of beauty was ultimately compatible with a utopia of freedom, the contemporary aestheticization of life turns out to be a prime guarantor of order. Art becomes the extension of politics, as the system of domination modernizes its mechanisms of control; not even the most argus-eyed cop-on-the-block could compete with the omnipresence of music, the most romantic of arts. Stores, markets, shopping centers, bars, restaurants, and airplanes are alive with the sound of muzak, and tunes regularly drone out over loudspeakers in public parks and pools, from hypertrophic radios at the beach and in the city, and even in the relative privacy of the telephone, when one is placed "on hold." The behaviorist thesis that the musical supermarket stimulates the consumer's will to buy is a crudely mechanistic trivialization of a profound restructuring of the public sphere. The ubiquity of muzak tends to obliterate communication and to break down individual resistance, constructing instead the beautiful illusion of a collective, singing along in dictatorial unanimity. Yet because it is a false collective in which no one is ever at home, it constantly collapses in a sado-masochistic antinomy: on the one hand, the autistic pseudo-privacy of the walkman, on the other, the megalomaniacal self-assertion of the ghetto blaster. The former apparently retreats into a self-enclosed passivity, while the latter imposes itself aggressively on its surroundings, and each of these gestures stands in an inverse relationship to the social status of the groups associated with the respective technical devices: the poorest sound the loudest. This contradiction indicates how, even in the context of the aestheticization of daily life, the post-auratic work still operates with a vestige of autonomous aesthetics, the non-identity of appearance and reality. The power of the music does not reflect the power of the recipient — the reverse is rather the case — and the corresponding principle of illusion is located at the intersection of aesthetic resources and political control.

Yet the hypothesis that the intonation of society acts as a vehicle for illusion is only an external explanation. The destruction of the public sphere through muscial blockage is not only manipulation but also the desublimation of a desire for isolated passivity, speechlessness and silence which are demanded of the recipient precisely by the overwhelming volume of the music. The deadening roar of the underclass radios conjoins with the catatonia of the walkeman victims in a mimesis of death. The libidinal economy is revealed in the locus of post-modern sociability, the dating bar, in which the decentered individual moves relentlessly from union to union, while the electronic noise guarantees the obsolescence of language and the vanity of communication. The specific constellation of sexual desire and deathly silence, eros and thanatos, indicates a new logic. For the difference between Odysseus and his men has dwindled, all hear the sirens and row toward them, knowing full well that it may mean their demise. Yet it is in fact the sirens who have disappeared; live performance has survived only in nostalgic enclaves — Dixieland in New Orleans or high school bands at football games — elsewhere music has fled the earthly bodies of musicians and reached the heavenly spheres. In this form, as dead labor, it envelops the contemporary listener who, still alive, pursues death through imitation in a new political economy. As passive as the absent producers, he fully understands the violence of the productive system, and precisely that violence fascinates the instinctual aggression, even when it is directed against himself. The aestheticization of life apparently appeals to a death desire that redefines artistic consumption as cannibalism; the exponential violence in the mass media and in spectacular crimes reflects a fundamental revision of the political-instinctual foundation of social organization. If music be the food of love, play on, but after the collapse of the ethic of worldly asceticism (Aschenbach's work), eros is not the only instinct to come to the fore.

The architectural counterpart to the abstraction of music is the concrete organization of space in definitively solid forms: shopping centers, airports, housing developments, convention halls, and the other accessories of city planning that overwhelm and overpower their inhabitants. The modernist relationship between the body and its spatial environment was determined by the discovery of sensuous plasticity (Rodin, Isadora Duncan) as a gesture against Victorian repression and by the dissolution of the oppressive nineteenth-century architectural shells that were replaced by the transparency of glass in order to flood the new interiors with the light of natural truth (Bruno Taut). In contrast, post-modern anti-subjectivity denies the presence of the body, while arbitrarily erecting concrete structures that compress space, channel movement and decisionistically affirm their own power as epistemic paradigms. The borderline between the two models separates the still modernist Hancock Building in Boston, dissolving into the sky and reflecting on the history of its local environment, from the Portland Building with its historicist facade signifying nothing, its reassuring coloration and its oppressively cozy lobby. After the escape of the work of art from the rigors of form, the aestheticization of everyday life pursues the imposition of form onto the recipient as victim, and this formative imperative draws from the same authoritarian source as does the rival of neo-classical language in painting. The new architecture does not open a public space; instead it encloses it in a carapaceous covering designed to insure order. Its stable solidity, historicist timelessness, and dark opacity all reveal its tomb-like character, providing the appropriate setting for the desublimation of thanatos.

The tendency to aestheticize space in terms of a death-like order extends as well to the reorganization of the body, which mirrors its new environment. As buildings take on an anti-modernist solidity and the power of mausoleums, body-building produces a muscular shell; beneath the ostensible intent to improve one's health lies an indisputable imitation of rigor mortis, the mimesis of death in the aestheticization of flesh, the symbol of which is the earthbound chunkiness of Arnold Schwarzenegger. Like the mythic references in painting and the formal imperative of architecture, the contemporary cult of the body and athletics draws on a neo-classical, hellenistic language; beauty and appearance are central categories in the new sports, but so are aggression and competition. The belligerent content in the martial arts and weight training is blatant, while even the apparently innocuous jogging culture is surrounded by an aura of violence, as anyone who has heard joggers berating drivers or drivers cursing out joggers will attest. The new athlete has trained his body to imitate machines, not to overcome them like John Henry. Competitiveness and survivalism abound; because he can run like hell, he looks forward to an imminent catastrophe, be it cancerous, ecological or nuclear, from which he alone, like Bunyan's Christian, will escape, while all the rest will be damned, deliciously enough. Conversely it is this expectation of catastrophe, a fixation on death, that fuels the health cult as the inverted camouflage of the latent content. Just as the Victorian repression of sex communicated with a distorted erotic desire, the contemporary insistence on health and the hysterical fear of disease point toward a deeper desire, as the joggers get ready for boot camp.

In addition to the aestheticization of the formerly public sphere via muzak, architecture and sports, a more encompassing aestheticization with particularly destructive consequences for the private sphere takes place through the process of commodification. The illusion of commodity aesthetics was always inherent in the capitalist relationship between use-value and exchange-value, and it has no particular, logical relationship to social organization in the late twentieth century. However in the pre-taylorist phase of the nineteenth century, the market mechanism still remained largely external to a multiplicity of traditional formations, such as peasant and working class culture, religious and regional heritages and family loyalties. These identities, which could provide the individual with at least partial protection from commodification, become exhausted during the long transitional period from 1905 to 1968; the relationship of avant-gardist modernism to social modernzation is ambivalent, since it contributes to the erosion of tradition, while frequently protesting against the consequences. With the demise during the seventies of the last generation that had known a non-commodified culture, the stage was set for the final invasion of the remaining private sphere by the logic of commodities, accelerated by the delegitimation of traditional gender roles and the crisis of the nuclear family. The atomistic individual, denied any inherited mechanism of self-identification, finds a helping hand in the world of commerce which proceeds to organize private lives in aesthetic terms: the life-style as the new colonial dumping ground for industrial overproduction. The atomized life that has been denied an authentic social context (family, community) becomes the object of commodified aestheticization. One consequence is the internal diversification of department stores where the multiplicity of tastes and tendencies quickly outdoes the touted polyphony of any post-modernist novel. Yet the process of life-stylization does not only apply to the department store set; it refers instead to the universal disappearance of an outside to art. There is no pre-aesthetic dimension to social activity, since social order has become dependent on aesthetic organization. Similarly nature, which art once imitated, has become secondary to art; any given piece of coastline, any single craggy peak cannot measure up to the standards set by the nature photographers and the Sierra Club calenders.

The double tendency examined so far, the desublimation of art in the wake of the avant-garde attack on the work and the extensive aestheticization of everyday life as a central strategy of capitalist progress, points out the anachronism of the position of critical theory outlined by Adorno. Obviously this contention is not made in order to resurrect Benjamin's modernist optimism, as has become fashionable in left post-modernism. On the contrary, the purported discovery of utopian elements in the manipulative aestheticization of social activity represents little more than a capitulation before the force of commodification. This statement however is itself dependent on a critique of Adorno that initially adopts his framework in order to trace its ageing. Adorno's argumentation is based on the two assumptions that, first, culture (both high and low) represented a separate sphere of activity distinguishable from the rest of society, especially the realm of production and, secondly, that a distinction between high and low culture was still tenable. Neither of these claims remains plausible today. A multi-faceted transformation of cultural organization has robbed Adorno's modernist aesthetics of much of their relevance for the contemporary situation: the denigration of technique, the accelerated commodification of artistic production, the destabilization of the institutional discourse, and the loss of faith in the objectivity of the art work. High art has rapidly integrated culture industrial forms in its works (Lichtenstein, Warhol) as well as in its mechanisms of distribution (televised concerts, mass marketing of subscriptions). One can speak less of a dialectical elevation of popular culture (although rock operas might be a relevant example) than of a transformed character of the culture industry. For Horkheimer and Adorno, the culture industry provided normative role models to integrate the masses into a conformist homogeneity through the identification with indistinguishable stars. Today the culture industry flaunts the outrageous and abnormal, the violent and the tabooed, although in the end it is all just good clean fun, so Michael Jackson can be received at the White House. In contrast to the golden age of Hollywood with its unwrinkled uniformity, contemporary commercial culture generates an artificial alterity: as entertainment, as a show of pluralism and as an effort to counteract the deadly sameness that advanced capitalism constantly produces. This internal diversification of the culture industry corresponds to an external flexibility; no longer directed largely toward white America (as was the case at the time of the writing of the seminal analysis in *Dialectic of the Enlightenment*), it has penetrated the black subculture and quickly coopted indigenous cultural forms: rap music, break dance. Historically the culture industry sapped off the energies of black culture since the days of minstrel shows; today the industry is assimilating that culture in a manner that promises to put an end to its autonomous character. Simultaneously the culture industry continues to succeed in foreign markets, with the ability to penetrate into the socialist east and to coopt the productive talents of any potential competitors (Caribbean music, German film). The first line of defense of American world power is culture, not the Cruise missiles.

Adorno's antinomic account of a clearly separated autonomous art and a manipulative culture industry fails to address the relevance of post-modernity as the culmination and supersession of the avant-gardist project. The erstwhile imperative of modernity — il faut être absoluement moderne — has ceased to represent a viable project. For the historical avant-garde, despite its revolutionary gestures, still depended on features of nineteenth-century cultural life that have since disappeared in the course of social modernization: the public's faith in the objectivity of art, the hermeneutically competent recipient, an acceptance of the work as the locus of an aesthetic otherness. The personality type of bourgeois culture (who alone was the object of dadaist shock), the associated structure of the public sphere and the institutional credibility of the work no longer support the modernist revolt, and this defines post-modernity as a new version of the end-of-art thesis. This does not mean that poems and paintings will soon become scarce, but it does mean that they lose their emphatic character as "works," the public ceases to treat them with the reverence still common two decades ago as potential sources of values, and the inherited generic identities quickly give way to hybrid forms. It is precisely this desublimation of works of art, no longer subjected to formal rationalization and increasingly expressive, that corresponds to the aestheticization of everyday life which too initiates a desublimation that revises the fundamental instinctual economy by agitating a death instinct that takes the aestheticized form of an aggressive collective. The renunciation of control and rigor leads Aschenbach to his encounter with the new community: "His heart throbbed to the drums, his brain reeled, a blind rage seized him, a whirling lust, he craved with all his soul to join the ring that formed about the obscene symbol of the godhead, which they were unveiling and elevating, monstrous and wooden, while from full throats they yelled their rallying cry. Foam dripped from their lips, they drove each other on with lewd gesturings and beckoning hands. They laughed, they howled, they thrust their pointed staves into each other's flesh and licked the blood as it ran down. But now the dreamer was in them and of them, the stranger god was his own. Yes, it was he who was flinging himself upon the animals, who bit and tore and swallowed smoking gobbets of flesh — while on the trampled moss there now began the rites in honour of the god, an orgy of promiscuous embraces — and in his very soul he tasted the bestial degradation of his fall."[26] The end of autonomous art as a vehicle of truth, which is the substance of post-modernism, engenders the violence of the desublimated collective held together only by myth. Mann's dionysian cult as an alternative to classical art therefore anticipates the contemporary predilection for mythic material: Christa Wolf, Michael Ende, Michel Tournier, J.R. Tolkien as well as that wing of "spiritual feminism" that dabbles in the purportedly pre-patriarchal mythology of the distant past in order to cement a subcultural community.[27] The national revolutionary Hennig Eichberg argues for the political revitalization of Germanic mythology, and Joseph Beuys, engaged for the Green Party, invokes the magic numinosity of the German oak.[28]

---

26. Mann, p. 68.

27. Cf. Christa Wolf, *Cassandra* (New York, 1984), Michael Ende, *The Never Ending Story*, (New York, 1983), Marion Bradley, *The Mists of Avalon* (New York, 1983), Michel Tournier, *The Ogre* (New York, 1972), J.R.R. Tolkien, *The Lord of the Rings;* (Boston, 1965); also Charlene Spretnak, *Lost Goddesses of Ancient Greece* (Berkeley, 1978).

28. Beuys comments: " . . . oak trees had a specific role to play not only during the Nazi period but even before then in the Wilhelmine era; it is certainly possible to misuse all these traditions but even when abused they do reveal another kind of factor and that is the polarity between the culture of the North and that of the South. Once again, under the sign of the oak, flowers the ancient contrast between the decentralized, almost barbarous culture of the Germanic peoples and the Celts, and the Latin conscience of urban character. The decentralized, itinerant and nomadic element in the Celtic and German nature is today current once again.

"It will naturally now be possible to prevent there being initiated any manipulation intent on opening the way to a historical and regressive conquest of a barbarous and inhumane past. We, on the contrary, intend with a new production of organic architecture to take action devoted to the future. We are perfectly aware that the most remote past and the most distant future come together under this sign." Joseph Beuys-Bernhard Blume, "Interview on Trees," in *Quartetto* (Milan, 1984), p. 105. Hennig Eichberg criticizes the constellation of patriarchy, monotheism and Christianity (which appears to be a sort of Roman colonialism when viewed from a neo-Germanic perspective) and points out the current ubiquity of myth even within the allegedly progressive subculture: "The renaissance of Celtic druids and Indian medicine men corresponds to the reappearance of witches in Germany (and elsewhere). Beside its liberal egalitarian wing, the feminist movement has generated a decidedly anti-egalitarian perspective, based on female

These final examples point toward the potential social consequences of the post-modernist end of art. The avant-gardist attack on the autonomous work finally succeeds in delegitimizing the aesthetic institution, while the desired aestheticization of quotidian experience stimulates a latent aggression no longer held in check by traditional cultural mechanisms. From modernism to nationalism to war? If one considers Marinetti as a model, the thesis can appear plausible, and the "menace" that hangs over the head of international politics turns out to have very much to do with Aschenbach's seeking "the open soon after tea." Three mechanisms in particular mediate the passage from cultural transformation to the aggressive nationalist collective. Firstly, after the disappearance of high art as a credible source of values, the propagandistic potential of the culture industry grows rapidly, carried on by the full aestheticization of everyday life. The propagandistic mobilization of nationalist identity is nothing new, as the role of Hollywood during the Second World War makes clear. Yet the relationship between cultural propaganda and nationalism has undergone an important change. The anti-fascist film redirected libidinal energy from erotic fulfillment (Bogart's self-denial in *Casablanca*) to substantial values of solidarity, i.e., nationalism operated with alibis like the defense of civilization, democracy or culture. The new nationalist propaganda, which emerged clearly during the Olympics, is linked to no such values. Instead an unmediated narcissistic egoism, fully oblivious to the competitiors (which is why the absence of the Russians made no difference), celebrates itself, as it directs a blind aggression toward any otherness it might encounter. The new nationalist mobilization has no pathos of values, and it no longer depends on a traditional bourgeois oedipal socialization leading from family to the state. On the contrary, the propaganda is informal and unpretentious, aggression in shirtsleeves, unmediated selfishness turning into absolute misanthopy. The increasingly violent character of culture industrial manipulation is evident not only in the bloodlust of films like *Friday the Thirteenth* and *Halloween* but in the murderous sociability portrayed in daytime soap operas or prime time series *(Dallas, Dynasty)* in contrast with which the television figures of the fifties and sixties seem endearing in their naive accounts of humanistic values.

This transformation of culture industrial nationalism depends on a second mechanism: a revised libidinal economy in the wake of the counter-culture. If the counter-culture represented a late stage in the modernist demontage of Victorian repression, it was also a vehicle for the aestheticitization of everyday life, since its hedonist critique of the Protestant ethic eventually contributed to an acceleration of consumerism and the colonialism of life-styles. Depsite this

specificity. Consequently the witches of the past recur as midwives and popular healers. The suppression of their paganism by Christianity (the father religion) and the science of male experts turns out to be a chapter in a comprehensive battle of the sexes." Eichberg goes on to point out how formerly leftist publishing houses have travelled from Marxism via anarchism and third-worldism to popular religions, shamanism and myths. See his "Kommen die alten Götter wieder? Germanisches Heldentum im 18./20 Jahrhundert — Zur Genese alternativer Mythen,: in: *Unter dem Pflaster liegt der Strand* Nr. 13, pp. 9-10.

unintended consequence, it argued that a breakdown of traditional structures and prohibitions would have desirable political results; "make love, not
war" means that the spread of the sexual revolution would undermine discipline and block military belligerence. The argument assumes a traditional
model of authoritarianism in which excessive instinctual denial produces the
potentially violent personality. It is a liberal argument insofar as it posits a fundamentally good human nature and treats the discontents of civilization as
unnecessary deformities caused by reformable social structures. The later
Freud, however, located a different tendency: the natural potential for violence and aggression that is kept in check only by a displacement of erotic force.
The thesis sheds an important light on the changed character of nationalist
voilence after the counterculture. For the new nationalism is fully compatible
with a non-ascetic, post-sixties life-style. It does not depend on restrictive high
schools, macho football coaches, fifties fathers and limited petting; it thrives
instead on the culture of selfhood, jogging marcissism, multiple divorces and
the absence of sexual prohibitions. The instinctual desublimation unleashes
innate aggression that is transfered from the personal self to the national self,
where it takes on the character of a global threat.

This appears at first to be paradoxical. The hedonist project, that stretches
from the emphatic eroticism of modernist art and literature (Klimt, Lawrence)
to its social realization in the counter-culture, does not lead to an authentic
increase in pleasure or a genuine hedonism (as the neoconservatives com-
plain). The emancipation of eros has been short-circuited as the "sexual
revolution," the main of benefits of which have accrued to the culture industry. Its main consequence has been the delegitimation of the institution of
erotic union (marriage) and a heightened experience of social atomization.
Traditional pleasure probably had to do with a victory over aggression in the
exceptional moment of a clandestine union when individuals escaped the
hostile logic of competitive individuality. The attack on erotic restriction has
turned into its opposite: the restriction of eros to universal competitiveness
and a weakening of the structures with which eros held thanatos in check.
The modernist promise of unlimited pleasure (Hesse's ball) has been realized
as a constantly increasing aggressive potential.

This magnification of aggression as it becomes nationalized can be explained with reference to a third mechanism. The dual process of cultural
transformation — the aestheticization of life and the desublimation of art —
carried an inherent violence which, after the completion of the process, is
occupied by the new nationalism. The aestheticization of life depended on
this violence because an organic resistance to consumerism (for example
within the multigenerational family structures that formerly preserved historical consciousness) had to be overcome; the concretization of that violence took
the form of generational conflicts with extraordinarily destructive outcomes.
In addition, because consumerism and the counter-culture insisted on the
model of a basically harmonious instinctual nature, they directed a repressive
force toward instinctual aggression to the extent that authentic conflicts and

differences were denied (cf. the suppression of particularity in Hesse's diony-sian crowd). An economy that wavers between cult of self and visions of unmediated solidarity fails to articulate genuine tensions which are sup-pressed and consequently nourished by the violence of their own suppres-sion.

Yet aggression accrues as well from the modernist process itself, i.e. the critique of autonomous art. Avant-garde iconoclasm, the hostility toward traditional modes of representation, reveals a basic antipathy toward beauty, pleasure and rest. The attack on the institution of art is not only a consequence of the specific character of the turn-of-the-century; it simultaneously rep-resents the remobilization of a self-destructive hatred endemic to modernity in the larger epochal sense. The derision directed toward bourgeois art, the contempt for contemplative satisfaction, and the hostility to peace that characterize the historical avant-garde all echo elements familiar from Savanarola's auto-da-fés and the Puritans' polemics against the theater. Para-doxically the artistic movement that accompanies the aestheticization of life is implicated in a profound denial of pleasure, inherent in all anti-aesthetic gestures. This hostility to pleasure, in turn, engenders the increased violence in the nationalist collective. Despite the ideology of hedonism and the demise of restrictive codes, the instinctual desublimation remains repressive, as pleasure is constantly promised and always withheld. The logical response to this frustration is aggression, misdirected, however, against irrelevant outsiders: the accumulated marital crises of 1984 fuel the invasion of Grenada.

Yet the anti-mimetic program cannot be reduced to this one anti-aesthetic element. Modernism was above all an effort to break the spell of the enchan-ted work and light up the world with the glow of Joyce's roman candles, not Savanarola's Florentine bonfires. The utopian desublimation of art, the pro-mise of the early twentieth-century avant-gardists, can still be articulated as a desideratum, no matter how its social ramifications have been misdirected by commodity aesthetics and the culture industry. If the avant-garde has failed to reach the envisioned emancipation precisely because of the coopted success of its dual strategy, then criticism ought at least preserve that vision as a standard with which to measure the culture that contemporary society declares suc-cessful. The modernist utopia, which was concretized in the aesthetic theory of the Frankfurt School, can — despite its obsolescence — be preserved and renewed in a critical appraisal of both the aestheticized society and the poten-tials for new artistic production.

After the completion of the avant-garde project, works of art have lost their privileged status and are no longer a safe harbor for the utopian image of a successful civilization, but the principle of aestheticization expands through-out society as a crucial medium of manipulation. In turn, however, social con-traditions are transferred directly into the aesthetic sphere. Critical theory always insisted that society recurred within the autonomous work, inscribed in the constellation of aesthetic categories. The congruence of society and art remains valid today, but in a new sense. The work of art which once appeared to be the final enclave of truth and resistance has been dismantled, and the end of the work means the end of art, understood in terms of the traditional bourgeois institution. Yet the aestheticization of everyday life as a crucial mechanism of control suggests the ubiquity of the signs of political power. As aesthetic manipulation expands into all facets of social activity, manipulation can be confronted from any point within aestheticized society. In the wake of the deautonomization of art, culture may potentially undergo a politicization, transforming it into the primary terrain for social conflict and revealing the fundamental weaknesses in a cultural defense of the heteronomous order. The "aesthetization of politics" and life, which won out over the "politization of aestehtics," does not generate a monolithic stability. The conflation of art and politics may certainly operate as deception to the extent that issues of substance are hidden by a charade of signs. However, this distinction between rhetoric and power is hardly new. The point is that in the wake of the aestheticization of everyday life, political power is dependent on a thoroughly transformed language of parliamentary reason, and becomes perhaps more labile. It is therefore crucial to ask where new points of tension emerge along with new structural deficiencies.

Firstly, while aesthetic culture might seem to provide a natural legitimation for a system of commodity aesthetics, all aesthetic claims have in fact been wounded by the avant-gardist attack on art. The collapse of objective notions of beauty, the lack of credible experts in (high or low) cultural matters, and the constant destruction of the auratic claims of culture industrial figures add up to an immanently labile mechanism of manipulation. Bourgeois aesthetic taste was remarkably stable during the nineteenth century, in marked contrast to the speed of technological innovation. Today the velocity with which the fashions of the aestheticized life-world are transformed is a function of revolutionary capitalism, and the perpetuity of change robs the social order of the signs of traditional legitimation. Not long ago, the domestic interior was dominated by inherited objects, laden with family memories; today they have been liquidated or return solely in the weak form of commodified antiques. While this transformation is undoubtedly a symptom of social amnesia and dehistoricization, it also implies an extraordinarily flexible present; it can engender either an easily malleable victim for manipulation or a potential subject that might finally free itself from the nightmares of the past.[29] The disappearance of history in post-modernity is clearly not by itself a radical project. The point is rather that a new political terrain is emerging. Traditional signs of authority tend to lose their effectiveness, which leads to anti-authoritarian opportunities. Such possibilities must, however, necessarily compete with non-traditional signs of authority as well as with the erosion of subjectivity no longer able to constitute itself through a critique of tradition.

Secondly, the aestheticization of everyday life tends to erode its own credibility by never fulfilling its promises. Neither the shining temptation of con-

---

29.   Russell Jacoby, *Social Amnesia* (Boston, 1975); Jean Baudrillard, *La Societe de Consommation* (Paris, 1974).

sumer goods nor the irresistable aura of the culture star anticipates the perpetual experience of disappointment on the part of the consumer or spectator; the sensuous gratification promised by the aestheticized object is never adequate. This dynamic is related to the exaggerated self-esteem of the narcissist who can never be satisfied by his environment. The resulting aggression need not become an object of manipulation in the new nationalist collective. On the contrary, the more illusion becomes the predominant characteristic of commodity production and marketing, the more susceptible does the system become to criticism from consumer groups. The limit to capitalist abstraction is the concrete use-value demanded of the product. This points to various forms of politicization: regulation of advertising, heightened safety standards and — more radically — a desertion from the dictated life-style of consumerism. The limits to these strategies are equally obvious: eventual conflicts with producers (unions), the shift in the economy from concrete goods to abstract services, and the pending alliance between anti-consumerism from below and austerity measures from above.

Thirdly, the transference of social conflict into the cultural sphere due to the aestheticization of everyday life implies that societal contradictions will take on a visible concreteness. The tendency of the bourgeois public sphere to subject politics to a process of abstraction and restriction, both in a temporal (election year) and geographical sense (the parliament as the sole forum of debate), gives way to the immediate presence of the signs of social membership. If image has replaced substance in the new social spectacle, then any struggle over images becomes a struggle for power.[30] The ideological conflict between the major parties is overshadowed by the competition between alternative strategies of self-representation and display: the classic simplicity of Republican unanimity or the gothic diversity of Democratic pluralism. Political commentators direct their attention nearly exclusively to image production and ignore substantive difference. While sensuous appearance displaces conceptual debate as the primary medium of national politics, the same principle of aesthetic concretization forces the subcultural opposition to a similar localization of its concerns: instead of a general critique of, for example, nuclear power, campaigns against single plants. The aestheticization of everyday life promises an escape from the abstract universality of traditional politics and a recognition of the primacy of particularity, a category previously reserved for works of art. It could therefore potentially engender a reinvigora-

---

30. "In the midst of a half-hour of American good feeling and praise for Ronald Reagan that the Republican campaign aired on television this week, there was one woman who looked into the camera with a sun-struck conviction and summed up the impression that is the strength of the Reagan Presidency, and the way the President creates it.

'I think he's just doggone honest.' she said. 'It's remarkable. He's been on television — what have I heard, about 26 times, talking to us about what he's doing? Now he's not doing that for any other reason than to make it real clear. And if anybody has any question about where he's headed, it's their fault. Maybe they don't have a television.' " (*New York Times*, Sept. 14, 1984, p. 12). In fact, Reagan has had fewer televised interviews and news conferences than his predecessors. The point is rather that aestheticized politics tends to drop the traditional dialogic forms, remnants of a liberal parliamentary ethos of political responsibility, and replaces them with the power of the cosmetic image.

tion of political conflict. However, it is unlikely to generate emancipatory political values from within; while it may successfully mobilize aestheticized crowds, they will have difficulty escaping the tide of collective aggression that has emerged from the process of cultural transformation.

By shifting social conflict into the cultural sphere, aestheticization consequently initiates at least these three new sorts of political developments: the iconoclastic delegitimation of the signs of authority, the expressionist critique of (commodity) illusion and the sensuous concretization of practice. Similarly the other aspect of the dual strategy of the avant-garde, i.e., the attack on autonomous art, may open up possibilities for contemporary artistic innovation that ought not be surrendered prematurely to the culture industry. To the extent that innovation continues to generate qualitatively new works, it is first of all crucial to provide a critical defense of their authenticity as exceptions to the rule of commodification. Critical theory's traditional insistence on aesthetic autonomy retains its relevance, despite the levelling of the difference between high and low culture and the dissolution of the work. In fact, these factors make a defense of authenticity all the more urgent, even if it no longer credibly represents a full strategic opposition to the administered society. In the complex landscape of contemporary artistic production, it is necessary to differentiate and locate the singular works which continue to shelter utopian alternatives; this critical project amounts to a theoretically conservative allegiance to genuine innovation against regressive forms of progress.

Secondly, outside the magic circle of genuine works, non-autonomous artistic production has become the watchword of the art market instead of fulfilling the promises of the avant-garde. A reversal of this situation would entail an emancipatory reauraticization of art, which may in fact be evident already in the most extreme stages of art's self-alienation: the radicality of minimalist formalism and the post-modernist scrutiny of traditional contents. Is it possible to imagine an art that participates in society neither as commodity nor as ornament nor as an engaged exponent of politics but as the placeholder of a radical otherness which is therefore utopian? A genuine retrieval of aura, which would necessitate a reversal of the trajectory of bourgeois culture, might counteract the perpetually heightening aggressive potential and articulate a project of community. Contemporary aesthetic theory faces the task of articulating an account of reauraticization that neither capitulates to the culture industry by designating its schmalz as utopian nor demands a civilizational regression by linking aura exclusively to rebarbarization. To overcome the extirpation of culture by reinvoking Weber's new prophets is neither theoretically honest nor politically desirable.[31] The problem remains, however, that the charisma of community has disappeared, while false collectives constantly generate self-destructive aggression, mobilized by a plethora of would-be charismatic leaders.

Finally, a reauraticization of art that would escape the force of the culture

---

31.   Max Weber, *The Protestant Ethic and the Spirit of Capitalism* (New York, 1976), p. 182.

industry cannot return to the traditional elitism of the liberal bourgeois period. In fact, it was precisely that elitism that provoked a populist hostility which avenged itself through the victorious culture industry (the Marx brothers at the opera). The same dynamic determined the demise of the political avant-garde and epic leftism: the Leninist elitism of the twenties liquidated by the pseudo-popularity of socialist realism in the thirties (Lukács contra Brecht). Clearly the future of art depends on an escape from both elitist conspicuous consumption (the culture vulture as recipient) and mass manipulation (putative realism and naive art). The alternative for authentic art would be authentic democratization, the necessary corollary to the theory of reauraticization. If art is to resist the aggression of a self-destructive society, then it has to reject any heteronomous institutionalization that appropriates the aesthetic object as a weapon against the excluded social groups. The bourgeois reification of culture transformed the aesthetic utopia into a sign of class privilege in order to wage a domestic war: the work of art as the mechanism of barbarism. To escape the logic of violence, art would have to renounce its elitist elevation, which was always an abuse. Because the hidden agenda of elitism was commodification, reducing art to a fully secular object of investment, a retrieval of aura today can only mean a renunciation of privilege and a democratic culture. It is a tendency already anticipated by subcultural transformations where works of art become increasingly accessible and the notion of the artist, stripped of much of its romantic pathos, is turned into a universal potential, "an art *per du* with humanity."[32] A reconciliation of the isolated artist and the bourgeois philistine — the antinomic poles of the classical modernist project — could emancipate the sense of the citizen. For now, however, the false reconciliation has only aestheticized the lackluster forms of capitalist relations.

32.   Thomas Mann, *Doctor Faustus* (New York, 1971), p. 322.

Books from:
Telos Press

Lucien Goldmann

Cultural Creation in Modern Society
$5.50 paper; $14 cloth

Essays on Method in the Sociology of Literature
$5.50 paper; $14.50 cloth

Jean Baudrillard

For a Critique of the Political Economy of the Sign
$5.50 paper; $14 cloth

Mirror of Production
$4.50 paper only

Marx and Engels on Literature and Art

Lee Baxandall, Stefan Morawski, eds. $4.50 paper; $12 cloth

Towards a New Marxism
Bart Grahl, Paul Piccone, eds.
$4.50 paper; $14 cloth

Essays on the New Working Class
Dick Howard, Dean Savage, eds.
$5.50 paper; $14 cloth

Political Plays for Children
Jack Zipes, ed. $5 paper only

Send with check or money order (U.S. currency only) to TELOS PRESS, Box 3111, St. Louis, Mo. 63130 USA. *Foreign order add 10%.*

FOUNDATIONS AND
THE SUPREME COURT

by Joan Roelofs

The literature of "power elite" theory is surprisingly silent on the role of the judiciary. This is particularly strange as the judiciary was designed to be *the* elite institution in the federal system, and there is a good deal of evidence that it has functioned as planned: "The Court's power is a natural outcome of the necessity for maintaining capitalist dominance under democratic forms; . . . - judicial review has proved to be a very convenient channel through which the driving forces of American economic life have found expression and achieved victory."[1] The elite backgrounds of the judges have been much studied, and might explain a predisposition to respond to elite interests and values. However, the "input" channels remain mysterious. The Court has been seen as an agent of corporate capitalism.[2] It remains to be shown how the Court receives and processes elite demands. Foundations have been oddly neglected. There are probably more studies of foundation garments than of the massive institutions overpinning our society. Most works on foundations are commissioned by the subject and are highly self-congratulatory.

Foundations do not want to look as if they were trying to arrange the world to suit themselves. In fact, they even go as far as to sponsor some "artificial negativity."[3] An early device to hide their hands was the creation of universities (e.g., University of Chicago, Johns Hopkins) and research institutes (e.g., American Law Institute, Brookings) whose findings would be regarded as detached and objective.[4] More recently, there has been the creation or vital patronage of "grassroots" organizations. What is striking about such groups (e.g., Planned Parenthood, Mexican-American Legal Defense and Education Fund) is the passivity of membership (where there is any), reliance on professionals, and focus on litigation techniques.

The major foundations studied here (Ford, Rockefeller, Carnegie, Sage, Twentieth Century Fund) are interested in reform, but they seek to control it and channel it in ways that will promote "modernization" and social rationalization. They are also interested in establishing civilized standards of justice

---

1. Max Lerner, "The Divine Right of Judges," in *The People, Politics and the Politician,* ed. Asher N. Christensen and Evron M. Kirkpatrick (New York: Henry Holt, 1941), p. 578.
2. Joan Roelofs, "The Warren Court and Corporate Capitalism," *Telos* 39 (Spring 1979), pp. 94-112.
3. Paul Piccone, "The Crisis of One-Dimensionality," *Telos* 35 (Spring 1978), pp. 43-54.
4. Stanley Katz and Barry Karl "The American Private Philanthropic Foundation and the Public Sphere: 1890-1930," *Minerva* 19 (1981), pp. 236-270. This is a publication of the International Association for Cultural Freedom.

to legitimate the system, which they see threatened by "alien redemptive ideologies." They are primarily interested in bureaucratizing and "depoliticizing" social change; organizing the masses is not their style. "Foundation funding tends to support the use of lawyers . . . rather than organize citizens to act on their own behalf."[5]

The foundations are closely interlocked with each other and with many important institutions of American life: corporations, universities, charities, cultural organizations. They also create satellite foundations, think-tanks, and "grassroots" organizations to carry out their work. They are closely linked with the public sector, not only through the frequent donation of personnel, and the steady supply of public policy ideas, but also as financial benefactors of a great variety of public projects, e.g., funding for covert actions abroad, for Great Society "Mobilization for Youth" programs, and for Senator Hennings Subcommittee on Constitutional Rights during the 1950s. They consequently attain the power associated with horizontal and vertical integration in the marketplace. However, while foundations and their critics (mostly right-wingers) acknowledge their vast power, they disagree over whether this is benevolent.

Clearly, the foundation network is not the *only* influence on Supreme Court policymaking, but it is a very important one which has generally been overlooked. It helps to shape the judicial environment in which even the "conservative" Burger Court is compelled to play the role of judicial activism, for "activist legal forces control feeder processes to the Supreme Court."[6] Furthermore, the foundations are not all-powerful; their efforts do not always succeed. A good example is in school finance reform on which millions have been spent by foundations. Nevertheless, a majority of the Supreme Court would not declare that unequal financing of schools is in violation of the equal protection clause *(San Antonio v. Rodriquez* 411 U.S. 1:1973). Foundation-supported litigants did win ten significant cases on the state level, which may indicate the direction of future law reform efforts.

The following, while not ignoring interesting connections in time and space, will concentrate on the ways in which major foundations influenced or attempted to influence Supreme Court decision-making, especially during the intense period of judicial activism, approximately 1952 to 1975.

Foundations and Culture

The great foundations arose in the early twentieth century when the new millionaires sought a systematic way to dispose of their fortunes. There was more than enough to leave to their families, and retail giving to charity was an administrative nightmare. The Carnegie Corporation, for the promotion of broad educational purposes, was chartered by New York State in 1911. John

---

5. Mary Anna C. Colwell, *Philanthropic Foundations and Public Policy: The Political Role of Foundations,* Ph.D. Dissertation, (Berkeley, 1980), p. 88.

6. Marvin Schick, "Judicial Activism on the Supreme Court," in *Supreme Court Activism and Restraint,* ed. Stephen C. Halpern and Charles M. Lamb, (Lexington: Lexington Books, 1982), p. 45.

D. Rockefeller decided ". . . to establish one great foundation. This foundation would be a single central holding company which would finance any and all of the other benevolent organizations, and thus necessarily subject them to its general supervision."[7] The Rockefeller Foundation failed to obtain a Congressional charter because of the odium of the name, but was chartered by New York State in 1913.[8] Russell Sage and Cleveland Foundations, Baron de Hirsch Fund and others were created at about this time. The Ford Foundation was established in 1936, and funded Michigan charities: "When the old man died in 1947, the Foundation acquired nearly 90 percent of the company's stock in the form of nonvoting shares, while the family retained the (voting) balance. Some $300 million in inheritance taxes thus shrank to a few million, and it was arranged for the Foundation to pick up even this modest tab; no FMC stock had to be put up at public auction."[9] With increasing value of the Ford stock, the Foundation's wealth outgrew its local focus and prompted its search for purposes national and international in scope.[10]

Tax evasion and public relations have been the motivations for most foundations (along with indeterminable quantities of guilt and benevolence). However, the most ominous product of the giant foundations is their translation of wealth into power. They can create, sustain and disseminate an ideology protective of capitalism; they can deflect criticism and mask or actually correct damaging abuses of the system; they can hire the best brains, popular heroines, even left-wing political leaders to do their work. One way in which they influence Supreme Court decisions as through their shaping of public opinion, especially elite opinion, which of course includes judges, lawyers, law students and professors. "Another motive for establishing the foundation, to which Rockefeller gave high priority, was a desire to show socialists that capitalism was capable of promoting the greatest 'general good'."[11] Foundation ideology makes certain litigation conceivable, certain arguments believable and certain decisions receivable, by the relevant public opinion.

There is great agreement among non-foundation-sponsored observers, whether of the right or left, on the way foundations function in our society. A leading contemporary critic, Robert Arnove, states: ". . . foundations like Carnegie, Rockefeller, and Ford have a corrosive influence on a democratic society; they represent relatively unregulated and unaccountable concentrations of power and wealth which buy talent, promote causes, and, in effect, establish an agenda of what merits society's attention. They serve as 'cooling-out' agencies, delaying and preventing more radical, structural change."[12] On

---

7. Barbara Howe, "The Emergence of Scientific Philanthrophy 1900-1920," in *Philanthropy and Cultural Imperialism,* ed. R. Arnove (Boston: G.K. Hall, 1980), p. 29.

8. *Ibid.,* p. 30.

9. Leonard Silk and Mark Silk, *The American Establishment* (New York: Basic Books, 1980), p. 126.

10. Ford Foundation, *Report of the Study for the Ford Foundation on Policy and Program* (Detroit, 1949).

11. Merli Curti and R. Nash, *Philanthropy in the Shaping of American Higher Education* (New Brunswick: Rutgers University Press, 1965), p. 215.

12. *Philanthropy and Cultural Imperialism,* R. Arnove (ed.), p. 1.

the other side, Birchite Gary Allen observes: "The terrible part of this business is that the economic fraud permitted the Rockefellers through their foundations — though maddening to the middle-class taxpayers who are aware of it — is the *least* malignant part of the foundation picture. It is the political and social impact of these foundations which is devastating."[13] These views show continuity with the attitudes of middle class progressive reformers of the early twentieth century. A congressional investigation was undertaken in 1915, seeking to unmask the activities of the Rockefeller Foundation, which were then regarded as a snow job to dispel nationwide horror at the Ludlow Massacre. The Walsh Commission found that: "The domination by the men in whose hands the final control of a large part of American industry rests is not limited to their employees, but is being rapidly extended to control the education and 'social service' of the nation. This control is being extended largely through the creation of enormous privately managed funds for indefinite purposes, hereinafter designated 'foundations,' by the endowment of colleges and universities, by the creation of funds for the pensioning of teachers, by contributions to private charities, as well as through controlling or influencing the public press." And it concludes "As regards the 'foundations' created for unlimited general purposes and endowed with enormous resources, their ultimate possibilities are so grave a menace, not only as regards to their own activities and influence but also the numbing effect which they have on private citizens and public bodies, that if they could be clearly differentiated from other forms of voluntary altruistic effort, it would be desirable to recommend their abolition."[14]

The Commission's recommendations were forgotten after the First World War. The mood of the country had changed and the foundation image was improving. This can be attributed in some measure to their role in fighting diseases and providing war relief. A more unusual tactic was the pension plan for college professors established in 1905 by the Carnegie Foundation for the Advancement of Teaching.[15] Furthermore, foundation methods became more subtle. The American Council of Learned Societies (1919) and Social Science Research Council (1924) were created as academic holding companies to distribute research funds slightly laundered of the Rockefeller and Carnegie stains.

The cleanup has been remarkable. In the pre-World War I period, all pro-

---

13. *The Rockefeller File* (Seal Beach: '76 Press, 1976), p. 42.

14. U.S. Congress. Commission on Industrial Relations. *Report.* (Washington, D.C.: Government Printing Office, 1915), pp. 118-125.

15. "This foundation was essentially a $10 million trust which financed pensions for aging college and university professors in a number of elite private east coast institutions . . . Similar arrangements were demanded by faculty and supported by trustees at other leading public and private universities. Once established, the plan worked to insure loyal service from grateful faculty and thus encouraged stability, compliance, and conservatism on the part of the academic labor force . . . By 1931 . . . Carnegie financial advisors shifted the program to a contributory plan administered by the Teachers Insurance and Annuity Association (TIAA)." David E. Weischadle, "The Carnegie Corporation and the Shaping of American Educational Policy," in *Philanthropy and Cultural Imperialism, op. cit.,* pp. 364-366.

gressive thought (and Progressivism was the ideology of the elite) regarded the name Rockefeller in all its manifestations as a synonym for the devil. The socialist-anarchist "Reds" crowd, to which Margaret Sanger belonged, doubled this in spades. Yet by the eve of World War II, Sanger is working hand-in-glove with the Rockefeller Foundation birth-control subsidiaries.[16] Thus does a movement for liberation become entangled and supported by the elite, whose interest in population control is related, but very different in nature.

By the late 1940s, many socialist intellectuals had been absorbed into the foundation orbit. Now Congressional committees were accusing foundations of promoting communism![17] This was because they identified communism not with proletarian revolution or the overthrow of capitalism, but with the concept of social engineering. René Wormser, counsel to the Reece Committee[18] saw a vast bureaucracy composed of the major foundations and their satellite organizations (SSRC, ACLS, American Council on Education, etc.): "The ideas and concepts of this bureaucracy are based heavily on the assumption of a cultural lag — the need to adjust law, values, and human affairs in general to a tempo dictated by our rapid technological progress."[19] This perception is accurate as far as it goes, but the right-wing critics never focus on the goals of the foundations: to preserve the power and wealth of the present ownership class and to make whatever social and political changes are necessary to insure this. The elite embraces such "radical" ideas as economic planning, world federalism, social responsibility of corporations, social responsibility of the legal profession and racial integration, because they hope to make them work for their own purposes. On the other hand, the foundations do not sponsor research or issue pamphlets on the desirability of supplanting the multinational corporations with collective or cooperative ownership.[20] On the contrary, they have made respectable the idea that public "seed" money should be provided to revitalize capitalism, e.g., the Ford Foundation's Community Development Corporation idea. As one former President of the Ford Foundation (Pifer) stated: " . . . foundations should anticipate the streams of social change and facilitate the adaptation of major institutions to such change."[21]

The objectives and operations of foundations are not confined to the United States. This was clearly stated when the Ford Foundation announced its goals for the future of mankind in 1949. Ford had intervened in grassroots political movements at home and abroad and sought to shape institutions and to influence public policy from above and below. A major function of the

16.   David Kennedy, *Birth Control in America* (New Haven: Yale University Press, 1970).

17.   U.S. Congress, House, *Hearings before the Select Committee to Investigate Tax-Exempt Foundations and Comparable Organizations,* 83rd. Cong., 2nd Sess., 1954 (Reece Committee).

18.   *Ibid.*

19.   *Foundations: Their Power and Influence* (New York: Devin-Adair, 1958), p. 81.

20.   But the Ford Foundation did give a grant to Critical Legal Theorist Roberto Unger of $104,400 for the development of a New Social Theory. Ford Foundation, *Annual Report,* 1979.

21.   Waldmar Neilsen, *The Big Foundations* (New York: Columbia University Press, 1972), p. 45.

foundations is to serve as sophisticated strategists of the Cold War. This has been their role since they sought to deflect the attack by populists and socialists on the "robber barons." It is not suprising that they share methods and leading personnel with the CIA. As one student of foundations has perceived it: "The political territory throughout the world which is principally prized and sought by the CIA is what it usually calls the NCL (the Non-Communist Left). Its policy is to infiltrate — and, if possible, take over the leadership of — moderate reform movements to prevent them from moving further leftwards, and in this way to safeguard American interests — not excluding the economic ones. Hence its field of interest has a useful overlap with the catchment-area of foundations."[22]

The foundations find their task in promoting social change to prevent discontent and disequilibrium, channeling protest movements into harmless directions, and providing ideology for whatever they do. Litigation is one particularly promising technique for these operations: it can produce some change when legislatures are sluggish; it is safe and conservative; it involves the public only as spectators, and it does not violate IRS rules for tax-exempt organizations.

There has been little serious attempt to develop a theory of the foundations in American society.[23] Right-wing critics perceive their effects on culture and policy but do not like to consider the implications of their foreign activities and CIA involvements. Liberal critics often focus on the trees — the foundations which exist merely to evade taxes or those active in extreme right-wing causes — and miss the forest — the power of the "benevolent" large "progressive" foundations. At a recent Congressional investigation of foundations, the Director of the Tax Reform Research Group (Naderite) Thomas Stanton asked: "Are we, the American people, really getting our money's worth for the immense tax subsidies which we grant to foundations and donors?"[24] He was the major critical witness; he approved of the well-staffed, active big foundations. It was the ones that did not do much that he faulted.

One recent theory, part of a major study of public interest law sponsored by the Ford Foundation, maintains that: "We have shown that there are likely to be both efficiency and equity failures in the private market, and we have suggested that government, which might be expected to correct such failures, is not always able to do so . . . Failures in the government sector, might give rise to a need for a voluntary sector, including public interest law (PIL) activities."[25]

22.   Ben Whitaker, *The Foundations* (London: Methuen, 1974), p. 163. See also Edward Berman, *The Influence of the Carnegie, Ford and Rockefeller Foundations on Foreign Policy* (Albany: SUNY Press, 1983).

23.   The best is the work in the Arnove volume.

24.   U.S. Congress, House, *Hearings on Exempt Foundations and Charitable Trusts before the Subcommittee on Domestic Finance of the House Committee on Banking and Currency.* 93rd Cong., 1st Sess., 1973 (Patman Committee), p. 15.

25.   Burton Weisbrod, "Conceptual Perspectives on the Public Interest: an Economic Analysis," in *Public Interest Law*, ed. Weisbrod, Joel Handler and Neil K. Komesar, (Berkeley: University of California Press, 1978), p. 25.

Critics on the left are scarce. A few journalists have taken on the foundations; those with academic connections rarely.[26] Foundations give grants to leftists and may employ them on their staffs, but they do not finance studies of foundations from radical perspectives.

Ideology

Many who discuss the American ideology — pluralism and its variants — assume that it comes from the air we breathe. Yet, ideology is a way of looking at the world; it is not scientifically derivable. In the past, ideology may have emanated somehow from the "ruling class." Today ideology can be produced, updated, and disseminated, using modern technology and psychology. Specialized institutions — the foundations and their satellites — provide this service.

The ideology that emerges from the foundations has roots in the Progressive movement. This was a response to populist and socialist protest against the evils of the late 19th century.[27] Notions of class struggle and social classes were transmuted by the Progressives into "social problems" and tasks for social scientists. "The elitist and technocratic dimensions of foundations — their imperious and imperial stance — inhere in their belief that social change can occur and social ills can be redressed by highly trained professionals (scientists and technicians) who produce knowledge and proffer solutions."[28]

Before the First World War, the Sage Foundation was particularly active in financing the professionalization of charity and promoting the idea (through publications, conferences and the journal *Survey*) that poverty was an individual problem requiring the intervention of social workers.[29] At the same time, the National Municipal League, and its affiliates, supported by the Rockefeller Foundation, were advocating reforms which tended to depoliticize local government: "The council-manager form of government was a general device to depoliticize city government. It was part of a mystique of efficiency and expertise that brands the average person as incompetent to make political judgements."[30]

During the interwar period, socialist theories gradually lost all respectability in the academic world. Foundation-supported (through SSRC, ACLS or directly) empirical social science rushed in to become the conventional wisdom, to the consternation of traditionalists. The Rockefeller Foundation and the Rockefeller-financed University of Chicago took a leading role in fostering this new orthodoxy. Rockefeller funds even managed to transform the London School of Economics, an institution created by the Fabian Socialists to

---

26. David Horowitz and David Kolodney, "The Foundations," *Ramparts*, (April and May 1969).

27. Samuel P. Hays, *The Response to Industrialism: 1885-1914* (Chicago: University of Chicago Press, 1957).

28. Arnove, *op. cit.*, p. 18.

29. Sheila Slaughter and Edward T. Silva, "Looking Backwards: How Foundations Formulated Ideology in the Progressive Period," in *Philanthropy and Cultural Imperialism*, p. 59.

30. G. William Domhoff, *The Powers That Be* (New York: Vintage, 1979) p. 155.

train administrators for a socialist Britain, into an outpost of American social science.[31] The Carnegie Corporation was supporting the psychological studies of Thorndike, which concluded that differences in social status were based on measurable innate differences of ability. This idea was incorporated into the Carnegie-initiated reforms of higher and general education, in the form of tracking and sorting systems.[32]

After the Second World War, the Ford Foundation defined and shaped the field of behavioralism through its own programs and through institutions it created, such as the Center for Advanced Study in the Behavioral Sciences.[33] This was not a value-free science but an instrumental ideology, meant to forestall anticipated social disorder on a national and international scale. The best statement of the policy orientation of behaviorism is the Ford Foundation's 1949 *Report*.[34] This was produced by a study committee chaired by Rowan Gaither (a lawyer who headed the Rand Corporation), charged with discovering which problems of mankind to solve, and how. The aim was to employ the vast discretionary funds of the Foundation ". . . to assist democracy to meet [the] challenge." The only way to fight communism was to meet all needs: ". . . to help man achieve his entire well-being . . ." The dignity of man, equal rights, and equal opportunity to develop capabilities were of great importance. The *Report* does not show an uncritical acceptance of the American political system. On the contrary, there are many problems to be solved with the foundation funds. There are defects in political institutions and a shortage of competent people in government. Red-baiting, with its trampling on civil liberties, is found to be counterproductive. Certain faults are particularly ominous: maladjusted individuals, lack of political participation and ". . . intergroup hostilities weaken our democratic strength by dissipating important resources of energy in internal conflicts, and by swelling the ranks of malcontents who constitute the seedbed for undemocratic ideologies."[35] The Ford Foundation, which, they claim, represents no interests and is not partisan, will be the agent to bring about the democratic utopia and universal peace. To further the latter aim: "Foundation success in this field may at times require activities in public education long in advance of official policy formulation. In fact, a foundation can make a most significant contribution by anticipating critical issues and by stimulating awareness and understanding of them in advance of governmental action."[36] Democracy will be promoted and apathy defeated by employing scientists or educators in the role of social engineers to stimulate and mobilize an interest in public affairs.

The Foundation conceives of democracy in terms of "results." This is the

---

31.   Donald Fisher, "American Philanthropy and the Social Sciences: the Reproduction of a Conservative Ideology," in *Philanthropy and Cultural Imperialism, op. cit.*

32.   Frank Darknell, "The Carnegie Philanthropy and Private Corporate Influence on Higher Education," *ibid.,* p. 405.

33.   Peter Seybold, "The Ford Foundation and the Triumph of Behavioralism in American Political Science," *ibid.*

34.   *Op. cit.*

35.   *Ibid.,* p. 46.

36.   *Ibid.,* p. 59.

same defense made today for judicial activism. The *Report* suggests that it would be useful to impose a welfare state, meritocratic education system, personal adjustment and constructive citizen participation. Economic planning may even be necessary. However, the authors of the *Report* never question the system of power, privilege, and hegemony.

To further the goals outlined in the *Report*, the Ford Foundation created the Fund for the Republic in 1952. The focus of the Fund's activities was the attempt: ". . . to assist the promotion of a national security based on freedom and justice."[37] One study financed by the Fund, Samuel Stouffer's *Communism, Conformity and Civil Liberties* (1955), promoted the idea that the masses have no respect for civil liberties, which would be more carefully preserved by an elite. This work has been a major support for the elitist point of view in political science.[38] A recent retrospective study of the Ford Foundation (by one of its officers) reaffirms their commitment to promoting social change. The philosopher-kings do not always show their hands, and may choose to work through others: ". . . we may feel that public policy is neither well formed nor well carried out, in which cases we try to support responsible critics despite the risk that they and the government may perceive each other as adversaries. We sometimes have supported institutions and individuals in an adversary role (especially as they employ litigation and other active means short of lobbying and political campaigning) when we felt the public interest would be served."[39]

By dispensing millions in discretionary funds, the major foundations achieve oligopolistic control over reform. They may foster existing movements or create new organizations (including "grassroots" ones) as they need them. The well-financed organizations tend to cannibalize those which are struggling along. Control is enhanced as the directorates of the foundations interlock with each other and with all major public and private institutions. Their money goes far; grants tend to stimulate others to support an organization. The foundations hope that ultimately the government will continue to support their projects, so that they can use their funds elsewhere. This has happened in many cases (e.g., the NEH, NSF, etc. are modeled on SSRC, ACLS; the OEO on Ford's Grey Areas program).

The promotion of reform from above relies on sophisticated cooptation techniques. For example, by 1975, the Ford Foundation Leadership Development Program had spent $11.5 million on identifying and training rural educators and community workers who showed leadership potential.[40] In addition, $2 million was spent on the National Center for Education in Politics, to involve college students in community affairs and political party activities. The Parvin Foundation, which worked closely with the Ford

37. Thomas Reeves, *Freedom and the Foundation* (New York: Knopf, 1969), p. 30.

38. Thomas Dye and L. Harmon Zeigler, *The Irony of Democracy* (Monterey: Duxbury, 1981).

39. Richard Magat, *The Ford Foundation at Work: Philanthropic Choices, Methods, and Styles* (New York: Plenum, 1979), p. 83.

40. *Ibid.*, p. 43.

Foundation-supported Center for the Study of Democratic Institutions, existed to educate ". . . Latin American leaders who opposed communism and supported democratic ideas."[41] (Justice William Douglas was a director of Parvin). A common CIA technique was to identify and attempt to co-opt student activists throughout the world, and bring them to this country for conferences or longer term education. The same methods used by foundations can induce radicals to pursue litigation for "rights" rather than attempting to change the system.

These are ways that the "innocent, benevolent" use of vast funds can influence choice. The aims, as well as methods of the foundations, are in accord with B.F. Skinner's positive reinforcement theories. (Skinner was a participant at the Center for the Study of Democratic Institutions.)

Behaviorism and Progressivism are chief elements of the elitist social engineering promoted by the foundations. Pluralism is the mask that the foundation ideology wears.

Foundations and the Legal System

Progressives of the early twentieth century did not emphasize litigation strategies, as courts were considered the most reactionary of governmental institutions. Foundation interest in the legal system increased enormously after the Second World War: courts are now more sympathetic to "social engineering" and have several other advantages for foundations — litigation is a safe and conservative outlet for activists and does not jeopardize foundation tax-exempt status. Furthermore, even failed litigation can absorb energies of hotbloods.

The major early effort of foundations directed specifically at the legal system was support (by the Rockefeller Foundation and Carnegie Corporation) of the American Law Institute for its restatement of the law. This was begun in the 1920s and was to encourage uniformity of all states' laws.[42] In the 1950s the possibilities of using courts to promote social reform became evident. The example of *Brown v. Board of Education* (foundations contributed to the litigation funds) indicated that the Supreme Court might play a progressive role. Subsequently, the Ford Foundation began to create programs and institutes and to fund projects in the hopes of reforming every aspect of the legal system. Other foundations participated in specific policy areas, but Ford has been interested in all processes and all issues.

These efforts complemented the general goal of the foundations in promoting and controlling social change. They were specifically interested in such changes as (1) Removing conditions which could lead to dangerous "intergroup hostilities." Racial tensions as well as Third World disdain for the United States as a "model" in race relations were threats to the system. (2) Conducting an effective fight against Communism without destroying the civil liberties of ordinary (i.e., non-communist) U.S. citizens. This was the

---

41. Frank Kelly, *Court of Reason* (New York: Free Press, 1981), p. 204.
42. Erwin Griswold, "Philanthropic Foundations and the Law," in *United States Philanthropic Foundations,* ed. Warren Weaver, (New York: Harper and Row, 1967).

major purpose of the Fund for the Republic. (3) Insuring criminal defendants a fair shake, through public provision of lawyers and expansive interpretation of the concept of due process. Those, e.g., criminals, who adopt individualist solutions to the problems of being disadvantaged, are to be reassured that the system is benevolent and that elaborate due process will prevail in their case. Thus, this potentially dangerous element is channelled into "beating the system" rather than changing it into one which offers more options. (4) Channelling protest into safe and conservative outlets. This aim became paramount with the disruptions of the New Left and race riots of the 1960s. Litigation modeled after the NAACP LDEF has many advantages. First of all, it reinforces the foundation idea that the major problem with our system is that there are disadvantaged groups which are underrepresented in normal political processes. Blacks, women, Chicanos, gays, environmentalists, consumers, the poor, are all examples of the disadvantaged. They are different, and do not carry weight in the system. Foundation literature assumes that there is nothing wrong with the system that representation cannot cure, there is no link between various disadvantaged minorities, and poverty is merely another peculiar circumstance in which some people happen to find themselves.

In sum, the Foundation-supported efforts at legal reform aim to remove glaring inequalities, but: ". . . will not disturb the basic political and economic organization of modern American society."[43] Cold war objectives remain important. While indigent rapists must receive every legal advantage, the Constitution is not literally interpreted to aid political dissenters. On the contrary, at the suggestion of the Ford Foundation, the CIA collaborated with New York City and other police departments in intelligence operations.[44]

Methods of Influence

In addition to the foundation influence on the climate of opinion, especially elite opinion, specific channels of influence include the financing (and the concommitant opportunities for control) of: (1) Social science research directly funded. (2) Creation or major support of research institutes, think tanks and public interest organizations (which produce supporting material or enter litigation as parties or amici). (3) New programs in legal education, especially the clinical education movement. (4) Law reviews. (5) Legal aid. (6) Public interest law firms. There is also an indeterminate amount of direct contact between Supreme Court Justices and foundations. Justice Douglas was a frequent conferee as well as a director of the Fund for the Republic. Justice Thurgood Marshall wrote the Foreword to the Ford-ABA study of public interest law.[45] Justice Robert Jackson was a trustee of the Twentieth Century Fund. Justice Warren Burger conferred at the Aspen Institute in 1976. Supreme Court Justices have a freedom to hang out at foundations which is denied to them in relation to the public sector and the private profit-making sector.

43. Joel Handler, *Social Movements and the Legal System* (New York: Academic Press, 1978), p. 233.

44. U.S. Congress, (Patman Committee), p. 171.

45. *Public Interest Law: Five Years* (New York, 1976).

They must stay away from politicians and capitalists, but how natural for them to mingle with our other guardian angels.

Social Science Research

Modern social science research has been almost entirely funded by foundations. Two examples are especially relevant. Gunnar Myrdal's *An American Dilemma*, in which many researchers participated, was directly sponsored by the Carnegie Corporation.[46] As most works of social science, it is both empirical and normative. The plaintiff's briefs in *Brown v. Board of Education,* as well as the Court's opinion, cite this work. It has been regarded as a powerful argument for the decision. The message of Myrdal's book is that not only does justice demand an end to segregation, but both national and international security will be threatened by the continued suppression of blacks.

A major study of legislative reapportionment was sponsored by the Twentieth Century Fund, a foundation deriving from Filene wealth.[47] Appearing after *Baker v. Carr,* it was intended to influence the Court to adopt the principle of one-man, one-vote, as well as to prepare public opinion for the acceptance of such a decision.

In addition, foundations (especially Fund for the Republic, Twentieth Century Fund, Ford and Sage) have sponsored research in civil rights and liberties, criminal justice, corporations, unions, public opinion, religion — every aspect of our economy, politics and society. Most of the "classic" studies which have shaped the post-1945 mind have been aided and abetted by the funds. It might be instructive to compile a bibliography of non-foundation-supported research and journals.

Research Institutes

Social science research that provides ammunition for social change through litigation or otherwise, is generally funded through research institutes created by the foundations. Some early examples are reported by Clement Vose.[48] The 1927 case of *Buck v. Bell,* in which the Supreme Court upheld the sterilization of an allegedly feeble-minded woman, was supported by research produced at the Cold Spring Eugenics Record Office, funded by the Carnegie Institute of Washington. The Sage Foundation financed the "Brandeis briefs" prepared by the National Consumers League in the attempt to have regulation of women's hours of labor declared constitutional. The American Law Institute, in support of a variety of issues, promoted centralization and uniformity in state laws. This facilitated the Supreme Court's "legislative" pronouncements, as in the abortion and criminal justice cases.

After 1945, foundation supported institutes provided social science evidence on a variety of issues under consideration by the Supreme Court. Some of these institutes also initiated or joined in the litigation. An important channel of social science to the Court is through amicus briefs. Marvell reports: "In

---

46. (New York: Harper and Bros., 1944).
47. Robert McKay, *Reapportionment* (New York: Twentieth Century Fund, 1965).
48. *Constitutional Change: Amendment Politics and Supreme Court Litigation Since 1900* (Lexington: Heath, 1972).

a study of briefs and opinions in over 200 United States Supreme Court cases decided from 1954-1974, it was found that over 40% of the citations to social science works in the briefs were in amicus briefs, as opposed to the parties' briefs, and that the Court was as likely to cite the works mentioned in amicus briefs as those in the parties' briefs."[49]

There is not a clear demarcation between research institutes, pure or applied, and public interest organizations which have both a research and advocacy role. This is not surprising, as social science, since Aristotle, has had a reformist orientation. Furthermore, these distinctions are not important for purposes of this study — all these organization are concerned with influencing public policy and all are supported by foundations.[50]

Some examples of how such organizations provide input to Supreme Court decision-making are: (1) The Metropolitan Applied Research Center, headed by Kenneth Clark, provided busing and school integration studies to litigants in these cases. (2) Ford-backed Brookings Institute sponsored Andrew Hacker's *Congressional Districting.*[51] The National Municipal League, which produced extensive studies on reapportionment, was also heavily supported by Ford. The multiplicity of studies provides more information, and also functions to generate acceptance: "Everyone's talking about it — it must be what everyone wants." (3) Ford and Rockefeller-supported Planned Parenthood organizations were involved as litigants in abortion cases. (4) The Education Law Center (Ford) and the Education Finance Reform Project (Carnegie) did extensive research in support of equal school financing litigation. The campaign lost in the Supreme Court, but has won significant victories in state courts. (5) The Fund for the Republic (Ford) dominated the liberal side of the civil liberties debate in the 1950s and 1960s. Everyone was talking about the rights of Communists, but not their ideas.

It is somewhat strange that the Fund for the Republic contributed funds to support Senator Hennings' Subcommittee on Constitutional Rights.[52] However, there is nothing in foundation charters which prevent them from making grants to governmental agencies. As the Walsh Commission noted: "Under the terms of this broad charter there is scarcely anything which concerns the life and work of individuals or nations in which the Rockefeller Foundation would not be authorized to participate. As the safety of the State is

---

49.   Thomas Marvell, *Appellate Courts and Lawyers: Information Gathering in the Adversary System* (Westport: Greenwood, 1978), p. 308.

50.   These are some examples of funded organizations, chosen at random from the Ford Foundation 1970 *Annual Report:* American Bar Association Fund For Public Education; American Law Institute; Law Students Civil Rights Research Council; Institute for Local Self-Government; Council on Legal Education for Professional Responsibility; Assoication of American Law Schools; Educational Testing Service; National Urban League; Center for Community Change; White House Conference of Food, Nutrition, and Health, Inc.; League of Cities/Conference of Mayors; Urban Institute; Metropolitan Applied Research Center; American Political Science Association; American Society for Public Administration; Council of State Governments; Regional Plan Association; National Municipal League; Rand Corporation; Brookings Institute; Citizens' Research Foundation; National Academy of Sciences.

51.   (Washington: Brookings, 1963).

52.   Reeves, *op. cit.,* p. 135.

the supreme condition of national civilization the foundation might in time of war use its income or its entire principal for the defense of the Republic. In time of peace it might use its funds to effect economic and political reforms which the trustees deem essential to the vitality and efficiency of the Republic. The foundation might become the champion of free trade or protection, of trusts or of the competing concerns out of which they grow, of socialism or individualism, of the program of the Republican Party or the program of the Democratic Party. It might endow the clergy of all religious denominations or it might subsidize any existing or any new religious denomination. Tomorrow it might be the champion of the Christian religion and a hundred years hence furnish an endowment for the introduction of Buddhism into the United States. It might build tenement houses for the poor in New York City or carry the results of science to enrich the exhausted soils of the East or the arid tracts of the West. It might set up an art gallery in every State of the United States or endow universities which would rival the great state universities of the West. With the consent of the legislature it might relieve any State of the care of its insane, pauper, and dependent classes or construct roads for the benefit of farmers and motorists. These may not be likely objects for the application of the funds of the Rockefeller Foundation. I am not, however, attempting to forecast its work but to understand its charter. If the object of the Rockefeller Foundation is to be coextensive with human civilization, then it may do anything and everything which its trustees think likely to effect reform or improvement in the material, economic, intellectual, artistic, religious, moral, and political conditions of the American people or of mankind."[53]

Joint foundation and government support occurs in a broad range of policy areas. Many "Great Society" programs were based on pilot projects financed by the Ford Foundation. When the government took over funding, the Foundation often retained a financial and program interest, as in Mobilization for Youth. The interplay between foundations and the CIA is a fascinating tangle, as yet to be unravelled.

In the criminal justice field, the Vera Institute and the Police Foundation are two among many Ford-sponsored research arms. They promote procedural due process, along with greater centralization and coordination among police forces, FBI and CIA. The Police Foundation was the model for the Law Enforcement Assistance Administration.

Research directly sponsored by the Ford Foundation and funds granted through the American Bar Foundation in the mid 1950s led to five volumes on detection, arrest, prosecution, conviction and sentencing. This was the first comprehensive study of the criminal justice system since the Wiskersham Commission (1931), which had been cited in *Miranda v. Arizona*.

Legal Education

Erwin Griswold attributed nearly all innovations in legal education since

---

53.   *Op. cit.*, pp. 120-121.

the Second World War to the Foundations.[54] The most significant development has been that of clinical legal education, with its network of institutes and policy-oriented law reviews. In 1957, the Ford Foundation began funding: ". . . a national series of experiments exposing law students to 'social practice' through internships with welfare agencies, police departments, prosecutors' offices, lower courts, and civil rights groups. The program was institutionalized in 1959 in the National Council on Legal Clinics, assisted with Ford grants totalling $1,750,000."[55] This later became the Council on Legal Education for Professional Responsibility, for which Ford had granted $10.9 million by 1979. "By the 1970-1971 school year, 100 law schools were administering 204 clinical programs in fourteen different fields of law. In the next five years the clinical movement swelled so that by 1975-1976, CLEPR could 'conservatively' estimate 'that slightly more than 90% of the American Bar Association-approved law schools provided some form of credit-granting clinical education.' "[56]

Institutes were created within law schools which taught and researched advocacy and law reform in civil rights and liberties; poverty, environmental, women's rights, consumer, and school finance law; and criminal justice. Some examples are: Center on Social Welfare Policy and Law at Columbia Law School, the Institute for Criminal Law and Procedure at Georgetown, and Center for Studies in Criminal Justice at the University of Chicago. Among the law reviews founded and funded were: *Law and Society* at Northwestern (grant from Sage Foundation), Vanderbilt's *Race Relations Law Reporter* (Ford), *Columbia Journal of Environmental Law* (Ford) and *Harvard Civil Rights Civil Liberties Law Review* (several foundations).

Although foundation money created these institutes and journals, their maintenance was sometimes later absorbed into the regular budget of the host institution. This gives the foundations all the more power: they are then free to use their assets to innovate elsewhere. The foundations' power comes not only from vast wealth which may be allocated at the directors' discretion; they are also virtually alone in the role of national planning institutions.[57] Obviously, law students and professors wanted these new programs; they were in the "spirit of the times." But that "spirit" was in many ways shaped by the networks directed and financed by foundations.

Clinical legal education has an impact on Supreme Court decision-making in several ways. Judges are mostly too old to have experienced it directly, but they are aware of its impact through law reviews and contacts with law professors. Law review articles, including students' work, are cited in Court opinions.[58] Scholars have found many influences outside of case materials

54. *Op. cit.,* p. 291.

55. Magat, *op. cit.,* p. 110.

56. Joel Seligman, *The High Citadel: The Influence of Harvard Law School* (Boston: Houghton Mifflin, 1978). p. 162.

57. Barry Karl, "Philanthropy, Policy Planning and the Bureaucratization of Democratic Ideal," *Daedalus* 105 (1976);129-149.

58. Neil Bernstein, "The Supreme Court and Secondary Source Material: 1965 Term," *Georgetown Law Journal* 57 (1968):55.

which are not cited.[59] The law clerks at the Supreme Court, said by Rehnquist to be mostly "leftists," are really just full of the latest thing.[60] ". . . [T]he clerks . . . are a conduit from the law schools to the Court. They bring with them . . . the intellectual atmosphere from which they are newly come."[61]

The latest thing in the law schools (from the 1950s to the 1970s) was to find some new right to be achieved by constitutional litigation. For example, Joel Klein, Justice Powell's new clerk in 1974, had been at Stanford's Center for Advanced Study in the Behavioral Sciences and at the ACLU's Mental Health Law Project.[62] He would presumably be familiar with the concept that mental patients should be subjects of special rights, e.g., to treatment. The Court was receptive to many of these assertions: the right to equal representation as a facet of equal protection, the right to integrated education, the right to privacy, the right to counsel at pre-trial proceedings, etc.; although it rejected others: e.g., the right to equally funded education and the right to welfare. Nevertheless, all of these claims could appear as reasonable subjects for litigation; public opinion, especialy elite opinion, had been prepared. Furthermore, the Court expanded the concept of standing and thus encouraged these suits. At another time, none of these claims might have been given a day in Court. The "backgrounds" of the justices do not explain why they entertained an expanded notion of what the Constitution demands. It can, however, be accounted for by the "climate of the times" created by the foundation network of think tanks, research institutes and legal education and practice innovations.

Another major connection between changes in legal education and Supreme Court decision-making was the development of public interest law. Legal clinics and law school institutes acted as "feeders" to public interest law firms. Students were also directly involved in litigation; the in-school institutes and public interest firms were often interconnected. Furthermore, such organizations as the Law Students Civil Rights Research Council of Washington, D.C. (supported by Rockefeller Bros. Fund among others) provided student assistants for lawyers in the civil rights movement.

Public Interest Law

Public interest law, which is almost entirely a creation of the foundations, helped to shape the agenda of the Supreme Court. The goals of this undertaking, as described by the Ford Foundation, are: ". . . to constructively advance necessary social change. It seeks to demonstrate that representation of those otherwise unrepresented in legal actions not only advances specific class or general public interests but also strengthens public confidence in the process of law."[63]

---

59. Charles M. Lamb, "Judicial Policy-making and Information Flow to the Supreme Court," *Vanderbilt Law Review* 29 (1976):45-124.

60. "Who Writes Decisions for the United States Supreme Court?" *U.S. News and World Report,* Feb. 21, 1958, pp. 114-116.

61. Alexander Bickel, *Politics and the Warren Court* (New York: Harper and Row, 1965), p. 143.

62. Bob Woodward and Scott Armstrong, *The Brethren* (New York: Avon, 1979), p. 419.

63. *Law and Justice* (New York: Ford Foundation, 1974).

PIL is premised on the policy-making role of the courts: "Public Interest Law has been a response to the problem that policy formulation in our society is too often a one-sided affair — a process in which only the voices of the economically or politically powerful are heard."[64] Enter the foundations and it becomes a 1½-sided affair: elitism masquerading as pluralism.

PIL was modeled after the NAACP/LDEF. That organization, as well as the ACLU, now receives crucial support from foundations, although they have dues-paying membership bases.[65] The following organizations were either created or vitally sustained by the Ford Foundation between 1967 and 1975: Center for National Policy Review; Lawyers Committee for Civil Rights Under Law; Legal Action Center; Mexican-American Legal Defense and Education Fund; NAACP/LDEF; National Committee Against Discrimination in Housing; Native American Rights Fund; Puerto Rican LDEF; Women's Law Fund; Women's Rights Project; National Resources Defense Council; Center for Law and Social Policy; Center for Law in the Public Interest; Citizen's Communications Center; Education Law Center; Environmental Defense Fund; Institute for Public Interest Representation; International Project; League of Women Voters Education Fund; Legal Action Center; Public Advocates; Sierra Club Legal Defense Fund; Research Center for the Defense of Public Interests (Bogotá, Colombia).

Foundations such as Carnegie, Rockefeller Brothers Fund and Clark also contributed, but Ford's share was preponderant. Naturally, control was also exerted: ". . . *each firm's* board of trustees stays in close touch with the foundation's declared policies on public interest law."[66] A foundation-created holding agency, the Council for Public Interest Law, reported that some firms lose funding if their activities threaten the interests of the foundations: "For example, an environmental law center is convinced that it failed to secure the renewal of a grant from a major foundation because of a suit it filed to prevent clearcutting in a national forest."[67]

The firms intervene in administrative proceedings as well as litigate and enter cases as amici. In certain cases, there is statutory provision for award of fees to successful plaintiffs; nevertheless the foundations provide the essential support. Ralph Nader and his public interest groups have collaborated and coordinated efforts with the foundation supported public interest law organizations, and foundations have increasingly supported Nader's work.[68]

The motives of the foundations in backing legal reform can be inferred from the long range goals of the foundations. Disorder and disruption in the mid and late 1960s and early 1970s — in the form of New Left, civil rights, anti-war and anti-nuke demonstrations and urban riots — had to be channelled into safe reformist activities: "Foundation officials believed that the

64.   Council for Public Interest Law, *Balancing the Scales of Justice: Financing Public Interest Law in America* (New York, 1976), p. 8.

65.   Robert McKay, *Nine for Equality under Law: Civil Rights Litigation* (New York: Ford Foundation, 1977) p. 12.

66.   Ford Foundation-ABA, *op. cit.,* p. 14.

67.   Council for PIL, *op. cit.,* p. 237.

68.   Alan Stang, "Foundations Pay the Way," *American Opinion* 20 (1977):35.

long-run stability of the representative policymaking system would be as-
sured only if legitimate organizational channels could be provided for the
frustration and anger being expressed in protests and outbreaks of political
violence during this period."[69]

The "cold war" is not merely an international crusade; it has its domestic
counterpart. Public interest law was an ideal channel for these radical energies: "Claims of legal rights envision a process of peaceful, orderly adjustment
that can be confidently left in the hands of professionals."[70] The clients who
receive representation in this manner are passive onlookers; neither popular
control nor political activity is fostered.[71] Elite interests are hardly threatened,
as the outcome of even successful cases is often merely "symbolic reassurance."
This is because PIL focuses on dramatic decisions and pays little attention to
problems of enforcement.[72] This is also a problem with the older public
interest reformers: Halpern reports that the incentives for ACLU litigation
lead to attempts at dramatic "breakthroughs" and neglect of enforcement.[73]

A further advantage of this approach is the support it gives the foundation
ideology that social problems are disparate problems of disadvantaged
"groups." Blacks, women, the poor, Chicanos, handicapped, mental patients, consumers, environmentalists — even children — are regarded as
"potential" interest groups. The political system has some defects which prevent them from getting their "rights." Fortunately, the role of the courts is to
protect these neglected "minorities"; with a little legal assistance, everything
will be fair again. Recent literature supporting judicial activism also expresses
this theme.[74]

Legal Aid

Legal aid is related to PIL in that it seeks to provide representation for the
underrepresented. There is also a tendency among more activist lawyers to
move from representation of the poor in individual cases to class action suits
challenging laws themselves. Normally, legal aid is merely supposed to help
the poor to get a fairer shake from the adversary system (whether in criminal
or civil proceedings) and not attempt to change the laws. In one area, however, legal aid can promote change in the rules: those rules relating to the circumstances under which defendants must be provided counsel. Ford and

69.   Jack Walker, "Origins and Maintenance of Interest Groups in America," *American Political
Science Review* 77 (June 1983): 401.

70.   Handler, *op. cit.,* p. 217.

71.   David Trubek, "Review of 'Balancing the Scales of Justice,' " *Wisconsin Law Review* 77
(1977):309.

72.   Neil Komesar and Burton Weisbrod, "The Public Interest Law Firm: A Behavioral
Analysis," in *Public Interest Law,* p. 89; Handler, *op. cit.,* p. 209.

73.   Stephen Halpern, "Assessing the Litigative Role of ACLU Chapters," in *Civil Liberties,* ed.
Stephen Wasby (Carbondale: Southern Illinois University Press, 1977), p. 165.

74.   Jesse Choper, *Judicial Review and the National Political Process* (Chicago: University of
Chicago Press, 1980); John Hart Ely, *Democracy and Distrust: A Theory of Judicial Review* (Cambridge:
Harvard University Press, 1980); Aryeh Neier, *Only Judgment: The Limits of Litigation in Social Change*
(Middletown: Wesleyan, 1982); Richard Neely, *How Courts Govern America* (New Haven: Yale
University Press, 1981).

Rockefeller funds were poured into legal aid during the 1950s, well before the Supreme Court's *Gideon* decree in 1963. Between 1953-1972, the Ford Foundation alone gave $7.4 million to the National Legal Aid and Defender Association. The existence of legal aid and public defenders can induce courts to expand the rights to counsel, just as court-ordered expansion will create the need for legal aid. The accused get lawyers and the lawyers get paid. This keeps everyone out of trouble (until next time).

Influence in Specific Policy Areas

"Justice Holmes and Brandeis are credited with having broadened the field of judicial decision by interpreting legislation in the light of historic and social conditions, but one asks oneself whence did these great judges derive their humane and enlightened point of view? Were they in their growing years given to reading the multitudinous studies in social science, so-called, patronized directly or indirectly by the great foundations?[75] Foundation ideology sustained and reinforced the trend on the post-war Supreme Court toward social engineering, derived from the progressive movement as well as the sociological jurisprudence of Pound, Brandeis and Cardozo.[76] The stream became a river, headed the way the foundation network sought. In at least three general ways, landmark court decisions reflected foundation aims: (1) The result-orientation of court decisions was a method of directing social change from above. (2) The centralizing tendencies of court decisions can be seen as a response to American Law Institute models for uniform state laws as well as the ideology of the network of foundation-supported public administration and planning organizations (National Municipal League, Regional Plan Association, American Society for Public Administration, International City Managers Association, National Planning Association). (3) The distinction between public and private was increasingly blurred.[77] Corporations were required to conform to certain constitutional norms, particularly in regard to civil liberties and rights issues. Laws such as the Civil Rights Act of 1964 aided the process, but the court has interpreted it expansively. This tends to legitimize corporate actions, giving them the mantle of public bodies, although they are not accountable to the public in any effective way (except via the courts, on occasion). The myth of "corporate responsibility," a major promotional item in the foundation product line, is nevertheless bolstered. During the 1960s and 1970s, the Twentieth Century Fund undertook a multi-volume study of property and power, directed by P. Harbrecht, S.J. In the Fund's 1965 *Annual Report*, the following statement appears: "While elements of the private property system remain, the institutions which now direct the use of capital wealth — our corporations, financial organizations and insurance and investment companies — are to a significant degree public or quasi-public institutions."[78]

---

75.   Abraham Flexner, *Funds and Foundations* (New York: Arno, 1952), p. 135.

76.   Roelofs, *op. cit.,* p. 95.

77.   Arthur S. Miller, *The Supreme Court and American Capitalism* (New York: Free Press, 1968), p. 146.

78.   *Op. cit.,* p. 27.

Civil Liberties

In 1952, the Ford Foundation established the Fund for the Republic: ". . . to assist the promotion of a national security based on freedom and justice. The fund would take into account: (a) The persistent Communist effort to penetrate and disrupt free nations; (b) The effects in international tensions on national security in the forms of hatred and suspicion; (c) The effects of short-sighted or irresponsible efforts to combat domestic Communism; (d) The need to better understand the spiritual and political significance of freedom and justice in the United States; (e) The need to rededicate ourselves to the vision of a free, just and unafraid America."[79] The Fund was active until 1957, when it metamorphasized into the Center for the Study of Democratic Institutions, which emerged in 1959. Its mission was the intelligent waging of the Cold War, without the McCarthyite excesses. Its methods included direct sponsorhsip of studies, e.g., Samuel Stouffer's *Communism, Conformism and Civil Liberties* (1955), Clinton Rossiter's series on communism in America John Cogley's report on black-listing; and grants to a wide variety of organizations, from New York City Bar Association for a study of loyalty-security programs to American Friends Service Committee to produce radio programs, to Senator Hennings' Subcommittee on Constitutional Rights. Awards were given to those "defending individual freedom," e.g., $5,000 to Plymouth Quaker Meeting for retaining their librarian, Mary Knowles, who had refused to sign a loyalty oath.[80] Pamphlets and books were supplied for study groups in schools, colleges, libraries, churches, civic organizations, etc. Legal defense was provided in specific cases, through such organizations as bar associations and American Friends Service Committee. Altogether, $11 million was spent by the Fund for the Republic (on civil rights as well as civil liberties issues).

The Fund virtually dominated the liberal side of the civil liberties discussion. It promoted the idea that the danger to civil liberties came from the masses, who felt threatened by the "urban power structure."[81] The elite — especially a national elite — was the natural protector of civil liberties.[82] People should be protected against *unjust* accusation of being communists. There was much discussion of liberties and due process but there was little room in this great national seminar for serious discussion of communism — or capitalism.[83]

The Supreme Court decisions in the civil liberties area during the 1950s

---

79.   Reeves, *op. cit.,* p. 30.
80.   Kelly, *op. cit.,* p. 124.
81.   Reeves, *op. cit.,* p. 284.
82.   Samuel Stouffer, *Communism, Conformism and Civil Liberties* (New York: Doubledy, 1955).
83.   The author can attest from personal experience to the effects of "sanitizing" of anti-communism. There was a small but vital left-wing movement among high school and college students in the late 1940s. By the early 50s the message had gotten across that *both* McCarthy and any flirtation with socialist or communist ideas were abominations. The student left disappeared in most places, replaced by crusades for "Atoms for Peace" and "Technical Assistance to Backward Nations."

and 1960s closely followed the Fund for the Republic line. This is hardly surprising, as one of the Court's leading civil libertarians, Justice William Douglas, was a director of the Fund during this period. The worst excesses of
Congressional investigations were curtailed and the Smith Act became unen-
forceable (although not found to be in conflict with the First Amendment
[Yates v. U.S. 354 U.S. 298:1957]). Procedural due process rather than freedom of speech was vindicated: "In *Watkins* [354 U.S. 178:1957] despite the
stirring rhetoric of Chief Justice Warren's opinion, the actual decision was
keyed to the technical requirement that the pertinancy of the Committee's
questions must be made clear to a witness if he is to be legally compelled
to answer."[84]

Even these victories were symbolic in an important sense: ". . . By 1954
most voices of dissent had long been shackled. The Communist Party and the
Progressive Party were in ruins, radical strength in the labor movement had
been almost completely destroyed, opposition to American cold war foreign
policies was practically unheard of, and suggestions of radical alternatives to
the existing political and economic structure in America were almost
equally rare."[85]

Civil Rights

The foundations, and their forerunners, the "industrial philanthropies"
had long been interested in race issues. The Peabody Educational Fund
(1867) and Slater Fund (1881) attempted to shape Southern black education:
"The General Education Board, established in 1902 by John D. Rockefeller,
served as a clearinghouse for industrial philanthropy and disbursed grants to
educational institutions and state departments of education."[86] The GEB
absorbed old and new foundations: Peabody and Slater Funds, Jeanes Foundation, Phelps-Stokes, Julius Rosenwald, Carnegie Corporation and Laura
Spelman Rockefeller Memorial Fund. "The industrial philanthropists were
more concerned with black education as a means to economic efficiency and
political stability than with equal rights for southern blacks."[87] The NAACP,
(founded in 1909), represented a conservative, elite-led approach to racial
integration and was aided during its formative years by the Rosenwald and
Peabody Funds. During the 1920s, the NAACP was regarded as a counterweight to the Communist Party, which was wooing Negroes.[88] The early
donors were joined by J.D. Rockefeller, Jr., Edsel Ford and the Garland Fund,
among others. "By 1928, on the eve of the Depression, the NAACP had

---

84.   Harry Kalven, Jr. "Uninhibited, Robust and Wide-open — A Note on Free Speech and the
Warren Court," in *The Warren Court: A Critical Analysis,* ed. Richard Saylor, Barry Boyer and Robert
Gooding (New York: Chelsea House, 1968), p. 110.
85.   Robert Justin Goldstein, *Political Repression in Modern America: 1870 to the Present* (Cambridge: Schenkman, 1978) p. 406.
86.   James Anderson, "Philanthropic Control over Private Black Higher Education," in
Philanthropy and Cultural Imperialism, op. cit.
87.   *Ibid.,* p. 154.
88.   Wilson Record, *Race and Radicalism: The NAACP and the Communist Party in Conflict* (Ithaca:
Cornell University Press, 1964).

amassed a sufficient surplus of funds to invest part of its income in an impressive array of stocks and bonds . . ."[89]

In the late 1930s, the racism of the white elite (e.g., eugenic movement) was overtaken by a recognition of the need for racial integration. The Carnegie Corporation financed the massive study by Gunnar Myrdal, *An American Dilemma* (1944). Kenneth Clark, Otto Klineberg, Howard Odum and many other researchers participated in the project. This work was a prime shaper of the post-war civil rights debate, as well as an authority cited in briefs, amici briefs and opinion in *Brown v. Board of Education*. Financial resources provided by the Ford Foundation were regarded as critical by one authority on foundations: "Without the help Ford gave through the NAACP, the litigation which led to the United States Supreme Court's 1954 schools decision could not have been pursued."[90] (Justice Frankfurter had been a member of the NAACP as well as ACLU until he joined the Court; whether this swayed his decision to join the majority is not known.)

The Fund for the Republic had originally considered race relations part of its domain: Harry Ashmore's report, *The Negro and the Schools,* appeared May 16, 1954, one day before the *Brown* decision. However, the urban disorders prompted the Ford Foundation to begin massively funding civil rights in 1967, when McGeorge Bundy became its president. Grants were given to a variety of civil rights organizations: National Urban League ($17.8 million between 1966-1977); Southern Regional Council ($8.6 million between 1953-1977); open housing organizations ($11.3 million between 1961-1977). Ford's grant to CORE helped to elect the conservative Mayor Stokes in Cleveland, and prompted the Tax Reform Act of 1969 restricting political activities of foundations.

Grants for civil rights litigation amounted to $18 million, including vital support for the NAACP and NAACP LDEF. Ford funds created and/or sustained the organizations listed above under Public Interest Law. Of particular interest was the Ford-funded Metropolitan Applied Research Center, headed by Kenneth Clark, which engaged in equal educational opportunity research, providing ammunition for school integration and busing litigation.

Foundation-financed organizations have been active in all civil rights areas. The NAACP and NAACP LDEF: "contributed to the landmark decision in *Griggs v. Duke Power Co.* (401 U.S. 424: 1971)," which found irrelevant tests to be a mask for employment discrimination.[91] Voting rights litigation was undertaken by Common Cause (among others) with funds from the Stern Fund (which also supported the Suburban Action Institute, a middle-income housing lobby).

The whole array of Mexican-American LDEF and cognate firms have been supported by the Ford Foundation. Late in the game, Ford discovered sex dis-

89.   B. Joyce Ross, *J.E. Springarn and the Rise of the NAACP: 1911-1939* (New York: Atheneum, 1972), p. 106.

90.   Whitaker, *op. cit.,* p. 171.

91.   Joel Handler, George Edgar and Russell Settle, "Public Interest Law and Employment Discrimination," in *Public Interest Law, op. cit.,* p. 272.

crimination, and began to support women's rights litigation, through Women's Law Fund, NOW LDEF and other organizations.

Criminal Justice

The activities of foundations in this area highlight the weaknesses of the American political system. By the post-World War II period, the "standards" of criminal "justice" in a number of states compared unfavorably with those in "backward" countries. Change was necessary, to validate the claim of the United States that it was not only a civilized nation, but in fact the leader of civilization. Of considerable significance was the persistent entrance of the Communist Party into ordinary criminal cases (often with black defendants, as in the Scottsboro case) to illuminate the inequities prevailing.

The lack of significant pressure groups at the state or national level, the weaknesses of political parties, and the restrictions of federalism meant that the situation could persist indefinitely. Here is where "social engineering" fills the bill. The Supreme Court was receptive to the reformers' initiatives, even though the resulting degree of control by the federal government over state criminal justice procedures amounted to a revolution. "It is to the credit of the Supreme Court that it recognized that the nation was in the midst of a social revolution before this became apparent to most of the elected representatives of the people, and that it sought to eliminate the basic defects in our system for the administration of criminal justice within our present structure. The result of this perceptive approach has been to immunize the Court from much of the alienation expressed against other institutions of our society, not only by the disadvantaged, but also by large numbers of our youth, upon whom the future of the nation depends."[92]

The Court received a great deal of technical assistance in this area. The American Law Institute's model codes made it easier for the Court to require standardized practices in the states. By the late 1960's millions had been granted by Ford and other foundations for criminal justice studies. Support for Legal Aid insured a good supply of criminal justice cases to the Supreme Court. Police Foundation, Vera Institute, American Bar Foundation and criminal justice institutes funded at many major law schools were at work refining concepts of due process. Ford monies were also employed to improve the efficiency of police and criminal justice processes, through better equipment, computerization and coordination of local and national police, e.g., encouraging CIA-NYC Police cooperation.[93] Another important element in shaping Supreme Court attitudes was the development of clinical legal education in the criminal justice field, whereby the energies of brighter students were enlisted in this formerly neglected specialty and criminal law gained a challenging constitutional dimension.

---

92.   Kenneth Pye, "The Warren Court and Criminal Procedure," in *The Warren Court: A Critical Analysis, op. cit.,* pp. 66-67.

93.   U.S. Congress. House. *Hearings on Exempt Foundations and Charitable Trusts before the Subcommittee on Domestic Finance of the House Committee on Banking and Currency.* 93rd. Cong., 1st Sess., 1973, p. 171.

Reapportionment

The reapportionment decisions also lacked a mass constituency, although politicians (generally Democratic) who felt underrepresented supported the litigation. The groundwork was prepared by the National Municipal League (Ford and Rockefeller-funded) and the Twentieth Century Fund.[94] *New York Times* reporter Anthony Lewis, while a Fellow of the Nieman Foundation at Harvard Law School, wrote an influential article for the *Harvard Law Review*, in which he argued that unequally drawn districts for legislatures violated the Fourteenth Amendment guarantee of equal protection of the law.[95] This was cited in the Supreme Court opinion in *Baker v. Carr*. The National Municipal League, which received "emergency funds" from the Ford Foundation for the project, then worked to obtain a "one-man, one-vote" ruling from the Supreme Court. The *Baker* case had triggered reapportionment litigation in state courts and the NML aimed to circulate favorable rulings as rapidly as possible to build up a convincing body of legal opinion. "The National Municipal League obtained, reproduced, and published opinions on all [state] cases and distributed them rapidly to litigants and defendants alike. The league learned of new cases through contacts it had in each state — universities, citizen groups, and lawyers. It wrote to court clerks in all states in which decisions were pending. Each opinion had to be duplicated on a special mahine, since only an exact reproduction could be used as court evidence. As soon as there were enough cases, the league bound and published them. For a while, during the feverish period of 1962-65, the league each month brought out a 100- to 200-page volume, *Court Decisions on Legislative Apportionment.* Its availability was announced to a mailing list of 1,000, which included Federal judges, state attorneys general and legislators, interested lawyers, the U.S. Department of Justice, state research bureaus, and civic organizations such as the League of Women Voters. Today, there are thirty-two volumes totalling 6,122 pages."[96]

Many other studies, such as the Twentieth Century Fund volume on Reapportionment, were sponsored to promote acceptance of the idea that the Constitution required "one-man, one-vote" in legislative districting.[97]

It is puzzling as to why Chief Justice Warren believed that the reapportionment decisions were the most important of his tenure. Certainly they were an enormous generator of litigation, which still goes on. Politicians have been kept busy, and political scientists employed by the various foundation-supported research-in-reapportionment institutes. The actual effect of the reapportionment decisions was a shift in political power from legislatures and parties to bureaucrats, judges, and academic researchers who were henceforth engaged in drawing boundary lines determining the extent of "natural"

94.   Neier, *op. cit.,* p. 86.

95.   "Legislative Apportionment and the Federal Courts," *Harvard Law Review* 71 (1958), p. 1957.

96.   Ford Foundation, *The Near Side of Federalism: Improving State and Local Government* (New York: 1972), p. 10.

97.   Robert McKay, *Reapportionment* (New York: Twentieth Century Fund, 1965).

communities, and so forth.[98] Studies of the impact of reapportionment have shown little effect on policy, even in those states where the most shocking malapportionment had existed.[99]

Oddly, the rationale for the Court's decision in *Reynolds v. Sims* (377 U.S. 533:1964): "Legislators represent people, not trees or acres. Legislators are elected by voters, not farms or cities or economic interests," bore little relation to the current doctrines of foundation-sponsored social science, which stressed that ordinary citizens are represented in the political process through group affiliations, not geographical constituency. The reapportionment venture seems primarily designed to keep people busy while conveying the illsuion of equality.

Abortion

Organizations studying sex and birth control have all been babies of the foundations. In the 1950s Rockefeller and Ford funded the Population Council, which conducted research into contraception and undertook a policy-planning role. In addition, ". . . efforts were begun to restructure public opinion regarding population control through the use of the mass media."[100] In 1959, the American Law Institute published a draft model state abortion law which: ". . . focused public opinion on the need for change, dramatized the issue, and aggregated support for new policies."[101] Throughout the 1960s and early 1970s, foundation money, sometimes specifically designated for abortion studies, was injected into Planned Parenthood local chapters. Litigation for the right to abortion was conducted by Planned Parenthood, American Civil Liberties Union and women's rights organizations, as well as a number of bodies oddly called James Madison Constitutional Law Institute. This fine name was borne by abortion litigation firms throughout the country; shy foundations could discreetly make their grants. An entry in the Foundation Grants Index of 1973 indicates that in 1972 the Rockefeller Foundation granted $50,000 to James Madison Constitutional Law Institute of New York City for "population law."

Studies of Justice Blackmun's opinion in the abortion cases have indicated that judicial notice was liberally employed and: "The Court based its opinion on only one school of thought."[102] The "school of thought" was that of the foundation-funded population policy-planning network.

Poverty Law

Poverty became a "problem" after Michael Harrington published *The Other America* in 1962.[103] Harrington, while working on projects at the Center for the Study of Democratic Institutions, had become aware of the submerged nation

---

98. Ward E. Elliott, *The Rise of Guardian Democracy: The Supreme Court's Role in Voting Rights Disputes: 1845-1969* (Cambridge: Harvard University Press, 1974), p. viii.

99. Timothy O'Rourke, *The Impact of Reapportionment* (New Brunswick: Transaction Books, 1980), p. 153.

100. Thomas Dye, *Who's Running America?* (Englewood Cliffs: Prentice-Hall, 1983), p. 259.

101. Eva Rubin, *Abortion, Politics and the Courts* (Westport: Greenwood, 1982), p. 20.

102. Charles Lamb, *op. cit.,* p. 72.

103. (New York: Macmillan).

of the poor. "Harrington wrote a book based on his findings — entitled *The Other America*" at Cogley's suggestion — which caught the attention of President Kennedy and led to the planning of the "war on poverty," which was waged by Lyndon Johnson after Kennedy's assassination. Thus the Center study convinced these presidents that the nation's economic policies were not bringing benefits to millions of Americans."[104]

Poor people, in the foundation view of the world, were simply another disadvantaged group that needed more adequate representation. Accordingly, in 1963 Ford funded a community law office in New Haven which later became the model for OEO legal centers. In 1965, Ford money helped to establish the Center on Social Welfare Law and Policy at Columbia Law School. The Center's objective was a landmark Supreme Court decision declaring welfare a right.[105] This was not bought by the Court, but the Center's efforts yielded some successes: invalidation of "man in the house" laws (*King v. Smith*, 392 U.S. 309:1968); outlawing of residency and requirements (*Shapiro v. Thompson*, 394 U.S. 618:1969); and the requirement of due process before beneifts were terminated (*Goldberg v. Kelly,* 397 U.S. 254:1970).

School Finance

This is another instance in which foundation efforts did not result in the desired Supreme Court decision: that unequal funding of schools by states violated equal protection of the laws. Nevertheless, state court victories achieved some of the objectives. The Carnegie Corporation has sponsored some school finance litigation, while the Ford Foundation has spent more than $14 million on the efforts to equalize funding of school districts. The money has been channelled through the Lawyers Committee for Civil Rights Under Law, National Urban Coalition, League of Women Voters, Massachusetts Advocacy Center, National Conference of State Legislatures, Stanford University Law School, the University of California Law School at Berkeley, and other groups. Public Advocates, Inc. a California public interest law firm supported by Ford: ". . . became chief counsel in *Serrano v. Priest* after OEO funding ran out."[106]

In 1974, the Ford Foundation established the Education Law Center to specialize in this type of litigation and the Foundation claims that: ". . . litigators partially supported with our funds have helped to win perhaps ten significant state school finance cases on state constitutional grounds. . . "[107]

As with the reapportionment decisions, the school finance cases gave rise to a minor industry of lawyers, school finance experts and other specialists. The "positive" results in the state cases have also had a centralizing and depoliticizing effect: "Ford efforts to make school finance and the delivery of educational services more equitable have produced unanticipated outcomes. The

---

104.   Kelly, *op. cit.,* p. 201.

105.   Jack Greenberg, *Cases and Materials on Judicial Process and Social Change: Constitutional Litigation* (St. Paul: West, 1977), p. 591.

106.   A. James Lee and Burton Weisbrod, "Public Interest Law Activities in Education," in *Public Interest Law, op. cit.,* p. 318.

107.   Magat, *op. cit.,* p. 147.

emerging role of state educational bureaucracies in monitoring these reforms has increased their authority relative to that of local school districts. Consequently, it has become more difficult for parents and citizens to have a voice in school governance and policymaking on the local level."[108]

The Supreme Court was not ready to declare equal educational expenditure a requirement of the Fourteenth Amendment. Such a decision could have had interesting implications, beginning with the notion that all require equally expensive lawyers for equal protection to prevail, and perhaps ending with a socialist revolution from above.

Other Areas

Foundation-supported public interest law firms have been active in many policy areas: environmental, consumer, housing, mental health, communications law, etc. However, no momentous Supreme Court cases have resulted. On the other hand, the presence of foundation influence in certain landmark cases, e.g., school prayer decisions, has not been investigated. Perhaps study of foundation influence could become a minor industry. On second thought, who would finance it?

This study has shown considerable influence of foundations on Supreme Court decision making; through wide dissemination of ideology supporting social engineering, law school innovations which encourage social reform through law, provision of social science justifications and data for law change, and funding of litigation through public interest law firms and other organizations. Judicial activism can thus be regarded as a channel for elite demands developed through a "policy-formation" process. So what? Who is helped and who is hurt?

Some tentative speculative conclusions will be ventured, considering that the questions raised have enormous implications about the nature and direction of our polity. We can ask (1): have the goals, express or implied, of the foundations been achieved? and (2): what have been the costs of their attempts to promote social change through litigation?

To begin to determine whether social change has in fact occurred requires an analysis of "impact" studies.[109] Changes have occurred where they coincided with elite interests, i.e., civil rights and abortion rights. Reapportionment has been happening, but with little impact on policy.[110] Civil liberties have been defended by the Supreme Court, at the same time that anti-communism has become clean and respectable. Repression now takes other forms, e.g., military surveillance of protesters (upheld by the Supreme Court in *Laird v. Tatum* 408 U.S. 1:1972) and cooperation between local police, FBI and CIA. Criminal justice is hard to evaluate: it seems that we have devised the perfectly fair trial, and plea bargaining has become the norm.

---

108. Dennis Buss, "The Ford Foundation in Public Education: Emergent Patterns," in *Philanthropy and Cultural Imperialism*, p. 356.

109. E.g., Stephen Wasby, *The Impact of the United States Supreme Court: Some Perspectives* (Homewood: Dorsey, 1979).

110. O'Rourke, *op. cit.*

Where the resolution of social ills presented a basic challenge to the system, there have been no landmark decisions, e.g., concerning the environment, consumers or poverty. Environmentalists, consumers and the poor are not simply disadvantaged minorities on the model of blacks. They are not demanding integration into the system, but a different allocation of resources.

In areas where significant court victories have been won, the results have often been symbolic only.[111] Organizations and lawyers have strong incentives to achieve dramatic declarations of rights, but receive few rewards from monitoring enforcement, which is what might affect the lives of ordinary people. Symbolic reassurance might well be an aim of the foundations, which seek to reduce ". . . the ranks of malcontents who constitute the seedbed for undemocratic ideologies."[112]

Judging by the massive financial response to the riots and New Left protests of the 1960s, and knowing the consistent motives of the foundations, we can assume that one objective is to channel discontent into harmless waters. Certainly some of the energies of the protestors and their radical upstart leaders went into litigation campaigns for rights. A.S. Miller claims that this is precisely the function of judicial activism: "By helping to siphon off discontent and channel it into innocuous forms, the Court enables that [ruling] class to remain on top while giving up only the barest minimum necessary to quell disastrous social disorder."[113]

We can't know if this diversion of discontent will be permanent — that depends on whether we are headed for *Friendly Fascism, The Backyard Revolution,* chaos, or something else.[114] However, even the defense of "rights" may someday to expanded to include the right to a job, housing, health care, clean air, etc. It is hard to imagine that the foundations and the Supreme Court would sponsor that revolution.

The foundations' aims have been realized to some degree, but what have been the costs? First of all, there has been an increase in centralization and depoliticization — government has been removed even further from the people. Ironically, even reapportionment, which was supposed to strengthen state government, has had this effect, by shifting political power from legislatures and parties to bureaucrats, judges and academic researchers.[115] The litigation process leaves little role for non-professionals, popular control of organizations or political activity.[16] According to the common wisdom this is a good thing, as the masses are prone to authoritarianism.[117] However, when we realize the extent to which our "social science" has been produced under

---

111.   Halpern, *op. cit.,* Handler, *op. cit.,* Donald Horowitz, *The Courts and Social Policy* (Washington: Brookings, 1977).

112.   Murray Edelman, *The Symbolic Uses of Politics* (Urbana: University of Illinois Press, 1964); Ford Foundation, *1949 Report, op. cit.,* p. 46.

113.   Arthur S. Miller, *Toward Increased Judicial Activism* (Westport: Greenwood, 1982), p. 8.

114.   Bertram Gross, *Friendly Fascism* (Boston: South End Press, 1980); Harry Boyte, *The Backyard Revolution* (Philadelphia: Temple, 1980).

115.   Elliott, *op. cit.,* p. viii.

116.   Trubek, *op. cit.,* p. 309.

117.   Stouffer, *op. cit.;* Dye and Zeigler, *op. cit.*

elite auspices, we may begin to question what is commonly accepted. Perhaps it is the elite which is repressive after all.

Another cost of "reform from above," which includes but is not limited to court decisions, is that elitism is masked, and appears as pluralism. This is very much in the interest of the elite; they bend over backyards [sic] to deny their power. "Healthy" pluralism is a mirage when most functioning "grass-roots" organizations are either created, or crucially funded by the foundation network. McKay claims that even the NAACP LDEF is vitally sustained by the Ford Foundation: ". . . Foundation grants have been essentially "free" money, to be used where the litigation needs were great . . . Secondly, the Foundation's grants signaled confidence in the LDEF and that helped trigger other gifts."[118] Organizations which do not serve the purposes of the elite may die from lack of funding or alter their purposes to become more grantworthy. A wide variety of organizations can qualify; it is in the interests of the elite to have every type of "disadvantaged" person join a separate organization; each neighborhood, block, or backyard to have its own revolution. They can fight against rural oppression or windmills (probably *for* windmills). What foundations will not support is an organization composed of all the oppressed, which takes its aim not at a particular abuse or discrimination, but at the system of corporate capitalism as such. Thus a major effect of reform from above is that energies are diverted from more basic changes.

---

118. McKay, *Nine for Equality, op. cit.,* p. 12.

TRUTH, SEMBLANCE, RECONCILIATION: ADORNO'S AESTHETIC REDEMPTION OF MODERNITY*

by Albrecht Wellmer

No one has succeeded better than Theodor W. Adorno in analyzing modern culture with all its ambiguities — ambiguities which herald the possibility of an unleashing of aesthetic and communicative potentials as well as the possibility of a withering away of culture. Since Schopenhauer and Nietzsche — with whose aesthetics and epistemology Adorno's thought secretly communicates — no other philosophy of art, at least in Germany, has had such a sustained influence on artists, critics, and intellectuals. The traces of his influence on the consciousness of those who, be it in a productive, critical, or purely receptive capacity, are involved with modern art cannot be overlooked. This is true in particular of his musicology, where Adorno, in Carl Dahlhaus' formulation, has defined the very level on which it is possible to talk about modern music at all.[1] Adorno's authority can even be felt in more recent musicology, where music has gone beyond those boundaries which Adorno set for it. I am thinking, for instance, of something like K.H. Metzger's plea for John Cage's "anti-authoritarian" music.[2]

However, whereas Adornian ways of thinking have left profound traces in the consciousness of artists, authors and intellectuals, his *Aesthetic Theory* has met with a less happy fate in academic philosophy of art and literary theory: after some ten years of critical reception, it now seems as though only remnants and fragments of Adorno's aesthetics have survived philosophical, literary and musicological criticism. It is not its esoteric character that has hindered the reception of the *Aesthetic Theory*. The problem lies rather in its sys-

---

*Translated by Maeve Cooke. The following abbreviations and editions have been used throughout the text: T.W. Adorno and M. Horkheimer, *Dialektik der Aufklärung* (Amsterdam, 1955) — 'DdA'; Translation: *Dialectic of Enlightenment (New York, 1972); Adorno, Ästhetische Theorie* (Frankfurt am Main, 1973) — 'AT'; Translation: *Aesthetic Theory* (London, 1983); Adorno, *Negative Dialektik* (Frankfurt am Main, 1973) — 'ND'; Translation: *Negative Dialectics* (New York, 1973); Adorno, *Philosophie der neuen Musik* (Frankfurt am Main, 1975) — 'PhdNM'; Translation: *Philosophy of Modern Music* (New York, 1973).

1. Carl Dahlhaus *et al.,* "Was haben wir von Adorno gehabt," *Musica* 24 (1970).
2. See above all H.K. Metzger, "John Cage oder die freigelassene Musik" and "Anarchie durch Negation der Zeit oder Probe einer Lektion wider die Moral. Hebel-Adorno-Cage (*Variations I*)," both in H.K. Metzger and R. Riehn, eds., *Musik-Konzepte. Sonderband John Cage* (Munich, 1978); Metzger, "Musik wozu," in Riehn, ed., *H.K. Metzger, Musik wozu. Literatur zu Noten* (Frankfurt am Main, 1980). Of course, Adorno's authority as a musicologist was never uncontested in circles of the musical post-avantgarde. See H. Eimert, "Die nowtwendige Korrektur," in *Die Reihe* 2 (Anton Webern), 2nd edition (Vienna, 1955), where Eimert represents a sharp antithesis to Adorno's skeptical judgment of Webern's successors.

tematic aspects: the aesthetics of negativity has revealed its rigid features: in Adorno's aporetic constructions something artificial has become visible, and in his aesthetic judgments a latent traditionalism has become apparent. As so often happens in philosophy, the critics (or at least those who do not regard the matter as over and done with) have divided the spoils among themselves: fragments of the complex interrelationship of negativity, semblance, truth and utopia, in terms of which Adorno conceived artistic phenomena, can be found in Jauss' aesthetics of reception, in Bürger's sociology of literature and in Bohrer's aesthetics of "rupture" ("Ästhetik der Plötzlichkeit"). That this is not merely the result of an eclectic appropriation of Adorno's thought is made clear by the philosophical criticisms of Adorno — in particular, those critiques by Baumeister/Kulenkampff and Bubner[3] which are directed towards the systematic aspects of Adorno's aesthetics. That all the above-mentioned critics are at least partially correct seems to me indisputable. At the same time their critiques leave one with the feeling of a disproportion between the results of critique and its object: as though the real substance of Adorno's aesthetics had escaped the critics. The latter is a danger of all partial critiques, i.e., those which ultimately remain detached from their object. The danger might possibly be avoided in the case of Adorno's aesthetics if one succeeded in setting the central categories in motion from the inside out as it were, thus rescuing them from their dialectical rigidity. The precondition for this would be an accentuation rather than a moderation of critique. In the essay that follows I will try to take a positive step in this direction.

I

The *Dialectic of Enlightenment* by Adorno and Horkheimer remains a key text for the understanding of Adorno's aesthetics. The dialectic of subjectification and reification is developed in it, and the dialectic of aesthetic semblance is at least anticipated. The mutual intertwining of these two dialectics is the moving principle of *Aesthetic Theory*.

The extraordinary character of *Dialectic of Enlightenment* resides not only in its literary density — prose illuminated by flashes of lightning, as it were — but even more in the extreme daring of the authors' attempt to fuse two disparate philosophical traditions: one which leads from Schopenhauer via Nietzsche to Klages,[4] and another which leads from Hegel via Marx and Weber to the early Lukacs. Lukacs had already integrated Weber's theory of rationalization

---

3. See T. Baumeister and J. Kulenkampff, "Geschichtsphilosophie und philosophische Ästhetik. Zu Adornos *Ästhetische Theorie*," *Neue Hefte für Philosophie*, no. 5 (1973). R. Bubner, "Kann Theorie ästhetisch werden? Zum Hauptmotiv der Philosophie Adornos," in B. Lindner and W.M. Lüdke, eds., *Materialien zur ästhetischen Theorie. T.W. Adornos Konstruktion der Moderne* (Frankfurt, 1980).

4. Axel Honneth has called my attention to the relation between several of the basic theses of *Dialectic of Enlightenment* and the philosophy of Ludwig Klages. See Honneth, "Der Geist und sein Gegenstand. Anthropologische Berührungspunkte zwischen der Dialektik der Aufklärung und lebensphilosophischen Kritik," manuscript (1983). In this connection see above all, L. Klages, *Der Geist als Widersacher der Seele* (Munich, 1960). On the direct connections to Nietzsche, see J. Habermas, "The Entwinement of Myth and Enlightenment," *New German Critique*, 26 (Spring-Summer 1982), pp. 13-30.

into a critique of political economy; the *Dialectic of Enlightenment* may be understood as an attempt to appropriate in addition Klages' radical critique of civilization and reason for Marxist theory. The stages of emmancipation from the spell of nature and the corresponding stages of class domination (Marx) are therefore understood simultaneously as stages in the dialectic of subjectification and reification (Klages). For this, the epistemological triad of subject, object and concept has to be reinterpreted as a relationship of repression and domination, where the instance of repression — the subject — at the same time becomes the overpowered victim. The repression of inner nature, with its anarchic desire for happiness, is the price paid for the formation of a unified self; this in turn being necessary for the sake of self-*preservation* and for the mastery of external nature. The idea that concepts are "mental tools" goes back not merely to Klages, but to Nietzsche, and even Schopenhauer; that is, tools for the adjustment and domination of reality by a subject motivated essentially by desire for self-preservation. For this reason not even formal logic is an organ of truth, but rather merely the connecting link between the unity of the subject — the "system-generating ego principle" (ND, p. 36) — and the concept which "prearranges and truncates reality" (ND, p. 21). Mind, bent on objectifying and system-constructing, and operating according to the law of non-contradiction, becomes in its very origins — by virtue of "the splitting of life into mind and its object" — instrumental reason. This instrumental spirit, itself part of living nature, can in the end understand itself only in the categories of a *dead* nature. As an agent of objectification, it is in its very origins "*forgetful* of itself." Being oblivious of itself, however, instrumental spirit has manifested itself as a universal system of delusion, as a closed universe of instrumental reason.

To be sure, Adorno and Horkheimer, in good Marxist (and Hegelian) fashion, adhere to the belief that the process of civilization is simultaneously one of *enlightenment*; "reconciliation," "happiness" or "emancipation" can be conceived of only as its *result* (cf. DdA, p. 71). Regression to Klages' archaic realm of images is thus blocked off as a merely illusory path to reconciliation. Reconciliation can only be conceived of as a *sublation* of the "disunion" of the self and nature, to be achieved only in the process of self-constitution of the human species as a history of work, sacrifice and renunciation. Consequently, the process of enlightenment can only be surpassed and perfected in its own medium — that of spirit bent on controlling nature. The enlightenment of misguided enlightenment, the "subject's recollection of its own origins in nature," is only possible in the medium of the concept. The precondition for this is that the concept turns against the reifying tendency of conceptual thought; Adorno recommends this for philosophy in *Negative Dialectics*: "it (philospohical thought) must strive, by means of the concept, to get beyond the concept" (ND, p. 27, translation, p. 15).

In *Negative Dialectics* Adorno has tried to characterize this self-conquest of the concept as the incorporation of a "mimetic" moment into conceptual thought. Rationality and mimesis must come together to deliver rationality from its irrationality. Mimesis is the name for those modes of behavior which are receptive, expressive, and communicative in a sensuous fashion. It is in art that mimetic modes of conduct have been preserved as spiritual ones in the course of civilization: art is intellectualized mimesis, i.e., mimesis which is both transformed and objectified by rationality. Art *and* philosophy thus denote the two shperes in which mind, by linking the rational with a mimetic moment, breaks through the crust of reification. To be sure, this process of intertwining occurs in both cases from opposite poles: in art, the mimetic moment assumes the form of spirit, while in philosophy, rational spirit tones itself down to take on a mimetic-reconciliatory character. "Reconciling spirit" is the medium common to art and philosophy, and at the same time it epitomizes their common relation to truth, their vanishing point, their utopia. Just as the concept of instrumental spirit implies not merely a cognitive relationship, but also a structuring principle of the relationship between human beings, and between human beings and nature, so too does the concept of reconciling spirit stand not merely for the "non-violent synthesis of the diffuse" in the beauty of art, but also for the non-violent unity of the diffuse in a reconciled relationship of all living things. In the cognitive forms of art and philosophy, this reconciled relationship of all living things is prefigured as the non-violent bridging of the gap between intuition and concept, between the particular and the general, between part and whole. And only to this form of spirit, prefiguring within itself a state of reconciliation, can knowledge be granted at all; this is the sense in which the sentence from *Minima Moralia* may be understood: that "knowledge (has) no other light than that which shines down from redemption onto the world."[5]

Thus, conceived from a utopian perspective, both art and philosophy are related antithetically to the world of instrumental reason; hence their constitutive negativity. However, whereas both art and philosophy, each in its own way, set out to bridge the hiatus between intuition and concept in a non-violent way, their relation to each other, a relation between two fragments of a non-reified spirit, is itself also a relation between intuition and concept; a relationship to be sure which cannot be stabilized by the articulated unity of a cognitive judgment. The presence of reconciling spirit in an unreconciled world can only be thought of aporetically.

This is the aporia: both non-discursive and discursive knowledge desire knowledge in its entirety; but the very fact of knowledge being spit into non-discursive and discursive knowledge means that they can each only grasp complementary fragmented forms of truth. It would only be possible to join together these complementary fragmented forms of truth, to make truth entire and unabridged, if the division itself were resolved and reality were reconciled. In the work of art truth makes its appearance as an object of the senses; this accounts for its superiority over discursive knowledge. But precisely *because* truth appears by means of the senses in the work of art, truth remains inaccessible to aesthetic experience; since the work of art cannot

---

5. Adorno, *Minima Moralia* (London, 1974), p. 247.

express the truth which it makes manifest, aesthetic experience does not know what it experiences. The truth which flashes forth in the moment of aesthetic experience, though a concrete presence, at the same time eludes comprehension. Adorno has compared works of art with riddles and picture puzzles in order to make clear this simultaneous relationship between the existence and impenetrability of truth as it apears in the aesthetic experience. Works of art are like picture puzzles to the extent that "that which they hide, like the letter in Poe's story, appears, and in this very appearing hides itself" (AT, p. 185, translation, p. 178).

Should one try to grasp what cannot be grapsed through an interpretive penetration of the work of art, then it disappears like a rainbow to which one has come too close (AT, p. 185, translation, p. 178). However, if the truth content of works of art were locked into the moment of aesthetic experience, it would be lost and the aesthetic experience itself would be vain. For this reason, works of art are dependent on "interpretive reason" (AT, p. 193, translation, p. 186), on the "production of their truth content" through interpretation, for the sake of that something in them which points beyond the fleeting moment of aesthetic experience. For Adorno, interpretation means *philosophical* interpretation; the need for interpretation which is inherent in the work of art is the need which aesthetic experience has for philosophical illumination. "Genuine aesthetic experience must become philosophy or it fails to exist at all" (AT, p. 197, translation, p. 190). Philosophy, however, whose utopia it is "to open up the non-conceptual by means of concepts, without making it equivalent to these concepts" (ND, p. 21, translation, p. 10), remains tied to the medium of conceptual language,[6] in which the immediacy of truth as it appears in the aesthetic experience cannot be restored. Just as a moment of blindness adheres to the immediacy of aesthetic intuition, a moment of emptiness adheres to the 'mediacy' of philosophical thought; only in tandem can they approximate a truth which neither of them can express. "Truth lies unveiled for discursive knowledge, but for all that it does not possess it; the knowledge which art is, has it (truth), but as something incommensurable to it" (AT, p. 191, translation, p. 183). In the "Fragment on Music and Language," Adorno described this mutual insufficiency of aesthetic and discursive knowledge as follows: "Discursive language wishes to express the absolute in a mediated way, and the absolute escapes it at every turn, leaving each attempt behind in its finitude. Music touches the absolute directly, but the very moment it does so, the absolute is obscured, just as a light that is too strong may blind the eye and prevent it from seeing what is perfectly visible."[7] The language of music and discursive language appear as the lacerated halves of "true language," a language in which "the content itself would become manifest" as Adorno puts it.[8] The intrinsic idea of such a language is "the

---

6. Adorno, *Gesammelte Schriften,* 16, p. 254.
7. *Ibid.*
8. *Ibid.,* p. 252.

figure of the divine name."[9] The aporetic relationship of art and philosophy sublates a theological perspective: art and philosophy combine to form a negative theology.

II

The antithetical relation of artistic beauty to the world of instrumental spirit — i.e., to empirical reality — resulted from a utopian conception of art. This accounts for Adorno's inversion of the theory of imitation: art does not imitate reality but at most that aspect of reality which points beyond reality, i.e., natural beauty (cf. AT, p. 113, translation, p. 107). In natural beauty Adorno sees the cipher of a nature which does not yet exist, that is, a reconciled nature, a nature therefore which has gone beyond the diremption of life into mind and object, and which has sublated this division, now reconciled, into itself; a nature which is to be thought of as the non-violent unification of the manifold, with the particularity of each individual entity remaining unharmed. Thus the work of art, as imitation of natural beauty, becomes the image of a nature which has found its voice, which is freed from its dumbness, is redeemed; and likewise the image of a reconciled humanity. The radical nature of the antithesis between instrumental spirit and aesthetically reconciled spirit explains the fact that the utopia of reconciliation refers to nature as a whole: both, instrumental spirit and reconciling spirit, signify an order of living nature as a whole.

This relationship between negativity and the utopian concent of the beauty of art is also implied by the basic categorial framework of Adorno's aesthetics, that is, by the interrelated categories of truth, semblance, and reconciliation. But just as the interrelationship of art and philosophy turned out to be aporetical, now the relationship of truth, semblance, and reconciliation in artistic beauty is found to be antinomical. This is the dialectic of aesthetic semblance.

Traces of the dialectic of aesthetic semblance are to be found as early as *Dialectic of Enlightenment*. The separation of artistic beauty from life-praxis (*Lebenspraxis*) appears there from a double perspective: firstly as the *demotion* of the beautiful to mere semblance (as depicted through the 'siren episode'), then as the *severing* of the beautiful from magical means-ends relationships, and thus with its *emancipation* as an organ of knowledge. The truth and untruth of the beautiful are inextricably linked. Now, to grasp the dialectic of semblance as Adorno developed it, above all in the *Aesthetic Theory*, we must define his concept of aesthetic truth. We might express the basic thought here as follows: what art makes manifest is not the light of redemption itself but *reality* in the light of redemption. Aesthetic truth is concrete, aesthetic truth is pluralistic — tied to the concreteness of individual works. In other words: it is one truth, which can at any one moment only manifest itself in particular form. Each work of art is a unique mirror of reality, like a Leibnizian monad. The truth content of works of art, as a *specific* one, depends on whether or not

---

9. *Ibid.*

reality is falsified, that is, on whether or not reality appears in the work of art as it really is. If one wanted to separate analytically what Adorno thinks dialectically in tandem, one could distinguish truth$_1$, as aesthetic rightness or validity from truth $_2$ as representational truth. The unity of both moments thus means that art can only be knowledge of reality (truth$_2$) by virtue of aesthetic synthesis (truth$_1$), and that on the other hand, aesthetic synthesis (truth$_1$) can only succeed if through it reality comes to appearance (truth$_2$). Now, however, art — as the sphere of apparent reconciliation — is by its very concept the "Other," the negation of unreconciled reality. Therefore it can only be true in the sense of being faithful to reality to the extent that it makes reality appear *as* unreconciled, antagonistic, fragmented. But it can only do this by letting reality appear in the light of reconciliation through the non-violent aesthetic synthesis of the diffuse — a synthesis which produces the appearance of reconciliation. This means, however, that an antinomy is carried into the *very interior* of aesthetic synthesis: aesthetic synthesis can, by definition, only succeed by turning against itself and calling its own principle into question — it must do this for the sake of truth which may not be had except by means of this principle. "Art is true to the extent that art itself and that which speaks through it is discordant and irreconciled; but it establishes this truth when it synthesizes the discordant, for only thereby can it define the latter in its unreconciled state. Paradoxically, art must testify to what is unreconciled and nonetheless tend toward its reconciliation. . . ." (AT, p. 251; translation, p. 241).

This antinomical structure of art is contained from the very beginning within the historical separation of image and sign, of non-conceptual and conceptual synthesis, even if it only arrives at self-consciousness with modern art, under conditions of a fully developed rationality. Art must, by its very concept, turn against its own principle, must rebel against aesthetic semblance.

I had said that the mutual penetration of the two dialectics — the dialectic of subjectification and reification, and the dialectic of aesthetic semblance — is the moving principle of Adorno's aesthetics. What has to be shown in detail is how the antinomies and aporias of modern art grow out of the intermingling of these two dialectics in Adorno's reconstruction: that is, the ambivalence of the principle of construction, the aporias of open form, the antinomy of the nominalistic principle. We must remember that, for Adorno, the dialectic of subjectification and reification, as a dialectical constellation, is written into the concept of subjectification itself: this concept denotes on the one hand a strengthening of the subject vis-à-vis the compulsions of inner and the constraints of outer nature as well asl vis-à-vis the force of objectively binding meaning; that is, vis-à-vis quasi-natural social rules, norms and conventions. The same concept depicts on the other hand the price at which these emancipatory advances alone can succeed: an increase in "subjective," that is, instrumental rationality, progressive reification terminating in self-destruction. Adorno then tries to show that even the emancipation of aesthetic subjectivity, in which an unleashing of art, an aesthetic "state of freedom," seems to be anticipated, is being overtaken by this dialectic. As he portrays it, reification seeps into the pores of modern art from all sides: from society, whose technical rationality rubs off upon the methods of aesthetic construction (Adorno's standard example is the degeneration of the twelve-tone principle into a method of composition); from the weakened subjects, who show themselves to be unequal to art's potential for freedom; and finally from the aesthetic material itself, the development of which causes theindividualization of language to turn into its disintegration. But these tendencies towards aesthetic decay which penetrate art from the outside and from "below" as it were, are only brought to a head by the compulsion towards the intra-aesthetic destruction of aesthetic meaning: art must, for the sake of its truth, turn against the principle of aesthetic synthesis: "negation of synthesis becomes (its) principle of organization" (AT, p. 232, translation, p. 222). This paradoxical formulation means that art can only survive as authentic if it succeeds in articulating the negation of synthesis as aesthetic meaning, and in effecting aesthetic synthesis even through its own negation. The modern work of art must, in one and the same movement, produce as well as negate aesthetic meaning, balance itself as it were on the razor's edge between affirmative semblance and illusionless anti-art.

What Adorno says about advanced modern music at the end of the Schönberg chapter of the *Philosophy of Modern Music* implicitly refers to authentic modern art as a whole: "It has taken all the darkness and guilt of the world onto its shoulders. Its entire happiness consists in recognizing unhappiness; all its beauty consists in denying itself the semblance of beauty" (PhdNM, p. 126). The antinomy of modern art, however, is expressed in the fact that we no longer have a concept which would allow us to conceive of that balancing act of which I have just spoken as successful: it is in the strict sense of the word impossible. For where art still succeeds in articulating the negation of meaning in an aesthetically meaningful way — in literature, Beckett's work is Adorno's most important example of such an achievement — it is apparent that even art which survives, that is, art which has taken the darkness and guilt of the world on its shoulders, does not escape the antinomy. The very means by which it remains art becomes simultaneously the occasion of its untruth. Aesthetic success, that is, the truth and authenticity of art, cannot be separated from a remnant of aesthetic semblance, i.e., untruth: "Art, in the end, is semblance, in that it cannot escape the suggestion of meaning in the midst of meaninglessness" (AT, p. 231; translation, p. 222). Art must, however, for the sake of the hope of reconciliation, take this guilt upon itself: this is what Adorno means by the "redemption of semblance."

III

In his "Theses on the Philosophy of History," Benjamin had suggested that the "puppet 'historical materialism' " must take theology into its service.[10]

---

10. Cf. W. Benjamin, *Illuminations* (New York, 1969), p. 253.

Adorno's philosophy might be understood as an attempt to fulfill this desideratum. However, a fissure between messianic-utopian and materialist motifs in Adorno's thought cannot be overlooked; the same fissure, moreover, appears once again in the materialist elements of his theory as one between historical materialism and utopian sensualism. Thus Adorno's aesthetics stand closer in many respects to a Schopenhauerianism interpreted from an eschatological *and* sensualist point of view, than it does to a theologically enlightened Marxism. The light of redemption which, according to Adorno, is to be cast on reality through the medium of art is not only not of this world, but, to express it in Schopenhauerian terms, comes from a world beyond space, time, causality, and individuation. At the same time, however, Adorno adheres to a sensualist concept of happiness as the epitome of sensual fulfillment. The interlacing of the theological motif with the sensualist one indicates a utopian perspective in which the hope of redemption nourishes itself on a longing for paradise lost. In a certain sense, one could say that Adorno devoted his entire intellectual energies to the task of rehabilitating this dream of reconciliation — if not as a philosophical category, then as a philosophical idea that would contain all truths within it. Only in this context could aesthetic synthesis become for Adorno the prefiguration of a reconciled relationship of people, things, and creatures of nature.

The eschatological-sensualist utopia allows the gap between historical reality and the state of reconciliation to become so profound that bridging it can no longer be a meaningful goal of human praxis. The gap becomes, as Adorno puts it, "an abyss between praxis and happiness" (AT, p. 26; translation, pp. 17-18). Concepts are no longer possible in which we could *think of* the state of reconciliation; the *idea* of reconciliation appears only *ex-negativo* on the horizon of art and philosophy — most tangible when, "in the emotional shocks of aesthetic experience," "the self peeps out for a moment over the walls of the prison that it itself is" (AT, p. 364; translation, p. 347). Thus aesthetic experience is, for Adorno as for Schopenhauer, rather an ecstatic experience than a real utopian one; the happiness it promises is not of this world.

On the other hand, the immensity of the gap between reality and utopia means that reality, prior to all experience — transcendentally as it were — is pinned to negativity. If it is only possible to gain access to the truth if we see the world as "needy and distorted as it will one day stand exposed in the messianic light,"[11] then the murderous character of the course of the world is already sealed, before our experience of it can lead to despair. The fact that the necessity of such despair is built into the basic categories of Adorno's philosophy may explain the peculiar predetermination of the question of truth in Adorno's interpretations of modern art.

It cannot of course be overlooked that within this utopian-messianic perspective elements of a genuine materialism maintain an obstinate and powerful life of their own. Here, a relation to social praxis lives on. These provide the

---

11. Adorno, *Minima Moralia*, p. 247.

vantage point from which the theological perspective would have to be reinterpreted once more: only then would the "puppet 'historical materialism' " have taken theology into its service. What is required here is a type of critique which would set the system of Adorno's philosophical categories as a whole in motion and thereby permit a materialist deciphering of Adorno's aesthetics.

The basic elements of such a critique of Adorno, i.e., one which sets out from the fissure between the materialist and the messianic motif, has been developed by Habermas in his *Theory of Communicative Action*.[12] Habermas' basic argument is as simple as it is convincing: the intersubjectivity of communication is as much an integral part of the sphere of mind attached to language as is the objectification of reality in contexts of instrumental action; likewise a symmetrical, communicative relationship between subject and subject is as much a part of this sphere as is an asymmetrical, distancing relationship between subject and object.

In contrast, the paradigm of a philosophy of consciousness which must explain the world-disclosing function of language on the basis of an asymmetrical subject-object model of knowing and acting leaves no room for the communicative moment of mind. The latter is forced into an extraterritorial position vis-à-vis the sphere of conceptual thought. This is what happens in Adorno; his name for the sphere of communicative behavior extraneous to the sphere of conceptual thought is *mimesis*. In contrast to this, reflection on the basis of instrumental spirit from the standpoint of linguistic philosophy necessitates the recognition of a "mimetic" moment in conceptual thought itself: a mimetic moment is sublated in ordinary life just as much as in art and philosophy. This fact must remain hidden to a philosophy which understands the function of the concept on the basis of the polarity between subject and object; such a philosophy cannot perceive, behind the objectifying functions of language, the communicative capacities as conditions of their possibility. For this reason it can conceive of mimesis only as the "Other" of rationality, and the coincidence of mimesis and rationality only as the negation of historical reality. To become aware of the *ongoing* unity of the mimetic and the rational moment in the foundation of language a change of philosophical paradigm is required: "The rational core in these mimetic capacities only reveals itself if we give up the paradigm of a philosophy of consciousness, that is, that of a subject which *represents* objects and *works upon* them, in exchange for the paradigm of philosophy of language, i.e., the paradigm of intersubjective understanding and communication; and such as to incorporate the partial aspect of cognitive-instrumental rationality into a more comprehensive *communicative rationality*."[13]

If, however, the intersubjectivity of understanding — communicative action — is just as much constitutive for the sphere of mind as is the objec-

12.   J. Habermas, *Theory of Communicative Action*, vol. 1 (Cambridge, Mass., 1983), "The Critique of Instrumental Reason," pp. 366 ff.

13.   *Ibid.,* p. 390.

tification of reality in contexts of instrumental actions, then the utopian perspective which Adorno seeks to elaborate through the concept, taken from the philosophy of consciousness, of a "non-violent synthesis," emigrates as it were to the sphere of discursive reason itself: uncorrupted intersubjectivity, the non-violent togetherness of the manifold, which would make possible a condition of simultaneous closeness and distance, identity and difference of individual beings; these are the key words of a utopian projection, the elements of which discursive reason extracts from the conditions of its own foundation in language. This utopian projection does not describe the "Other" of discursive reason, but its own idea of itself. Because this utopian projection remains attached to the conditions of language, what is at issue here is an inner-worldly — in this sense a "materialist" — utopia.

The consequence of this recognition of a communicative moment in conceptual thought is that the dialectical relationship of subjectification and reification dissolves *as* a dialectical one. Habermas has shown this in the *Theory of Communicative Action*. The point of his arguments there may be clarified through a comparison with two of Adorno's formulations. In the *Aesthetic Theory*, Adorno speaks at one point of the "epistemological insight that subjectification and reification are correlative to each other" (AT, p. 252; translation, p. 242). This formulation is admittedly ambiguous; it would be compatible with Habermas' thesis that "communicative rationalization" on the one hand, and "systemic rationalization" and natural-scientific-technological progress, on the other, stand in a "correlative" relationship in the modern world. This thesis refers to the categorial distinction of two types of rationalization and their reciprocal *possibilities of structuration* in the modern world. What is left open by this thesis is the way in which the structures of communicative asnd instrumental-functionalist rationality, which may be conceived of *conceptually* as correlative, will concretely penetrate the general structure of a social life-context. This is an empirical-historical question; Habermas' own explanation for why structures of communiation are threatened in modern society, and why systemic rationality is taking over is, in the final analysis, a Marxist one. In contrast, the two levels of analysis in a sense coincide for Adorno, as the second formulation, also from the *Aesthetic Theory*, shows. There Adorno says that subjectivity works, by virtue of its own logic, "towards its own extinction" (AT, p. 235; translation, p. 225). Since the communicative share of the subject in the subject-object model has become invisible, only the tendency to reification by virtue of a conceptual logic remains visible as the correlate of the subject which grows ever stronger. Thus, as a result of the interrelationship between subjectivity and reification in Adorno and Horkheimer, a *dialectic* of subjectification and reification has to emerge. However, even if in the end the consequences for social criticism in Habermas' writings on the one hand, and in Adorno and Horkheimer's on the other, were not so very different, what is crucial is that as a result of their conceptual differences, history *itself* wins back a degree of freedom which it had lost for Adorno and Horkheimer, through their choice of basic categories, and without which the idea of a potential for freedom within the historical process becomes void. The direct consequence for aesthetics is that the transition from the "negation of objectively binding meaning" to the "meaninglessness" of late-capitalist reality can no longer be deduced dialectically from the "impossibility of meaning generated by the subject"; this deduction is however central for Adorno's construction of the antinomy of modern art. To the problem, bound up with this construction, of the aesthetic meaning of "open form," I shall return later.

IV

The question arises as to how the constellation of the aesthetic categories of truth, semblance, and reconciliation may be set in motion if these categories are severed from the dialectical relationship between subjectification and reification. As I have indicated, the meaning of these categories cannot for Adorno be separated either from the a priori polemical relationship of art to reality, or from the vision of a redeemed nature. Even if we give up just one of these presuppositions, the relationship between truth, semblance, and the utopian content of the work of art as constructed by Adorno will begin to disintegrate. This may be illustrated by reference to three critiques of Adorno, in which three different aspects of the problem are brought to the fore:

1) H.R. Jauss[14] has, against Adorno, made an appeal for the communicative functions of art. There are good reasons why these do not appear in Adorno: problems of reception and communication can only emerge with respect to art, if the unilinear conceptual relationship between reality, the work of art, and utopia, as constructed by Adorno, is called into question. Conversely, where this schema is presupposed, problems of reception and communication are reduced to the problem of an adequate comprehension of the philosophical schema itself: all that matters is the genuine experience of works of art and unravelling this experience philosophically. Once the communicative functions of art are brought into play, the conceptual triad of reality-art-utopia is replaced by that of reality-art-subject of reception. This relationship can no longer be thought of as a linear one, rather merely as a circular one. Art is accorded a function in the life-praxis; it is thought of as something which *re-acts* upon reality.

2) P. Bürger[15] has criticized the relationship between the categories of truth, semblance, and reconciliation in Adorno from another point of view. Adorno's defense of aesthetic semblance as a paradigm of reconciliation is seen by Bürger as an attack on avant-garde attempts to set the relationship between art and life-praxis in motion.[16] And indeed it is true that Adorno's "redemption of semblance" is directed against tendencies to falsely sublate art, which for him follow the development of modern art in the 20th century like a shadow. Bürger to be sure does not take the Adornian schema of the aesthetic cate-

---

14. Cf. H.R. Jauss, *Aesthetic Experience and Literary Hermeneutics* (Minneapolis, 1982), pp. 15 ff.
15. See P. Bürger, *Zur Kritik der idealistischen Ästhetik* (Frankfurt am Main, 1983).
16. *Ibid.,* pp. 67-72 and 128-135.

gories truth, semblance, and reconciliation any more seriously than Jauss does; otherwise, he would have had to notice that Adorno's reservations concerning a *false* sublation of art are based on the idea of the *authentic* sublation — i.e., as a realization of its promise of happiness. What is, however, correct is that the idea of a historical transformation of the constellation of art and life-praxis, in which Bürger sees the real productive core of avant-garde attempts towards a sublation of art, is indeed hardly compatible with Adorno's "paradigm of reconciliation." For this reason Bürger once again replaces the explanatory schema of reality, art and reconciliation by that of reality, art and life-praxis, whereby admittedly the production-aesthetic meaning of this schema, as opposed to the reception-aesthetic meaning, now dominates in a problematic way. This finds expression not least in the fact that Bürger would like to completely eliminate the category of aesthetic semblance and replace it with the category of "rupture."[17] The only part of the edifice of Adornian aesthetics which he seeks to defend is its foundation — art's claim to truth. To be sure the attempt to occupy this foundation seems especially pointless from the point of view of philosophical aesthetics when access to the utopian splendor of aesthetic semblance above is blocked off.

3) In contrast to Bürger, who wants to do away with the category of aesthetic semblance for the sake of that truth, K.H. Bohrer,[18] following Nietzsche, has attempted to save the category of aesthetic semblance by severing it completely from its relationship to the concept of truth: the idea is an emancipation of aesthetic semblance so that now even the *other* pole of the basic Adornian schema of truth, semblance, and utopia resolves itself into aesthetic semblance: utopia emigrates to the moment of aesthetic experience, whose "utopian" element thus loses its reference to a real future. Bohrer resolves in an aestheticist way an ambiguity in Adorno's thought which results from the tension between Schopenhauerian and Marxist aesthetics: art's promise of happiness is redeemed in the ecstatic moment of aesthetic experience itself. Bohrer retains the notion of the subversive function of aesthetic experience; for this reason one could also understand what he says about the "allegorical" role of the messianic-eschatological imagery in Benjamin and Musil as a de-mythologizing interpretation of Adorno: "They invoke . . . with reverence, the allegorical power that may not be lost of a bygone cultural-religious image for a 'now,' which logically and psychologically cannot exist as a total presence, and which nonetheless must be dramatized as such, if one does not want to fall prey to the constraints of cultural norms and of history that has already been written, or of ideas which are no longer valid."[19] Bohrer is the only one of the three authors mentioned who definitely holds onto the utopian quality of

---

17. *Ibid.*, p. 67.
18. See K.H. Borer, *Plözlichkeit. Zum Augenblick des ästhetischen Scheins* (Frankfurt am Main, 1981). See especially the following sections: "Ästhetik und Historismus: Nietzsches Begriff des 'Scheins,' " p. 111 ff.; and "Utopie des 'Augenblicks' und Fiktionalität. Die Subjektivierung von Zeit in der modernen Literatur," pp. 180 ff.
19. *Ibid.*, pp. 211 ff.

aesthetic semblance. He couples this, however, with an emphatic rejection of all attempts to abolish the boundaries between art and life, be it in a "political-moral," a "surrealist-destructive" or a "utopian-sentimental" way.[20] While negating any truth claim of art, he simultaneously negates the real, futuristic meaning of its utopian element. One could say that Bohrer occupies the strategically important middle floor in the edifice of Adornian aesthetics; the accesses above and below, which have become unviable, he surrenders.

The basic explanatory schema of the aesthetic categories truth, semblance, and reconciliation has, for each of the three authors mentioned, fallen apart. This is indeed unavoidable if one gives up the polemical utopian perspective of Adorno's aesthetics. In this the three authors concur. Each preserves a fragment of Adorno's aesthetics: Jauss and Bohrer retain the subversive character of aesthetic experience as "the negation of objectively-binding meaning" which is contained within it; Bohrer holds on to the utopian splendor of aesthetic semblance; Bürger to the truth claim of art. It seems to me that these fragments of Adorno's aesthetics might very well be brought together again to form a whole, whereby admittedly, the linear, one-dimensional explanatory schema of the categories truth, semblance, and reconciliation would have to be transformed into a more complex, multidimensional constellation of categories. Doing this would mean setting Adorno's dialectically frozen categories in motion from the inside outward. I shall try to indicate what such an attempt might look like, though the result of the experiment still remains a matter of conjecture.

V

I shall now consider Bohrer's reduction of the utopian concept of art to the moment of aesthetic semblance. I see in this a legitimate resolution of an ambiguity which remains unresolved in Adorno, in so far as Adorno interprets the ecstatic moment of aesthetic experience as simultaneously a real utopian one. However, with the demythologization of the relationship between semblance and utopia, the idea of aesthetic synthesis pointing to a possible form of social synthesis (which for Adorno is implied in the former) does not simply become meaningless; rather it may now be conceived of in a new way if we give up the thesis of a dialectical relationship between subjectification and reification and with this the polemical-utopian overloading of the concept of aesthetic synthesis.

We have seen that Adorno understood the "negation of objectively binding meaning" as the epitome of the emancipatory potential of modern art. By this he meant the questioning of those traditional norms, conventions, syntheses of meaning and forms of life in which the Enlightenment discovered something unreflected, illegitimate, and violent. In retrospect, even the formal conventions and aesthetic norms providing unity and meaning in the traditional work of art also appear as unreflected, violent syntheses of meaning. Here it is not a question of *specific* formal conventions and aesthetic norms.

---

20.   *Ibid.,* p. 95.

What is rendered problematic is rather a *type* of unity and all-embracing meaning, which in the era of great bourgeois art was represented by both the unity of the self-contained work and the unity of the individual ego. The aesthetic enlightenment discovered both in the unity of the traditional work of art and in the unity of the bourgeois subject is something violent, unreflected, and inauthentic: i.e., a type of unity that is only possible at the price of the suppression and ostracism of things disparate, non-integrable, and repressed. What is at issue here is the "inauthentic" unity of a fictitious totality of meaning, analogous to the totality of meaning represented by a cosmos created by God. The open forms of modern art are, according to Adorno, an answer on the part of an emancipated aesthetic consciousness to all that is inauthentic and violent in such traditional totalities of meaning. The moments of *inauthenticity* and *violence* in the meaning-syntheses of this tradition is what Adorno is referring to when he characterizes modern art as a "case against the work of art as a totality of meaning" and when he claims for modern art a principle of individuation and of an "increasing elaboration-in-detail."

These claims suggest that with the incorporation of that which is unintegrated, alien to the subject, and meaningless into modern art, a correspondingly higher degree of flexible and individualized methods of organization is required from the artist. The "opening-up" or "expansion of the boundaries" of the work of art is thought of as a corollary to an increasing capacity for aesthetic *integration* of all that is diffuse and has been split off. Adorno himself saw a strengthening of the aesthetics subject as precondition of this kind opening-up of art to the "refuse of the world of appearance." Therefore Adorno links the open forms of modern art to a form of subjectivity which no longer corresponds to the rigid unity of the bourgeois subject but rather displays the more flexible organizational form of a "communicatively fluid" ego-identity. Adorno could not push this thought one step further because he denied modern society that which he ascribed to modern art: the ability of enlightenment to emancipate a potential "expansion of subjective limits" (G. Schwab) as well as a potential for reification. Here too the outcome of the enlightenment is not yet decided. Against this background it is plausible to connect the reflexively unbound forms of modern art with an unbounded subject, not only in a historical but also a *functional* sense, especially in regard to the subject of *reception*. Such a study has recently been undertaken by G. Schwab with examples from Woolf, Joyce, Beckett and Pynchon.[21] Schwab claims that the reflexive opening of the form of literary representation generates a playful dynamic of identification and differentation in the reader, leading tendentially to a real expansion of the borders of the subject. One could conclude that new forms of aesthetic synthesis in modern art point to new forms of psychological and social "synthesis." This is the *emancipatory* potential of modernism: a new type of "synthesis" appears — with aesthetic, psychological-moral and social ramifications — incorporating diffuse, non-

---

21.   G. Schwab, *Entgrenzungen und Entgrezungsmythen. Zur Anthropologie der Subjektivität in modernen angloamerikanischen Roman* (Konstanz Habilitationsschrift, 1982).

integrated, senseless and excluded material into a space of domination-free communication, both in the unbounded forms of art as well as in the open structures of a no longer rigid type of individuation and socialization. Of course, we can only reach this conclusion if we no longer take the "in-itself" of artistic form as primary and as a chema of reconciliation: only as the medium of a communicative mediation betwen subjects, as something which is produced and received, can the work of art catalyze changes in forms of individuation and socialization.

I can now clarify why Adorno offers such a one-sided interpretation of the "negativity" which he attributes to the "shattered unity" of the modern art work: Adorno, both in his theory and in his interpretations of modern art (e.g., in his magnificent interpretation of Beckett's *Endgame*), saw in great works of art an increasing disintegration both of meaning and the subject in social reality, not unlike his opponent Lukacs, in this respect. However, art's "path of progressive negativity" also contains the opposite moment: inherent in the negation of "objectively binding meaning" is a growing capacity for the aesethetic assimilation of that which now, by virtue of its embodiment in the work of art, is *not* merely negated — that is, is no longer excluded from the sphere ofsymbolic communication.

If one acknowledges this moment, however, the "move away from the work of art as a totality of meaning" may be no longer automatically identified with the increasing disintegration of meaning in capitalist society; an objection to which Lukacs is open as much as Adorno. Clearly, a distinction must be made between increasing disintegration of meaning and of the subject in reality — on the horizontal plane of historical time, on the one hand, and between an aesthetic appropriation of layers of experience which are extraneous to the subject and its universe of meaning — on the vertical plane of psychological organization — on the other. That modern art is concerned with both seems to me indubitable; the fact that Adorno neglected the second moment, however, is not blindness on his part — his interpretations of the expressionist Schönberg prove that — but is rather the expression of a philosophical preconception.

Upon examining the relationship between the opening up of subjective and aesthetic boundaries, it becomes clear that what Adorno called "aesthetic synthesis" may ultimately be reintegrated once more with a true utopia of nonviolent communication This is however only true if one attributes to art a *function in connection with* forms of non-aesthetic communication and with real transformations of the self and social conditions respectively. To the extent that the work of art refers to a real reconciliation, it is not the inauthentic embodiment of a non-existent situation, but the catalytic potential of a process that begins with "the transposition of aesthetic experience to symbolic or communicative action" (Jauss).

If the work of art is now related functionally instead of ideally to "reconciliation," then the relationship between art and philosophy also must be conceived in a new way. Aesthetic experience still requires illumination through interpretation and critique, but it no longer requires a kind of philosophical elucidation teaching it what aesthetic semblance is all about. For works of art which by virtue of their *effect* rather than their intrinsic being point towards an emancipation of communication no longer fulfill their cognitive functions (as organs of illumination) as forms of philosophical *knowledge*, but rather in the subjects' relationships to themselves and to the world, where works of art intervene in a complex interrelationship of attitudes, feelings, inter-pretations, and value judgments. In this intervention what might be called the cognitive character of art fulfills itself. The fact that the knowledge which art brings about cannot be captured in words does not result from the concept's deficiencies, but from the fact that the 'enlightenment of consciousness,' which is implied by the word "knowledge," here includes in equal measure cognitive, affective, and moral-practical aspects. "Knowledge" here denotes a result which stands closer to a knowing-how than to a knowing-that. It is more of an ability to speak, to judge, to sense or to perceive, than the result of a cognitive undertaking.

We can now attempt to unravel Adorno's concept of the truth of art. I assume with Koppe that we can only speak of the truth of art if we already know what it means to speak of truth independent of the aesthetic context.[22] I would like to take as the starting point of my considerations Habermas' language-pragmatic differentiation of the everyday concept of truth; in Kop-pean terms, this means the distinction between "apophantic" truth, "en-deetic" truth (truthfulness/authenticity) and moral-practical truth. The three concepts of truth denote dimensions of validity of everyday speech, that is, a preliminary understanding of truth which every speaker has at his or her dis-posal. If one starts out from this kind of differentiated *everyday* concept of truth, then the concept of the truth of art seems to assume a mysterious quality initially. It transpires, however, that art is bound up with questions of truth in an extremely peculiar and complex way: not only in that it reveals, corrects, and broadens our experience of reality, but also in that aesthetic "validity" — i.e., aesthetic "rightness" (*Stimmigkeit*) — *touches on* questions of truth, truth-fulness/authenticity and moral-practical rightness in an intricate way, al-though this does not mean that it may be equated with any one of the three dimensions of truth, or even with all of them together. It seems reasonable to suppose that the notion of the "truth of art" will only be redeemed in terms of the interplay between the various dimensions of truth.

Now Adorno himself always emphasized the interrelationship of the vari-ous dimensions of truth in artistic truth; this finds expression both in the idea of the association of the mimetic-expressive with a rational moment in the work of art, and in his conceptualization of the relation between truth, sem-blance, and reconciliation. The interpretation of the truth of art in terms of the interplay between the various dimensions of truth is to this extent initially merely a language-pragmatic reformulation of a thought which is central for Adorno. More important than the reformulation itself is, however, the ques-

---

22.   See F. Koppe, *Grundbegriffe der Ästhetik* (Frankfurt am Main, 1983), p. 88.

tion as to the consequences that follow from it. I have already hinted at some of these consequences when I distinguished between a "functional" and an "ideal" relation of the work of art to "reconciliation" and consequently emphasized the *practical* character of aesthetic knowledge. If we apply this to our earlier analysis of Adorno's concept of the truth of art, it seems to be a question of separating two aspects in this concept which for Adorno combine dialectically: "truth$_1$" (aesthetic validity) and "truth$_2$" (cognitive truth). This is not supposed to imply that aesthetic *validity* has nothing to do with aesthetic *truth*: it implies rather that aesthetic synthesis does not as such *mean* reconcilliation. Through the idealization of the work of art's relation to reconciliation, the latter becomes for Adorno a central moment of its truth *content*. For this reason Adorno can only conceive of the appropriation of the truth of art in the sense of a transformation of aesthetic experience into philosophical insight. The attempt to unravel the truth content concealed in the work of art is for Adorno nothing but the attempt to rescue the truth of art, which would otherwise be lost. *What*, however, is rescued here through conceptual articulation is the polemical-utopian concept of art as such — art's relation to reconciliation as something which is knowable: it is a truth *about* art and not the truth content of the particular work of art. It is only because for Adorno the two levels of 1) an analysis of the *concept* of the truth of art and 2) the appropriation of each concrete truth of art, coincide, that he has to conceive of aesthetic knowledge as philosophical insight and the truth of art as philosophical truth. In this way, the apophantic dimension of the truth of art does, finally, become dominant in Adorno: his aesthetics becomes one of apophantic truth.

The language-pragmatic interpretation of the truth of art in terms of the interplay between the various dimensions of truth clearly implies more than a mere reformulation of Adornian insights. For now a conceptual distinction between the truth content of works of art and their relation to reconciliation becomes possible; between the two poles of art's relation to truth (which in Adorno coincide dialectically) the subject of reception now enters as mediating agency. With this, however, the meaning of the notion of the truth content of the work of art is bound to change. According to what has been said earlier, it might reasonably be supposed that the truth of art, rather than being truth in the literal sense of the word, will be a truth *potential*: the truth potential of works of art would then be the epitome of their potential for *disclosing* truth. To be sure this kind of interpretation of the truth of art as the epitome of its "truth *effects*" remains unsatisfactory as long as we cannot define what it is in aesthetic products that makes them bearers of truth potentials. In other words, the relationship between aesthetic *validity* and the truth of art remains to be clarified.

Since no philosopher from Kant to Adorno has been able to satisfactorily explain the intricate relationship between beauty and truth, the prospects of a language-pragmatic reconstruction in the case of this central aspect of Adorno's aesthetics do not admittedly seem very favorable. Nonetheless it seems to me that a direction may be indicated in which we can look for a solution to the problem.

I would like to formulate the problem as follows: there is something about art which tempts us to think that works of art are bearers of truth claims; these *truth* claims of works of art are bound up with their *aesthetic* validity claim. I will restrict myself in the following to apophantic and endeetic truth; that is, to apophantic and endeetic "truth claims" of art.

If one starts out from the intuitive core that underlies the apophantic concept of artistic truth, then one could characterize it with metaphors such as "disclosing," "making visible," "showing" reality. The idea is that art "discloses," "makes visible" or "shows" reality in a particularly effective way. Such metaphors are interesting because they are, in certain aesthetic contexts, as unavoidable as they are misleading. They are unavoidable because reality can only be shown and not said; misleading because that which shows *itself* can, in the case of art, only show itself (i.e., become present to the senses) in that which does the showing (i.e., in the work of art), and not as reality showing itself unmediated. Therefore, what shows itself in the work of art must be recognized as something showing itself on the basis of a familiarity which does not have the character of intuitive self-evidence; as though, for instance, a certain mirror had the power to reveal to us the "true" face of others: we can only know *that* it is their *true* face on the basis of a familiarity with them which assumes the form of an unconcealed sensual presence only on the appearance of the mirror image. We can only recognize the "essence" which "appears" in the apparition if we already *know* the essence as something which does not appear.

With the help of the imagery of "appearing" and "showing-itself," the relationship between aesthetic validity and the power of the beautiful to disclose reality may be made clearer: in an aesthetic object (at least traditionally) every detail is crucial; just as a tiny change in facial features would change a facial expression, so too would the reality which reveals itself in the aesthetic object be a different one if the sensual configuration of the object were to change. Alternatively, one could say that an aesthetic object more or less appropriately, more or less faithfully, more or less authentically, manifests that which appears within it. To be sure the decision as to whether reality is manifested in an appropriate way may not be an easy one. Or rather, where intuitive judgments are controversial, the corresponding (aesthetic) discourses may be interminable.

What is at stake in aesthetic discourse of this kind is the right understanding, the right perception of the aesthetic phenomenon. Such discourse points backward towards aesthetic experience itself, simultaneously correcting and expanding it. Aesthetic "validity" must in the final analysis be *perceived*; and to the extent that aesthetic "validity" is connected with reality showing itself, the work of art must be perceived *as* reality showing itself in the work as the medium of this showing, and reality must be *recognized* as showing itself. That is, recognized not in the way that the truth of a statement is recognized, but in the way that a face is recognized. In contrast, however, to the way in which we recognize a face, in the recognition of reality in the aesthetic phenomenon (for which for Adorno, the formula "that's how it is" stands as the ostensible gesture of the work of art), all that is realized vaguely, experienced unclearly, and known implicitly, quickens for the first time into the suggestiveness of a sensuous phenomenon. The pre- and subconscious, which has always been present, though obscurely and indistinctly, combines in the manifestation of an image, and thereby becomes as it were "tangible"; or what amounts to the same thing: uncomprehended experience is illuminated by condensing itself into a type of second order experience; experience becomes experienceable.

Heretofore, I have relied on a Platonic model in which the notion of "being acquainted with" has an ontological precedence over that of "re-cognizing." However, obviously art works in *both* directions: art also *transforms* our experience of the thing with which we are acquainted, with the result that this only *retrospectively* becomes the thing which is recognized. Art not only reveals reality, but also opens our eyes. This opening of eyes (and ears), the transformation of perception, is the healing of a partial blindness (and deafness), of an inability to perceive and experience reality as we learn to experience and peq ceive it by means of aesthetic experience. With modern art, one might say, this moment of *transformation* of perception through aesthetic experience becomes increasingly dominant.

But now what does all of this have to do with aesthetic *truth?* Evidently the temptation to aesthetically expand the concept of truth has its origin in the power of the beautiful to open up reality for us. This power *manifests* itself in those *effects* of art which are relevant to the notion of truth; at the same time it *confronts* us with an aesthetic *validity* claim. In the light of what has just been said, we can now explain the sense in which a truth *claim* corresponds to the truth *potential* of works of art — a truth claim which cannot be distinguished from an *aesthetic* validity claim. Obviously, we cannot explain what this truth claim might be on the basis of an apophantic concept of aesthetic truth. We can, however, try, as Seel has suggested,[23] to grasp the connection between an aesthetic validity claim and a truth claim in terms of the structure of aesthetic discourse: in aesthetic discourse the question of the "authenticity" of the "presentation" is dealt with simultaneously with the question of aesthetic rightness or validity. Aesthetic discourse is the mediating instance between the apophantic imagery from which we started out, and questions of aesthetic validity. For this reason, we can only grasp the truth *claim* of art if we start out from the complex interdependence of the various dimensions of truth in aesthetic discourse: in case of dispute as to the truth or falsity of aesthetic constructs, which is at the same time supposed to be a dispute as to their aesthetic validity, those taking part in the discourse have to bring to bear their own experience. Their own experience, however, may only be mobilized for dispute and transformed into arguments in all three dimensions of truth *simultaneously*, that is, in the three dimensions of truth, truthfulness/authenticity, and moral-practical rightness. Thus both the truth *potential* and the truth *claim*

---

23.   In a recently completed Konstanz dissertation: *Die Kunst der Entzweiung. Zum Begriff der ästhetischen Rationalität.*

of art may only be explained by appeal to the complex interdependence of the various dimensions of truth in life-historical experience, as well as in the formation and transformation of attitudes, ways of perceiving and interpreations.

Thus "truth" can only be ascribed to art metaphorically. But this metaphorical ascription of "truth" to art has a basis in the connection between aesthetic validity and the truth potential of works of art. If one pursues this thought further, one sees that a metaphorical intermingling of the truth dimensions in the work of art itself may be related to the intermingling of the various truth dimensions in the *effects* of art as well as in aesthetic discourse. For it is no coincidence that the imagery of "showing" and "making visible" is effortlessly bound with that of "saying" and "giving expression to." Reality comes to light in art, to quote F. Koppe, in a "mode of being affected"; the notions of "making visible" and "giving expression to" are inextricably bound. As something which speaks and expresses, art transforms that which is vaguely experienced into the presence of a sensuous phenomenon; by making reality visible, art becomes eloquent and expressive. For this reason, one could also see the immanently utopian quality of aesthetic semblance in the (overwhelming) experience that it can be verbally articulated, and that "that which is about to slip away can be objectified and cited to permanence" — as Adorno once expressed it.[24] To the extent that the imagery of "saying" and "giving expression to" comes to the fore, one will attempt to explain what is authentic in the work of art not in concepts of apophantic truth, but in terms of endeetic truthfulness. I notice this tendency in Habermas and to a certain extent in Koppe. Both attempts, however, the attempt which relies on concepts of apophantic truth, and that which uses concepts of endeetic truthfulness, have the common weakness that they are forced to interpret the work of art on the analogy of a special type of speech act. But in the work of art the artist does not literally *say* something; therefore what is authentic in a work is not determined by whether or not the artist was authentic; insofar as we can speak of authenticity at all, it is revealed in the work itself. Neither truth *nor* truthfulness may be attributed *unmetaphorically* to the work of art — at least if "truth" and "truthfulness" are understood in the sense of a pragmatically differentiated everyday concept of truth. That truth and truthfulness — and even normative rightness — are instead *metaphorically* bound up with each other in the work of art may only be explained by the fact that the work of art, as a symbolic construct with an aesthetic validity claim, is at the same time the object of an *experience* in which the three dimensions of truth are linked *unmetaphorically*.

If the concept of aesthetic truth is reconstructed according to the above schema, then even Kantian insights may be combined with motifs of an aesthetics of truth. In a discussion of truth aesthetics, R. Bubner[25] has tried to set off Kant's concept of the beautiful *against* the notion of an aesthetics of truth. I do not find this alternative compelling; that it is not is indeed already

---

24. AT, 114; translation, p. 108.
25. R. Bubner, "Über einige Bedingungen gegenwärtiger Ästhetik," *Neue Hefte für Philosophie*, no. 5 (1973).

suggested by the transition from the analytic of the beautiful to the theory of the beauty of art in Kant's aesthetics. Kant's idea of characterizing the experience of the beautiful as an indefinite and free interplay of imagination and understanding is certainly irreconcilable with an apophantic truth aesthetics, since the free play of *faculties* is *not* supposed to become a fixed determinate relationship between concept and intuition. The very *extension* of faculties, however, which results from the pleasurable and free interplay of imaginative and intellectual-reflective moments in aesthetic experience, may be related back to truth. One only has to apply the character of the potentiality which is contained in the word "faculties" to the concept of truth: the truth content of a work of art would actually be its truth *potential* — in the sense I have indicated above.

If aesthetic semblance may be understood as the locus of that pleasurable and free interplay of imaginative and intellectual-reflective capacities, then even the utopian "splendor of semblance" would not in the end be barred from truth and a real utopia. The ecstatic moment of aesthetic experience, in which the continuum of historical time is exploded, may be understood as the "setting free" of forces which in their non-aesthetic use can re-establish a continuum between art and the life-praxis. It is just this which Jauss probably has in mind when he establishes a connection between "aesthetic pleasure" and the "shift from aesthetic experience to symbolic or communicative action."[26] However, if this changeover from aesthetic experience to communicative action indicates that the work of art is bound up with questions of truth, then the emancipation of semblance cannot be complete. It (semblance) communicates secretly — though not quite in the way that Adorno assumed — with truth and reconciliation.

VI

I have tried to suggest a sense in which the conceptual interrelationship between Adorno's categories of truth, semblance, and reconciliation might be transformed into a more complex categorial schema, so that the philosophical potential and critical implications of Adornian aesthetics might remain intact. If one expands communicatively Adorno's concept of rationality, then his truth aesthetics may also be expanded "pragmatically." The inclusion of aesthetically experiencing, communicating, and acting subjects into the categorial schema of art, reality, and utopia produces an effect of "multidimensionality" as against Adorno's dialectical one-dimensional constructs. It would be worth discussion questions of actionist, aleatory, and popular art from this point of view — forms of art to which Adorno was as a rule unfavorably disposed — as well as the question of the "dissolution of the concept of the work of art," which has been discussed so often in recent times. I think that here too central arguments of Adorno which are nowadays frequently criticized as "traditionalist" (not entirely without some justification) would have to be given a new turn. However, I will restrict myself here to two

---

26. Jauss, *Aesthetic Experience and Literary Hermeneutics,* pp. 19 and 39 ff.

sub-problems: i) the question of the possibility of variations in the constellation of art and life-praxis, which has in particular been emphasized by P. Bürger, on the one hand, and ii) the question of the aesthetic value of popular art forms, on the other.

(i) If one understands (as I have done following Habermas up to now) the process of differentiation of the spheres of validity of science/learning, law/morality, and art, in which problems are dealt with according to an inner logic corresponding to the validity claims in question — if one understands this process of differentiation (as conceived on the abstract level of spheres of validity) as the expression of an irreversible cultural learning process, then phrases such as "the sublation of art in life-praxis," if taken literally, can offer no possible escape from the situation of an ideological *separation* of art from the reality of life. The failure of the avant-garde movements, as analyzed by Bürger, which actually tried to achieve the sublation of art in life-praxis,[27] thus *also* had its roots in an illusory self-understanding. Bürger points out correctly that "that which ahs been split off historically as the aesthetic sphere cannot be turned into the organizing center of a liberating and liberated life-praxis."[28] At the same time, as Bürger himself insists, we can think of the constellations in which art and life-praxis are related to each other as amenable to transformation. The differentiation of spheres of validity must be distinguished from specific forms of an *institutional* differentiation. Bürger says of the "bourgeois institution of art": "art as fully individuated subsystem is, at the same time, one whose individual products no longer tend to assume a social function."[29]

Consequently Bürger demands a *transformation* of the "institution of art," or of the norms which govern it,[30] as a result of which art would win back its social relevance. Bürger's utopia of an avant-garde transformation of the institution of art "so that everyone, freely producing, might be able to develop his/her capacities to the full,"[31] seems to me, however, to interpret the "praxis of art" — its social function — in an overly production-aesthetic way; it is only for this reason that Bürger can play off the "praxis of art" against Adorno and his notion of the (great) work of art.[32] If, in contrast, one takes the reception-aesthetic side into consideration, then it is not clear why a change in the function of art which would be related to a democratic expansion of society should exclude the idea of the great work of art. The opposite indeed seems to me to be true: without the paradigmatic products of "great" art in which the imagination and the accumulated talent of obsessed artistic virtuosos objectifies itself, a democratically generalized aesthetic production would presumably lapse into an amateur arts-and-craftsism. Something akin to what is true for the improvsisatory elements of modern music is also true here; Boulez and Dahlhaus have pointed out that the attempt to absolutize these improvisatory

---

27. P. Bürger, *Theory of the Avantgarde* (Minneapolis, 1984).
28. P. Bürger, *Zur Kritik der idealistischen Ästhetik*, p. 189.
29. P. Bürger, *Theory of the Avantgarde*, p. 42.
30. See P. Bürger, *Zur Kritik der idealistischen Ästhetik*, p. 187.
31. *Ibid.*, p. 135.
32. Cf. *Ibid.*, pp. 128 ff.

elements would lead to a regression in musical development. Improvisation is, as a rule, merely the varying activation of that which has already been sedimented in memory, or, as Boulez puts it, "manipulated memory."[33] Even John Cage seems to have hit upon the same problem when he says: "I must find a way to set people free without making them silly."[34]

I assume that a "transformation" of the "institution of art" cannot imply an elimination of the "culture of experts,"[35] but that it would result in the production of a denser net of associations between the culture of experts and life-world, on the one hand, and the culture of experts and popular art, on the other. Adorno and Horkheimer, in their critique of the culture industry, had already described barriers to such a reconvergence of aesthetics and practical life, or of the lofty and the base. However, if one grants to history an ambiguity sufficient to allow it emancipatory potentials, then traces of a transformation in the constellation of art and life-world are already to be found in reality. On the basis of these traces we can defend the idea of a transformed relationship between art and life-world, in which a democratic life-praxis would productively exhaust the innovative and communicative potentials of art. My reflections on the truth of art are intended to show that the prospect of *this kind* of "sublation" of art in life-praxis is in fact contained in the concept of the beauty of art: here too a thought of Adorno's may be won back from the realm of the unthinkable to that of the thinkable.

(ii) We can only gloss the question of popular art — a question that was of particular interest for Adorno. Adorno's critique of Benjamin is well known. His writings on jazz may be understood as an answer to Benjamin's optimistic assessment of modern popular art in his essay on "The Work of Art in the Age of Mechanical Reproduction." In a letter to Benjamin regarding this essay, Adorno does, it is true, speak of Schönberg and of the American film as the "torn halves of an integral freedom,"[36] but he makes it clear in the very same letter that he can, in popular art, discern no freedom, but *only* reification and ideology. By the formula of the torn halves of freedom, Adorno basically means once again the polarity within art between the sensual-mimetic and the intellectual-constructive. The formula might be related to a passage from *Dissonanzen*, where Adorno emphasizes the liberating role played by the "sensual-expressive-superficial" in the development of the Viennese classical period and thus of all great music after Bach: "Thus these deplored moments became part of great Western music: sensual stimulation as gateway to the harmonious dimension and finally to the coloristic one; the unrestrained individual as bearer of the expressive and humanizing dimensions of music;

---

33. Cf. P. Boulez, *Wille und Zufall. Gespräche mit Célestin Deliège und Hans Mayer* (Stuttgart/Zürich, 1976), p. 131.

34. Cited in D. Schnebel, "Wie ich das schaffe/," in H.K. Metzger and R. Riehn, eds., *Musik-Konzepte. Sonderband John Cage*, p. 51.

35. Cf. J. Habermas, "Modernity vs. Postmodernity," *New German Critique*, 22 (Winter 1981), pp. 3-14.

36. T.W. Adorno, letter to W. Benjamin of March 18, 1936, in *Aesthetics and Politics* (London, 1977), p. 123.

"superficiality" as critique of the dumb objectivity of forms. . ."[37]

Mozart's *Magic Flute* is, for Adorno, a moment of perfect coincidence of the serious and the light in music; at the same time, however, the last of these. "After the *Magic Flute* serious and light music could no longer be forced into a common framework."[38] "Light" contemporary music remains for Adorno ideology and cultural refuse — a product of the culture industry like the film. Adorno's judgment of jazz is damning.

It seems to me that when Adorno makes these kinds of judgments, he not only expresses a legitimate critique of the culture industry, but also at the same time a conservative prejudice that prevents him from perceiving the productive elements in Benjamin's interpretation of popular art. To be sure, Adorno had strong theoretical arguments in the background: for example, the basic theses of the *Dialectic of Enlightenment*, though they leave room for a certain ambivalence as regards "great" art, leave none as regards popular art. This apparently fits in completely with the universal system of delusion. But in this instance Benjamin's approach seems to be more productive in that it is an exploratory one, is equipped with fewer theoretical safety mechanisms, and does not shy away from contradictions. Whereas Adorno measures the products of modern popular art according to standards by which it can only appear as primitive, silly, or cynical, Benjamin believes that something *aerthetically* new grows out of the interplay of the modern technological process and new modes of reception; that new forms of aesthetic processing of reality come into being, the aim of which is the achievement of a state of "equilibrium between individuals and the technological apparatus."[39] The American grotesque films, to give an example of Benjamin's position, effect a "therapeutic exploding of the unconscious" which finds its expression in "collective" laughter.[40] Mechanized art becomes a vaccine against collective psychoses, in which otherwise the enormous tensions which mechanized reality produces in the masses would have to vent themselves.[41] Benjamin sees in mechanized popular art elements of an antidote to the psychological destruction of individuals through industrial society; whereas Adorno understands it principally as a medium of conformity and psychological manipulation. Only the antithesis as such is interesting: I think that Benjamin's analysis points to *potentials* of modern popular art at least — from film to rock music — which Adorno, due to conservatism as well as to theoretical prejudice, was not able to see. Rock music as "industrial folk music" would be a test case;[42] I think that in rock music, and in the attitudes, modes of perception and

37.   Adorno, "On the Fetish Character of Music and the Regression of Listening," in *The Essential Frankfurt School Reader,* A. Arato and E. Gebhardt, eds. (New York, 1978), p. 272.

38.   *Ibid.*

39.   Cf. Benjamin, "Das Kunstwerk im Zeitalter seiner technischen Reproduzierbarkeit," *Gesammelte Schriften*, vol. I.2 (Frankfurt am Main, 1974), p. 460. This passage is missing from the second draft of Benjamin's "Work of Art" essay, i.e., the only version available in English translation. Cf. *Illuminations*, pp. 217-252.

40.   *Ibid.,* p. 462.

41.   *Ibid.*

42.   Cf. T. Kneif, *Einführung in die Rockmusik* (Wilhelmshaven, 1979).

abilities which have developed in connection with it, there are as many potentials for a democratization and liberation of the aesthetic imagination as there are for a cultural regression. It would be worth defending such *ambivalences*, as in the case of jazz, against Adorno.

An analysis of modern mass culture which pursued Benjamin's approach would at least have to examine the explosive mixture of aesthetic and political imagination which has, since the sixties, defined a new quality in the subversive behavior of protest movements. One argument of Benjamin's might be extrapolated here: Benjamin believed that the dadaist impulse had found its artistic medium in film: in the same way one might be able to argue that actionist art and the "happening" have only found the context in which they can develop their aesthetic explosive power in the new political forms of action which have come out of the alternative and resistance movements. This politicization of aesthetics would have to be sharply distinguished (Benjamin saw this clearly) from the aestheticization of politics through fascism: the latter implies the destruction of politics through the expropriation of the masses, which are degraded to the status of supernumeraries in a cynically directed theatrical show; the former, on the other hand, implies, by virtue of its potential, the appropriation of politics by the now self-aware masses. Seen as ideal types, these two views are extreme opposites. The fact that the extremes meet occasionally in concrete phenomena is part of the physiognomy of a social structure that contains within it equally the possibilities of political regression and of new potentials for freedom.

VII

We have now, following various paths, come nearer to a new interpretation of the interrelationship of the categories truth, semblance, and reconciliation in Adorno. The truth of art appeared as a phenomenon of interplay of the various dimensions of the everyday concept of truth. The latter is, to be sure, linked to a utopian perspective: that of non-violent communication. The *specific* utopian aspect, however, which art contributes, is also present already in each of its authentic productions: the surmounting of speechlessness — the sensual crystallization of meanings as they are dispersed in everyday experience. Non-violent communication does not, however, imply the *sublation* of art: the beauty of art does not stand for reason in its entirety; rather reason requires art for its illumination: without aesthetic experience and its subversive potentials, our moral discourse would necessarily become blind and our interpretations of the world empty.

At the end of the *Aesthetic Theory*, Adorno at least hinted at a similar way of looking at things; in the concluding passage he emphasizes the communicative potentials of emancipated art over against its "progressive negativity." He says, "Perhaps a pacified society will reappropriate the art of the past which at present is the ideological complement of an unpacified one; however, if newly evolved art were then to return to a condition of peace and order, to affirmative representation, this would be the sacrifice of its freedom" (AT, p. 386; translation, p. 369). What is worthy of note is not that here too Adorno

defends modern art against traditional art, but that he accords an emancipated art a place in an emancipated society. In sentences such as these, the
solidarity of Adorno the Marxist, the theorist of modern art, and the theorist
with his own time, breaks through the conceptual constraints of an overly
narrow construction of history. The intention guiding me in my considerations here was to set free the truth content of Adorno's aesthetics from
this construction of history and to develop it through critique and interpretation — as Adorno postulated for the work of art. The allusion to Adorno's
understanding of art interpretation is not merely meant as an analogy: Adorno's texts on aesthetics have something of the work of art about them, and to
this extent can neither be exhausted nor surpassed by interpretation and critique. However, interpretation and critique might well take on, with respect to
these texts, the function of a magnifying glass. If one reads the texts with the
help of a magnifying glass, it is possible that layers of meaning which to the
naked eye blend into each other will now separate and gain an independence
from each other. The image of a stereoscope would be better still: it would
here be a question of producing a three-dimensional picture that would
reveal the latent depth of the texts. Through this kind of "stereoscopic" reading of Adorno one will discover that his incomparable capacity for penetrat-
ing experience philosophically has permitted him — even in the limited
representational medium of a philosophical subject-object dialectic — to give
expression to much that in fact resists representation in this medium. My considerations here were intended, not least of all, to encourage just such a
stereoscopic reading of Adorno.

THE DECLINE
OF THE MODERN AGE*

by Peter Bürger[1]

> "There is no protection against
> the misuse of dialectical con-
> siderations for restorative ends."
> Adorno

For some time sociologists and philosophers have tended to label present-day society "post-industrial" or "post-modern."[2] Understandable as the wish is to set off the present from the age of advanced capitalism, the terms selected are no less problematic. A new epoch is introduced before the question is even asked, let alone answered, as to how decisive current social changes are, and whether they require that a new epochal boundary be set. The term "post-modern," moreover, has the additional disadvantage of only naming the new period abstractly. There is an even more drastic disadvantage. Of course, deep economic, technical and social changes can be observed when compared with the second half of the nineteenth century, but the dominant mode of production has remained the same: private appropriation of collectively produced surplus value. Social democratic governments in Western Europe have learned only too clearly that, despite the increasing significance of governmental intervention in economic matters, the maximization of profit remains the driving force of social reproduction. We should therefore be cautious about intepreting the current changes and not evaluate them prematurely as signs of an epoch-making transformation.

Even in art, talk of the "post-modern" shares the defects of the sociological concept of the "post-modern." From a few quite accurate observations, it prematurely postulates an epochal threshold which, however, can be indicated only abstractly, since a concrete definition obviously fails. Despite this general objection to the concept of the "post-modern," it is difficult to deny that in the last 20 years have taken place in the aesthetic sensitivity of those strata which were and are the carriers of high culture: a positive stance toward the architecture of the *fin de siècle* and hence an essentially more critical

---

*Translated by David J. Parent. Originally published in J. Habermas and L. von Friedeburg, eds., *Adorno-Konverenz* (Frankfurt, 1983).

1. Since the historical avantgarde-movements have undermined confidence in art as a sphere of pure aesthetic experience, the question of how to deal with art has been a disputed one. I have attempted to deal with it systematically in my book *Zur Kritik der idealistischen Ästhetik* (Frankfurt, 1983).

2. A Touraine, *La Société post-industrielle* (Paris, 1969); German translation by Evan Moldenhauer: *Die postindustrielle Gesellschaft* (Frankfurt, 1972). Also J.-F. Lyotard, *The Postmodern Condition* (Minneapolis, 1984).

judgment of modern architecture;[3] the softening of the rigid dichotomy between higher and lower art, which Adorno still considered to be irreconcilably opposed;[4] a re-evlauation of the figurative painting of the 1920s (e.g., in the great Berlin exposition of 1977); a return to the traditional novel even by representatives of the experimental novel. These examples (they could be multiplied) indicate changes that must be dealt with. Is it a question of cultural phenomena that accompany political neo-conservatism and therefore should be criticized from a consistent modern standpoint? Or can so unambiguous a political classification not be ascertained, and do the aforementioned changes compel us to draw a more complex picture of artistic modernity than even Adorno did?

If, starting from the post-modern problematic, one returns to Adorno's writings on aesthetics, and especially music, one discovers, not without surprise, that he was very much preoccupied with the problem of the decline of the modern age at least since World War II.[5] Adorno first encountered this problem in the early 1920s in his first composition teacher who, as an opponent of atonal music, sought to lead his pupils back to tonality by portraying the former as old-fashioned. Adorno tells of this in his *Minima Moralia*: "The ultra-modern, so his argument went, is already no longer modern, the stimuli which I was seeking had already become dull, the expressive figures which excited me belonged to an old-fashioned sentimentality, and the new youth had more red blood corpuscles, to use his favorite phrase" (MM, 291). The idea, which strikes us as a little absurd, that modern art was already at an end by the early 1920s, could at that time have claimed a certain plausibility. As early as 1917 Picasso had abruptly broken off his cubist phase with his portrait of his wife ("Olga in the Reclining Chair") that smacked of Ingres. In subsequent years, he alternately painted cubist and "realistic" pictures. In 1919, Stravinsky, who just two years earlier had written the avantgarde *Histoire du soldat*, returned to 18th century music with the ballet *Pulcinella*. And in 1922 Paul Valéry, with his collection of poems *Charmes*, sought to re-establish the ideal of a strict, formal classicism. Not only second-rate artists rejecting their own age oriented themselves by the classical model, but with Picasso and Stravinsky (Valéry's case is somewhat different) it came to include precisely those who had contributed decisively to the development of modern art. That makes the problem of neo-classicism a touchstone for every interpretation of artistic modernity.

3.   Cf. e.g. P. Gorsen "Zur Dialektik des Funktionalismus heute" in J.Habermas eds., *Stichworte zur 'Geistige Situation der Zeit'* (Frankfurt, 1979), p. 688 ff.

4.   Cf. e.g. the critique of Adorno in J. Schulte-Sasse and F. Jameson, *Zur Dichotomisierung von hoher und niederer Literatur* (Frankfurt, 1982) p. 62 ff. and 114 ff.

5.   For Adorno's following works I use the abbreviations: *AT* — *Aesthetic Theory,* Christian Lenhardt, trans. (London, 1984).

Diss — *Dissonanzen. Musik in der verwalteten Welt* (Göttingen, 1969).

MM — *Minima Moralia. Reflexionen aus dem beschädigten Leben* (Frankfurt, 1969). The citations have been drawn from the appendix of the German edition, which was not included in the English translation.

MS — *Musikalische Schriften I-III*, ed. R. Tiedemann, *Ges. Schriften* Vol. 16 (Frankfurt, 1978).

PMM — *Philosophy of Modern Music* (New York, 1973).

Adorno did not avoid the problem but — as he so often did — he advanced two contradictory interpretations of it. The first, which could be called polemical, can be found in the above-quoted text of *Minima Moralia*: "Neoclassicism, that type of reaction which does not admit being so but presents even the reactionary element itself as advanced, was the vanguard of a vast trend, which under fascism and in mass culture quickly learned to do without delicate consideration for the all-too-sensitive artists and to combine the spirit of Courths-Mahler with technical progress. The modern age has actually become unmodern" (MM, 291 f.). Sharply opposed to the modern spirit, neoclassicism is at the same time denounced as politically reactionary. Undoubtedly, this interpretation can be documented: Chirico's turn to fascism corresponds to his rejection of so-called mythical painting.[6] But such individual cases are hardly sufficient to support so far-reaching an interpretation as Adorno's, which excludes neo-classicism as a whole from the modern.

Adorno himself could hardly have missed the problematic character of so summary a viewpoint. At any rate, in his late essay on Stravinsky, where he corrects his portrayal of the Schönberg-antipode in the *Philosophy of Modern Music*, he proposed a completely different interpretation of neo-classicism: Stravinsky's music is not the reconstruction of a binding musical language but an artist's sovereign play with pre-given forms of the past. Winckelmann's classicism was not being set up as a norm, but it "appeared as in dreams, plaster statues on clothes-cabinets of his parents' apartment, scattered odds and ends and old paraphernalia, not a genre-concept. The scheme was shattered by this individuation of the formerly schematic into a scarecrow; it was damaged and disempowered by a patched-up arrangement of dreams" (MS, 391 f.). By explicitly locating Stravinsky's as well as Picasso's neo-classicism in the vicinity of surrealism, Adorno now assigns the latter a place *within* modern art. That the two interpretations are incompatible is obvious, and so is the superiority of the latter interpretation. Whereas the polemical interpretation proceeds in a globalizing fashion, understanding neo-classicism as a unitary movement, the second interpretation seeks differentiation. It leaves open at least the possibility of seeing more in neo-classical works than a sheer relapse into a reactionary thinking of order.

As for Adorno's evaluation of neo-classicism, however, one must not be deceived by the allusion to a common ground with surrealism. He compares even the montage-procedure of *Histoire du soldat* with the "surrealists' dream-montages made of everyday remnants" (PMM, 183), without thereby at all mitigating the negative judgment of this work. With an argument which he will take up in his dispute with Hindemith, he interprets the element of protest in the *Histoire* as regressive, as the expression of the ambivalent stance of a man who remains attached to the authority against which he rebels (PMM, 183 f.). "Close behind the wild behavior lurks identification with that against which

---

6. That Chirico in his metaphysical phase must be understood as a modern painter has been convincingly shown by W. Rubin: "De Chirico et la modernité," in *Giorgio de Chirico* [exposition catalogue] (Paris: Centre Georges Pompidou, 1983) p. 9-37; German Edition (Munich, 1982).

one is rebelling; excess itself, as it were, proclaims the necessity of moderation and order so that such a thing may at last cease."[7] Adorno sees a connection between Stravinsky's turning to so-called neo-classicism and the previous questioning of traditional musical language by reference to trivial forms and their consistent shattering in the *Histoire du soldat*; but he devalues both as "music about music" (PMM, 182). By taking up and disintegrating pre-given forms such as march music and ragtime, Stravinsky seizes "(literally) existing musical materials" and changes them (Stravinsky's neo-classical music uses the very same approach). Such a procedure runs counter to the principle postulated by Adorno of a complete pervasiveness of *form*. Just as the surrealistic collage first takes up the wood-cut, with its depiction of the *fin-de-siècle* bourgeois interior as a retrospective fragment of reality, so Stravinsky's *Histoire du soldat* takes up the tango or the waltz. And as Max Ernst alienates the interior by giving his humans beast-of-prey heads, so Stravinsky alienates the forms of entertainment music. This quite avantgardistic treatment of the pre-given, which does not settle just for the parody of these forms (as Adorno suggests in one passage; PMM, 186), but through it aims at a questioning of art, resists Adorno's concept of art. Holding firmly to the idea that artistic material reflects the state of total social development without the consciousness of the producer being able to see this connection, he can recognize only *one* material in a given epoch. Indeed he goes so far as to challenge the use of the concept of material for Stravinsky: "The concept, central for Schönberg's school, of a musical material innate in the work itself is, strictly speaking, hardly applicable to Stravinsky. His music is constantly looking at other music, which it consumes by overexposing its rigid and mechanistic traits" (PMM, 184). The concept of 'material' applied here, which eliminates the element of givenness from the material, absorbing it completely within the work and attaching it to the principle of the all-pervasiveness of form, is revealing because it stands at odds with the avantgardist principle of montage. Here we encounter what I have called Adorno's anti-avantgardism.[8] It is only apparently paradoxical that this anti-avantgardism lies at the basis of his rejection not only of the (in his own term) infantile Stravinsky, but also of the neo-classical one.

Here it is not a question of saving neo-classicism as a whole; this would be just a repetition of the mistake of the polemical interpretation from *Minima Moralia* under a different valency. Whether the recourse to past formal schemata merely reproduces them or they are made into a convincing means of expression for a current expressive need cannot be decided by theory, but only by meticulous, detailed analysis of individual works.[9] Adorno's magnificent one-sidedness consists in having demanded this decision of theory. Of

7. Th. W. Adorno, *Impromptus* (Frankfurt, 1970) p. 77.

8. Cf. P. Bürger *Zur Kritik der idealistischen Ästhetik, op. cit.,* pp. 128-135.

9. But the possibility will also have to be taken into account that the content of such a recourse cannot be understood from the individual work but only from a series of pictures. This is the case, for example, for the works of the Berlin painter Werner Hilsing, whose virtuoso readoption of the material stocks of the past, alienated by minature format, (precisely from the circle of "classical modernism") accompanies the perpetuation of art after its termination with a merrily ironical commentary.

course, increasing historical distance is also highlighting more and more its negative consequences which restrict the field of possible artistic activity. This is true especially of the thesis of the single-strandedness of the artistic material. But it also applies to the principle of the totally constructed character of the work, which assigns an eccentric place to the concept of montage within the system of Adorno's aesthetics; for this concept can be assimilated by Adorno only by absorbing Benjaminian motifs into his own thinking.

The abandonment of Adorno's thesis (ultimately based on the history of philosophy) of the most 'advanced artistic material,' does not merely allow the juxtaposition of different stocks of material to come into view (e.g., the painting of the "new objectivity" along with Picasso's or that of the surrealists), whereby theory no longer presumes to explain *one* material as the indicator of the historical moment. It also facilitates the insight that the later development of an artistic material can run into internal limits. This can be observed in cubism. The consistency with which Braque and Picasso draw certain conclusions from Cézanne's late work and carry them further has often been admired. Yet, it is not hard to observe in Picasso's paintings from 1914 a certain arbitrariness, whose most striking feature is the recourse to pointillistically shaped surfaces. This pointillism will then return in a few of the traditional figurative pictures of 1917 — a technical idea whose necessity is lacking in both cases. The idea that the possibility of a consistent continuation of the cubist material could have been exhausted is not far-fetched. It could probably also be supported by including the further development of the painting of Braque and Gris. If this is admitted, then the recourse to a different material which Picasso undertakes in "Olga in the Reclining Chair" is given a consequentiality which Adorno's aesthetics does not allow us to recognize. Neither the recourse to a neo-classical material is thereby aesthetically justified (for this, the quotation-character of the recourse would have to be cogently proven, which I consider impossible), nor is it adequately interpreted historically (for this, various possibilities of interpretation would have to be weighed against one another). But the necessity to break out of one type of material would be made evident as precisely the attitude which the modern artist feels compelled to adopt.

The free disposition over various stocks of materials seems at first sight to broaden creative possibilities immeasurably. This is indeed true in a certain sense, but at the same time it no less drastically restricts the chances of success. Here lies the moment of truth in the normative restrictions which Adorno and Lukács adopt (though in opposite directions). Valéry saw this correctly: the restriction of the field of productive possibilities can increase the chances of artistic success, because it compels concentration. But — and Valéry overlooked this — the restriction must not be an arbitrarily postulated one, but must be experienced by the producer as necessary. Because Valéry's poetic activity submits to coercions that are set only externally, it comes close to craftsmanship on more than a few occasions. Only where the free availability of various stocks of materials is not simply accepted as a given wealth, but is reflected in the work itself, can the producer hope to escape the illusion of unlimited possibilities.

Adorno's first composition teacher had falsely posed the problem of the waning of the modern age, namely, in terms of the obsolescence of the modern as a result of neo-classical anti-modernism. At least in the text of *Minima Moralia*, Adorno lets the statement of the problem be prescribed to him by the opponent when he condemns neo-classicism en bloc as reactionary. But not even in the *Philosophy of Modern Music* does he proceed much differently; only here he includes Stravinsky in his avant-garde phase in his negative judgment. Radical avantgardism and neo-classicism remain equally outside Adorno's concept of the modern. Only with the essay published in 1954 on the "Decline of the New Music" does he pose the problem which we have already cited with reference to cubism: the immanent boundaries in the development of the new music. "Decline" here does not mean the gradual process of adaptation on the part of at least certain strata of listeners to this music and the resulting dulling of the shock effect; it is rather a question of the central categories of the thing itself. What bothers Adorno could be called modernist conformism. It is first characterized by the works' loss of tension,[10] their lack of expression. The phenomenon is not limited to music. Who has not seen those abstract paintings, which are ideally suited to decorate managerial offices? All that can be said about such works is: they disturb nothing. As such, they betray the modern; as abstract, however, they also claim to belong to it.

Adorno does not blame the works' manifest loss of vigor on the subjective failure of the producers, but to an objective developmental tendency of modern art. This could be summed up in the statement that the modern primacy of artistic material turns into "material fetishism" (*Diss.*, 8). This goes right to the central category of Adorno's aesthetic: the artistic material, which is at the center of his historico-philosophical interpretation of the development of art. As sedimented content, it corresponds subterraneanly to the totality of the epoch. Hence, its transformation coincides with that of society; both belong to the principle of progressive rationalization: "The core-concept which set recent musical history in motion is that of rationality, immediately united with that of the social domination of extra- and intra-human nature" (*Diss.*, 123). This formulation is very radical, but precisely because of this, it casts a harsh light on a constant of Adorno's aesthetic: the refusal "(to isolate) from the process of enlightenment, art as a protected natural part of the unchangingly human and well-protected immediacy" (*Diss.*, 150).[11] This means an uncompromising advocacy of rationality in the artistic production process. Adorno must now recognize precisely these "tendencies toward total rationalization," combined with the "widespread allergy to all expression" (*Diss.*, 148) as the cause of all waning of the modern. Even "the emancipation from the pregiven formal categories and structures" (*Diss.*, 145), which he identifies as the

---

10.   Cf. T.W. Adorno, *Introduction to the Sociology of Music* (New York: 1976).

11.   I cannot in this context go into inaccuracies in Adorno's concept of aesthetic rationality.

ineluctable accomplishment of the artistic revolution at the beginning of our century, owes its expressive content not least to the traditional material from which it distances itself. Modernism, by not admitting that it is obligated to tradition by its very negation of it, succumbs to the "superstition of significant original elements, which in fact stem from history and whose very meaning is historical" (*Diss.*, 146).

Adorno's judgment is hard: not only does the technicized stance of the producers, their "infatuation with the material" (*ibid.*), associate them involuntarily with the art industry, but even their rationality becomes a superstition of the direct symbolism of colors and tones. Yet, the expectation that Adorno would draw the consequences from this radical critique of modernism, more precisely from his concept of modernity, is frustrated. He even sees himself compelled to rehabilitate the categories of expression and the subject. But this by no means goes so far that he would revise his own earlier statements. In the *Philosophy of Modern Music*, he says of Webern: "He saw the derivative, exhausted, irrelevant nature of all subjectivity, which music here and now would like to fulfill: the insufficiency of the subject itself"; and a little later: "the subject's right to expression itself succumbed" (PMM). No less categorical, however, are the statements in "The Decline of the New Music": "All aesthetic objectivity is mediated by the power of the subject, which brings a thing completely to itself" (*Diss.,* 157). Hence, "the symptoms of the waning of the new music" can be interpreted as symptoms "of the disintegration of individuality" (*ibid.*). The contradiction is surely not just one of theory; rather, theory captures something of the aporetic position of the modern artist. The artist is pledged to a subjectivity under conditions which are ever more unfavorable to the development of individuality.

The insights into the waning of the new music have, as far as I can see, evoked no thorough revision in Adorno's aesthetics. The closest to this would be the category of *mimesis* which in his *Aesthetic Theory* assumes an important position as a counterpoint to aesthetic rationality. It remains, however, unclear how mimesis becomes effective in the production process. This in turn depends on the fact that a theory of mimesis in the strict sense is impossible, since Adorno defines this as "archaic behavior," "a stance toward reality this side of the rigid opposition of subject and object" (AT, 162). Indeed, some formulations of *Aesthetic Theory* go so far as to subordinate aesthetic rationality to mimesis, so that the concept of rationality hardly has anything to do with Max Weber's employment of it, but means merely the artist's intervention: "With blindfolded eyes, aesthetic rationality must plunge itself into the process of formation, instead of steering it from the outside, as a reflection on the work of art" (AT, 168). But even this strong relativization of the concept of aesthetic rationality (Adorno speaks in one place only of a "quasi rational tendency of art"; AT, 98) does not call into question the construction of the development of art in bourgeois society based on the Weberian concept of rationality. Neither the theorem of the most advanced artistic material nor what could be called Adorno's purism (his refusal to consider the possibility of a recourse to trivial material) are revised.[12] The presence of a modernist conformism is, for Adorno, no reason to permit recourse to past stocks of material: "However, that radically abstract pictures can be displayed in exposition halls without annoyance does not justify any restoration of objectivism, which comforts a priori, even though for the sake of reconciliation one selects Che Guevara as object" (AT, 315 f.). One can ask whether the (unnecessary) jab at the student movement does not merely conceal a weakness of the argument. Today, at any rate, it should no longer be clear why neo-realism should be rejected simply because it uses an objective material, or Peter Weiss' *Aesthetic of Resistance* because it uses narrative techniques of the realistic novel.

If one seeks the reasons that prevent Adorno from drawing conclusions for his aesthetic theory from his insights into the decline of the modern, it makes sense to consider his belonging to the Schönberg school. In fact, in his 1960 essay *Music and New Music*, he tried to solve the problem with virtuosity: Here the waning of the new music is reinterpreted in the sense of the ascendancy of a new epochal style (MS, 484). "Its concept wanes because next to it the production of others becomes impossible, becomes *Kitsch*" (*ibid.*, 492). The restriction of the music of the present to "the variety which has a place in the Schönberg school" (MS, 177) must nonetheless not be explained just from the fact that Adorno's aesthetics is production-oriented. Such an interpretation would take too lightly Adorno's claim to have formulated *the* aesthetic theory of the modern. There is more behind this undeniable aesthetic decisionism than the dogmatism of a school. With it Adorno seeks to banish the danger of historicism, "the chaotic juxtaposition of music-festival authors, who in the same era embody historically different positions and whose syncretic coexistence merely continues the stylistic jumble of the nineteenth century" (*ibid.*).

Now it is easy to see that aesthetic decisionism and historical juxtaposition are just two sides of the same historical situation as long as there is failure to legitimate the decision for a specific material tradition. Adorno does this by associating artistic development in bourgeois society with the modernization process (in his terminology: with enlightenment). Art should by no means become the refuge of the irrational within a rationalized world. Only when art corresponds technically to the state of development of the forces of production can it be simultaneously an instrument of knowledge and a potential for contradiction. "But if art really would want to revoke the mastery of nature; if it applies to a state in which men no longer exercised mastery through the mind, then it reaches this point solely by virtue of the mastery of nature" (MS, 537). One is tempted to reproach Adorno with a mysticism of the dialectical reversal. In fact, he does not draw from the dialectic of enlightenment the con-

---

12.   However, especially in his studies on Mahler and Zemlinsky he tried to remove some of its dogmatic rigidity from the theory of the most advanced material. "At times the flight of the most progressive in art is the relic of the past which it drags along with it," he says of the "anachronistic element" in Mahler (*MS* 339). And in the Zemlinsky essay he finds that from later perspectives aspects "in what was once left behind" can be found that [prove to be] "more lasting than in the advanced [art] of the past" (*MS* 367). — He also rcognized in Mahler the quotation of the banal (*MS* 328).

sequence that it is a matter of slowing up the process of modernization. Rather, he holds firmly to the idea of the dialectical reversal: "in a rationally organized society, together with scarcity, the necessity of repression through organization [would disappear]" (*ibid.*). Such hopes (seldom expressed by Adorno) of an ultimately achieved rationalization might be difficult to share today.

Fear of regression remains the central motif for Adorno's aesthetic decisionism. It determines both his rejection of the avantgardist Stravinsky as well as of neo-classicism. This fear, understandable because of the experience of fascism which knew how to channel and legitimize the regressive wishes of the masses, however, strips modernism of one of its essential modes of expression. Diderot had realized this when he wrote: "Poetry wants something monstrous, barbaric and savage."[13] The longing for regression is an eminently modern phenomenon, a reaction to the advancing rationalization process. It should not be tabooed, but worked out. Bloch's warning not to leave irrationalism to right-wingers has today reacquired an urgency which can hardly be overestimated.

Adorno's thoughts on the waning of modernism are formulated from the perspective of production; they should therefore be complemented by a remark on changes in the area of reception. Among younger persons today one can often notice a way of dealing with literary works that can only be characterized as low-brow from Adorno's standpoint. I mean the widespread renunciation of any discussion of aesthetic form in favor of a discussion of the norms and patterns of behavior which are the basis of the actions of the characters portrayed. The questions which are asked of the work then do not read: How are the aesthetic form and content of the work communicated? But: Did this or that character act correctly in this situation? How would I have behaved in a comparable situation? Such an attitude of reception can be dismissed as inadequate to works of art and can be judged as a sign of a cultural decline. But one can also ask whether the reading of a realistic novel that is interested mainly in procedures of narrative technique does not miss precisely its specific achievement. One can even go further and ask whether the novel does not become primarily an autonomous work of art detached from the living practice of individuals by the fact that a particular discourse marks it as such. What first seemed to be only a lack of culture could prove to be the starting point of a new way of dealing with works of art that overcomes the one-sided fixation on form and at the same time places the work back in relation to the experiences of the recipients.

Do these observations justify the characterization of the art of the present as one of post-modernism, and what implications does this have? To answer these questions, I would like to distinguish three different readings.

1. *The anti-modern reading:* It could use Adorno's theorem that there is in every epoch just *one* advanced stock of material, and turn it against Adorno. The signs of a waning of the new music which he noted, turned, it could be

---

13.   D. Diderot *Oeuvres Esthétiques,* ed. P. Verniere (Paris, 1959) p. 261.

argued, away from twelve-tone music and returned to tonality. Since comparable processes of decline can be seen in abstract painting and modern literature, a return to objectivity or to realistic forms of narration is suggested here too. Of course, metaphysical validity could no longer be attributed to the traditionally normative genres, but they had their place as artistic means. As Valéry repeatedly showed, artificially posed difficulties (for instance, the fulfillment of a complicated verse scheme) acted as stimulants to artistic achievement. In brief, one could formulate a theory of post-modernism as a pleading for the new academicism and in so doing appeal once again to Adorno who has regretted the loss of the "pedagogical virtues of academicism" (*Diss.,* 155).

That Adorno was as far from thinking of a return to academicism as he was from any call for moderation (he calls "the ideal of moderate modernism" disgusting; *Diss.,* 156) is not adequate to refute the above argument. Its strength consists precisely in that it — rightly, it would seem — raises the claim of drawing from Adorno's reflections the conclusions which he evaded. Also the argument drawn from Adorno's critique of Lukács that realistic forms are *as such* affirmative, has become unconvincing, since non-objective paintings have become the decor of managerial suites and are used as montages for magazine covers. If one does not want to settle for a political critique of aesthetic restoration, then one will have to try to show its weakness by way of immanent critique. It lies in an *aporia* that is otherwise typical of neoconservatism. For it can attain its own standpoint (here: the return to tonality, to objectivity and to traditional literary forms) only by the abstract negation of modernism. But this approach contradicts its own conservative self-understanding, which values not new beginnings, but preservation and development. Since the anti-modern version of the post-modern theorem can preserve nothing of modernism, it comes to contradict its conservative self-understanding. That unmasks it as a badly secured polemical position which has nothing to contribute to the comprehension of the possibility of art today.

2. *The pluralistic reading:* It could be formulated approximately as follows: Theorists of the modernism have held the objectively illegitimate thesis that only modern art has attained the heights of the epoch. They thereby devalued implicitly or explicitly all rival artistic movements. The decline of modernism shows the onesidedness of a concept of tradition which recognizes in music only the Schönberg school, and in narrative literature only a few authors such a Proust, Kafka, Joyce and Beckett. The music and literature of the 20th century were, however, much richer. The consequence of this position for the present reads: there is no advanced material, all historical stocks of material are equally available to the artist. What counts is the individual work.

This position has a series of arguments in its favor. There can be no doubt that a construction of tradition such as Adorno's is onesided. We should, however, not forget that it owes to this onesidedness its capacity of making connections recognizable. That today, however, no particular material can still be regarded as the historically most progressive is indicated not only by the motley array of different things, so confusing for the outsider, which every local fine arts exhibit documents. It is demonstrated mainly by the intensity with which some of the most conscious artists explore the use of the most varied stocks of materials. A few of Pit Morell's etchings contain reminiscences of Renaissance drawings along with the expressive directness of the paintings of children and the insane. And Werner Hilsing paints at the same time surrealist, expressionist and cubist miniatures, thus reflecting the possibility of a multiplicity of material. If one wanted to try to draw any conclusion from this, it would be that aesthetic valuation today must detach itself from any link with a particular material. Less than ever does the material guarantee in advance the success of the work. The fascination which correctly emanates from periods of consistent development of material (say, in early cubism) must not mislead one into making it the supratemporal criterion of aesthetic valuation.

The insight into the free availability of different stocks of material which exists today must neither blind us to the resulting artistic difficulties nor to the problematic of the position which is here called pluralist. Whereas Adorno would single out almost all of current artistic production as worthless, the "pluralist" runs the danger of recognizing everything equally and falling prey to an eclecticism which likes everything indiscriminately. Art thus threatens to become an insipid complement to everyday life, i.e., what it always was to the popularizations of idealist aesthetics.

Instead of drawing from the questioning of the theorem of the most advanced material the false conclusion that today everything is possible, one would have to insist on the difficulties which confront works today. If reliance on the correspondence between the artistic material and the epoch has vanished, a reliance which is the historico-philosophical basis of Adorno's aesthetics, then for the productive artist too the abundance of possibilities can appear as arbitrariness. He cannot counter it by surrendering to it, but only by reflecting upon it. That can be done in many different ways: by radical restriction to *one* material, but also by the attempt to use the multiplicity of possibilities. The decison is always legitimated only afterwards, in the product.

3. *Toward a contemporary aesthetic:* I would explicitly not like to place this third reading under the auspices of post-modernism, because the concept suggests an end to the modern era, which there is no reason whatever to assume. One could instead claim that all relevant art today defines itself in relation to modernism. If this is so, then a theory of contemporary aesthetics has the task of conceptualizing a dialectical continuation of modernism. It will strive to affirm essential categories of modernism, but at the same time to free them from their modernist rigidity and bring them back to life.

The category of artistic modernism par excellence is form. Sub-categories such as artistic means, procedures and techniques converge in that category. In modernism, form is not something pre-given which the artist must fulfill and whose fulfillment the critics and the educated public could check more or less closely against a canon of fixed rules. It is always an individual result, which the work represents. And form is not something external to the content; it stands in relation to it (this is the basis of interpretation). This modern conception of artistic form, which originates in the modern age with the victory of aesthetic nominalism, ought to be irreplaceable for us. Though we can imagine a work of art in which individual elements are interchangeable (from a picture of Pollock's one can cut off a part without essentially changing it, and in a paratactically constructed narrative individual parts arranged in succession can be interchanged or even left out); but we cannot imagine a work in which the form as such would be arbitrary. Irreplaceability means that in the act of reception we apply a concept of form that grasps the form of the work as particular, necessary within certain limits, and semantically interpretable.

But irreplaceability must not be confused with unchangeability. The aesthetics of idealism grasps the work of art as a form/content unity. "True works of art are such, precisely by the fact that their content and form prove to be completely identical," says Hegel in his *Encyclopedia* (§ 133; Supplement). But in this positing of a unity of subject (form) and object (content) history did not come to a stop. Rather, the development of art in bourgeois society burst asunder the idealistically fused elements of the classical type of work. The concept of the work held by idealistic aesthetics was itself already an answer to the modern phenomenon of the alienation of individuals from themselves and the world. In the organic work of art, the really unresolved contradictions are supposed to appear as reconciled. Hence, the demand of a form-content unity that alone can generate the appearance of reconciliation. Now, to the extent that bourgeois society develops into a system that is subject to crises, but none the less closed, the individual increasingly feels impotent *vis-à-vis* the social whole. The artist reacts to this by attempting to prove, at least in his own field, the primacy of the subject over against the given. This means the primacy of the subjectively set form, the primacy of material development. The result is achieved first in aestheticist poetry: the striving for purity of form, which has characterized the idealist conception of art since its earliest formulations, threatens to annihilate that which makes producing a work worthwhile, i.e., the content. The novel, which can absorb the fullness of reality, for a long time proves to be resistant to the coercion to formalization. Only with Robbe-Grillet's *nouveau roman* is the aestheticist project of a "book about nothing" realized also in this genre. Here too the emancipation from the matter as something given and withdrawn from the control of the subject leads to emptiness.

The earliest answer — unmatched to this day despite all contradictions — to the developmental tendencies of art in bourgeois society is given by the historical avantgarde-movements. The demand for a return of art to life, the abolition of the autonomy of art, marks the counterpole to that tendency which extrapolated the status of autonomy right into the work. The aestheticizing primacy of form is now replaced by the primacy of expression. The artist-subject revolts against form, which now confronts him as something alien. What should master the facticity of the given, proves to be a coercion which the subject inflicts on himself. He rebels against it.

And where do we stand, we who are both the heirs of aestheticist formalism and of the avantgarde protest agsinst it? The answer to the question is made more difficult by the fact that we have had to confirm both the decline of the modern (in Adorno's sense) and the failure of the avantgarde attack on the institution of art.[14] Neither anti-modernism nor historical eclecticism can be considered adequate designs for the aesthetic theory of the present. But merely clinging to the theory of aesthetic modernity, as Adorno has formulated it, also fails to see relevant phenomena of contemporary artistic production, e.g., the *Aesthetic of Resistance,* in which Peter Weiss uses the narrative techniques of the realistic novel throughout. Instead of propagating a break with modernism under the banner of the post-modern, I count on its dialectical continuity. That means that aesthetic modernism must also recognize as its own much that it has until now rejected. That is, no more tabooing of tonality, objectivity, and traditional literary forms; but at the same time distrust of this material and of the appearance of substantiality which emanates from it. The recourse to past stocks of material must be recognized as a modern procedure, but also as an extremely precarious one (Picasso's *Olga in the Reclining Chair* is not a successful picture). The modern is richer, more variegated, more contradictory than Adorno depicts it in the parts of his work where he sets up boundaries out of fear of regression, as in the Stravinsky-chapter of *Philosophy of New Music.* The artist can rely on what seems to him to be immediacy of expression which yet is always mediated. Since the expressive strength of the painting of children and of the insane is recognized, there can no longer be any taboo against regression. But it would be mistaken to believe that it is enough to imitate the clumsy drawings of first-graders to produce good paintings. The dialectics of form and expression must be executed as something irreducibly particular, whereby the latter no longer means individual situation but social experience refracted through the subject.

Already Hegel prognosticated the free disposition over forms and objects for art after the "end of art." This prospect becomes cogent at the moment when there is no longer any generally binding system of symbols. To the question of a criterion for putting a stop to the bad wealth of historical eclecticism, first a distinction would have to be made between an arbitrary toying with past forms and their necessary actualization. Secondly, after the attack of the historical avantgarde movements on the autonomy of art, the reflection on this status ought to be an important trait of important art. To the extent that this reflection is translated into artistic conduct, it encounters the historico-philosophical place of art in the present. If this is plausible, then Brecht's work should have a place within the literature of our century which Adorno does not concede to it.

On the side of reception, the dialectical continuation of modernity means the striving to combine the above-mentioned reception stance oriented to living

14. Cf. On this and prior topics, my book *Theory of the Avantgarde* (Minneapolis, 1984).

practice with sensitivity for the specific achievement of forms, which modern art has taught us since impressionism and aestheticism. With the risk of being misunderstood, what is meant can be characterized as the re-semanticization of art. This term is misleading because it does not appeal to the formal a priori of art. What Adorno criticizes as "material fetishism" in a modernism consistent in its rational tendencies has as its complement on the side of reception — the readiness to celebrate even the monochromatically painted canvass as an extraordinary artistic event. Against this, the semantic dimension of the work of art must be emphasized.

In closing, let me return to the concept of "post-modernism." Perhaps, the problematic of the concept can be most readily delineated if one says that it is both too broad and too narrow. Too broad, because it relegates to the past the modern concept of form, which is irreplaceable for us. Too narrow, because it restricts the question of contemporary art to the question of a material decision. But that is not permissible because the changes which are currently taking shape are also precisely changes in the way of dealing with art. If the claim formulated by avantgarde movements to abolish the separation of art and life, although it failed, continues as before to define the situation of today's art, then this is paradoxical in the strictest sense of the word: If the avantgardist demand for abolition turns out to be realizable, that is the end of art. If it is erased, i.e., if the separation of art and life are accepted as matter-of-course, that is also the end of art.

PRAXIS

INTERNATIONAL

Editors: Ferenc Feher and Mihailo Marković

Volume 4 no. 4   January 1985

Social Theory and Modernity
Albrecht Wellmer, *On the Dialectic of Modernism and Postmodernism*
Lolle Nauta, *Historical Roots of the Concept of Autonomy in Western Philosophy*
Militarism, Federalism, and Contemporary Societies
Jorge A. Tapia-Valdés, *Security Crisis and Institutionalized Militarism*
Philip Resnick, *Federalism and Socialism: A Reconsideration*
Marxism and the Workers
Wolf Schäfer, *Unlicensed Brainwork: A Case Study in Suppressive Discourse from Above*
Lyman H. Legters, *Who Speaks for the Workers?*
Critical Review
Richard Schmitt, *Marxism and Psychoanalysis*

Published quarterly: April, July, October and January
Subscriptions to Volume 4 (1984/85)
Individuals: £13.95 (UK); £16.75 (Overseas); $33.50 (US); $40.50 (Canada)
Institutions: £38.00 (UK); £46.50 (Overseas); $85.00; $104.50 (Canada)

Please send orders, with payment to: Iris Taylor, Journals Department,
Basil Blackwell, 108 Cowley Road, Oxford OX4 1JF, England.

Basil Blackwell · Oxford · England

HIERARCHY AND THE HUMANITIES:
THE RADICAL IMPLICATIONS OF
A CONSERVATIVE IDEA

by Martin Jay

It is customary to begin essays of this kind with an arresting quotation from an eminent source, a practice that both displays the author's ostensible erudition and covertly betrays his need to draw on an external authority to support the argument he is about to make. In order to remain true to this time-honored convention, I have chosen as my opening text for today the following passage from Theodor Adorno's *Negative Dialectics,* written in 1966: "All culture after Auschwitz, including its urgent critique, is garbage. In restoring itself after the things that happened without resistance in its own countryside, culture has turned entirely into the ideology it had been potentially — had been ever since it presumed, in opposition to material existence, to inspire that existence with the light denied it by the separation of the mind from manual labor. Whoever pleads for the maintenance of this radically culpable and shabby culture becomes its accomplice, while the man who says no to culture is directly furthering the barbarism which our culture showed itself to be."[1] In short, to put it even more bluntly, the Holocaust has finally and irrevocably exposed the lie that supporters of culture and the humanities have promulgated for centuries in order to justify their existence: the claim that the pursuit of what we usually call "high culture" is somehow a humanizing endeavor, nurturing what R.S. Crane once called "the virtues and knowledge that separate men most sharply from the lower animals."[2] The harsh truth, according to Adorno, is revealed instead in what he called a "magnificent line" of Brecht's: "the mansion of culture is built of dogshit."[3]

If we unpack the implications of Adorno's bitter outburst, three specific points seem to me paramount. The first is his typically Marxist admonition to avoid separating culture from society, or what he calls mental from manual labor. No materialist theory can countenance the alleged superiority of the former over the latter. The ascetic, anti-hedonist moment in what his friend Max Horkheimer called "affirmative culture"[4] was in fact partly responsible

---

1. Adorno, *Negative Dialectics*, trans. E.B. Ashton (New York, 1973), p. 367. Translation slightly altered.
2. Crane, *The Idea of the Humanities,* vol. I (Chicago, 1967), p. 7.
3. Quoted in Adorno, p. 366. Similar sentiments were voiced by their mutual friend Walter Benjamin, who claimed in a frequently cited remark that "there is no document of civilization which is not at the same time a document of barbarism." *Illuminations; Essays and Reflections*, ed. with introduction, Hannah Arendt, trans. Harry Zohn (New York, 1968), p. 258.
4. Horkheimer, "Egoismus und Freiheitsbewegung," *Zeitschrift für* Sozialforschung, V, 2 (1936), p. 219; see also Herbert Marcuse, "The affirmative Character of Culture," in *Negations; Essays in Critical Theory*, trans. Jeremy J. Shapiro (Boston, 1968).

for the life-denying practices of modern totalitarianism. Insofar as culture is still honored at the expense of gratifying man's material needs, it must be exposed as repressive.

The second point is more directly historical. For Adorno, whose philosophy of history had long since abandoned any Marxist or even liberal belief in progress, Auschwitz was the final confirmation of Western culture's failure to lead to genuine emancipation. Like George Steiner, who gave wide currency to the same idea in his *Language and Silence* of 1967, Adorno expressed not only the guilt of the survivor, but also the anguish of the mandarin whose faith in the saving powers of high culture had been irremediably shattered. The threat that had been latent in the claims of earlier defenders of humanism like Irving Babbitt, who boasted that what they were defending was not equivalent to "sentimental naturalism" or "humanitarianism,"[5] was thus now realized. For us Steiner put it in a well-known lament, "we know now that a man can read Goethe or Rilke in the evening, that he can play Bach and Schubert, and go to his day's work at Auschwitz in the morning."[6] Indeed, and this is perhaps an even more frightening thought, the tears spent weeping for fictional victims may diminish our capacity to react to the misfortune of real ones.

The third and most indirect implication of Adorno's argument concerns a more general issue, and the one on which I want to dwell today: the apparently sinister effect of cultural hierarchy. For it seems at first glance that Adorno is challenging the very claim culture and the humanities make to nurture an appreciation of truth, goodness and beauty, an appreciation that separates humans at their best from what Crane and many others call "the lower animals." There is, Adorno seems to be suggesting, a covert complicity between the alleged superiority of mental over manual labor and society's collective domination over the natural world, that disastrous "dialectic of the enlightenement," he and Max Horkheimer traced in their most influential book.[7] To hold on to such an elevated view of culture, Adorno implies, is to be an accomplice of the barbarism it failed to prevent. The great chain of being thus turns out to be a shackles for those allegedly lower on the scale of virtue or worth. Only a total levelling of such a hierarchical vision of reality, Adorno seems to be saying, will prevent such a complicity from continuing.

And yet, as anyone familiar with Adorno's work will readily attest, he doggedly refused to eschew judgments of value in his criticism of both social and cultural phenomena. Certainly no friend of popular or mass culture, the "culture industry" as he scornfully called it, Adorno had little tolerance for those who retreated into a pseudo-democratic relativism in their eagerness to escape the guilt of high culture. Thus, as he insisted in the final line of the remarks I quoted a few moments ago, "the man who says no to culture is

5. For a discussion of these distinctions in Babbitt, Paul Elmer More and other "New Humanists," see J. David Hoeveler, Jr., *The New Humanism; A Critique of Modern America, 1900-1940* (Charlottesville, 1977), p. 128f.

6. Steiner, *Language and Silence; Essays on Language, Literature, and the Inhuman* (New York, 1967), p. ix.

7. Horkheimer and Adorno, *Dialectic of Enlightenment*, trans. John Cumming (New York, 1972).

directly furthering the barbarism which our culture showed itself to be."

If Adorno seems to be contradicting himself, both attacking culture as garbage and rejecting the implications of that very attack, the explanation is that he was attempting to confront without flinching one of the thorniest aporias of the modern condition: the impossibility of finding a stance, on intellectual as political issues, that is free of some sort of self-contradiction. In particular, he wanted to remain true to the inherently ambiguous nature of high culture, at once a false consolation for real suffering and an embattled refuge of the utopian hopes for overcoming that very misery. He wanted, moreover, to avoid finding a conciliatory middle ground between these two incompatible truths, following instead his dictum in *Minima Moralia* that "the dialectic advances by way of extremes, driving thoughts with the utmost consequentiality to the point where they turn back on themselves, instead of qualifying them.[8]

Adorno's tormented attempt to hold on to both extremes without trying to forge a consistent position out of them offers an important lesson today when the delicate balance or, as he would call it, the negative dialectic of culture is threatened in new ways. If before Auschwitz, to use his shorthand expression, there was a general tendency to accept the elevating self-image of the humanities uncritically and thus ignore their covert complicity with barbarism, in the most recent period the opposite inclination seems to have gained the upper hand. From many sides, we are now constantly reminded that high culture does not save, indeed that it might do the opposite. Cultural elitism, we are insistently told, is the handmaiden of social elitism and thus has no place in a pluralist democracy, let alone in any more radically egalitarian polity. What hitherto had been the rallying cry of disgruntled populists and their unexpected allies among the more dadaist elements of the avant-garde has now become a widespread complaint.

The task today therefore is to make a case for the ambivalent virtues of hierarchy in order to redress the balance. In so doing, I will try to establish what can be seen as the covertly radical or at least critical dimensions of an idea that is normally considered conservative. Misunderstood, the argument I will make may appear to be a perverse plea to resist progressive change through a defense of tradition, a call to retreat from the "infinite universe" of modernity to the "closed world" of premodern hierarchical order.[9] To avoid this inference, let me stress my intention to "refunction," in Brecht's sense, rather than merely defend the value of cultural hierarchy. I am not, in other words, really trying to say that the mansion of culture is built of precious jewels and rare metals, and that as a result we would be unwise to try to disrupt its sturdy foundations.

In order to make my case, what must first be done is to establish the validity

8. Adorno, *Minima Moralia; Reflections from Damaged Life*, trans. E.F.N. Jephcott (London, 1974), p. 86.

9. The transition from the pre-modern to modern world view in these terms is classically expressed in Alexandre Koyré, *From the Closed World to the Infinite Universe* (Baltimore, 1957). The challenge to the hierarchical ordering of the universe presented by the new emphasis on infinity in the work of Nicholas of Cusa and others is spelled out in C.A. Patrides, "Hierarchy and Order," *Dictionary of the History of Ideas*, vol. II (New York, 1973).

of my observation that there is a greater tendency today to denigrate than defend cultural hierarchy. To do so with any thoroughness would try your patience, however, as there has been a plethora of attacks launched by victims of the current version of that hierarchy. I am referring, of course, to the crescendo of criticism directed against "white, male, heterosexual" culture by those who fall outside those categories. It would be callous to deny the legitimacy of many of their complaints and condescending to advise them to be patient in trying to remedy them. What perhaps may be less out of order is a plea to examine more closely the ambiguities of the anti-hierarchical solution many of them propound. To defuse the inevitable suspicion that I may be doing so in order to protect my vested interest in the maintenance of Eurocentric, patriarchal culture, let me direct my remarks against two recent critics of hierarchy who cannot be construed as being among its most obvious victims. By focusing on their work, I hope to demonstrate two points: first, that the critique of hierarchy is now so widespread that it has permeated the ranks of those at the top and second, that the quarrel over its implications should not be construed as a mere class (or perhaps better put, status) struggle between the victims and victimizers of the current version of cultural inequality.

The two targets I have chosen are very different, one a distinguished senior historian rarely given to polemical bloodletting and the other a younger literary critic, who clearly often is. The former is William J. Bouwsma, recent president of the American Historical Association, currently Sather Professor and Chairman of the Department of History at the University of California, Berkeley, and a world-renowned scholar of the Renaissance and Reformation. He is also the author of a provocative essay in the *Journal of Interdisciplinary History* published in 1981 entitled "Intellectual History in the 1980s: From History of Ideas to History of Meaning." My second exemplar is Michael Ryan, who teaches English at Northeastern University and is the author of a book entitled *Marxism and Deconstruction*, published in 1982.[10] Taking these two scholars together is particularly instructive because they come from very different intellectual traditions, yet arrive at a similar destination in their attitude towards hierarchy. Bouwsma, from what might be called the perspective of a Christian anthropologist, and Ryan, who presents himself as a Marxist-feminist advocate of deconstruction, both vigorously denounce the evils of cultural elitism.

The stimulus to Bouwsma's reflections is what he sees as the current crisis of intellectual history, whose decline he calls "obvious and probably irreversible."[11] Rather than mourn this state of affairs, however, he celebrates it

---

10.   Bouwsma, "Intellectual History in the 1980's; From History of Ideas to History of Meaning," *Journal of Interdisciplinary History*, XII, 2 (Autumn, 1981); Michael Ryan, *Marxism and Deconstruction; A Critical Articulation* (Baltimore, 1982).

11.   Bouwsma, p. 279. This obituary may, however, be premature. In his summary remarks in a recent volume dedicated to *Modern European Intellectual History*, eds. Dominick LaCapra and Steven L. Kaplan (Ithaca, 1982), Hayden White notes his surprise at "the general air of buoyancy and self-confidence in [the earlier essays] — a pervasive sense that a renaissance of a field that had been, to say the least, recessive with respect to that social historiography which has predominated in our discipline in the last two decades, was in the offing" (p. 280).

because he feels that the traditional basis of intellectual history was an idealist anthropology. "According to this view," he writes, "the human personality consists of a hierarchy of discrete faculties, among which the intellect — more or less closely identified with reason — is highest. In the earlier stages of this tradition, the intellect was believed to constitute the divine element in man and so to distinguish him from the other animals . . . The association of the intellect with the brain gave the head ethical significance and converted it into a potent metaphor; the highest became best."[12] Drawing on the lessons in humility taught recent mankind by Darwin, Marx and Freud, he concludes that it is no longer possible to define man as an essentially intellectual animal. This is not, however, to say that man is undifferentiated from other animals; his uniqueness, according to Bouwsma, lies in his capacity to invest the world in which he lives with meaning. But, he writes, "these efforts are not the work of the 'intellect' or of any particular area of the personality. They are rather a function of the human organism as a whole."[13] Contemporary cultural anthropologists are thus particularly useful for historians who want to construct what Clifford Geertz calls "thick descriptions"[14] of the webs of meanings in which we are suspended. They provide us with a model of the human condition, which "rejects the conception of man as a hierarchy of discrete faculties . . . [and] the assignment of privileged status *a priori* to one or another area of human activity. Since it conceives of the human personality as a mysterious whole, it is opposed to all reductionism."[15] In short, the traditional distinction between intellectual and other forms of history should be discarded, as must that between a privileged sphere of high culture and culture in the broader anthropological sense.

In this essay, Bouwsma's vantage point seems to be that of contemporary anthropology, but, as I mentioned a moment ago, there is a deeper, more religiously motivated premise underlying his argument. In an earlier essay to which Bouwsma kindly drew my attention, he probed the concept of "Christian Adulthood" for a *Daedalus* volume on the theme of maturity.[16] In this piece, he defends the Christian ideal of adulthood against what he calls the alternative model of "manhood," which is derived largely from classical antiquity. In that latter view, whose gender connotation was by no means an accident, are embedded "both the metaphysical distinction between form and substance, with its hints of anthropological dualism, and a characteristic distinction, within man, among the several elements of the human personality: soul and body, or reason, will, and passion."[17] Manhood was associated

12. Bouwsma, pp. 280-281.

13. *Ibid.,* p. 283. The argument that intellectual history should be the history of meaning is now widespread. See, for example, the articles by Roger Chartier and Keith Michael Baker in LaCapra and Kaplan.

14. Geertz, *The Interpretation of Cultures* (New York, 1973), p. 6. The term is actually Gilbert Ryle's but it is Geertz who has popularized it. For a critique of his impact on historiography, see Ronald G. Walters, "Signs of the Times: Clifford Geertz and Historians," *Social Research,* XLVII, 3 (Autumn, 1980).

15. Bouwsma, p. 289.

16. Bouwsma, "Christian Adulthood," *Daedalus,* CV, 2 (1976).

17. *Ibid.,* p. 78.

closely with the domination of reason, which was absent in the child. Human rationality was a sign of man's participation in the divine, as well as a tool to order the chaotic ambiguities of the world.

Through a characteristically learned acount of the Christian response to this legacy from the classical world, Bouwsma shows that alongside one tradition, which adopted the ideal of manhood and pitted man's allegedly higher soul against his baser passions, another tradition developed, which did not. This second Christian ideal was one of "adulthood," a term without the gender connotations of its classical predecessor. Rather than privileging sober maturity over playful childhood, this ideal recognizes the valuable residues of our pre-rational selves in our adult lives. Growth does not mean leaving our capacity for play behind, but rather remaining open to the possibility of divine foolishness. Nor does the Christian adult in this view place the soul above the body, whose ultimate resurrection is a sign of its value. "Adulthood," Bouwsma writes, "does not recognize real qualitative and hierarchical distinctions *within* the personality; it sees man, whether child or adult, as living whole.[18]

What is especially striking about Bouwsma's reconstruction of this holistic vision of Christian adulthood, at least for our purposes, is the use to which he implicitly puts it in his more recent essay on intellectual history and the history of meaning. In the original *Daedalus* article he admits that it is a normative view, which has found only occasional realization in history as an antidote to the classical ideal of manhood whose hierarchical discriminations were also embodied in social forms. In the second essay, however, he bases his argument for the absolescence of intellectual history on the implicit assumption that something like Christian adulthood in fact describes the way men really are: "we can hardly any longer define man as an intellectual animal. However we regard him, he is both less and more than this — and infinitely more interesting, which is the major explanation for the fact that an autonomous intellectual is now likely to seem, like the discrete intellect of the old anthropology, at best an irrelevant abstraction from real life."[19] Or in other words, our disciplinary distinctions need no longer be hierarchical because a holistic meaning-giving man has in fact replaced the hierarchically divided man of the classical ideology, at least in our self-understanding of the human condition. Thus, paradoxically, the blows to human pride in the work of Darwin, Marx, and Freud, with their anti-idealist debunking of rationality, has led to a less elitist vision of our status, which approaches the Christian model of adulthood.

Why this new vision should be extrapolated back into history is not, however, completely clear for two reasons. First, if the classical view held sway as long as Bouwsma concedes it did, historians cannot hope to understand the past unless we acknowledge its powerful formative effect on the cultural differentiations that were the lived experience of our ancestors. Second, and more important, the social hierarchy that in some sense was the underpinning

18. *Ibid.,* p. 81.
19. Bouwsma, "Intellectual History in the 1980's," pp. 282-283.

of those distinctions must be taken into account in any attempt to reconstruct how meaning was made in history. As Antonio Gramsci once put it, "All men are intellectuals . . . but not all men have in society the function of intellectuals."[20] The same might be said of men as meaning-givers, which Geertz's "cultural idealism,"[21] as Marvin Harris has called it, often fails to register. To cite another critic of this position, Ronald Walters: "Ideally, thick description says something about society. In practice, it often describes reality as a drama in which the focus is upon symbolic exchanges, not social consequences. Words like 'class,' 'exploitation,' and — most important — 'power,' recede, drop out of the analysis or take new, less strident meanings."[22] It is, in fact, ironic to hear Bouwsma argue that "an autonomous intellectual is now likely to seem . . . at best an irrelevant abstraction from real life" just at the time when contemporary sociologists like Alvin Gouldner, George Konrád and Ivan Szelényi are presenting the intellectuals as a "new class" or on "the road to class power."[23] The point is not to return to an idealist defense of pure intellect above the fray or to construct watertight divisions between high and low culture, but rather to acknowledge that social differentiation has effected in the past and still continues to effect the means through which webs of meaning are created and sustained. As sociolinguists like Basil Bernstein and others have demonstrated,[24] the linguistic codes of different social groups are decisive in the ways in which they interpret and reproduce their cultural reality. That some, whom we call intellectuals, depend on what Gouldner terms a "culture of critical discourse," which is relatively more reflexive and context-independent than the discourse of non-intellectuals, means that we must still be aware of the ways in which the model of Christian adulthood is thwarted in the modern world. In fact, I would argue that pretending it is not is itself a contributing factor to the maintenance of the very hierarchical distinctions that it hopes to overcome.

Before commenting on the reasons I think this pretense functions in this way, let me turn to Michael Ryan's no less impassioned critique of hierarchy. Ryan would not doubt have little but scorn for Bouwsma's model of Christian adulthood as a holistically integrated personality. To the St. Augustine who cried "I want to be healed completely, for I am a complete whole,"[25] he would probably reply that the only thing from which you really suffer is the old logocentric myth of perfect presence. Relief can come only from a willingness

20. Antonio Gramsci, *Selections from the Prison Notebooks,* ed. and trans. Quintin Hoare and Geoffrey Nowell Smith (New York, 1978), p. 9.

21. Marvin Harris, *Cultural Materialism; The Struggle for a Science of Culture* (New York, 1979), p. 281f.

22. Ronald G. Walters, p. 553.

23. Alvin W. Gouldner, *The Future of Intellectuals and the Rise of the New Class* (New York, 1979); George Konrád and Ivan Szelényi, *The Intellectuals on the Road to Class Power; A Sociological Study of the Intelligentsia in Socialism,* trans. Andrew Arato and Richard E. Allen (New York, 1979).

24. Basil Bernstein, *Class Codes and Control,* vol. I, *Theoretical Studies Towards a Sociology of Language* (London, 1971), vol. II, *Applied Studies Towards a Sociology of Language* (London, 1973), vol. III, *Towards a Theory of Educational Transmission* (London, 1975). See also, William Labov, *Sociolinguistic Patterns* (Philadelphia, 1972).

25. Quoted in Bouwsma, "Christian Adulthood," p. 86.

to engage in the infinite, explosive, transgressive play that makes a mockery of any pretension to centered subjectivity, a play that is far more Dionysian than that envisaged in the Christian model by Bouwsma. And yet, tacitly in tandem with Bouwsma, Ryan is unremittingly hostile to the elitist privileging of reason or the soul over the other aspects of the human personality. Radical deconstruction and Christian anthropology thus both converge in their distaste for the evils of cultural hierarchy.

In *Marxism and Deconstruction,* Ryan's general intention is to present what he calls a "critical articulation" of these two traditions in order to fashion a libertarian intellectual and political position that will avoid the authoritarianism of earlier leftist efforts. In his eagerness to win the energies of deconstructionist intoxication for the revolution, as Watler Benjamin might have put it,[26] he tends to gloss over many of the very substantial differences that pit Derrida against Marx. It is difficult, for example, to know how to reconcile his typically Marxist Humanist call for a politics that treats people as "responsible and creative agents"[27] with the deconstructionist demolition of any self that could conceivably be the center of such agency. Nor is it very clear how Derrida's philosophy can really support the Marxist demand, which Ryan seems to champion, for a "full development of all human faculties,"[28] a slogan that recalls the very ideology of classical *Bildung* that deconstructionists have had so much fun debunking. Inconsistencies of this type abound in his argument,[29] which may trouble those of us still hung up on the virtues of logical coherence.

But rather than multiply examples of Ryan's questionable reasoning, I will return to the more basic animus that motivates his attempt to force the marriage of Derrida and Marx, an animus directed against hierarchy of any kind. What he finds most attractive in deconstruction is its resistance to a politics of exclusion, which he claims has a "necessary relationship"[30] with the hierarchical conceptual thinking Derrida has sought to undermine. Most important among such conceptual hierarchies are the distinctions between transcendence and immanence, consciousness and the body, mental and manual labor, theory and practice, reason and the irrational, efficiency and chaos, science and ideology, works of art and ordinary texts, and speech and writing. All of these privilege the first term over the second, which leads to the

---

26. Benjamin spoke of the Surrealist project as winning the energies of intoxication for the revolution. See his essay on "Surrealism," *Reflections; Essays, Aphorisms, Autobiographical Writings,* ed. with introduction, Peter Demetz, trans. Edmund Jephcott (New York, 1978), p. 189.

27. Ryan, p. 203.

28. *Ibid.,* p. 136.

29. To take just one other example, he argues against Althusser that "for Marx, at least, communism meant human control over human life" (p. 99), but elsewhere admits that "it is easy to see how [Derrida's] emphasis on the passivity of the subject could underwrite a conservative traditionalism" (p. 37). He tries to explain away what he admits is Derrida's exaggerated-writing off of the subjective factor by saying it was an understandable reaction against the "excessively subjectivist humanism of the various phenomenologies and existentialisms" (p. 36) which preceded deconstruction on the French intellectual scene. The result is to trivialize the very fundamental challenge to humanism presented in Derrida's philosophy.

30. *Ibid.,* p. 8.

domination, marginalization or exclusion of the latter. Deconstruction, as Ryan defends it, goes so far as to call into question all conceptual thinking as an essentialist suppression of difference and the non-identical; "in fact," he writes, "all knowledge operates through acts of exclusion and marginalization."[31]

Following Derrida's arguments in his essay, "The White Mythology,"[32] he further contends that the major victims of such hierarchically tainted knowledge have been women and third world peoples who are excluded from the patriarchal version of rationality promoted by European men. So-called feminine hysteria, therefore, is a therapeutic corrective to male rationality, "a sign of moral and philosophical goodness"[33] which, to be sure, ought not to be enthroned in a new hierarchical position of domination. Any intellectual or cultural hierarchy, Ryan argues, is immediately complicitous with political repression. Thus, for example, "there is an analogy in Lenin between his practice of reading and theorizing — locating the center, the paradigm, the master theme, the essence through exclusion, manipulation and suppression — and his theory of socialist practice — order, discipline, central authority, exclusiveness."[34] The truly libertarian alternative, Ryan argues, is a politics of permanent revolution, which is analogous to the infinite, transgressive play supported by deconstruction.

Regardless of whether or not this vision should be denounced as an updated version of what Lenin damned as "infantile leftism," it is unlikely to appeal to many observers today, especially after the recent discrediting of the romantic image of the Chinese Cultural Revolution held in certain quarters a decade ago. Nor will it seem very attractive to those with longer memories who recall the disturbing links between a totally relativist cultural nihilism and the decisionist politics of will that contributed to fascism. In fact, one of the most influential interpretations of fascism, that of Ernst Nolte,[35] understands it precisely in terms of a reaction against the very same transcendence that Ryan also so despises.

What, however, seems even more fundamentally questionable in Ryan's argument — and here I think there is a parallel with a weakness in Bouwsma's — is the ultimately ahistorical assumption on which it is based. Perhaps because Ryan is so hostile to hierarchy of any kind, he refuses to privilege any historical cause in explaining the source of present inequalities. Instead he supports a holistic relationism in which nothing is prior to anything else. Although helping him to avoid the pitfalls of reductionism, this methodological bias makes it impossible for him to ask the difficult question: are some hierarchies more basic and irremediable than others? It also prevents him

31. *Ibid.,* p. 140.

32. Derrida, "The White Mythology: Metaphor in the Text of Philosophy," in *Margins of Philosophy,* trans. Alan Bass (Chicago, 1981).

33. Ryan, p. 121.

34. *Ibid.,,* p. 172. Ryan is fond of these kinds of linkages. Thus, for example, he talks of "the circuit that leads from John Searle's reactionary philosophic study to David Rockefeller's bank office, to the torture chambers of Santiago de Chile" (p. 46).

35. Nolte, *Three Faces of Fascism,* trans. Leila Vennewitz (New York, 1969).

from acknowledging that merely seeing through the hierarchical distinctions of our cultural and social life as harmful illusions does little to dispell them in reality. Thus, he engages in a kind of magical thinking in which he contends that "mental labor is always manual,"[36] "theoretical knowledge is immediately practice,"[37] and " 'the political' and 'the economic' cannot even be considered as separate categories for the sake of theoretical exposition."[38] In other words, in his haste to deconstruct the hierarchical distinctions he dislikes, he fails to grasp their tenacious rootedness in an objective world created over time and deeply resistant to change. Like Bouwsma's contention that the hierarchical separation between mind and body underlying the distinction between intellectual and other forms of history is no longer operative, Ryan's arguments present a desideratum as if it were already a fact. And in so doing, they occlude our understanding of why in reality it is not. In short, the obstinately real hierarchical differentiations produced by history cannot be undone by positing an egalitarian process of "differencing" that exposes their illusoriness. The Marxist in Ryan is, to be sure, aware of this dilemma, but too often the deconstructionist in him acts as if the only task were "showing how public institutions and public power are cultural conventions sustained by acculturated personal belief."[39]

Even if we share all of the radical egalitarianism of these critics of hierarchy, we cannot hope to realize their aims by short-circuiting the painstaking process through which the obstacles to that realization might be overcome. Interpreting social institutions, structures and practices as mere texts to be decoded and then discarded is akin to the mistaken culturist view of reification that certain Hegelian Marxists like Lukács sometimes held in their more idealistic moods. Although a de-naturalizing consciousness of the subjective origins of the social world may be a necessary moment in the struggle to change society, it is not a sufficient one. Indeed, pardoxically, by assuming that public institutions are merely "cultural conventions" that can be changed by exposing their artificiality, we may blind ourselves to the deeper more varied sources that generated them and the still potent functions that they now serve.

In fact, any attempt to locate those sources is bound to be a daunting endeavor, which perhaps accounts for the self-protective deconstructionist dismissal of any search for origins. A wide variety of divergent hypotheses has, of course, been offered in the hope of accounting for social, cultural, political and sexual inequality. The intellectual historian Arthur Lovejoy traced the great chain of being to Plato's denigration of the sensible world in favor of the intelligible.[40] Durkheim sought an answer in the religious distinction between the sacred and the profane, which itself reflected the opposition be-

---

36.   Ryan, p. 23.

37.   *Ibid.,* p. 62.

38.   *Ibid.,* p. 99. Yet another example of his conflation of two categories is his argument that the personal should be "seen as already being public, as a social text" (p. 220).

39.   *Ibid.,* p. 221.

40.   Arthur O. Lovejoy, *The Great Chain of Being; A Study of the History of an Idea* (New York, 1960), chap. II.

tween collective moral life and individual material existence.[41] Freud conjectured that when men stood erect and lost their ability to react positively to olfactory stimuli, they began to feel shame about their "baser" sexual and excretory functions.[42] Privileging the sense of sight over that of smell thus was congruent with the sexual repression that is the bedrock of cultural hierarchy. Rousseau, with his more primitive understanding of the psyche, blamed it on psychological proclivities towards pride and envy, while Marx pointed his finger at the division of labor and private property. A more recent Marxist, Alfred Sohn-Rethel, argued that the invention of an abstract money economy in classical Greece led to the distinction between pure, abstract thought and its impure concrete opposite.[43] This in turn created the fateful distinction between mental and manual labor, which still persists today. Foucault claims that it is our inevitable fall into language, which gives us the ability to say two things with the identical word and the same thing with different words, that makes hierarchical distinctions possible.[44] Louis Dumont, who self-consciously defends the *Home hierarchicus* he sees in Indian caste society over the *Home aequalis* of the West, traces hierarchy to what he calls the "encompassing of the contrary."[45] There is, he claims, a necessarily hierarchical relationship between a whole or set and an element within it, which is expressed, for example, in the biblical myth of Eve created from Adam's rib. Hierarchy is thus not a chain of superimposed commands or even the ranking of different values, but rather an expression of a holistic unity of opposites that is as much a part of the structure of human thought as the binary oppositions posited by Lévi-Strauss. And there is, of course, a plethora of explanations, biological, demographic, social, for the hierarchical relations between men and women that many feminists now claim is the fundamental inequality of civilization.

All of these explanations are, of course, highly speculative and I cannot pretend to offer any genuine guidance in choosing among them. What they suggest, however, is the extraordinary difficulty of overturning hierarchy, which, to put it mildly, is an overdetermined phenomenon derived from a vast number of possible sources. It may seem that unless we get down on all fours, give up language, private property and the division of labor, undo all social

41. Emile Durkheim, *The Elementary Forms of the Religious Life*, trans. Joseph Ward Swain (New York, 1965).

42. Sigmund Freud, *Civilization and Its Discontents*, trans. James Strachey (New York, 1961), pp. 46-47.

43. Alfred Sohn-Rethel, *Intellectual and Manual Labor; A Critique of Epistemology* (Atlantic Highlands, N.J., 1977).

44. Michel Foucault, "The Discourse on Language," in *The Archaeology of Knowledge,* trans. A.M. Sheridan Smith (New York, 1972). For a discussion of Foucault's tacit emphsais on the trope of catechresis, which recognizes the ambiguous meanings of all signifiers, see Hayden White, "Michel Foucault," in *Structuralism and Since; From Lévi-Strauss to Derrida,* ed. John Sturrock (Oxford, 1979). In his more recent work, it should be noted, Foucault emphasized power relations more than linguisticality.

45. Louis Dumont, *Homo Hierarchicus; The Caste System and its Implications,* trans. Mark Sainsbury, Louis Dumont and Basia Gulati (Chicago, 1980), p. 239. See also his *From Mandeville to Marx; The Genesis and Triumph of Economic Ideology* (Chicago, 1977), which is the first installment of a projected series of books on *Homo aequalis.* Contrary to Ryan, Dumont argues that holism entails hierarchy, while individualism leads to equality.

abstractions like money, stop thinking in terms of parts and wholes, and over-come our biological differences, it is highly probable that hierarchy in one form or another will be around for some time to come. In fact, even its enemies tacitly fall back on hierarchical evaluating thinking. Thus, for exam-ple, Ryan claims that deconstruction shows that difference is "in fact more primordial and more general"[46] than the tradition of logocentric indentity thinking that has tried to exclude it. From this priority, he implies, it then follows that privileging difference over sameness is somehow liberating.[47] This may be true, but it subtly restores the very type of hierarchical thinking that it is designed to overturn.

What may then be more useful — and is certainly less depressing — than speculating about the putative origins of hierarchy or struggling to find the perfectly consistent formula to express one's distaste for it is considering the present function or functions it fulfills. For, if the now celebrated genealogical method bequeathed to us by Nietzsche is right, there may be no necessary connection between origins and current significance or function. In fact, if we take the general post-structuralist attack on the search for origins to heart, then it is really only the present function that matters. Such an attitude may go too far in severing that function entirely from its historical roots, but it is useful to remember if we are to avoid being paralyzed by the impossibility of revers-ing all of the possible sources I listed a few moments ago.

In probing the contemporary function of hierarchy, we are, however, con-fronted by the problem of bracketing or holding in abeyance our visceral egalitarian inclinations, which prevent us from acknowledging the ambigu-ous dialectic of culture suggested in the remarks of Adorno cited earlier. In particular, we have trouble avoiding the type of premature conflation of all types of hierarchy into variations on the theme of domination that Ryan, for all his stress on difference, exemplifies. For such an homogenization prevents us from considering the possibility that some may not work in tandem with others, but rather against them.[48] It is in fact precisely this possibility that brings us back to our initial question, the implications of Adorno's claim that

---

46.   Ryan, p. 10. See also his argument against Althusser that "the determination in the last instance of the economic is itself a determined effect of a metaphysical and patriarchal culture, which institutionalizes both philosophical and sociopolitical points of authority" (pp. 101-102). Whether or not this causal hierarchy is true, it demonstrates Ryan's inability to escape thinking in hierarchical terms.

47.   That it may also lead to nihilism has been argued by Stanley Rosen, *Nihilism; A Philosophical Essay* (New Haven, 1969). Rosen's targets are Nietzsche, Heidegger and, to some extent, Witt-genstein, but his arguments can just as easily be applied to post-structuralism.

48.   An excellent example of Ryan's inability to grasp this possibility is his treatment of reason. "The homology, correspondence, adequation and compatibility between rational knowledge and the rationalized world is not likely to promote anything but an acceptance of that world as 'reasonable' " (pp. 149-150). He bases this argument on the belief that "logocentric reason . . . is by nature asocial. It privileges the individual mind and the individual actor" (p. 154). What Ryan thus ignores is the variety of rationalities that compete in the modern world: substan-tive, formal, instrumental, functionalist, communicative, etc. That some of these may be in ten-sion with the way in which the world has been rationalized eludes him, as his inadequate discussion of Habermas illustrates. For the latter's distinction among forms of rationality, see *Theorie des kommunikativen Handelns*, 2 vols. (Frankfurt, 1981).

all culture after Auschwitz is garbage. Taken at face value, this charge suggests that cultural hierarchy is indeed complicitous with the pervasive social domination that Adorno abhorred. But if we recall Adorno's contrary admonition that "the man who says no to culture is directly furthering the barbarism which our culture showed itself to be," it is clear that in his mind something potentially emancipatory was still preserved in elite culture despite its tainted status as false consolation. It is difficult, after all, to imagine Adorno, or anyone else for that matter, claiming that all garbage after Auschwitz is culture, a reversal whose absurdity is even more blatant if we apply it to Brecht's scatological observation about the mansion of culture.

What Adorno felt should be salvaged from the traditional elitist notion of high culture as superior to everyday life was evident in many places throughout his work, but perhaps nowhere as clearly as in his debate with Benjamin over the implications of Surrealism.[49] Without spelling out all its ramifications, the following points should be made. For Benjamin, Surrealism represented a revolutionary attempt to reintegrate radical art and life. Or to put it in terms of his now celebrated concept of the aura, the Surrealists tried to obliterate the cultic, ritually derived distance between unique works of art and prosaic reality in order to harness the emancipatory power of art to transform society. The de-auraticization of art, a process abetted by the technological innovations of the 20th century, was thus a healthy development, which would help bring about the overturning of both cultural and social hierarchy. Surrealism was the prototype of other similar modernist movements, like the *neue Sachlichkeit,* and of what we now sometimes call post-modernist ones, in its desire to collapse art back into the life-world from which it originally emerged.

Although sharing his friend's sensitivity to the de-auraticization of much recent art, Adorno was far less sanguine than Benjamin about its revolutionary potential. Instead, he championed that current in aesthetic modernism which remained esoteric rather than exoteric in its appeal. Figures like Schoenberg and Beckett, who resisted the demand to make their art immediately effective in political or social terms, were more genuinely revolutionary in the long run than those, like the Surrealists, who did not. There were, of course, costs in such a choice, as Adorno's more activist leftist critics never tired of reminding him. A totally inaccessible artistic elitism might never find the way to reunite its emancipatory potential with the social forces that could help realize it.

But at least in the years since their quarrel was first joined, I think it can be said that Adorno has gotten the better of the argument. For rather than leading to anything demonstrably revolutionary, the integration of de-auraticized art and life has led to the cooptation of artistic negativity by new variants of affirmative culture. The once disturbing techniques of movements like Surrealism have shown themselves to be easily adaptable to the demands of con-

---

49. For a good summary of the debate, see Eugene Lunn, *Marxism and Modernism; An Historical Study of Lukács, Brecht, Benjamin and Adorno* (Berkeley, 1982).

sumer advertising. In other words, the attempt to break down a hierarchical cultural relationship may unintentionally have contributed to the maintenance of a still hierarchical social one. What Herbert Marcuse once called "repressive desublimation"[50] in reference to the pseudo-liberation of sexuality in our seemingly hedonist culture has thus had its analogue in aesthetic terms. The conclusion that Adorno reached was that an art which resists reabsorption into everyday life in the short run may help prepare the way for a more genuinely liberating unification in the future. The same might perhaps be said of other variants of hierarchy that now pervade our cultural life, such as the distinction between intellectual and other forms of history which Bouwsma with his premature plea for an ecumenical history of meaning wants us to reject.

My point in conclusion is not that we should be simply complacent about the elitist aspects of the humanities as they are now conceived. Nor am I pleading for some timeless canon of great works existing in an ahistorical Arnoldian realm of the best and most beautiful. The exact content of what we privilege as higher than other aspects of our cultural experience must constantly be rethought and challenged. So-called high culture has been and will continue to be renewed from below, just as popular or even mass culture derives much of its energies from above. The boundaries shift and dissolve, the categories harden and soften, each era defines itself both through acceptance of and rebellion against the values of the past. No specific received hierarchy is immutable, nor should any be defended as such. Esoteric art is not forever superior to exoteric, whatever its present function may be.

What I would argue, however, is that the process of establishing new hierarchical evaluations itself remains, at least for the foreseeable future, inescapable and indeed worthy of our approbation. For all the efforts of anti-elitists of whatever kind, whether deconstructionist, feminist, populist or even Christian anthropologist, to debunk it, there seems little likelihood of their success. Even the much ballyhooed demise of the avant-garde, which has led some critics to question Adorno's faith in esoteric modernism, has not really lead to the flattening out of all cultural inequalities. If there are genuine reasons to bemoan the specific implications of the types of hierarchy that now exist, and I think there are, there are also reasons to be thankful that we have not entirely lost our capacity to make distinctions of quality and rank. For as the Hungarian critic Sandor Randoti recently put it, "The *revocation* of [the] alienation [of high art from society in general] is not only impossible in dynamic societies, but is not even desirable. It is not desirable because the exclusive character of a demand for recognition as belonging to the world would annihilate the criticism that the art work exercizes over the world."[51] It is as the much-maligned guardians of this alienation that the humanities, not despite but because of their inevitable elitism, can justify whatever emancipatory role they may still play even in the grim aftermath of Auschwitz.

---

50.   Herbert Marcuse, *One-Dimensional Man; Studies in the Ideology of Advanced Industrial Society* (Boston, 1964).

51.   Radnoti, "Mass Culture," *Telos*, 48 (Summer, 1981), p. 46.

LUKÁCS AND THE HOLY FAMILY

by Agnes Heller

In January 1968, Lucien Goldmann organized a conference on aesthetic theory in Royaumont, France.[1] Adorno was one of the keynote speakers; I delivered a lecture on Lukács's *The Specificity of the Aesthetic,* which then was still not well known. Of course, we were immediately entangled in passionate discussions arguing for three different, and apparently irreconcilable, positions. Then something entirely unexpected happened. A young man took the rostrum and spoke with anger and irritation: Lukács, Goldmann and Adorno are all the same. They are members of the Holy Family. By standing for the autonomy of art work, they seek salvation in a celestial image of the world. They are equally old-fashioned, bourgeois and despicable. We need Arrabal instead. A chorus of young people echoed his words. "Arrabal, Arrabal," they chanted. That was when post-modernism was born. In a minute, the whole scene changed. Adorno, Goldmann and myself (representing Lukács) ended up on the same side of the proverbial barricade. Instead of criticizing, we started to support one another. The common elements in our position turned out suddenly to be more important than what divided us. The defense of the autonomous art work implied the defense of a possible unity of subjectivity and objectivity: the defense of aesthetic judgment of a kind which was not simply a matter of personal taste. It implied the assumption that *there must be* certain standards for judging the quality and the relevance of art works, that the distinction between "high" and "low" is valid, and that it is the matter of the highest importance, even a matter of life and death, to stand for one kind of art work and to reject others. The commitment to the autonomous work of art seemed then to be more important than any particular judgment. Today, I still believe that an evaluation of Beckett's plays is definitely not a matter of life and death. But for Adorno, Beckett was almost a savior, the only one who succeeded (at least in literature) in coping with problems of modernity and expressing them in the most supreme artistic form possible. For Lukács, on the contrary, Beckett was close to the devil — the writer of a self-complacent adjustment to an alienated world. For both Lukács and Adorno, however, it was almost a matter of the survival of humanity to pass these and similar judgments.

In a sense, the young man in Royaumont was right. Lukács, Adorno and Goldmann did indeed belong to the Holy Family, and one could also add Bloch to the list. The following, however, will focus mainly on Lukács.

After his turn to Marxism and the collapse of the philosophy of *History and Class Consciousness,* Lukács eventually repackaged his ideas in the shabby gar-

---

1. For a discussion between Goldmann and Adorno during this conference, see "Appendix 3" in Lucien Goldmann, *Cultural Creation* (St. Louis: Telos Press, 1976), pp. 131-147.

ments of an official *Diamat*. He began speaking in a language that concealed rather than revealed the message he meant to convey. Sometimes this language was used as a camouflage, while at other times, it merged with the message itself and distorted it. Here, the method of some post-modernists becomes useful. Lukács — especially the later Lukács — has to be read "against the text." This simply means to disregard the language of *Diamat* and all its distortions. What is to be redeemed is Lukács' attitude towards modernity. Today, Lukács' aesthetic writings are not read in the way they should be. Let us try, then, a different reading.

Lukács' so-called "conservatism" did not result from any compromise with communist authorities and their cultural policy. Rather, it was the outcome of a fundamental choice made in his early youth. Lukács was brought up in the cultural atmosphere of the *fin de siècle,* during the first great upsurge of cultural relativism. His immediate environment, the Budapest Jewish bourgeoisie, made frantic attempts at assimilation and had uprooted itself, purposely losing contact with its own tradition. This milieu was in complicity with cultural relativism. When the young Lukács first read Homer and James Fenimore Cooper's novels, he discovered a world of authenticity — a world he saw as "real" in comparison with his own environment, which he regarded as unreal. This was the fundamental experience that shaped Lukács' attitude to culture the rest of his life. The stage was set for cultural conservatism. But this cultural conservatism was later coupled with a messianism that gave it a radical twist. Along with so many others, Lukács bet on the future, on salvation, on the arrival of a this-worldly Messiah who would destroy the world of "absolute sinfulness," redeem culture from the abyss of a cynical relativism, and restore the old in the form of the new. In a world in which the sharp division between false and true had vanished, there is also no way to tell good from evil. But if this is the case, then the world of relativism is doomed. Redemption thus meant the restoration of the distinction between true and false, good and evil. This is why the sharp distinction between high and low, authentic and inauthentic, good and bad, progressive and regressive art work became a matter of life and death for Lukács. It was precisely the feeling that without an absolute division, an absolute standard, we lose all standards, that motivated Lukács' quest for redemption.

Wolin has referred to certain postmodernist attempts to blur the distinction between high (autonomous) art works and the products of the culture industry, on the one hand, and substituting everyday "cultural practices" for the creation and reception of autonomous art works, on the other hand, as a "sham democracy."[2] But democracy can only be called "sham" if there is an alternative, real democracy, which is both desirable and viable. But can culture, under present conditions, be both authentic and democratic at the same time? Can the creation and reception of the autonomous art work be democratic? If the answers to this question are in the negative, one has to accept the postmodern condition as a fact, as *the* condition of an *empirical* democracy. Let

2.   See Richard Wolin, "Modernism vs Post-modernism" in this issue of *Telos*.

us rephrase the crucial questions: can modern Western culture be at the same time authentic and democratic? Can the creation and the receptio of the modern autonomous art work be really democratic? Undoubtedly, the answers to these questions are generally negative.

Both Lukács and Adorno take up this challenge and sacrifice *one* norm, in order to meet the requirements of the other. Adorno defends authentic modern art work and relinquishes thereby the norm of democracy. Lukács rejects authentic modern art. He makes a case for traditional "realism" and, in so doing, he sides with democracy. Adorno is an elitist, Lukács is not. Adorno defends the best artistic efforts of modern culture precisely insofar as he is an elitist, while Lukács does them grave injustice by siding with works of art within the reach of everyone. For Lukács, a novel has to have a story, as well as characters. The story has to start at the beginning and proceed to the end. A painting has to be figurative and convey a message interpretable by all. Music must have a *collective*, not just an idiosyncratic, melody that can be "sung" by all. Not so for Adorno. Lukács does not sharply differentiate between low and high art in the same way Adorno does. For Lukács, there should be a constant capillary movement between "high" and "low," a constant interplay. He does not dismiss the "culture industry" completely. The culture industry, says Lukács (without using the term) may become a means of refined manipulation, but it can also produce real stories with real characters about real life. Lukács was the advocate of what he termed the "normal" relation between everyday life and art works. The artist has to be inspired by the daily experience of average people, by the shared experience of a historical epoch. The work of art has to penetrate the everyday life of everyone, make people reflect upon their own life-style, illuminate their own problems in providing standards for reflection and understanding — including self-understanding. If this happens, the reception of works of art can contribute to the transformation of our lives for the better. The readiness to rise to the level of a utopian reality has to be present before reception. A readiness of this kind need not be conscious. It can be in the form of a mute dissatisfaction, of a longing or quest for something different, higher, more sublime. Lukács' model is the story of Judith, the peasant woman in Gottfried Keller's novel *The Green Heinrich*. Judith who is uneducated but endowed with a good common sense came to read Ariosto's *Orlando Furioso*. The epic poem led her to understand herself and her love of Heinrich. She underwent what Lukács called "catharsis": an insight into the essence of life that shakes one's personality and sheds new light on every life experience in one's past, present and future.

Both Adorno and Lukács agreed at least on one crucial point: in the modern world, only the work of art can embody a "defetishized" reality. Lukács went even further in rejecting modern social science than Adorno. In his view, modern (bourgeois) science expresses rather than critically illuminates the fetishized world. Modern "bourgeois" philosophy follows suit. Instrumental reason (termed metaphysical reason by Lukács) has gained the upper hand in both science and philosophy and challenges to metaphysical reason culminate in irrationalism. Philosophy proper must become *aesthetics*, for a defetishizing message can only be deciphered from the language of the work of art. What made Lukács a *radical cultural conservative* was his commitment to democracy. He stood by his belief that modern art works express, rather than unmask, a fetishistic reality, in a fashion similar to social science of philosophy. A text that cannot be deciphered by everyone endowed with common sense is foreign to men of common sense. What is alien from human beings is alienated. The more elitist a work of art is, the more alienated it is. When speaking of *realism*, Lukács did not have in mind a literary or artistic style. A realistic art work is defetishizing insofar as it addresses everyone endowed with common sense and ready for catharsis. Further, it encourages the belief that life can be conducted otherwise, can be changed, that human beings are not subjected to an unalterable fate, that they are still free to do something about this fate. But are they?

This is an article of faith with Lukács. He emphatically denied that modern bourgeois life was completely alienated and that modern man's consciousness is completely fetishized. For him, the dialectic never became negative. If life were completely alienated, art and literature could not help but express this alienation. The expression of alienation would then be a kind of defetishization. Yet people are still confronted with real choices, real options, real alternatives. They are still able to reassert their real (albeit relative) freedom by deciding for one option rather than another. The modern world is not closed, but still open. If this is true, works of art presenting the world as closed do not defetishize it, but rather they contribute to its fetishization. Realist art works constitute worlds in which there is freedom. There are individuals who put their freedom to use or fail to do so, who confront their fate *because* they are committed to something and not as a result of an inescapable human condition. It is *their* fate, not fate "as such." Realist artists swim against the current. They are not necessarily superior to other artists as far as artistic brilliance is concerned. Yet, they are superior in the sense that they live up to the historical mission of art: defetishization. This is the reason why for Adorno and Lukás, the division between "high" and "low" cuts across the map of cultural practices in entirely different regions.

At times, Lukács seems astonishingly close to certain postmodern theoretical positions. A man so attracted by the unity of life and culture in popular festivities would be the last to raise objections to "happenings." Similarly, he would be in deep sympathy with the idea of "artistic practices" in everyday life. Lukács would not have shed a tear for the demise of elitism, nor would he have denounced "reading against the text," which he practiced himself. He did not even treat fashion with contempt. He distrusted the "high priests" of culture and detested the cultural market far more than the street corner as the appropriate *locus* of art and literature. And yet, he does belong to the "Holy Family." As I already mentioned, Lukács' attitude towards life, the basis of his philosophy, can be understood as a reaction to the *fin de siècle*, to the first emergence of the postmodern condition. His whole work is the outright reaction to the postmodern condition, despite occasional coincidences between his sympathies and those of certain postmodernists.

Moreover, Lukács was a philosopher of the Enlightenment far more resolutely than Adorno. Or, more precisely, as he aged, Lukács was increasingly committed to the promise of the Enlightenment. Without disregarding the contradictions inhrent in the Enlightenment project, he argued that its work was not yet finished. His critics often reproached him for defending bourgeois art. So he did. Lukács could have paraphrased Rosa Luxemburg's well-known creed: "there are no bourgeois rights, only human rights," in the following way: "there is no bourgeois art and literature, only art and literature." He regarded the emergence of the autonomous artistic sphere as a process of *emancipation*. "Real history" in Lukács does not begin with communism, as with Marx: it begins with the full emancipation of art and literature, with the fusion of decoration and representation in art forms which follow no laws but their own. As far as art and literature were concerned, Lukács was both ultra-Hegelian and anti-Hegelian. With all his respect for the cave drawings of Altamira and the refinement of ancient crafts (a respect paid all human achievements), Lukács never subscribed to cultural relativism concerning art and literature. He believed in *progression* in the creation of art. He saw the birth of the independent sphere of art, the autonomous art work, as the end result of a long progression. For it is exactly here that "real history" begins. Of course, he did not conceive of this progression in a unilinear fashion. Ancient Greek art, the self-expression of our entering real history, always preserved its paradigmatic character. He even subscribed to the Hegelian theory that all great epochs promote one art form as against others, that each has a "dominant form of art." But Lukács never subscribed to the Hegelian prediction about the end of art. This for Lukács would have meant the end of history. Rather, the period of art was not about to end, it had just begun. As early as *The Theory of the Novel*, Lukács made a case for the rejuvenation of the novel in Dostoyevsky. He saw bourgeois society *sensu stricto* as a short period of history that was supposed to usher in a new epoch in which all genres of art and literature could come to full bloom. The setbacks in this progression are only temporary. Art is not defeated and it will fulfill its promise. Lukács stuck to this position till the very end of his days.

Indeed, there was something in Lukács' account which, at first glance, resembles the "deification of art." It was, however, a deification that went along with deep contempt for the "priests of art." The combination sounds strange, but here is the clue for comprehending Lukács' thoroughgoing commitment to the Enlightenment.

"Works of art exist, how are they possible?" This was the question raised by Lukács' first aesthetics — a question that, in Weber's view, completely changed our approach to aesthetics. Every art work, Lukács insisted, is a *world* of its own, a total world he called a "work individuality." Every work individuality expresses the historical consciousness of an epoch, but remains a totality, an individuality. Each and every work of art presents and represents uniqueness.

Historicity and ubiquity, the fusion of both, is what the "world" of an art work is all about. Moreover, every individual work of art *embodies universality*. This is neither an idea nor a principle; it is actually *embodied* in works. Universality does not *regulate* the creation of the art work, but it is co-constitutive of it. The three major Hegelian categories, individuality, particularity, and universality, are homogenized in the work of art. Moreover, it is historicity (particularity) which, as the overarching category, carries the other two. The more historicity carries universality and individuality, the more coherently historicity *fuses* the other two categories, the higher the work of art ranks. The model of the supreme work of art is the model of the supreme human personality. The more a person of a particular historicity can become a unique *individual* and *embody* universality (humanity) in one person, the more sublime, the "higher" he or she becomes. Moreover, one cannot have the one without the other. One cannot become an individual without embodying universality, and the quest for the universal does not make us "sublime," should we fail to become complete and unique individuals. Lukács made no secret about his taking the model of personality from German classicism — especially Goethe. He used to quote frequently that, according to Goethe, every human being can be "complete." This "completeness" does not depend on refinement, formal culture or good taste. Sometimes rather the opposite is the case. Moreover, the individuality of the autonomous work of art and the classical idea of personality are not simply considered "parallel" phenomena. It was Lukács' firm conviction that the "more complete" someone is, the more one will become the true recipient of the work of art; and conversely, the reception of the autonomous work of art helps to transform the person into an autonomous personality. Lukács would have hated the idea of the deconstruction of personality, because it was precisely personality, as the unity of the individual and the human-universal, he stood for throughout his life.

Lukács was deeply aware of the social constraints at work to deconstruct the self. This is why he became a radical cultural conservative. He believed that the modern work of art makes a case for a deconstruction of the self or, at least, that it does not make a case against it. This is why the reception of modern art cannot be cathartic, cannot even be the point of departure for the construction of personality. For him it was obvious that only works of art generally conceived prior to the 20th century can perform this task. Since our world is not completely fetishized or alienated, the construction of personality is still possible. However, this process can only be facilitated by works of art which are themselves autonomous, which embody both universality and individuality, and which can be grasped by everyone who may be or may become "complete," whether educated or non-educated, refined or unrefined.

As already mentioned real history begins for Lukács with the emergence of the autonomous work of art. Only where men attained consciousness of human essence can we speak of history proper. And this is exactly the moment when works of art become autonomous, when they become a "world" of their own. Works of art thus represent and embody the history of humanity.

For Lukács, the concept "humanity" is not empirical but normative, for he uses the term as equivalent to "generic essence" as distinct from "mute species." Our species became vocal in art and literature. This is why the *memory* of humanity is embodied in works of art. Lukács learned his hermeneutics well. All intepretations are misinterpretations, he wrote in his first aesthetics. But our relation to an individual object is our relation to that object. We read human history in different ways as we revive the past in a variety of interpretations. But not everything qualifies as an object of historical interpretation. Autonomous works of art best qualify for such interpretation. We unveil the past by *reading* such works, but we can unveil the past only by reading *them*. Human beings without a past, without memory, cannot be personalities. We reconquer our past in our memory via the reception of art works.

Two contradictions can be detected in this conception: one apparent and one real. First, how can one emphasize the democratic character of Lukács' aesthetics when his standards for the *sublimity* of works of art are so high that only a few art works can meet them? The answer is simple: no one cared less for the artists and the minutiae of art creation than Lukács. That contemporary artists could not perform the task he expected of them was the least of his concerns. Lukács' interest was solely vested in the process of reception. If Homer's, Shakespeare's or Balzac's works were the only ones to meet his standards, what difference would it make? People would read precisely these works, visit the statues of Michelangelo, listen to the music of Bach, Beethoven and Mozart. At the same time, Lukács did not perceive the recipient as a passive container of immortal artistic effects. He envisioned a constant "to and fro" between high art and everyday practices, a continuous interplay between cathartic reception and everyday creative-artistic activity. It was rather the professional artistic creation that claimed to be "high" while losing sight of the standard, on the one hand, and the pursuit of everyday practices without the capacity for the reception of the sublime work of art, on the other hand, that he rejected. Thus, the contradiction between the highest standard and the democratic message in Lukács is only apparent.

This is, however, not the case with the second contradiction.

Lukács, as we have seen, drew a sharp line between true and false: the work of art that defetishizes is true, all other works of art are not only inferior, but false. Everyone who stands for the defetishizing (realistic) art work is right; everyone who defends fetishistic, anti-realistic art works is wrong. There are no nuances, no "more or less," there is only an "either-or." The art work is either true or false, it either stands for emancipation or for decadence, either for the fully developed personality or the decomposition of personality, either for alienation or for de-alienation. It was either swimming with or against the current, it is either friend or foe. Yet does such a sharp demarcation between true and false really help us distinguish good from evil? Does it provide us with a *moral* standard?

Lukács' main concern was not aesthetics, but ethics. He wanted to construct a wall separating true and false in order to be able to tell good from evil. He shared Adorno's view (as well as Benjamin's) that modern philosophy must become a *philosophy of art*, it must have recourse to the only defetishizing objectification. It must do so, Lukács argued, in order to circumvent the moral deadlock of our century, the disappearance of collective morality: *Sittlichkeit*. But do aesthetics or any kind of philosophy of art qualify for such a task? Despite his sharp distinction between true and false, despite raising a strict standard of aesthetic judgment, Lukács did not provide any standard for differentiating good from evil.

The art work should be autonomous; so should human personality. But the insistence on the full development of human personality, on swimming against the current, on defetishizing, does not provide a moral standard. The standards for the work of art can be established by applying the criterion of defetishization; however, art is autonomous precisely in that it has its *own* standards which are *not* moral standards, even if they have a moral implication. Human beings cannot achieve moral autonomy through the quest for autonomy as such. They must know *what* norms, *what* moral criteria they ought to observe, on the basis of what norms and criteria their personality should develop. Lukács does not provide any such criteria. Yet, searching for autonomy without observing any moral norms can make us evil as well as good. Lukács dreamt of an ethics of personality, an ethics based on Marx's messianic hope of total de-alienation. If the human species and the individual were to completely coalesce, no moral norms would be needed to make men good. But the total coalescence of individual and the species is nothing but the messianic hope of total redemption, and not a socially viable perspective, even from a utopian standpoint. An image like this does not provide us with moral guidance in the present, not even as a regulative practical idea. At this point, Lukács comes extremely close to postmodernism, despite his commitment to the contrary. He does not want to accept *any* external authority above and beyond the individual. But if all external authorities have to be rejected equally, if the personality has to obey only his or her own intrinsic laws, then *all* external authorities are alike, be they moral or immoral, despotic or democratic, universalistic or particularistic. And if one comes to the conclusion that the actualization of the idea is not yet viable, if one has to renounce the hope that heaven will come down to earth today or tomorrow, then one can reconcile oneself with *any* external authority; it no longer matters which.

The old Lukács came to realize that philosophy of art cannot be the clue to ethics. This is why he decided to write an ethics based on the ontology of social existence. Given that this ontology was organized on the paradigm of work and, as a result, all value patterns were duly derived from the patterns of purposive rationality, this last venture did not sound more promising than previous ones. But the change of attitude is still discernible. Previously, Lukács had reconciled himself with the reality of an external authority, although he was unaware of this reconciliation. This time, Lukács attains an awareness of reconciliation. But the latter is no longer the reconciliation with a political authority; rather, it is with our historicity, our being thrown into the present world. It is a reconciliation in the spirit of the Hegelian Preface to *The Philosophy of History*: to discover the rose on the cross of the present. The awareness that the present is a cross, but that one can still find a rose on it, elicited a theoretical attachment to a novel kind of stoicism. Always stoic in inclinations, never before stoic in ethics, the old Lukács finally sought to give a theoretical expression to his own inclinations. This new kind of stoicism may have eventually generated adequate moral philosophy.

Returning to the "postmodern condition," there is very little hope now for a cultural revival where works of art can be both autonomous and democratic. Adorno and Lukács formulated the two options of yesterday, which still remain the alternatives of today's postmodernism. They read as follows: either we have autonomous art works which express the sublimity of our human conditions — in which case we have to resign democracy and embrace elitism — or we accept cultural conservatism in which case we can still be democratic. In a way, Lukács' option gains momentum against Adorno's. If no new "sublime" modern novel were written, if no new autonomous sculpture or musical composition were created, the highest products of the Western tradition would still be appealing while preserving the standards and contrast a utopian reality to the present. As long as art has a place in daily life, a rise "upward" is not entirely ruled out. And Lukács' insistence that everything "at the top" comes from "deep down," provided there is a personality which carries it "upwards," provides hope. Lukács would add: the personality can never be unmade. So there is hope.

What has to be acknowledged as a complete failure in both Adorno's and Lukács' attempts is the grounding of philosophy in art. Philosophy, in particular moral philosophy, cannot be modelled after art. Everyday life is the only sound starting point. And here again, Lukács wins the day. A philosophy can only grow out of contemporary everyday life if one rejects the negative dialectic of complete alienation and total fetishism. But without a normative foundation, which at the same time is related to empirical life, this kind of work cannot be performed. But if this kind of work can be performed, it has to be performed in a stoic manner: without fear and hope, or, more modestly, without excessive fear and excessive hope.

The Holy Family stood for norms and standards: it stood for autonomy and personality. From this viewpoint, members of this family can serve as models. Yet, the Holy Family was not holy enough or, rather, its members were sometimes holy in the wrong way. They were not holy enough for they were either moral minimalists or moral maximalists. They failed to address the question of *normativity* in life, in politics, and in interpersonal communication. They were holy in the wrong way, for they did not accept plurality of life-styles, cultures and human personality. There are roses of different colors and scents on the cross of the present, and all of them can convey something that is true, good and beautiful. But a standard is needed, not so much to define which is the really true or good or beautiful rose, but to guide us in distinguishing the rose from the cross, as well as from those who would like to crucify us to that cross.

An Appeal For Justice In Turkey

Twelve founding members of the Turkish Peace Association are in jail. Six others are for the moment free on bail pending outcome of an appeal. These 17 men and one woman did nothing to earn their lengthy sentences — nothing that would be considered criminal in any Western democracy, at least. The TPA platform urged, among other things, a bilateral ban on nuclear weapons production, general disarmament, and respect for the territorial integrity of all nations. Last year, the defendants were nominated for the Nobel Peace Prize.

Those convicted are:

Orhan Apaydan, Chair, Istanbul Bar Association
Erdal Atabek, President, Turkish Medical Association
Husseyin Bas, Journalist
Niyazi Balyanci, Journalist
Mahmut Dikerdem, Former Ambassador, Author
Ergun Ergin, Engineer
Harun Goner, Engineer
Gundogan Gorsev, Publisher
Reha Isvan, Deputy Head, Istanbul Education Dept.

Metin Ozek, Psychiatrist
Ismail Oztorun, Former Member of Parliament
Ali Sirmen, Journalist
Gencay Saylan, Political Scientist
Ali Taygun, Director, Turkish State Theater
Orhan Taylan, Artist
Haluk Tosun, Professor
Melih Tumer, Economist, Former Dean
Cemal Usluoglu, Engineer

You *can* help. Please write letters appealing for the immediate and unconditional release and the cessation of prosecution of all TPA defendants to Turkey's prime minister. Readers in the United States are asked to send copies of letters to Turkey's ambassador to the United States and to Elliott Abrams of the U.S. State Department. Their addresses appear below.

Prime Minister Turgut Ozal
Başbakanlik
Ankara, Turkey

Ambassador Dr. Sukru Elekdag
Embassy of the Republic of Turkey
1606 23rd Street NW
Washington DC 20008

Elliott Abrams
Assistant Secretary of State
State Department
Washington DC 20520

SOVIET SOCIETY AND
THE WORLD SYSTEMS ANALYSIS

by Victor Zaslavsky

In his review of *The Neo-Stalinist State*,[1] Luke reproaches me for neglecting both "the new importance of the USSR's and Eastern Europe's niche in the world economic system" and the use of the East-West economic exchange by the Soviet regime to "sustain its 'neo-Stalinist' state." These criticisms are well taken. Yet, I deliberately concentrated on the inner workings of the Soviet state in its mature form without going into the problems of the Soviet position in the global system. After pointing to these weaknesses, Luke suggests his own interpretation of Soviet developments in the past decades. They can be summarized as follows.

After World War II, Soviet society failed to develop an advanced industrial political economy. As a result, the Soviet leadership had to abandon "Stalin's autarchic command economy . . . in favor of a partial re-integration into the world economic system as a semi-periphery economy." In improving Soviet economic performance, Soviet leaders had no choice but to assign a major role to foreign trade and technology, and from 1964 onward, the country has been expanding trade with the West. Correspondingly, "from 1964 to 1984, the Soviet systems in the USSR and CMEA have established comprehensive, systematic dependencies on foreign capital, expertise and technology to accelerate their domestic development." The USSR and its allies entered "the global market as integral components of a capitalist world economy" exemplifying, therefore, a "dependent development as upwardly mobile, semi-peripheral economies in the world economic system."

This analysis is flawed on several accounts. In order to discuss such an approach it is useful to spell out certain implicit but recognizable cultural attitudes and theoretical assumptions on which it is based. In this respect, Luke's approach to Soviet society appears profoundly ethnocentric.[2]

In analyzing Western approaches to Soviet foreign policy, Yergin contrasted the "Riga" and the "Yalta" axioms. He introduced these terms to distinguish between the image of the Soviet Union as "a world revolutionary state, denying the possibilities of coexistence, committed to unrelenting ideological warfare, powered by a messianic drive for world mastery" (the Riga axiom) and the image of the Soviet Union as a great power with traditional security concerns which strives to achieve its national state goals with-

---

1. Timothy Luke, "Review Symposium on Soviet-type Societies," *Telos*, 60 (Summer 1984), pp. 158 ff.

2. As Ken Booth points out, "ethnocentrism is used in the following closely related senses: 1) as a term to describe feelings of group centrality and superiority; 2) as a technical term to describe a faulty methodology in the social sciences; 3) as a synonym for being 'culture-bound'." Cf. Ken Booth, *Strategy and Ethnocentrism* (New York, 1979), pp. 14-15.

out overthrowing the international order (the Yalta axiom).[3]

In discussing American popular views of Soviet society and its economy, it will be useful to single out what could be called the "Moscow on the Hudson axiom" and the "military colossus axiom." The first has recently been forcefully presented in the movie from which I borrowed the title. It is a metaphor for Soviet society exemplified by an overcrowded room in a Moscow apartment where an extended family organizes a feast after someone managed to obtain some toilet paper. Having defected to the U.S., a member of this family found the same warmth, emotional support and overcrowded conditions in a Harlem black family. Soviets seem to be aware of their semi-peripheral status and crave to move up in the world. Even a privileged official prefers to remain in New York to sell hot dogs. The film portrays a slightly condescending image of warm and emotional Soviets populating an inefficient, almost pre-industrial and largely obsolete society.

In sharp contrast to this image, there is a tradition that portrays the USSR as a military giant seeking world conquest. This "military colossus axiom" was expressed, albeit in a very primitive form, in another American box office hit, "The Red Dawn." In this film, Soviet troops armed to the teeth with the most sophisticated military equipment and aided by Cubans, Nicaraguans, etc., succeed in occupying the U.S. and transforming the country into a huge concentration camp.

Today both axioms quietly coexist in American conventional wisdom, while theoreticians seek to explain how the Soviet regime manages to achieve military and space parity or superiority while simultaneously remaining a dependent and underdeveloped country. One solution has been suggested by Castoriadis.[4] He pictures the Soviet economy as consisting of a military sub-society (the military establishment proper and the armament industries) and a non-military sector. Accordingly, the military sub-society has emerged as 'the only live and effective sector of Russian society," while in the non-military sector "things do not work, do not function."[5] Castoriadis obviously does not address Soviet society as a system whose elements are interdependent and mutually condition each other. Certain analyses of Soviet agriculture represent a close analogy to this line of reasoning: huge and inefficient collective farms are contrasted to small but miraculously productive "private" plots. In reality, kolkhozes and individual plots coexist in a symbiotic relationship and cannot survive without each other nor be analyzed separately. Castoriadis, however, is not inclined to harp on Soviet underdevelopment. He recognizes that Soviet military build-up largely depends on its internal

---

3.   Daniel Yergin, *Shattered Peace* (Boston, 1977), pp. 11, 42-68.

4.   Cornelius Castoriadis, *Devant la Guerre* (Paris, 1981).

5.   Cornelius Castoriadis, " 'Facing the War' and 'The Socio-Economic Roots of Re-Armament': A Rejoinder," *Telos*, 53 (Fall 1982), pp. 193, 195. An exiled Soviet satirist, Yuz Aleshkovsky, arrives at the same conclusion in his recent, irresistibly funny novel *Maskirovka* (Ann Arbor, 1982). According to Aleskovsky, all this visible Soviet life, with shoddy work and drunken workers dragging their feet, is no more than a "mask," a cover to pull the wool over Western eyes whereas deep underneath, real and efficient Soviet plants are unceasingly producing elaborate missiles and other military hardware.

sources and he insists that growing trade and credit may even lead to increased Western dependence on Soviet society.

Pipes suggests a different explanation of the alleged Soviet ability to combine military superiority with industrial underdevelopment.[6] On the one hand, Soviet military superiority is temporary and due mainly to the loss of nerve and lack of determination on the part of American administrations. On the other hand, Pipes cites incontrovertible examples of sales by Western countries of certain equipment and technologies which directly contributed to increasing Soviet military capabilities. He concludes that technological transfer from the West is the basis of the successful USSR military build-up. Luke expands the latter part of Pipes' argument, applying it not only to military industries but to the Soviet economy as a whole. According to Luke, USSR technological underdevelopment makes key sectors of its industry "dependent upon Western firms to improve both their output and productivity."

This viewpoint seems to have become as widespread within the American academic community as it was before the Soviet Sputnik. In Pipes' words, "solid evidence that no one so far has been able to refute shows that the Soviet economy has never been self-sufficient and today is less so than ever."[7] This is certainly true. After all, there is no industrial nation-state in the world, including the U.S., Japan, and France, which can claim to be self-sufficient. Moreover, today's science and technology are truly international and it is a rare case when any major invention can be identified as a purely national effort. Judgments of this sort become a matter of degree and definition. Consider Luke's argument for Soviet technological underdevelopment: "Lacking the capability to develop many modern technologies from initial conception to eventual application, the USSR instead has concentrated on duplicating, scaling up and modifying basic designs borrowed from foreign sources." First of all, until recently, such arguments were made concerning Japanese science and industry. Now they seem to be out of fashion simply because it has not been demonstrated that the Japanese approach leads to inherently inferior results. Characteristically, a noted Japanese physicist, Makato Kiguchi, sees the reason "why Japan was able to catch up so rapidly to the U.S. level of achievement" in the Japanese practice of following the pioneering U.S. Thus, Japan could avoid retracing U.S. failures and save a great deal of time and money "that would otherwise have been spent looking into blind alleys."[8] More importantly, in many fundamental sectors of R&D the Soviet Union has never heavily relied on borrowing or imitating but rather on the creative strength of its native science and technology. Soviet achievements in space exploration, energy technology, in creating the most advanced types of armament and very efficient system of education hardly need to be proven. Ex-

---

6. Richard Pipes, "How to Cope with the Soviet Threat," *Commentary*, 78:2 (August 1984), pp. 13-30.

7. *Ibid.,* p. 26.

8. Makoto Kiguchi, "Creativity and Ways of Thinking: The Japanese Style," *Physics Today*, September 1981, p. 43.

plaining them in terms of buying and stealing from the West is tantamount to endorsing the old conspiracy theory, which claims that not Ioffes and Kurchatovs, Landaus and Sakharovs, but Fuchses and Rosenbergs were primarily responsible for Soviet nuclear developments.

The past decades have witnessed an enormous Soviet military build-up and a substantial increase of the role of the Soviet bloc in the international system[9] achieved simultaneously with a noticeable growth in the standard of living of the Soviet population. Attempts at accounting for this course of events through the Soviet "shift toward dependent economic development" and Soviet use of "Western expertise, industrial capital and foreign trade . . . to accelerate economic growth, compensating for the Soviet Union's underdevelopment"[10] appear as attempts to explain away the real problem. Moreover, proponents of this interpretation attach to it a sense of universal validity. If someone is going to ask about Soviet development before the 1960s when the Soviets did not trade with the West, Pipes has already answered that "the USSR imported little from the West because it needed time to absorb its Lend-Lease equipment and the immense quantities of war booty that it had seized in Germany and Eastern Europe."[11] Correspondingly, if tomorrow the Soviet bureaucracy would decide again to cut society off from world trade,[12] Soviet development could still be attributed to the beneficial influence of previous purchases from the West. Western industrial society is presented as the demiurge and the only source of creativity in the world while Soviet society is a military colossus with clay feet resting on Western trade and technology.

I disagree with this ethnocentric explanation not only because of its evident logical and historical flaws, but also intuitively, because of my personal background and experience. Having worked for some 15 years in the Soviet mining industry as a worker, engineer and middle-level manager, I can testify that almost all equipment, save South African diamonds for rock-drill bits, was both Soviet-made and world-wide, state-of-the-art at the time. As to the industry's (oil, gas, coal, ferrous and non-ferrous metals, etc.) output, it could be favorably compared with that of the U.S.[13]

---

9.   Roger E. Kanet, ed., *Soviet Foreign Policy in the 1980s (New York, 1982).*

10.   Luke, *op. cit.*

11.   Pipes, *op.cit.,* p. 27.

12.   The same Soviet leaders who several years ago stressed advantages provided by foreign trade today warn against the excessive reliance on East-West trade and emphasize self-sufficiency, especially in key economic sectors. See Thomas N. Bjorman and Thomas J. Zamostny, "Soviet Politics and Strategy toward the West: Three Cases," *World Politics,* 36:2 (January 1984), pp. 191-197. This changing approach does not result from any factional struggle within the Soviet leadership but rather is due to tactical changes based on the sober assessment of global economic realities. Moreover, neither increase nor decline in the format of foreign trade affected noticeably the nature of Soviet economy or the distribution of political power in the USSR.

13.   But I also recognize that any stable social system tends to produce its own ethnocentrisms and I will try to keep mine in check. I remember that we, students of the University of Leningrad, discussing in the course of political economy the situation of unemployment in the West, sought to solve the problem through the incorporation of Western unemployed workers into the Soviet economy with its permanent excess of jobs over the available workforce. The obvious absurdity of the solution escaped our understanding. The fact is that a person raised and educated within a certain social system tends to perceive a different system as unnatural and inferior. That certain

How did Luke reach the conclusion that the Soviets were unable to develop an "advanced industrialism"? He obviously defines advanced industrialism as the actual state of Western or, better, American society. Then he measures by this yardstick the Soviet economy and realizes that it does not pass muster. On the whole, the Soviet economy is obviously inferior to the Western one, especially in the consumer goods sector, and the Soviet population craves Western products. Correspondingly, technological transfer and Soviet dependence on the West come in handy as reasonable explanations of Soviet achievements in certain selected sectors of the economy. Today's claims that the Soviet economic system is "absurd"[14] or "anachronistic"[15] which abound in Western literature are a gross exaggeration. I sense some sort of cognitive dissonance in Luke's article because it seems to exemplify a frequent situation in which cultural, ethnocentric attitudes lead to positing one society's standards as universal and to distort rational analysis.

Luke accepts one of the major findings of the books he reviewed. He agrees that Soviet society as a social formation is "neither a novel, modified form of (state) capitalism, nor is it socialism — it is 'something else.' It is a social formation completely different from any that has existed in European or world history to date and it is equally different from any relevant conception in terms of which socialism, either 'scientifically' or in a utopian manner, has ever been conceived. Nor is this social formation a kind of transition between two states of social affairs, one existing (capitalism) and one not yet existing. It is a self-reproducing social order in which many elements declared to be 'transitory' (for reasons of camouflage) are constitutive of, and indispensable for, the functioning of the system. . . . This is, then, a universal system, or at least a system that has universalistic aspirations. It is not a regional solution."[16]

In other words, modern industrial society exists in two very different variants — Western-type and Soviet-type societies, each representing a stable and viable form of social organization and neither likely to collapse or disappear except in the case of a nuclear war, which would destroy both. Correspondingly, there are two types of industrial political economy, not one "advanced industrialism," which, as Luke postulates, the Soviet Union was unable to develop. Soviet economy is the "economy of shortages."[17] These shortages in themselves are not evidence of underdevelopment industrialism but

---

seemingly "unnatural" appearances may reflect essential characteristics of underlying social systems is not easily comprehended.

14.   Arch Puddington, "A Reply to Letters from Readers," *Commentary,* August 1984, p. 3.

15.   Marshall I. Goldman, "An Anachronistic System," *Society* (January-February 1984), p. 3.

16.   Ferenc Feher, Agnes Heller, Gyorgy Markus, *Dictatorship over Needs* (New York, 1983), p. 221. Incidentally, Luke misinterprets me when he says that "Zaslavsky sees the neo-Stalinist state as a particularly regional development confined within the multinational USSR." I always considered Soviet-type society as a new socio-economic formation leading to the creation of a new world system. As to the Soviet system's universal character, there is no difference between the views of Feher-Heller-Markus and my own. See F. Feher's review of *The Neo-Stalinist State* in *Soviet Studies,* 35:4 (1983), pp. 570-572.

17.   Janos Kornai, *Economics of Shortage,* 2 volumes (Amsterdam, 1981); Igor Birman, *Ekonomika nedostach* (Benson, Vermont: Chalidze Publications, 1983); Alec Nove, *The Soviet Economic Systems* (London, 1980).

rather an essential characteristic, a mode of operation unavoidable in this centrally planned economy. The "Moscow on the Hudson axiom" appears precisely as a result of applying market society's success indicators to the economy of shortages. In the Soviet-type "market," however, "the seller is not a genuinely independent, market-oriented firm. It is basically not led by profit considerations and it does not have to compete for the goodwill of the buyers. The 'seller' is a multi-level regulating organization motivated by a number of other factors, and it is able to impose its will upon the buyer."[18] This "dictatorship over needs" normally proves much inferior to the market industrial society from the viewpoint of the quality of life it provides for its population. Soviet-type economy has certain built-in mechanisms which produce shortages. At the same time, it is better protected from both the over-production of goods and over-production of needs. Many goods produced and many needs developed under the influence of the market economy simply do not obtain in a Soviet-type society without compromising its industrial advancement in other fields. On the other hand, central planners can always concentrate enormous human and material resources needed to achieve any particular goal within what is technologically possible at the time. To cite a characteristic example, the USSR lagged far behind the West in developing such sophisticated technologies as numerically controlled machine tools, the Soviet 1968 output being only 7 percent of that of the U.S. Having identified NC machines as a priority area, the Soviet output in 1971 exceeded that of the U.S.[19] The Soviet centrally planned economy adapts to certain types of tasks easier than to others. It will always produce consumer goods which, with some exceptions, will be intrinsically inferior in quantity, quality and variety to Western goods. As to goals such as the development of energy technology, space industry and armaments, however, major innovations or even breakthroughs can be expected not only from Western but also form Soviet-type societies. The Soviet economy operates in a qualitatively different way than its Western counterpart. This, however, does not necessarily lead to its dependent position in the global economy and does not entail the underdeveloped character of Soviet industrialization. Excessive reliance on largely ethnocentric evaluations of the Soviet performance resulting from the application of criteria not proper for a Soviet-type society may lead to a dangerous underestimation of Soviet capabilities. As V. Emelyanov, one of the major organizers of Soviet R&D, has recently stressed: "The Soviet economy, science and technology are now at such a high level that the country is able in the shortest period of time to create any new types of armaments."[20] This is not a bluff and both the Soviet industrial potential and the actual use of this potential should be analyzed without biases and preconceptions.

It would be unfair to discuss Luke's attributing the dependent, semi-peripheral status to Soviet society only in terms of largely unconscious cul-

18.   Z. Kapitany, J. Kornai, J. Szabo, "Reproduction of Shortage on the Hungarian Car Market," *Soviet Studies*, 36:2 (1984), p. 248.

19.   Stephen Woolcock, *Western Policies or East-West Trade* (London, 1982), p. 32.

20.   V. Emelyanov, "Osolaya opasnost," *Novi mir*, 5 (1984), p. 181.

tural attitudes and dispositions. It is also based on a new and promising theoretical paradigm developed by proponents of the so-called world systems analysis. Their approach to Soviet-type societies and the position assigned to the USSR by the world systems theorists requires, therefore, a special discussion.

Proponents of world-systems analysis advanced the thesis that a single capitalist world-economy has been developing sine the 15th century and that its development has been the driving force of global social change prompting, in particular, a rapid expansion of the state form of organization and the creation of the European state system. By the end of the 19th century the latter had become a global system with strong core states and weak peripheral states. From the world-system perspective, any theory of state formation and functioning should explain both the "historical development of the North Atlantic states and the historical underdevelopment of the African, Latin American and (excepting Japan) Asian states."[21]

According to Immanuel Wallerstein, "the capitalist world-economy was built on a worldwide division of labor in which various zones of this economy (the core, the semiperiphery, and the periphery) were assigned specific economic roles, developed different class structures, used consequently different modes of labor control and profited unequally from the workings of the system."[22] Taking the concept of world-economy as the point of departure, the world-systems approach posits a methodological principle: since states as a consequence of their different roles in the world-economy are structured differently, the structure and workings of an individual state can only be properly understood if the position occupied by this state in the system of the world economy will be taken into account. Correspondingly, particular patterns of state development in different areas of the world are determined not only by endogenous factors within these states, by historically pre-existing institutional patterns, by geopolitical pressures and constraints, but also by a given state's position in the larger setting of the world system, whose operation strongly influences the development of each single state.

This methodological approach offers a new distinctive paradigm which seems to be especially important when applied to state development in the 20th century. It draws our attention to two fundamentally different principles of organization that actually operate in the world-system: an essentially political principle organizes the world's population as the subject of various particular sovereign states; an essentially economic principle organizes the world's population as participants in a single world production system. Tensions between the worldwide and the local (national state) principles of organization, between the increasingly global structure of production with major production units cutting across state borders, and separate nation-states as distinct

---

21.   T.K. Hopkins, "The Study of the Capitalist World-Economy: Some Introductory Considerations,' in T.K. Hopkins, I. Wallerstein, *et al.*, *World-Systems Analysis. Theory and Methodology* (Beverly Hills, 1982), pp. 10-11.

22.   Immanuel Wallerstein, *The Modern World-System*, Vol. I (New York and London, 1974), p. 162.

political units, obviously condition many processes of state formation and development in the 20th century. Correspondingly, the world-systems approach helps to clarify our understanding of the effects of transnational structures on nature and functions of individual states.

The particular form which the world-systems paradigm has taken in the works of world-systems theorists and their approach to concrete transnational structures, however, call for serious criticisms. The world-systems analysts postulate the existence of the only one real world system: the system of world capitalism. In their excessive reliance on the concept of a single, all-encompassing system of worldwide economic division of labor, they overlook and misinterpret the emergence and the growing significance or a second world system of Soviet-type (or "socialists") states. Thus, Wallerstein dismisses the creation of socialist states as a pseudo-problem and refuses seeing a self-standing totality in the system of Soviet-type states.[23] It is not difficult to demonstrate that "there are today no socialist systems in the world-economy," but Wallerstein's conclusion that there is only one world-system which is by definition capitalist does not follow. "Soviet" and "socialist" are by no means synonyms. Wallerstein does not address himself to thorny problems of Soviet political economy, does not consider closely the nature of the Soviet mode of production, and fails to demonstrate the existence of a single global division of labor. He conceives of the Soviet regime as a specific way for a semi-periphery country to achieve core stateus. The Soviet state "using the classic technique of mercantilist semi-withdrawal from the world economy" reversed the declining trend of Russian economy and "at the end of the Second World War Russia was reinstated as a very strong member of the semi-periphery country to achieve core status. The Soviet state "using the classic Wallerstein characterizes Soviet internal policy as the "preparation for future competition in the world market as an exporter of manufactured goods"[25] — a prediction which would undoubtedly amaze both the leaders and the population of the Soviet Union.

According to the accounts of world-systems theorists, the world capitalist system derives its dynamics largely from world market processes and particularly from the development of international trade. This argument blows out of all proportion the influence of world market opportunities on socio-economic structures of nation-states. If we accept for a moment the idea that the relations of exchange and international trade might play a decisive role in shaping the character and internal workings of a social system, a mere glance at the character and scope of the East-West trade would immediately reveal the fact that the Soviet bloc's participation in the world capitalist market is almost negligible and by no means could determine or even influence the internal workings of either Soviet-type or Western societies.

23.   I. Wallerstein, "The Rise and Future Demise of the World Capitalist System: Concepts for Comparative Analysis," *Comparative Studies in Society and History*, 16:4 (1974), p. 415.

24.   *Op.cit.,* p. 411.

25.   I. Wallerstein, *The Capitalist World-Economy* (New York, 1979), p. 87.

In fact, in the Soviet Union's case, East-West trade as a percentage of GNP in 1979 was 1.3 percent while that for the U.S. (in 1980) was 0.2 percent.[26] There is no doubt that the Soviet Union and East European countries have been importing from the West noticeable quantities of goods and know-how to introduce new technologies and modernize existing industries. The overall impact of the transfer of Western technology to the USSR, however, is quite modest. According to Hanson's well-known study, productivity improvements from Western technology have possibly provided the Soviet Union with, at most, an incremental 0.5 percent of growth annually.[27]

Moreover, Soviet bloc countries as a whole purchase a relatively small share of the high-technology products exported by industrial Western countries. According to Gary Bertsch, "of the total Western high-technology exports in 1970, communist countries imported only 5 percent, the figure climbed to 7 percent in 1975 and dropped to 6 percent again in 1979."[28]

Soviet massive purchases of grain are often cited as the clearest evidence of the Soviet dependence on the West. Considering the following facts, however, will provide a better picture of the situation. The failure of kolkhozes as a form of organization of agricultural production is now taken for granted by both the Soviet leadership and the population.[29] The present leadership seeks to maintain the status quo and to avoid any drastic reforms that are deemed politically dangerous. Correspondingly, it has chosen the path of a slow but steady transformation of collective forms into state agricultural enterprises. This policy does not promise to rapidly solve Soviet agricultural problems nor to achieve a self-sufficiency in food products in the near future. Nevertheless, this is a conscious choice of the Soviet political elite based on realistic calculations.

First of all, the failure of the American grain embargo proved that the Soviets had no reason to fear a collective grain embargo that Western countries could afford neither economically nor politically. Moreover, even in a very unlikely case of such a collective action, the Soviet regime could successfully withstand this Western pressure by using internal reserves and increasing the level of social mobilization. It should be taken into account that Soviet 'real" grain requirements are not known even to the Soviet leadership. From the early 1960s, the government has been pursuing a policy of maintaining very low, political prices on staples, including bread. As a result, bread consumption in the USSR is exaggerated and extremely wasteful. (Soviet press accounts of peasants feeding cattle with bread, of urban families, cafeterias and restaurants throwing huge amounts of bread into the grbage could fill volumes). Even a gradual raising of those political prices would noticeably

26.   R.V. Roosa, M. Matuskawa, A. Gutowski, *East-West Trade at a Crossroads. The Trilateral Commission (New York, 1982), p. 21; Gary K. Bertsch, East-West Strategic Trade. COCOM and the Atlantic Alliance* (Paris, 1983), p. 24.

27.   Philip H. Hanson, *Trade and Technology in Soviet-Western Relations* (New York, 1981), pp. 144-155.

28.   Bertsch, *op.cit.,* p. 16.

29.   See Lev Timofeev, *Soviet Peasants* (Telos Press, forthcoming).

reduce the Soviet grain consumption. There is no doubt that the Soviet Union will soon raise all the political prices as has already been done by Eastern European countries.

Secondly, Soviet leaders learned through experience that buying grain abroad instead of reforming inefficient collective farms is not only more secure politically, but also cheaper economically. Throughout the West, key sectors of agriculture are heavily subsidized. As a group of experts has recently put it, "the Western exporting countries are in fact losing money with every bushel of maize or other crops that they sell to the Soviet Union and the countries of Eastern Europe."[30] Thus, the Soviet government operates under very favorable conditions of a buyer's market when being the only buyer with reserve hard currency resources permits a considerable control over world prices on grain. In order to obtain hard currency Soviet central planners have disproportionately developed extractive industries, especially oil and gas industries. Such a development has various implications for the Soviet economy as a whole.[31] The major short-term consequence, however, is the fact that the Soviet fuel exports to the West have doubled from 1979 to 1983 while the fuel exports share in the Soviet hard currency trade is now close to 80 percent. "The USSR has been able to reverse its hard-currency foreign trade deficits of $2 billion to $3 billion a year from 1980 on."[32] It helped the USSR to overcome the tight world credit market of the 1980s and assume a strong bargaining position, all this after unprecedented massive grain purchases of the past years.

The Soviet choice to concentrate efforts on developing extractive industries instead of introducing uncertain and costly economic reforms does not signify any Soviet dependence on the West. The Soviet regime depends on Western grain no more than the latter depends on Soviet energy resources. What can be discussed, therefore, is a certain degree of interdependence between the world systems. The central fact, however, is that both world systems are largely self-sufficient. This explains both why the volume of trade is relatively small and now declining[33] and why neither of the sides can use trade to shape internal developments and overall relations with the other. the opposing world systems have almost no economic or political leverage they can exercise over the opponent.

World-systems theorists tried to forestall such criticisms by postulating Wallerstein's thesis that class relations of production and forms of property within states are largely irrelevant. After all, for Wallerstein, as some reviewers have noted, "the trade-based division of labor is the primary independent variable of world history."[34] For those who share this approach, the essence of

30.   R.V. Roosa, M. Matsukawa, A. Gutowski, *op.cit.,* p. 51.

31.   See Boris Rumer, "Structural Imbalance in the Soviet Economy," *Problems of Communism* (July-August 1984), pp. 24-33.

32.   See *Soviet Analyst,* 13:19 (September 1984), p. 5.

33.   Thomas N. Bjorkman, Thomas T. Zamostny, *op.cit.,* pp. 191-197.

34.   James L. Ray, "The 'World-System' and the Global Political System: A Crucial Relationship?" in Pat McGowan, Charles W. Kegley Jr., eds., *Foreign Policy and the Modern World-System*

capitalism, the capitalist nature of the world system is determined by the sole fact that core states exploit peripheral and semiperipheral ones.

World-systems theorists are not prepared to deny that differences in internal structures in the U.S. and the Soviet Union result in different foreign policies.[35] But their failure to recognize the existence of a second world system compels them virtually to ignore major differences between the policies of economic exploitation of underdeveloped countries by Western states and multinationl corporations, on the one hand, and Soviet policies of political domination ("political imperialism") on the other.

Another theoretical consequence of raising the capitalist world to the rank of the solely existing global system is a virtual neglect of power relations and political-military conflicts in the world today. Thus, according to Wallerstein, the most difficult issues that confront U.S. policy-makers in the coming decades are neither East-West issues nor North-South issues. "Rather they are West-West issues that are based on the great economic and therefore political threat of the two significant U.S. rivals, Western Europe and Japan."[36]

This startling conclusion demonstrates both Wallerstein's theoretical consistency and the basic weaknesses of a model which allows such an underestimation of those political-military conflicts between the two existing world systems which threaten to destroy the world.

Criticizing the particular form which the world-systems analysis has taken in the works of Wallerstein, Hopkins, Gunder Frank, Chase-Dunn and others should not make us forget some positive and promising aspects of this new paradigm. Students of the state had previously been preoccupied mainly with the internal sources of state development. The intricate and truly dialectical interplay of internal and external factors of state development was too often neglected. The world-systems approach seeks to analyze both internal developments and external policies of states in their relation to a larger setting, to the external environment within which the state's development and operations are taking place. The world-systems approach brings to the fore new explanatory factors, by suggesting that characteristics and functions of states should be understood with reference to the particular positions they occupy within a wider context to which they belong. Nevertheless, the recognition of the fact that industrial society exists now in two very different variants, and the global system of today is composed of two world-systems based on different and often opposed organizational principles will enhance considerably the explanatory potential of the world-systems paradigm. In particular, the division of the world into two world systems helps to explain the different patterns of state structure and function in Western-type as against Soviet-type states, as well as the characteristics of the Western and the Eastern interstate systems. The struggle between the two political-military blocs which represent the two

(Beverly Hills, 1983), p. 19; see also Theda Skocpol, "Wallerstein's World Capitalist System: A Theoretical and Historical Critique," *American Journal of Sociology*, 82:5 (1977).

35.   Christopher Chase-Dunn, "Socialist State Policy in the Capitalist World-Economy," in McGowan, Kegley, *op.cit.*, pp. 63-88.

36.   I. Wallerstein, *The Modern World-System*, vol. 2 (New York, 1980), p. 125.

world systems constitutes the continuing antinomy of the postwar period. The process of the emergence of Western and Eastern world systems and of the division of the world after World War II known as the Cold War deserve, therefore, special attention.

A detailed analysis of the origins of the Cold War is beyond the scope of this article,[37] but a brief discussion of the emergence of a new Soviet-type world system might be useful. The postwar conflict between the U.S. and the USSR is not externally induced, accidental, or dependent on some psychological traits of their particular leaderships. The Cold War broke out because of a fundamental incompatibility of interests between Western and Soviet-type industrial societies. There was no objective basis for a lasting friendly cooperation between the pluralist market society of the United States, with private property as its central institution, and Soviet society set on sweeping away capitalism with all its arrangements and institutions. In the face of the destruction or exhaustion of several major world powers of the past, the American and Soviet policies of building their own spheres of influence, strengthening and stabilizing their interests and securing imperatives of the protagonists of the conflict. Conclusions that the "Soviet system was the true cause of the Cold War"[38] are as unwarranted as the opposite ones that blamed the Cold War on aggressive and imperialist policies of the U.S.[39] Both countries sought to maximize their powers by all means short of direct war and it is irrelevant whether particular policies were reactions to pressures from the outside or internally conditioned initiatives. The Cold War turned into a zero-sum conflict when any gain of one side signified a net loss for another.

The Soviet-type world system emerged as a byproduct of Soviet attempts to secure firm control over its zone of influence. There is no evidence that the Soviet leadership in the aftermath of World War II had any blueprint for world conquest and the imposition of world socialism. Sovietization of East European countries was set in motion by the inner logic of the Soviet state's working and by the exigencies of organizing a reliable system of control over the satellite buffer zone. The idea that Soviet security required a buffer zone of states whose foreign policy would be controlled by the Soviets was widely accepted by Western politicians. Moreover, the Soviet army, having done all the fighting, occupied the territory and the Soviet government did not need any Western approval for organizing its sphere of influence; at most, it sought "formal diplomatic sanction by the West of the postwar status quo in Eastern Europe."[40] The Soviet administration soon realized that any lasting control

37. For a useful analysis of this problem see John L. Gaddis, "The Emerging Post-Revisionist Synthesis on the Origins of the Cold War," *Diplomatic History*, 7:3 (Summer 1983), pp. 171-190; Elena Aga Rossi, "Introduzione," in E. Aga Rossi, ed., *Gli Stati Uniti e le origini della guerra fredda* (Bologna, 1983), pp. 11-82.

38. Vojtech Mastny, *Russia's Road to the Cold War: Diplomacy, Warfare and the Politics of Communism 1941-1945* (New York, 1979), p. 307.

39. William A. Williams, *The Tragedy of American Diplomacy*, 2nd edition (New York, 1972); D.F. Fleming, *The Cold War and its Origins, 1917-1960* (Garden City, 1961); cf. also Soviet official historiography.

40. Arpad Kadarkay, *Human Rights in American and Russian Political Thought* (Washington, 1982), p. 184.

could be effective if exercised not through external military force but rather through those social groups and segments of the local population which by virtue of their structural position had stakes of their own in keeping their country a Soviet ally. The economic integration and division of labor were another powerful means for seeking another country's strong dependence on the Soviet state. The logic of the emergence of the Soviet camp might be presented as a sequence of interrelated and mutually conditioned processes: Soviet victory and state security imperatives — Soviet zone of influence — Sovietization of this zone of influence — Soviet transnational camp. As a result there appeared a new superstate structure, the Soviet-type world system, with its own division of labor and largely internal developmental dynamics.

Both Western and Soviet-type industrial societies represent stable and viable systems of social organization with enormous developmental potentials which do not show any sign of economic or military decline. It cannot be excluded that, having achieved a certain size and certain degree of control over the Soviet-type world system, the Soviet Union might shift to the policy of isolationism and autarchy focussed on the system's security, stability and internal development. However, today such a change remains a remote possibility. All Soviet leaderships considered, consider and will consider the support of social movements and any other actions to destroy or at least weaken capitalism as its own political-strategic, ideological and systemic imperative. Thus, the basic and most authoritative definition of the policy of peaceful coexistence given by Soviet leaders is very revealing: "Peaceful coexistence in no way means reconciliation with capitalists or an end to the class struggle, but rather that the struggle would be waged by economic, political and ideological means rather than war."[41] The 1977 Soviet Constitution defines systemic goals in an unambiguous way stating, for example, that the duty of the Soviet government is "to consolidate the position of world socialism by supporting the struggles of the people for national liberation and social progress." But the right to label a social movement as a revolutionary or liberation movement remains with Soviet leadership. At the same time, there is no dearth of American high officials' statements which not only focus on the ideological roots or the totalitarian character of the Soviet system but also assert that "there is no place in the world so remote that it does not enter into the sphere of American concerns and interests." There is a general understanding that now the particular policy of the U.S. administration is to engage the Soviets in a sustained arms race that will break their economy and "then there will be just one superpower in a safe world."[42] Particular scenarios and policies can be changed, new agreements on curbing the arms race and pro-

---

41. B. Ponomarev, F. Konstantinov, Yu. Andropov, "Na starykh revisionistskikh pozitsiyakh," *Kommunist1* 3 (1960). Cited in *Survey,* 1 (1984), p. 33.
42. Nicholas Lemann, "The Peacetime War," *The Atlantic,* October 1984, p. 94; Russell J. Leng, "Reagan and Russians: Crisis Bargaining Beliefs and the Historical Record," *The American Political Science Review,* 78:2 (June 1984), pp. 338-355.

hibiting especially dangerous types of weapons can be reached, but a situation where rival social systems have in common not much more than their interest in survival remains largely immutable. Thus, a new form of world systems approach to international and national politics, one that addresses the global system as encompassing both a Western and a Soviet-type world system and considers their incompatibility, competition and contest as one of the major driving forces of today's historical process, is becoming indispensable.

The
Berkeley Journal
of Sociology

A Critical Review   Volume XXIX 1984

Individuals: $5.00   Discounts on Back Issues
Institutions: $12.00   and Multi-Volume Orders

THE BERKELEY JOURNAL OF SOCIOLOGY
Univ. of CA   458A Barrows Hall   Berkeley, CA 94720

DECONSTRUCTION'S USE AND ABUSE
OF NIETZSCHE

by Kenneth Asher

Sensitive to the fluidity of Nietzsche's thought, which often expresses itself in apparent contradiction, Karl Jaspers notes that "for nearly every single one of Nietzsche's judgements one can also find an opposite."[1] But Jaspers goes on to warn that the art of reading Nietzsche faithfully demands that we gradually locate the central axis of his philosophy so that seeming irreconcilables may be resolved into a hierarchy of importance. Not surprisingly, however, this painstaking study has seldom been performed, with the result that Nietzsche's paternity has been claimed by a wildly disparate band of selective readers. Thus in Wilhemine Germany the most radical wing of the SPD denounces rigid party orthodoxy by quoting approvingly Nietzsche's distaste for "herd morality," while completely ignoring the fact that Nietzsche considered socialism itself to be a late blooming variety of just such morality.[2] Little more than a generation later, right when the Nazis adopt Nietzsche as champion of the Aryan "blond beast" come to crush a decaying Jewish world order, they conveniently overlook not only Nietzsche's disapproval of German nationalism which culminates in his claiming Polish ancestry, but also his call to "expel the anti-Semitic loudmouths"[3] whose resentment "has always bloomed in hidden places, like the violet, though with a different odor."[4] A more flexible reader, Mussolini found in Nietzsche a call for action in the service of Life and, in a *tour de force* regarded himself as Nietzschean both as a young Marxist and later as fascist — the source of Life had merely been reinterpreted.[5] Those who saw themselves as apolitical, too, derived sustenance from Nietzsche. The Yeats who dreamed of an unperturbed high culture cloistered in ancestral houses, who saw the Anglo-Irish War of 1919 as nothing more than "weasels fighting in a hole," detects a kindred spirit in the aestheticism of Nietzsche's *Birth of Tragedy,* written under the influence of Wagner and Schopenhauer. Similarly, Thomas Mann, in his series of essays, *Reflections of an Unpolitical Man* (1918), cites Nietzsche on behalf of a Wagnerian *Kultur* which transcends the tinny, facile, vote-cadging world of politics. The more hard-headed Nietzsche of *On the Genealogy of Morals* who knew all too well that a political revolution was necessary to secure a moral revolution goes unremarked by both Yeats and Mann.

To this catalogue of misappropriations of Nietzsche must now be added that of deconstruction, a school of criticism currently the high fashion in literary studies. Like structuralism, which it has replaced in prominence, deconstruction was imported

---

1. Karl Jaspers, *Nietzsche: An Introduction to the Understanding of his Philosophical Activity,* trans, by Charles F. Wallraff and Frederick J. Schmitz (Tucson: University of Arizona Press, 1965), p. 10.

2. R. Hinton Thomas, *Nietzsche in German politics and society, 1890-1918.* (Manchester: Manchester Univ. Press, 1983), pp. 7-15.

3. Friedrich Nietzsche, *Beyond Good and Evil,* sec. 251.

4. Friedrich Nietzsche, *On the Genealogy of Morals,* trans. by Walter Kaufmann (New York: Vintage, 1969), essay II, sec. 11.

5. See Ernst Nolte, *Three Faces of Fascism,* trans. by Leila Vennewitz (New York: New American Library, 1969), pp. 218 ft.

from France and, again like its predecessor, traces its origins to other disciplines. In fact, the high priest of deconstruction, Jacques Derrida, is a philosopher who leaves the task of literary criticism largely to his disciples. Such interdisciplinary application of his work is, however, perfectly consistent with his philosophy. Since, as will be seen, the object world ceases to play any role in Derrida's thinking, the division of such a world into the subject matter of various disciplines is illusory in the first place.

Derrida emerged dramatically in Parisian intellectual life in 1967 with the publication of a trio of books, *De la grammatologie, L'Écriture et la différence,* and *La Voix et le phénomène,* all of which have now appeared in English. Despite the fact that these three volumes range over the work of a variety of authors from Plato to Freud and ultimately to recent structuralists such as Lévi-Strauss and Derrida's own (substantially rejected) mentor, Foucault, all rest on a single epistemological insight: language, which is our only means of knowledge, is a completely enclosed, self-referential system of signs; the concepts which our words convey are irrevocably cut off from the world they purportedly reflect. In Derrida's own terminology, there is no fixed "presence" in the world to which our words point. That we ever thought so is a function of the larger metaphysical delusion that there exists a First Cause which generates value, guarantees fixed meaning. Thus for the past two and a half millenia, or ever since Plato, we have been suffering from a mistaken belief in the power of words, when used judiciously, to approximate, perhaps even reach, objective Truth. Derrida, however, as unmasker of this long-lived hoax he calls "logocentrism," has come to herald a new, liberated age.

The aggressive skepticism which fuels this debunking of Western culture owes less to Hume and the tradition of British empiricism than to Ferdinand de Saussure, turn of the century Swiss linguist, best known for his lecture notes, posthumously published as *Course in General Linguistics.* The Saussure argued that the association between a word(signifier) and its related concept(signified) is arbitrary. We might, by convention, have designated our mental image of "tree" by the linguistic marker d-o-g with no loss of meaning. Significantly, Saussure does not interest himself in the way our concepts relate to the world. Instead, he argues that meaning occurs within the enclosed system of signs (sign = signifier + its signified), each sign intelligible only by its difference from other signs in the system. "Tree," for example, is intelligible insofar as it is part of a system where both acoustically and conceptually it is distinguishable from "dog," "cat," etc. The essence of a sign, in fact, resides *only* in this difference: "In language, as in any semiological system, whatever distinguishes one sign from the others is what constitutes it. Difference creates its characteristic just as it creates value and the unit itself."[6] The variety of the signs constitutes their significance, not their role as denoters of any extralinguistic reality.

In support of this rupture between words and things, Derrida and his fellow deconstructors continually allude to an early and previously little noted essay by Nietzsche entitled "Truth and Morality in an Extra-moral Sense" (1873), unpublished during his lifetime. In this essay, as in *The Birth of Tragedy* written just prior, Nietzsche is at pains to free European man from the straitjacket of scientific thought whose misguided optimism makes impossible anything like the tragic culture Nietzsche so admired in presocratic Greece. In order to undermine what he takes in to be the epistemological arrogance of science, Nietzsche first protests against the correspondence theory of truth. We cannot know things as they really are; our notion of truth, he argues, is merely a convenient fiction: "What then is truth? A mobile army of metaphors, metonymics, anthropomorphisms: in short, a sum of human relations which

---

6.   Ferdinand de Saussure, *Cours de Linguistique Générale* (Paris: Payot, 1982), p. 168.

become poetically and rhetorically intensified, transposed, adorned, and after long usage, seem to a nation fixed, canonic and binding; truths are illusions of which one has forgotten that they *are* illusions; worn out metaphors which have become powerless to affect the senses; coins which have their images effaced and now are no longer of account as coins but merely as metal."[7] Nietzsche goes on to call not for a new nonmetaphoric language, something which would be impossible he believed, but for a more intuitive, artistic use of metaphor, a new coinage, enabling a vibrant mythology to supplant the cramped rationalism of the nineteenth century.

What Derrida does with this essay of Nietzsche's is, in effect, to fuse it with Saussure. Whereas Saussure had claimed that the connection between words and concepts was arbitrary and Nietzsche that the connection between words and the world was metaphoric, Derrida proceeds as if the *connection between words and the world were arbitrary* and proscribes any serious attempt by language adequately to reflect the world as the worst kind of *mauvaise foi*. Nor can there be any middle ground for the faint-hearted who would waver between acceptance and rejection of Derrida's view. According to J. Hillis Miller of Yale, one of the most prominent American deconstructors, "A critic must choose either the tradition of presence or the tradition of 'difference,' for their assumptions about language, about literature, about history, and about the mind cannot be made compatible."[8]

To choose deconstruction is to enter into the vertiginous world of linguistic nihilism. There one is alienated, not only from the external world, but also from the self. No longer may we maintain traditional notions of ourselves as entities which shape language to our purposes as we weigh alternatives, reach decisions, express intentions, etc. In an extreme form of psycholinguistics, the deconstructors claim that our consciousness is rigidly determined by the language available to it, and further, seems to contain nothing but the flow of language. From there it is a short step to maintain that we are as non-centered, as much in flux as our language, with its infinite play of difference. And we are reminded that beyond just being constructed of words, our consciousness, like all other concepts, is also in turn a verbal construct — no knowable self exists apart from its fictionalized representation in language. Distinctions between subject and object dissolve as all is absorbed in the chase of signs. Unfortunately Derrida, betraying a Cartesian suspicion of the body, has little to say on the biology of the self. His followers, though, seem little troubled, and occasionally write as if human beings were merely Language's way of creating more speakers.[9]

What all this means in terms of literary criticism is that various forms of authority disappear. We may not ask questions about the author of a text, for that would imply that he stood magisterially behind his work as willful creator. An author's commentary on his own text is theoretically no more privileged than that of even the most casual reader, for meaning does not inhere in a text waiting to be teased out by the skilled critic. A text is rather defined by the interpretations it generates, and since these are infinite, the "meaning" of a test will never be resolved. Indeed, the newly minted

7.   Friedrich Nietzsche, "Über Wahrheit und Lüge im aussermoralischem Sinne," *Sämtliche Werke: Kritische Studienausgabe,* ed. by G. Colli and M Montinari (Berlin: Watler de Gruyter, 1980), pp. 880-1. The translation here is adapted from Oscar Levy *The Complete Works of Friedrich Nietzsche,* vol. II (New York: Macmillan, 1909), p. 180.

8.   J. Hillis Miller, "Georges Poulet's 'Criticism of Identification' " *The Quest for Imagination,* ed. O.B. Hardison, Jr., (Cleveland: Case Western Reserve Univ. Press, 1971), p. 216. See Vincent B. Leitch "The Lateral Dance: The Deconstructive Criticism of J. Hillis Miller" *Critical Inquiry* 6 (Summer 1980), pp. 593-607 for an excellent discussion of Miller's recent work.

9.   J. Hillis Miller, "The Critic as Host," *Critical Inquiry* 3 (Spring 1977), p. 444.

criticism immediately enjoys equal status with the original work, for both are likewise interpretations. The critic need not be seen any longer as parasitic on the work of art, but as a peer of the artist. Further, because the text, as just one more instance of discourse, offers no vantage point outside itself (whether author's intention, the discrimination of a hypothetical "ideal reader," or even the perspective of common sense) which might allow for firm judgement, parameters for criticism do not exist: anything may be said with equal validity. This constitutes the much vaunted exercise of "free play," the text as occasion for *le jeu* of the reader. Here again Nietzsche is invoked, this time as gleeful *Spieler* in the abyss, and much to be preferred to the joyless structuralists who still morosely seek the foothold of fixed meaning: "Turned towards the lost or impossible presence of the absent origin, this structuralist thematic of broken immediacy is therefore the saddened, *negative,* nostalgic, guilty, Rousseauistic side of the thinking of play whose other side would be the Nietzschean *affirmation,* that is the joyous affirmation of the play of the world and the innocence of becoming, the affirmation of a world of signs without fault, without truth, and without origin which is offered to an active interpretation. *This affirmation then determines the noncenter otherwise than as loss of the center.* And it plays with security."[10]

Now, the groundless relativism of the deconstructive project certainly bears resemblance, at first glance, to much of what Nietzsche writes on epistemology. He is quite clear that there can never be an objective, disinterested knowledge of the world, for we are all confined by nature to a "perspective." As for the deconstructors, for Nietzsche there are no facts, only interpretations. But a tension, the kind Jaspers warns us of, emerges here. For if truth, as Nietzsche seems to claim, is nothing but an illusion, why does he himself bother to expend so much energy disabusing us of various other illusions, as for example, in his attacks on the Judeo-Christian slave morality and its attendant ideals? And what of his own theory of the will to power? Would he be willing to concede in the last analysis that it too was just one more illusion? The deconstructors are content, when they notice such apparent contradictions, to regard them as a clever rhetorical device for proving one set of terms: if Nietzsche contradicts himself he does so to show that interpretations may run rampant, his point in the first place.[11] But such a strategy all too quickly gives priority to Nietzsche the epistemologist over Nietzsche the moralist. And it is in making Nietzsche primarily an epistemologist that the deconstructors misuse him.

This overemphasis on Nietzsche as epistemologist is necessitated by a strained effort to assimilate him to the tradition of French rationalism out of which the deconstructors themselves grow. They fail to see that he fits squarely in an opposite tradition, that of voluntarism, which regards the intellect as in service to the will, and busies itself much more with the disposition of desires than the acquisition of knowledge. *Why we will to know* this or that is more important than the accuracy of the knowledge. Nietzsche does bring truth into question, as the deconstructors claim, but only for the ultimate purpose of asking the value of truth for life, and life for Nietzsche is synonomous with will to power. Nietzsche spells out plainly his argument that the search for truth is a function of the will to power: "The so-called drive for knowledge can be traced back to a drive to appropriate and conquer: the senses, the memory, the instincts, etc., have developed as a consequence of this drive. The quickest possible

10. Jacques Derrida, *Writing and Difference,* trans. by Alan Bass (Chicago: University of Chicago Press, 1978), p. 292.

11. Paul de Man, *Allegories of Reading* (New Haven and London: Yale Univ. Press, 1979), pp. 116-18.

reduction of the phenomena, economy, the accumulation of the spoils of knowledge (i.e., of the world appropriated and made manageable) —."[12] Nietzsche regards as knowledge, then, that interpretation of phenomena which is beneficial to the interpreter. Here we can see that knowledge presupposes evaluation: since knowledge is nothing more than the gaze of self-interest, we tend to observe that toward which we have a predisposition and consequently have pre-judged important. The primacy Nietzsche accords the activity of evaluation leads him to the striking claim that "it cannot be doubted that all sense perceptions are permeated with value judgements (useful and harmful — consequently, pleasant or unpleasant)."[13] Building on this observation he speculates, "to what extent the basic epistemological positions (materialism, idealism) are consequences of evaluations: the source of the supreme feelings of pleasure ('feelings of value') as decisive for the problem of reality!"[14] Finally, since pleasure and power are intimately connected, Nietzsche can conclude: "How is truth proved? By the feeling of enhanced power —."[15]

What Nietzsche does here is to exempt his own theory of ever-questing wills from the relativistic swirl of illusions. He establishes a criterion, a fixed point, in deconstructive language a "presence," which allows him to organize a hierarchy of interpretations judged on the basis of their enhancement of power. Heidegger very astutely points out that by privileging his own insight — "The will to power is the last fact that we come down to" — Nietzsche himself has become a metaphysician, an establisher of first principles.[16] And certainly Nietzsche wastes little time passing judgement on the basis of these principles. What he assesses is the quality of an individual's will to power which, for Nietzsche, is measured along a spectrum extending from "healthy" to "diseased," "strong" to "weak." Using this measure further, he goes on to project an outline for a future society which would reflect these gradations of the will to power.[17] In this envisioned three-tiered utopia, reminiscent of Plato's *Republic,* class, he believed, would truly indicate worth. This, then, is the political form which guarantees his moral revolution, the "transvaluation of all values," which was the goal of his entire philosophic enterprise.

It is this Nietzsche, the one who posits the will to power as the essence of reality, the one who, having assessed individuals' levels of power, saves some, damns others with Calvinistic rigor, and finally, the one who designs a hierarchical society on the basis of his assessment, that differs so sharply from the autistic Nietzsche of deconstruction who perpetually juggles interpretations in issueless self-delight. To be sure, in attempting to show the faulty underpinnings of Western culture, Nietzsche does demonstrate that the objective truths on which we have relied are themselves merely interpretations beneficial to a particular group. But it is clear that Nietzsche only engages in deconstruction of this type as a kind of ground clearing for a new morality. The fluidity in Nietzsche comes about when he urges each of us to "[become] what one is," to exercise the will to power with no preconceived notions of where this should lead us. Of course, this advocacy presupposes that we are in essence will to power — and of this Nietzsche has no doubt. Were it not for this base of certainty, this metaphysical 'presence" (which the deconstructors deny him), his own vigorous

---

12. Friedrich Nietzsche, *The Will to Power,* trans. by Walter Kaufmann and R.J. Hollingdale (New York: Vintage, 1968), sec. 423.

13. *Ibid.,* sec. 505.

14. *Ibid.,* sec. 580.

15. *Ibid.,* sec. 455.

16. Martin Heidegger, *Nietzsche,* vol. I (Pfullingen: Verlag Günter Neske, 1961), p. 12.

17. See Friedrich Nietzsche, *The Antichrist,* sec. 57.

attacks on alternative positions would be gratuitous, his rhetoric bizarrely over-charged. It is rather precisely because he regards any interpretation as symptomatic of one's will to power that he is far from gazing on the variety of interpretations merely as infinite, effervescent play. The vast majority of men generate low levels of power; the vast majority of interpretations are pernicious.

One can only assume, then, that Derrida's book-length study of Nietzsche as a shape-shifter who affirms nothing, *Spurs* (1978), would not have pleased its subject. The ultimate focal point of Derrida's investigation is not something Nietzsche pub-lished, nor even his unpublished notes in rough form, but a jotting in quotation marks found among Nietzsche's papers: "I have forgotten my umbrella." Did Nietzsche overhear this remark, or perhaps quote it from a book, Derrida wonders. Was it a reminder to himself? A joke? Something in secret code? Maybe, after all, Nietzsche himself didn't even write it. Endless possibilities for speculation arise and we shall never be able to decide. Once this is granted, Derrida, by extension, would have us consider that the same can be said for everything Nietzsche wrote. The absoluteness of each of Nietzsche's claims is destroyed by succeeding claims as one after the other he deliberately reveals their status as so many plausible fictions. The elusiveness of truth, the "undecidability" of the text is the lesson his work conveys. Thus Nietzsche is to be especially valued because his works self-deconstruct: they are forever slyly cutting the ground out from under themselves.

In this regard Nietzsche's texts do more self-consciously what the texts of other authors do — or are made to do — despite themselves. In the hands of the deconstruc-tors every text can be made to point to its own fictionality. Oliver Twist, for example, does not derive its driving force from any concern on the part of Dickens for social con-ditions in mid-Victorian England, but rather from the tension which arises between the novel's convention of verisimilitude and passages of stagey melodrama.[18] By call-ing attention to the irreconcilability of these two sets of elements, the deconstructive critic, in this case J. Hillis Miller, makes explicit the text's inability to maintain its illu-sion of truth-telling, of reference to an extratextual world. This struggle between referential truth and fiction recapitulates a larger battle, we learn, for the two positions "might be associated with two grand antagonists in the history of philosophy: Plato and Nietzsche."[19] Similar heavy philosophical artillery gets wheeled up to deconstruct Wordsworth, Melville, Proust, and Kafka, to name but a few. Now, granted, certain authors, especially in the modern era, take the problem of language as their subject, but for the deconstructors to level *all* texts to the same linguistic dilemma is to demonstrate a reductionistic fervor that equals anything done by the structuralists, whose dogmatism they criticize. In the case of the deconstructors this sameness of res-ponse is even more troublesome, for it is they who boast of the dizzying play of inter-pretation. Ultimately we cannot help feeling cheated that *le jeu* always ends in the same score, that the liberators of criticism must know what a text will reveal before reading it. Plato the authoritarian is forever to be defeated by Nietzsche the anarchist.

Does this epistemological battle have political repercussions? Does linguistic libera-tion from metaphysical presence anticipate liberation from dominant political insti-tutions which must have been buttressed by the old logo-centrism? Derrida steps gingerly here. When asked point blank about deconstruction's affinity with Marxism, he tentatively concedes: "If one wished to schematize — but truly this is only a schema

18.   J. Hillis Miller, *Charles Dickens and George Cruikshank* (Los Angeles: Univ. of California Press, 1971), pp. 28-31.

19.   *Ibid.,* p. 29.

— what I have attempted can *also* be inscribed under the rubric of the 'critique of idealism,' " but claims that he is not yet ready to do a deconstructive reading of Marx.[20] However, Derrida is far less circumspect in the polemical rhetoric of his essays. In "Violence and Metaphysics," for example, he is quite willing to employ political terminology in discussing his linguistic revolt: "Thus, the thought or pre-comprehension of Being signifies nothing less than a conceptual or totalitarian comprehension"[21] "The best liberation from [metaphysical] violence is a certain putting into question which makes the search for an *archia* [i.e., first principle] tremble"[22] ". . . traditional 'philosophy' or 'metaphysics' . . . are therefore 'politics' which can escape ethical violence only by economy: by battling violently against the violences of the *an-archy*."[23] Not surprisingly, then, the radical implications of such prose have been seized upon by those who would link deconstruction to Marxist politics.

One of the main difficulties in such a connection is that if Nietzsche is to be retained as patron of deconstruction, he, too, must be made to seem compatible with Marx. If the deconstructors were to take seriously Nietzsche's moral and political thought, this, of course, would immediately preclude any such alliance with Marx. For while Nietzsche and Marx are both demystifiers of bourgeois pretensions and deplore the cash nexus of capitalist relations, their respective attacks are made on behalf of very different visions. Nietzsche's unembarrassed elitism in which the mass merely provides scaffolding to support a minority in the exercise of their superior wills to power is in obvious and irreconcilable opposition to the classless future foretold by Marx. Because, however, this Nietzsche is precisely the one the deconstructors never show us, their task becomes easier (although ultimately no more convincing). In making their connection to Marx they need only bring along Nietzsche the radical skeptic who overturns established hierarchies. The indiscriminate leveling they learn from Nietzsche is felt to be ample training for Marxism.

The most commonly advanced form of the case for deconstruction's affinity with Marxism is that made by Michael Ryan in his recent *Marxism and Deconstruction.* There Ryan, undoubtedly influenced by Derrida's appropriation of political terminology to the philosophy of language, argues that if we sever words from their referents and thus break down "absolutist concepts in the theory of meaning," we can destroy "all forms of macro- and microdomination."[24] As a result, he continues, Derrida's egalitarianism of interpretation implies a political egalitarianism perfectly consistent with Marxism. Ryan's anarchistic Babel, though, smacks much more of Dadaism than Marxism. The adolescent delight in jettisoning all meaning comes out even more plainly in the German deconstructor Norbert Bolz, who confidently announces: "The state is afraid of a philosophy that no longer makes sense and for which that which exists is not everything."[25] But one must wonder what sort of society could ever be grounded in the linguistic nihilism of Ryan and Bolz. And even if we were to view deconstruction as operative only in a transitional stage of history — something few of its politicizers would concede in the first place — why should what follows necessarily

---

20. Jacques Derrida, *Positions,* trans. by Alan Bass (Chicago: Univ. of Chicago Press, 1981), pp. 62, 63.
21. Derrida, *Writing and Difference,* p. 140.
22. *Ibid.,* p. 141.
23. *Ibid.,* p. 141.
24. Michael Ryan, *Marxism and Deconstruction* (Balitmore and London: The Johns Hopkins Univ. Press, 1982), p. 8.
25. See Robert C. Holub, "Politicizing Post-Structuralism: French Theory and the Left in the Federal Republic and in the United States" *German Quarterly* 57 (Winter 1984), p. 80.

be Marxist? The very fact that deconstruction can so easily be assimilated to Nietzsche ought to teach us that its association with Marxism would be far from inevitable.

Indeed, it seeems a much stronger case could be made for the basic antagonism of deconstruction and Marxism. In laying bare the economic laws which propel history, in detecting an infrastructure beneath the phenomenal superstructure isn't Marx, as his own terminology suggests, essentially a structuralist? As a positer of a reality beyond the linguistic isn't he, too, guilty of appealing to "presence" and thereby implicated in the metaphysical heresy? Why should Marx escape deconstructive censure where Lévi-Strauss, Freud, and Foucault have not? On the other hand looking at deconstruction, in turn, from a Marxist perspective, one must doubt the usefulness of a philosophy which insists on "undecidability," thereby robbing us of grounds for firm judgement, relieving us of all moral choice, and leaving us no basis for group action. Social injustices, on this view, can be regarded as no more than designs in the rich tapestry of textuality, occasion perhaps for further patterns of commentary, none of which, however, may enjoy prominence. *Who,* in fact, would there be to stand free as independent subject? So inveigling are the powers of textuality that any sense of a discrete self which might be seen as moral agent is also enmeshed in the linguistic web and rendered impotent. We are instances of language, not initiators of action. The self is just one more fiction. Understandably bothered by this abolition of the self, Marxist critic Terry Eagleton, who has become steadily more disenchanted with deconstruction, sees it as a desperate measure taken by bourgeois liberalism to preserve a sense of freedom. As individual autonomy becomes more constrained and implausible in late monopoly capitalism, the deconstructors try at least to salvage liberal delight in the freedom of plurality — even if it means doing away with the self which traditionally enjoyed the freedom.[26] Whether or not one accepts Eagleton's analysis, he is surely correct in his assessment of the political effect of deconstruction: "Political quietism and compromise are preserved, not by a Forsterian affirmation of the 'personal,' but by a dispersal of the subject so radical as to render it impotent as any kind of agent at all, least of all a revolutionary one."[27] Ultimately, then, despite the radical posturing of deconstruction's politicizers, who frequently use calculated eccentricity to disguise lack of substance, and despite the invocation of Nietzsche as the great liberator, deconstruction's implications for politics are distinctly conservative.

This conservatism shows up quite clearly in deconstructive literary criticism, though here again accompanied by a flamboyant radical gesture, this time signaling disdain for virtually all prior criticism. Special hostility is reserved for the New Criticism which dominated the Amercian academic scene in the 40s and 50s, subsequently giving way to structuralism in the 60s. Deconstructive attacks on this moribund foe are occasioned by the fact that the New Criticism represented the height of Anglo-American empiricism, the art of "close reading," something of which the structuralists with their large-scale schema are rarely guilty of. Now certainly, the New Criticism was conservative. By treating the work of art as a kind of holy icon which must be viewed only in terms of itself, the New Critics effectively ruled out contaminating considerations of the social milieu in which the work was created as well as the author's intentions (conscious or unconscious) which might have been retrieved from biography or deduced from other of his works. Each individual work in its integrity transcended all historical consideration. Thus severed from anything beyond itself, the work was compelled to derive its

---

26. Terry Eagleton, *Walter Benjamin or Towards a Revolutionary Criticism* (London: Verso Editions and JLB, 1981), p. 138.

27. *Ibid.,* p. 138.

tension internally. And in poem after poem, novel after novel, the New Critics discovered ambiguity, irony, and paradox, hallmarks of excellence. Later, weary of a criticism which seemed to them hopelessly entangled in the tightly textured surface of nuance and connotation, the structuralists sought out underlying patterns of organization. Behind this project was the desire, inherited from Lévi-Strauss' structural anthropology, to find *the* model or 'code' basic to all texts. As a result, structuralism, like the New Criticism before it, was blithely ahistorical. Homer's narrative pattern could be related by archetype to Kafka's; sociological and psychological differences between them are superficial. Like the New Criticism, then, structuralism was essentially static, conservative.

When looked at closely, however, the deconstructive criticism of these two earlier schools of criticism is not based on their ahistorical nature, but on their confidence in the existence of a knowable object. Both assumed that meaning inhered in the work — the New Critics in its totality, the structuralists in its informing elements. But if meaning were thus fixed, deconstruction free play would be banished. In order, therefore, to rob the work of its authoritarian presence," the deconstructors reduced it to the realm of general discourse. By letting the work of art flow into the continuum of all language use, the deconstructors opened up criticism (theoretically, at least) to inspection from philosophical, sociological, psychological, and other perspectives previously regarded as extrinsic. While this in itself held the promise of a more engaged criticism, the promise was not fulfilled, for their notion of textuality never allows us access to the world. Trapped in language, we become perpetual readers. In the last analysis, then, deconstruction is actually a continuation, even exacerbation, of the conservatism of the New Criticism and structuralism. Despite its Nietzschean delight in risk taking, ultimately it risks nothing.[28]

But Nietzsche had expected such counterfeiters. After having announced the death of God, Nietzsche realized that divested of its author the whole traditional moral structure must crumble and the cosmos revert to a seemingly meaningless chaos. "Nihilism stands at the door" he predicted feverishly. However, because the term "nihilism" has been comprehended in a variety of ways and Nietzsche uses it in two different senses without always distinguishing between the two, confusion has arisen concerning the extent to which he welcomed the advent of nihilism, or was himself a nihilist. The bulk of Nietzsche's remarks relevant to these questions occurs in the series of notes posthumously organized and published as *The Will to Power*. There he contrasts two types of nihilism, an "active" nihilism which struggles for the utter destruction of the decaying world order, and a "passive" or "negative" nihilism which entails "the radical repudiation of value, meaning, and desirability."[29] The first type, "active" nihilism, is taken by Nietzsche to be a welcome ground clearing of outmoded beliefs. "What is falling one should also push," Zarathustra had counseled, and the ability to do so is a manifestation of strength, a looking forward to the future, a deconstruction which anticipates construction. But in this interregnum between the destruction of the old world view and the creation of a new, the threat of "passive" nihilism presents itself. Because one interpretation of the world which for so long was considered *the* interpretation of the world is no longer believable, the temptation is to regard all interpretations as false and deny there can be any possible meaning to existence. It is this passive nihilism that Nietzsche refers to as "the danger of dangers," for it debilitates the will at just that his-

---

28. See Gerald Graff, *Literature Against Itself* (Chicago, Univ. of Chicago Press, 1979), esp. pp. 60-62.

29. Friedrich Nietzsche, *The Will to Power,* sec. 1.

torical moment when unusually great resilience would be needed to undertake the creation of new goals. But isn't this volitional impotence in the aftermath of the destruction of metaphysics exactly what characterizes deconstruction? When they lost metaphysics, the deconstructors, unlike Nietzsche, also ceded the world, and now wandering chartless, all signs pointing only to other signs, they are incapable of providing any direction toward new goals. And consistent, too, with Nietzsche's typical view of the powerless, they make a virtue of their weakness, for unwilling to choose among the welter of interpretations, deconstructors glorify "undecidability." Thus while it boldly masquerades as Nietzsche's *active* nihilism, deconstruction, in its paralysis of the will — today Derrida consoles us "the category of choice seems particularly trivial,"[30] — is clearly a perfect example of the *passive* nihilism Nietzsche warned against.

That the deconstructors fail to recognize this is due to their total disregard of Nietzsche's self-proclaimed role as transvaluer of all values, as instead they concentrate on his epistemological skepticism. Nietzsche, the organicist, regarded decadence as the taking of a part for the whole, and in viewing him merely as tablet breaker the deconstructors have offered us a truncated, decadent Nietzsche and based a philosophy of sterile hermeticism upon this reading. It is especially ironic, then, that Nietzsche, who would have been one of Derridolatry's most vigorous iconoclasts should be enlisted as prime defender of the faith.

---

30. Derrida, *Writing and Difference*, p. 293.

THE POLITICAL ORIGINS OF
ABSTRACT-EXPRESSIONIST ART CRITICISM

by James D. Herbert

The emergence of Abstract Expressionism as a predominant artistic style in the early 1950s was accompanied by a new critical image of the artist as a heroic individualist. This myth, according to which the artist created great works primarily by looking into the profound depths of his own soul rather than by responding to the world and society around him, has become the standard description of the Abstract-Expressionist artistic process. By such an account, the Abstract-Expressionist artist was an apolitical being, unconcerned with the conflicts in society due to his overriding concern with the explorations of the self.

This treatment of Abstract Expressionism began with the writing of two critics, Clement Greenberg and Harold Rosenberg. If Atstract Expressionsists such as Willem de Kooning and Jackson Pollock can be said to have pioneered new forms of visual expression, Greenberg and Rosenberg deserve credit for the creation of the critical ideas and vocabularies used to understand such works. Obviously, Greenberg and

Rosenberg differed in their interpretations of Abstract Expressionism; e.g., they did not always agree on such issues as the importance of tradition or the significance of the painting process. Yet, it was these very differences which defined the parameters of the Abstract-Expressionist critical discourse.

Although Greenberg's and Rosenberg's criticism, treated the Abstract Expressionists as apolitical figures, this image of the artist had a specific and definite political intent in its origin. Regardless of the actual motivations or beliefs of the Abstract-Expressionist artists themselves, Greenberg and Rosenberg each in their own way began by giving the Abstract-Expressionist artist a politically revolutionary role. The origins of this interpretation lie not in the first articles they wrote specifically on Abstract Expressionism, but earlier, in the late 1930s, when both men examined in depth the political importance of the cultural avant-garde.

During the late 1930s, Greenberg and Rosenberg were both closely associated with the radical leftist circle in New York City centered around *Partisan Review;* both shared this magazine's Trotskyist tendencies. Like many members of this circle, Greenberg and Rosenberg were concerned with the fate of progressive political movements in a time of increasing political regression. The emergence and frightening growth of Fascism in Germany and Italy, as well as the revelations of the repressive nature of Stalinism (further reinforced by the Hitler-Stalin Pact of 1939) confronted Marxists with a spectrum of world governments all of varying degrees to the political right. Faced with such bleak prospects in the political sphere, Greenberg and Rosenberg sought a safe haven for radical progress within avant-garde culture. Specifically, they attempted to endow Abstract Expressionism with a revolutionary political responsibility.

That is only part of the story, however, since just as the original political justification of Abstract Expressionism can be traced back to Greenberg and Rosenberg, its subsequent treatment as an apolitical artistic movement was also the result of the writings of these two men. Indeed, once a safe haven for progress in culture had been established, it became necessary to protect it by maintaining a distance between it and regressive political movements. As the possibility of political revolution waned through the 1940s and 50s, Greenberg and Rosenberg were forced to make the connection between their radical culture and the rest of society ever more tenuous and eventually to sever it altogether.

Greenberg's and Rosenberg's theoretical developments are sufficiently distinct to be examined separately, beginning with Greenberg, whose ideas developed and were codified earlier than those of Rosenberg. Greenberg's first article, "Avant-Garde and Kitsch," appeared in *Partisan Review* in 1939. There, Greenberg developed an image of the individual, not the mass, as the source of revolutionary change. Moreover, Greenberg depicted the antithesis between revolutionary individuality and the regressive mass not within politics but rather within culture, thereby treating the cultural conflict between avant-garde and Kitsch as the final battle for the continuation of social progress.

Greenberg made the connections between Kitsch (which he defined as "popular, commercial art and literature"[1]) and regressive political movements abundantly clear. Kitsch represented a way of thinking without reflection, of accepting without questioning. It was a form of consciousness particularly appropriate to the urban mass, members of which, according to Greenberg, lacked the time or cultivation to develop the ability to "reflect." This meant that Kitsch posed a double political threat. First, it

---

1.   Clement Greenberg, "Avant-Garde and Kitsch," *Partisan Review,* 6:5 (Fall 1939), p. 39.

stopped the development of consciousness in the mass. But second, it also offered itself seductively to world leaders as a means through which to control actions of entire nations since the mass unquestioningly did what their Kitsch culture told them they should. Greenberg argued that the governments of Germany, Italy and Russia used Kitsch in exactly this way, and that Western capitalists also used Kitsch as a means of manipulating the mass so as to insure continued profit. Throughout the world, then, Kitsch went hand in hand with conservative and reactionary politics.

Against this grim picture, Greenberg offered hope in the form of an avant-garde culture invested with a monumental political responsibility for it was the only existing institution with a social revolutionary ideology. Unlike Kitsch, the avant-garde insisted on continued development and this, for Greenberg had revolutionary implications. The avant-garde had emerged contemporaneously with Marxism and, like Marxism, recognized the need to move beyond the existing bourgeois order. Since no political movement in the 1930s was progressive, however, the avant-garde stood alone as the only institution in either the political or cultural realms which insisted on change. Neither the bourgeoise nor the mass, nor the mass culture of Kitsch shared this striving for movement. Isolated in its commitment to change, the avant-garde became responsible for the continuation of progress, not only in culture, but also in politics.

Greenberg argued that the avant-garde, a cultural entity, could serve as a politically revolutionary force since it corresponded to an individualistic consciousness, just as Kitsch did to the consciousness of the mass. To embody individual consciousness was itself a revolutionary act. Greenberg adopted much of this directly from Trotsky. He was familiar with Trotsky's theories on this matter through the 1938 *Partisan Review* article entitled "Manifesto: Towards a Free Revolutionary Art," which was signed by André Breton and Diego Rivera, but was actually written by Breton and Trotsky.[2] That article was largely a polemic against governmental control of art in general, and against Soviet control in particular. Trotsky and Breton argued that the artist by insisting on total freedom of artistic expression, advanced a revolutionary spirit seeking the complete emancipation of all people, which these two writers saw as the goal of revolution.[3] Moreover, in an open letter to Breton published in *Partisan Review* in 1939, Trotsky made it clear that this spirit of emancipation had to come strictly from within the individual. Revolutionary ideas in art, according to Trotsky, could not be imposed from without, even by the communist party.[4]

In "Avant-Garde and Kitsch," Greenberg adopted this Trotskyist analysis of art. Avant-garde artists were not revolutionary in that they delivered a message of revolutionary politics. They were revolutionary in that they expressed themselves freely and thereby insisted upon human freedom. The avant-garde was revolutionary in precisely the way in which Kitsch was anti-revolutionary: while the mass consciousness of Kitsch encouraged the continuation of existing conditions, the individualistic consciousness of the avant-garde recognized the need for change and offered a means of developing consciousness so as to make that change possible.

With the thriving of the avant-garde raised to the level of a political imperative, Greenberg went on to prescribe the artistic direction which the avant-garde should take within a hostile society. Since the avant-garde could not turn to the various

---

2. For documentation of Trotsky's authorship, see Breton's letter to Peter Selz, dated February 12, 1962, in Herschel B. Chipp, *Theories of Modern Art* (Berkeley, 1968), pp. 457n-458n.

3. André Breton and Diego Rivera (Breton and Leon Trotsky), "Manifesto: Towards a Free Revolutionary Art," trans. D. MacDonald, in *Partisan Review*, 6:1 (Fall 1938).

4. Leon Trotsky, open letter to André Breton, *Partisan Review*, 6:2 (Winter 1939), p. 127.

regressive ideologies within the society surrounding it as sources, the progressive artist had to find a source of content within the world of art itself. Only by so turning to a realm of one's own experience could the artist avoid regressive tendencies. This meant that art could not "depict" anything at all, but rather had to explore in paint the nature of painting. This assertion in turn led Greenberg to support self-referential abstract art.

In 1940 Greenberg expanded the concept of art taking itself as subject in specific application to painting, claiming that painting had to break away not only from bourgeois society, but also from the values of other artistic disciplines such as literature. Avant-garde painting had already taken this step by becoming abstract, freeing itself from the dependency upon telling a story inherent in representational pictures. Rejecting the canons of Renaissance perspective, Greenberg argued that avant-garde painters had to move towards the flat.[5] In this development towards flatness, Cubism served for Greenberg as the crucial historical link. According to Greenberg, Cubism broke up the complexity of three-dimensional space, returning the eye to the surface of the canvas. This endorsement of Cubism was coupled with an equally fervent rejection of Surrealism, which he saw as ". . . a reactionary tendency . . . attempting to restore 'outside' subject matter."[6] For Greenberg, there was only one legitimate standard-bearer for progressive art: Cubism. These ideas from 1939 to 1940 became the foundation of all of Greenberg's political and art critical writings for the next two decades.

In his critical reviews from 1942 to 1952, Greenberg championed various Abstract-Expressionist artists. Abstract Expressionism had inherited the mantle of revolutionary progress and stood as the only progressive force in society. Such a responsibility gave Abstract Expressionism the same political imperative which had graced the avant-garde in his 1939 essay. Yet, despite the manner in which Greenberg's theoretical ideas had weathered the war and become attached to the Abstract-Expressionist movement in the 1940s, by the late 1940s and early 1950s a problem had developed. The avant-garde in Greenberg's pre-war essays, after all, was to have caused a revolution. By the turn of the decade, however, it had become clear not only that a revolution in the United States had failed to materialize, but that the chances for one occurring were more unlikely than ever. The phenomenal success of Abstract Expressionism in American museums and art markets complicated the issue, for it seemed contradictory for revolutionary art to succeed while revolution itself failed. Greenberg was forced to reassess his political and aesthetic theories. Thus, in 1953 Greenberg reformulated the conditions for the preservation of the avant-garde so that the success of progressive culture in the form of Abstract Expressionism no longer depended on the occurrence of a revolution.

Two of Greenberg's pre-war characters reappeared with new names: The avant-garde had become "highbrow culture" while Kitsch was now the "lowbrow." But whereas Grenberg had described a strict dichotomy between these two cultures with nothing in between in 1939, in 1953 he argued that social developments following America's victory in World War II had caused a third form of culture, sandwiched between the other two, to emerge as well: middlebrow culture.[7] This was the culture of a

5. Clement Greenberg, "Towards a Newer Laocoon," *Partisan Review*, 7:4 (July-August, 1940).

6. Greenberg, "Avant-Garde and Kitsch," p. 49n.

7. Greenberg never provided a precise definition for these three categories. He wrote in a footnote: "I am afraid no other terms available fit the realities I am trying to deal with as well as these three. And the reader, I feel sure, will understand immediately what they mean . . ." Clement Greenberg, "The Plight of Our Culture: Industrialism and Class Mobility," *Commentary*, 15:6 (June, 1953), p. 563n.

new amorphous post-war middle class which turned culture into a vast, uninterrupted continuum. The political danger posed by this culture lay in the fact that it combined attributes of both highbrow and lowbrow culture so as to create a particularly socially stultifying mixture. From lowbrow culture, middlebrow culture assumed the inability to cause its audience to "interact" with its cultural products; like Kitsch, therefore, middlebrow culture stopped the development of consciousness. At the same time, however, middlebrow culture acquired from highbrow culture its claim to cultural authority. Greenberg argued that the new middle class was increasingly assuming political and economic control over society and therefore was asserting that its culture should occupy the controlling position over culture once held by the highbrow.

It was with these factors — the new continuum of culture, the lack of interaction between audience and culture inherent in middlebrow culture, and the middlebrow's assertion of cultural authority — that Greenberg accounted for the continuing tenuous position of true progressive culture. Whereas kitsch never pretended to be anything greater than kitsch, the middlebrow with its claim of cultural legitimacy exerted a drag on the progress of highbrow culture for it insisted that highbrow art be diluted down to its level of comprehension. Thus the triumph of Abstract Expressionism did not necessarily mean the triumph of Greenberg's pre-war ideas. Abstract Expressionism may have had its success on the American art markets and in the popular press, but for the middlebrow audiences of those media, its real message had been lost in the process of a popularizing dissolution.

Faced with the prospect of losing the real purpose of all progressive culture in this new post-war environment, Greenberg found one last sanctuary for highbrow culture. It could continue to progress, safe from the leveling effects of the middlebrow, only by completely isolating itself, rejecting all of society. The audience for this art, therefore, had to join the artists in their purity and isolation in order to support and understand this highbrow culture. The true art appreciator had to be a professional, recognizing the traditional standards of art strictly in their own right. Art became the province of a "self-assured, self-intelligible class of connoisseurs."[8] There was no social justification for these artists and professionals, no connection with the rest of society at all. For the sake of preserving progress, Greenberg sought to isolate artist and audience completely from the rest of society.

But in this last retreat, Greenberg had reformulated the problem in such a way as to have drastically altered the revolutionary potential of the avant-garde. He had forfeited the avant-garde's ability to precipitate a revolution. Complete isolation may have prevented society from crushing the avant-garde, but it also made it impossible for the avant-garde's message to reach the rest of society and revolutionize it. Thus the avant-garde, which Greenberg had entrusted in 1939 with the revolution needed to redeem society had by 1953 only the simple task of isolated self-preservation and protection of the traditional standards of art. "Today a large part of the essential activity of high culture consists simply in asserting a level, *its* level."[9] Through this process of the depoliticization of culture, the concept of "art for art's sake" took on a new significance. Stripped of its political justification, it simply became the axiomatic justification for Greenberg's support of the avant-garde.

In order to understand the origins of Rosenberg's treatment of Abstract Expressionism, it is necessary to return again to the pre-World War II period. In the face of a

---

8.   Clement Greenberg, "Art," *The Nation*, Dec. 28, 1946. At that time, however, Greenberg claimed that such a class did not yet exist.

9.   Clement Greenberg, "Work and Leisure under Capitalism: The Plight of Our Culture, Part II," *Commentary*, 16:1 (July, 1953), p. 55.

multitude of pre-war regressive mass movements, Rosenberg, like Greenberg, entrusted the continuation of political and social progress to the world of culture, specifically to individualistic Modernism. In 1940, Rosenberg argued that fascism threatened to bring historical advance to a halt by stopping the continued development of human consciousness and thereby "not only punish humanity for the sins of its past but also compel it to repeat them again and again."[10] The only way to combat fascism successfully was not through the "practical" solutions proposed by world political leaders — solutions which were just as stultifying to the development of consciousness as was fascism — but rather through Modernism. The Modern, for Rosenberg, was in its essence individualistic; it represented the individual's assertion of conscious control over human destiny, thus successfully breaking out of restricting patterns of the past.

Rosenberg, however, did not reach this alliance between individualistic Modernism and political progress through a description of an individual vs. mass confrontation, as did Greenberg; for him, the conflict in 1940 was between Modernism and fascism, not between individual and mass. For Rosenberg, the individual/mass dichotomy did not become the fundamental conflict in society until after World War II forced him to revise his description of politics and culture. The allied victory over Hitler, in fact, proved Rosenberg dead wrong. The elimination of fascism had come not at the hands of the Modern but rather from those nations which had based their opposition to fascism strictly upon the practical, not the Modern. Nor did the world, now free of the fascist threat, become a place where individualistic culture thrived; instead, practical culture continued to grow at an alarming rate.

From Rosenberg's perspective, practical culture, particularly in the capitalistic West, seemed to blossom into a myriad of diverse and often conflicting forms once it was free of the fascist threat, appearing in advertising, movies, popular literature, and so forth. Although such variety lacked the single-minded direct control of fascist (or anti-fascist) culture, in no case did it seem to take the form of the forward-looking individualistic Modernism that Rosenberg had championed in 1940. This lack of cultural focus made it impossible for Rosenberg to blame all regressive culture on a particular political institution, as he had done in 1940. In the late 1940s, the diversity and pervasiveness of the forces opposed to the Modern compelled Rosenberg to develop a much more complex description of cultural and political dynamics.

Around 1948, then, Rosenberg began to outline a new antithetical pole to individualistic Modernism, replacing that of fascism. This new force was an evolved form of "practical" culture. But since it was no longer primarily defined by its anti-fascist origins, Rosenberg gave it a new name: mass culture. This culture did not become the exclusive property of a specific class called The Mass; such an approach would have proved far too inflexible for a successful analysis of culture in an America characterized by increasing homogeneity and blurred class lines. It was, rather, a way of thinking available to all people, the mode of consciousness entered by all whenever they stopped thinking as individuals. Mass culture was thus any cultural artifact that communicated to a "mass," however large or small, by assuming a commonality of experience. In Stalinist Russia, only one form of mass culture existed, a centralized culture which had achieved universal domination, checking the creation of any other kind of culture. In the United States, on the other hand, the structure of mass culture was much more complex; it existed as a pyramid of conflicting and contradictory mass

10. Harold Rosenberg, "On the Fall of Paris," *Partisan Review*, 7:6 (November-December, 1940), p. 445.

cultures, much as the middlebrow had existed as a continuum in Greenberg's analysis. This commonality existed precisely because classes existed: All members of each class, be it the proletariat class or the intellectuals, shared the same experience precisely of being of that class.

This characteristic of mass culture made it an exceedingly dangerous political device. Mass culture assumed control over the part of the individual which had been converted into a class since no individual, capable of experiencing events only as an individual, could determine the nature of a mass reaction. Thus, the individual had to be told how the mass aspect of himself experienced reality, and this telling was done by mass culture. Regressive political regimes could therefore use mass culture to define the mass according to their own needs. In particular, mass culture could be used to define a reality in which the continuation of existing political institutions appeared essential to the mass. According to Rosenberg, regressive political systems such as Stalinist Russia or the capitalist West, could stop the progress of history by means of mass culture.

Against this, Rosenberg contraposed individual culture. For Rosenberg, to think with individual consciousness was to gain "a capacity for the historical,"[11] that is, the ability to perceive one's actual position in history. Of Course one was not either an individual or a member of a mass; individual consciousness existed, in varying degrees, in many people. Indeed, the degree to which one subscribed to individual consciousness served as an index of the degree to which one had avoided being forced to abandon individuality to the mass. It was to this part of consciousness which individual culture spoke. Individual culture concerned itself with "actual" experiences; the individual artist experienced something as an individual and recorded that something in a work of art. Since Rosenberg believed that the only way to experience reality was as an individual, this form of culture touched reality in a way in which the illusion of mass culture never could.[12] Individual culture therefore was the reassertion of the individual's control over his perception of reality.

Rosenberg's insistence that individual culture express only what each individual actually experienced seemed to imply that communication among individuals with different experiences was impossible. For Rosenberg, however, this clearly was not the case. One of the strengths of individual culture was its ability to address actual events which more than one individual experienced for themselves. Rosenberg called these "common situations" in contradistinction to the "common experiences" marketed by mass culture. Communicating "common situations" was a dynamic process, as various individual perceptions of a single event played off each other, furthering the development of self-knowledge. Thus, Rosenberg made the battle for the revolutionary progress of consciousness an entirely cultural conflict — a contest between mass-cultural concealment and individual-cultural revelation. But this account of Rosenberg's revolutionary process is not yet complete; still missing is his explanation of how revolutionary consciousness — preserved in culture — could be passed onto the proletariat, and in so doing, turn it into a revolutionary class.

Like Marx, Rosenberg believed that revolutionary change had to come from the proletariat as a class, not from individuals, and that the material preconditions for a revolution were ripe. A lag in consciousness, however, prevented the proletariat from seizing the moment. The inner alteration of the proletariat necessary for making it a

11. Harold Rosenberg, "The Pathos of the Proletariat," *Kenyon Review*, 11:4 (Autumn 1949), p. 610n.

12. Harold Rosenberg, "The Herd of Independent Minds," *Commentary*, 6:3 (September, 1948), p. 246.

revolutionary class was precisely its acquisition of the "capacity for the historical" that the individual possessed but the classes lacked. The barriers preventing the mass from acquiring this capacity, however, were greater than simply overcoming the domination of anachronistic political institutions. According to Rosenberg, the very nature of the revolution tended to separate the interests of individuals within a class from the needs of the class as an entity. A revolutionary had to be prepared to make the absolute sacrifice of his life. Yet any individual member of a class who possessed the "capacity for the historical" recognized the historical relativity of the revolution itself.[13] The absoluteness of the personal sacrifice seemed to outweigh the relativity of class interest. No historically self-conscious proletarian would have been willing to make this absolute sacrifice for the historically relative needs of the class. Obviously, then, for a class to be revolutionary, its "capacity for the historical" had to come from some other source than its members' self-consciousness.

Previous revolutionary classes had found this revolutionary "passion" by turning back into history veiling the relativity of their own historical position by acting in the name of abstract absolutes adopted from the past. Hence the resurrection of Roman ideals by the bourgeoisie in the French Revolution to justify their class interest in terms of "classical" eternal values. The proletariat, however, could not turn to the past as a myth for its revolution. To the extent to which the proletarian revolution represented the elimination of all illusions concerning the proletariat's historical position, it could not rely on myths from the past: the passion for revolution had to come from some other source.

That new source took the form of a new historical actor: "the American" (not, of course, as a real U.S. resident, but as a theoretical being). What made this American special was that, like the proletariat, he existed without a past; he had discarded both Europe's past and its habit of looking to the past. Yet, unlike the proletariat, the American could still act for he was the master, not the victim of the industrial epoch.. And this action became for Rosenberg the source of proletarian revolutionary passion, the missing link between the proletariat and the "capacity for the historical." By learning from the American how to act without reference to the past, the proletariat could become a revolutionary class. The American bridged the gap between the revolutionary consciousness of the individual and the revolutionary position of the mass. Once the proletariat acquired this ability to act, it could become a revolutionary class.

It was upon these theoretical foundations that Rosenberg built his description of Abstract Expressionism. In contrast to Greenberg, Rosenberg wrote very little about the movement. However his only major article on the subject, "The American Action, Painters" of M52, provided such a compelling account of the Abstract-Expressionist artist that his influence rivaled Greenberg's. According to Rosenberg, the Abstract Expressionists had two personalities: they were both artists producing individual culture as well as Americans of action. Like the practitioner of individual culture, the Abstract Expressionist rejected the common experience, both aesthetic and political, and thereby made an exploration of individuality possible: ". . . the foundering of Art and Society was not experienced as a loss. On the contrary, the end of Art marked the beginning of an optimism regarding himself as an artist."[14] For him, a true perception

---

13. It was in this context that Rosenberg wrote: "The historical is unendurable," Cf. Harold Rosenberg, "The Resurrected Romans," *Kenyon Review*, 10:4 (Autumn 1948), p. 611.

14. Harold Rosenberg, "The American Action Painters," *Art News*, 51:8 (December, 1952), p. 48.

of the world could come only through individuality, not from the "givens" of the mass. Thus, Abstract Expressionism, for Rosenberg, revealed the true individual and thereby continued the battle for revolutionary individualistic consciousness.

Even more pronounced than individuality, the overriding characteristic of Abstract Expressionists was their capacity for action. Rosenberg transformed Abstract Expressionists from artists to actors who treated painting as an act. Like the American, the Abstract Expressionist was able to act without reference to the past. Since the art historical tradition stood as a series of objects and Rosenberg considered the product of Abstract Expressionism to be an act not an object, the Abstract Expressionist needed simply to "act" in order to break from the past. "Call this painting 'abstract' or 'Expressionist' or 'Abstract-Expressionist,' what counts is its special motive for extinguishing the object, which is not the same as in other abstract or Expressionist phases of Modern art."[15] Whereas Greenberg sought to connect Abstract Expressionism with the Modernist — specifically Cubist — tradition, Rosenberg denied any connection with tradition.

For Rosenberg, artists alone were capable of fulfilling the role of "the American" in modern industrial society since they still controlled the means of their production. Thus, the Abstract Expressionist became not *a* possible "American," but *the only* possible "American" who could serve as a revolutionary model, both as promoters of individual culture and as Americans of action.

By placing the entire responsibility for the preservation of revolutionary consciousness upon Abstract Expressionism, Rosenberg was forced to protect this movement from regressive influences. The threat to impose some predetermined content on advanced art came not only from traditionally conservative camps, but also from political revolutionaries who attempted to control all other professions by tearing out and destroying "their self-concentrated centers."[16] Rosenberg went so far as to define totalitarianism as any system in which one profession (e.g., the revolutionary) dominates all others and forces them to devote their energies to "practical" ends. The revolutionary artist actively had to fend off the imperialist ideologies of such "professionals" in order to protect the "self-concentrated center" of art. Thus, art — or other action — should be practiced for its own sake. In order to fulfill his revolutionary role as protector of revolutionary consciousness and revolutionary model of action, the Abstract Expressionist had to preserve the self-concentrated center of art by making action painting an activity unto itself, isolated from the political and social issues of the rest of society. So, by a different route and later than Greenberg, Rosenberg had developed his own justification for the doctrine of art for art's sake. Despite their differences, both critics had sensed a threat to Abstract Expressionism and had sought to protect it by making it a self-referential and largely self-justified activity.

The manner in which Greenberg came to his defense of art for art's sake inevitably led him to treat the Abstract-Expressionist artist as an apolitical being. Initially, art for art's sake was a political imperative, necessitated by a need to protect the revolutionary artist. Greenberg had made the avant-garde artist, as the guardian of the continuity of progress, responsible for revolution. The lack of a revolution after the war, then, meant the failure of Abstract Expressionism as a revolutionary force. In 1953, therefore, Greenberg had to either denounce Abstract Expressionism as a failure or modify his evaluation in such a way as to free vanguard American artists from that revolutionary responsibility. He chose the second option and the Abstract Expressionists ceased to

---

15.   *Ibid.,* p. 23.

16.   Harold Rosenberg, "Everyman a Professional," *Art News,* 7:7 (Part I) (November, 1956), p. 66.

serve a revolutionary function. In so doing, he transformed the principle of art for art's sake from a protection mechanism for the revolutionary artist into the justification for an apolitical art of formalistic concerns.

For Rosenberg, on the other hand, the doctrine of art for art's sake did not lead him to make Abstract Expressionism apolitical since the action painter had never been responsible for revolution. Since Abstract Expressionists were only given the responsibilities of maintaining revolutionary consciousness and of standing as revolutionary models of action, the art for art's sake doctrine could have worked indefinitely to protect Abstract Expressionism as a dormant political force until the proletariat rose to its revolutionary role. In practice, however, Rosenberg's justification of Abstract Expressionism suffered the same apolitical fate as Greenberg's. Since individual culture operated within the common situation, not the common experience, action painting could only be appreciated by a small audience as advanced as the artists themselves — a special class of action connoisseurs. The limited size of this audience, however, endangered the revolutionary mission of Abstract Expressionism. The revolutionary character of action painting depended on its ability to break away from art and tradition. But only the connoisseurial elite could recognize this. The vast majority of society, those hopelessly burdened with mass consciousness, approached action painting within the framework of the common experience. In other words, they treated Abstract Expressionism as art and tacked it on to the tradition of Modern art. Such a treatment deprived action painting of any revolutionary viability.

This has been the fate of action painting over the last 30 years. Even Mary McCarthy, certainly a sympathetic intellectual and potential action connoisseur, could write in response to Rosenberg's action theories: "You cannot hang an event on the wall, only a picture."[17] — an attitude which returned action painting to the world of art. As Abstract-Expressionist works have continued to be "hung on the wall," they have been treated as art objects, complete with a tradition of their own. "Action" has simply emerged as an alternative label with which to discuss the formal characteristics of Abstract Expressionism within the hermetic confines of the world of art: The art work serves as a historical record of an action which accounts for the structure of the work of art. Thus, like Greenberg's, Rosenberg's version of art for art's sake has become not a device for revolutionary protection, but the justification for self-referential, autonomous artistic production, isolated from the world of politics.

17. Mary McCarthy, "An Academy of Risk," a review of *The Tradition of the New* by Harold Rosenberg, *Partisan Review*, 26:3 (Summer 1955), p. 480.

PAST OR POST MODERN IN ARCHITECTURAL FASHION

by Diane Ghirardo

If the historian has difficulty assessing events in the past, matters are worse for the contemporary critic who attempts to explore events which are still unfolding. Thus, it is not surprising that contemporary discourse about Post Modernism in architecture does not lend itself to a neat taxonomy, not least because the participants sometimes term themselves Post Modernists, and other times reject that label. It is possible, however, to distinguish between stylistic Post Modernism and theoretical Post Modernism.

Stylistic Post Modernism is that of the popular press — an architecture characterized by a departure from the stylistic canons of the Modern Movement. Its leading practitioners claim that the architecture of Modernism eschewed ornament, emphasized the expressive potential of functionalism only, and denied both history and the human element in architecture. Post Modernist buildings on the other hand celebrate ornament, historical allusions, color and humanity. To this extent, stylistic Post Modernism helped relax the stranglehold of orthodox modernism, but this primarily affected the lesser architectural talents who mindlessly repeated the dogmas articulated by Hitchcock and Johnson in *The International Style.*[1] Even Venturi, in the earliest text which Post Modernists claim as their own, repeatedly referred to the masters of the Modern Movement — Le Corbusier, Mies van der Rohe, Gropius — as having achieved the kind of complexity and interest which he argued should replace the boring boxes of modern architecture.[2]

Stylistic Post Modernism found an early expression in the Venice Biennale of 1980 organized by Paolo Portoghesi, which included the work of leading Post Modernists as well as that of younger architects. To the extent that it is possible to apply this term, Jencks is the leading "theorist" of this particular stream of Post Modernism.[3] Jencks argues that Modern Movement architecture shed its "plural traditions," but that Post Modernism, by being more "inclusivist" (that is, allowing the architect eclectic use of elements from the past), fulfills the primary goal of heightened communication. Of course, if communication is to be other than mindless babble, it must be conveying some message, but Jencks is silent on this score. Architecture has languages and conventions, says Jencks, and he suggests that these should be open to all architects to use according to their fancies.[4]

The leading practitioners of stylistic Post Modernism — Stern, Graves, Portoghesi, Tigerman — are unable to offer a richer definition of their version of Post Modernism. Their architecture constitutes a rebellion against the stylistic constraints of international modernism, as well as a return to domestic architectural practices of the late 19th century. Although they argue for a greater stylistic diversity, their architecture tends toward pastiche and, at that, a pastiche comprehensible only to the cognoscenti. One must know Boullée's fantastic designs in order to comprehend Jahn and Murphy Associates, "Argonne National Laboratories Support Facility" (1979), or Raphael in order to comprehend Tigerman's "A House Done in the Intention of the Villa Madama" (1980). The populist surface conceals a highly patrician substance.

At bottom, stylistic Post Modernism hinges on the belief that architecture is simply style, Post Modernism being the successor style of Modernism. A "classical language" of architecture, known and shared thoughout the western world, provided the secure elements for architectural composition until the twentieth century Modern Movement. From the preformulated elements of this language, architects since the Renaissance had been able to devise endless variations — but however they manipulated, distorted or played with it, they never abandoned that classical language. Modern Movement architects responded to the issue of style with the argument that since the materials, fabrication techniques, and production conditions of building had been profoundly altered, the old styles were no longer relevant or valid. A modern architec-

---

1.   Henry-Russell Hitchcock and Phillip Johnson, *The International Style* (New York, 1931).

2.   Robert Venturi, *Complexity and Contradiction in Architecture* (New York, 1966).

3.   Charles Jencks, ed., *Free Style Classicism: The Wider Tradition* (London, 1981); *Post Modern Architecture*, 2nd ed. (New York, 1977). See also my review essay, "Limitation as the Sincerest Form," *Design Book Review* 2 (Summer 1983), pp. 34-39.

4.   Jencks, *Free Style Classicism, op. cit.*, 5, p. 14.

ture, they believed, must come to terms with the reality of the new conditions of production as well as those of changed social circumstances.[5] Stylistic Post Modernism ignores all of these concerns and retreats to the security of the pre-modern, preformulated elements of the architectural language, taking a secure place as a consumer oriented enterprise in the cycle of consumption and production.

From this narrow conception of architecture as style emerges an architecture of picturesque effects aimed largely at a fashion-conscious well-to-do audience. Clients from this class can afford the elaborate and expensive decorations devised by their architects to "personalize" their houses. By its very association with the world of fashion, this is an architecture of consumption; as a plaything of the cultural Cosa Nostra, it represents a comforting retreat to the fanciful but nonetheless stable cultural images of the past. One need hardly add that these images are unblushingly aristocratic: rarely does this architecture allude to the peasant or working class past. Stern argues for the recovery of the old because, as he recently remarked, he distrusts the revolutionary in both art and in politics.[6]

Apart from the attack on the aesthetics of the Modern Movement, stylistic Post Modernists also explicitly divorce themselves from the political, social and utopian goals of the Modern Movement, such as the plans of Le Corbusier for the Radiant City or the Plan Voisin. Although such utopian visions have been largely discredited in the last half century (the suburbs of most major European cities are their worst progeny), the baby and the bathwater go down the drain together for Post Modernists. Architecture should have no political or social agenda, they argue; it is an art and a personal expression. Stylistic Post Modernists elect not to talk about ideas, or theories, but about aesthetic experiences and styles.[7] Emblematic of this tendency is a recent symposium at the University of Texas at Austin.[8] The symposium sought to explore the future of the natural and urban environment in America. Although such symposia are notoriously inconclusive, this one began promisingly enough with lawyer Henry Diamond raising the issue of Land Use legislation, Ian McHarg proposing environmental information laboratories to enable citizens to make informed decisions about issues which affect their communities, William K. Reilly exploring the tension between homogenization and the conservation of place in the shaping of American cities, and William Ruckleshaus urging a change from the ethos of produce and profit to one of preserve and protect. But when the architects came on the panel, the level of discussion sank to embarrassing lows: Stern argued for cities more like Disneyland than Lubbock, Texas; Nathaniel Owings (whose firm Skidmore Owings and Merrill has largely been responsible for the glass-box-skyscraperization of American cities) demanding height limitations on buildings which he characterized as noting more than expressions of ego; and Denise Scott-Brown, Charles Moore and Bernardo Fort-Brescia concluded the conference with squabbles about infringements on their aesthetic freedom enforced by local Design Review Boards. As in most of their in-house debates, the architects were able to divert attention from issues of substance to issues of surface. Questions about appropriate land use, the direction of urban change, and social priorities do not figure in the discourse of stylistic Post Modernists: only narrow aesthetic issues concern

5.   For a sound discussion of the Modern Movement, see Kenneth Frampton, *Modern Architecture: A Critical History* (New York, 1980), pp. 123-191, 210-223.

6.   "The Land, the City, and the Human Spirit," symposium at the LBJ Library, Austin, Texas, 12 - 13 April 1984.

7.   See Robert A.M. Stern's review of Frampton, *Modern Architecture*, in *Skyline* (October 1981), pp. 22-25.

8.   "The Land, the City, and the Human Spirit," *op. cit.*

them. Even worse, quality of construction often plays second fiddle to questions of image, as in Graves' Portland Public Office Building and Charles Moore's Pizza d'Italia in New Orleans. The position adopted by Post Modernists is as thin as their architecture; only rarely does any of their work yield sufficient substance to generate serious discussion. I have elsewhere drawn a comparison with junk food — easily digestible, cheap, lots of fat and little nutritional value — which still seems an acurate characterization of stylistic Post Modernism.

In the end, this brand of Post Modernism offers nothing more than flashy new packaging for the same old Modernist box which these same architects vigorously opposed. Part of the packaging, it would appear, is that of the architects themselves. Tom Wolfe immortalized them in *From Bauhaus to Our House, Time* featured Philip Johnson on its cover, and both *Time* and *Newsweek* regularly devote space to the latest antics of contemporary architects.[9] Architectural fashion magazines have exploded throughout the country, from the in-house *Progressive Architecture* to *Architectural Digest,* followed by *Metropolitan Home, Houston Home and Garden, Texas Homes,* and many others. Each regularly turns the spotlight on leading local or national architects, but nowhere was this accomplished with the *chiaroscuro* of *Vanity Fair's* portrayal of four leading American architects as contemporary Howard Roarks for a remake of *The Fountainhead.*[10]

Although at first blush it seems as if architects have finally arrived, in fact the profession is in crisis — a crisis which stylistic Post Modernism masks only thinly. The hoopla surrounding stylistic Post Modernism is compensatory: the architect finds himself a media darling just as his significance dwindles. For nearly every project, the architect in a sense arrives last on the scene. Contemporary practice shrinks the role of the architect from that of an active agent in the construction of the community and its structures to that of an exterior designer or an interiors specialist. Leasing agents, developers, commercial loan officers, planning and zoning commissions make the important decisions, leaving for the emarginated architect the trivial task of selecting finishes and glosses inside and out.[11] The utopian aspirations, social and political commitments, philosophical rigor and lofty self-confidence of the Modern Movement recede ever further into the distance. Stylistic Post Modernism's exclusive preoccupation with style can be seen as a pathetic acceptance of the trivialization of the profession.

Vague uneasiness and sense of crisis in the profession becomes, for the theoretical Post Modernists, almost total despair. This second branch of Post Modernism is as diverse as stylistic Post Modernism is blandly homogenized, as rich with theory as the latter is bereft of it. One strand in stylistic Post Modernism takes its cue from Italian architectural criticism and theory of the last twenty years, represented in this country primarily by Manfredo Tafuri, but which in Italy includes Massimo Cacciari, Francesco Dal Co., and others. Two major works by Tafuri have been translated into English: *Theories and History of Arhictecture* (1976, translated 1980), and *Architecture and Utopia,* (1973, translated 1976), in addition to several articles which appeared in the now defunct journal *Oppositions.*[12] Following the strategy proposed by Roland Barthes,

9.   Tom Wolfe, *From Bauhaus to Our House* (New York, 1981). See my review in *Archetype,* II, No. IV (Fall 1982), pp. 30-31.

10.   Suzanne Stephens, "The Fountainhead Syndrome," *Vanity Fair* (March 1984), pp. 40-45. The four architects celebrated in macabre black and white photographs were Peter Eisenman, Michael Graves, Richard Meier, and Robert A.M. Stern.

11.   See my forthcoming "Architecture of Deceit," in *Perspecta 21.*

12.   Manfredo Tafuri, *Architecture and Utopia: Design and Capitalist Development* (Cambridge, MA, 1976); *Theories and History of Architecture* (Cambridge, MA, 1980).

Tafuri's texts are assemblages of paragraphs loosely strung together which cannot be comprehended as a continuous, linear discourse. It is impossible to review here the complexities of his arguments or even to do justice to all of his ideas; but a few points are central for understanding his perception of architecture's place in contemporary society.

The opening words of *Architecture and Utopia* are as instructive as were those of an earlier discussion of utopia: Socrates opened *The Republic* with the words "I went down . . .", by which he signaled the duty of the philosopher to engage in the life of the polis. Tafuri begins with the words "Allontanare l'angoscia . . ." (To ward off anguish . . .), and far from engagement, Tafuri proposes detachment. Tafuri returns repeatedly to this anguish, an anguish which involves the intellectual's response to the confrontation with capitalist rationality, the motivation for bourgeois ideology, and indeed, despair at the loss of purpose for architecture. A tension exists between architecture's demand for order and the city's will to formlessness. Architecture is "a stable structure which gives form to permanent values and consolidates the urban morphology," but with the city fully open, Tafuri deems any attempt to seek equilibrium within it utopian.[13] In the wake of the Enlightenment, architecture renounced its symbolic role as well as its task of forming "objects"; it became instead the technique of organizing performed materials, only one link among many in a chain of production in the city. Both utopia and architectural ideas were instrumentalized by "capitalist rationality" in its early stages of development; and architectural ideology, contaminated by capitalism, could no longer hold out any hope for design: ". . . the entire cycle of modern architecture . . . came into being, developed, and entered into crisis as an enormous attempt to resolve, on the always more outdated level of ideology, the imbalances, contradictions, and retardations characteristic of the capitalist reorganization of the world market and productive development."[14] Tafuri also recognizes the previously mentioned crisis of the profession, and he insists that it is pointless "to propose purely architectural alternatives" within the (capitalist) "structures that condition the very character of architectural design."[15] Since capitalist rationality has robbed architecture of its historical tasks, Tafuri concludes that all that remains for architecture is to return to *"pure form"*, to forms without utopia; in the best cases, to "sublime uselessness." The profession, in Tafuri's words, now "navigates in empty space."[16]

Although he later denied that he had thus declared architecture dead, his book was widely understood as such in Italy and America; if nothing else, he had certainly established the groundwork for such an interpretation. In a sense, Tafuri turned the tables: where Modernism vested too much power in the architect to alter and redeem society, Tafuri grants none at all. Whether one must accept his either/or characterization of architecture is yet another point: must it be utopia or silence, redemption or loss, emptiness or meaning, with no possible navigation in a quieter arena somewhere between the extremes?

A more coherent, readable, and carefully explored position is offered by Perez-Gomez in *Architecture and the Crisis of Modern Science*.[17] He too discerns the death of

---

13. Tafuri, *Architecture and Utopia, op. cit.*, p. 42.
14. *Ibid.*, p. 178. Another problem in reading Tafuri is his unsystematic terminology: "capitalist rationality" and "architectural ideology" are particularly difficult to pin down to a precise meaning in his text.
15. *Ibid.*, p. 181.
16. *Ibid.*, pp. ix-x.
17. Alberto Perez-Gomez, *Architecture and the Crisis of Modern Science* (Cambridge, MA, 1983).

architecture, but in very different terms. Tafuri identifies the origins of architecture's crisis in the corruption by capitalism since the Enlightenment, while Perez-Gomez finds that the crisis took shape after the Galilean revolution, and especially after 1800, with the functionalization of architectural theory. Mathematical certainty became the goal in architecture as in other arenas of human conduct. The dominant assumption over the last two centuries has been that meaning in architecture derived from "functionalism, formal games of combinations, the coherence or rationality of style understood as ornamental language, or the use of type as a generative structure."[18] Perez-Gomez follows Husserl in detecting a split between two dimensions of meaning: the formal, or syntactic, and the transcendental, or semantic; it is the latter which architecture rejected. Scientific thought claimed the distinction of offering the only legitimate interpretation of reality, and when architecture accepted this primacy, it was ". . . deprived of a legitimate poetic content . . . reduced to either a prosaic technological process or mere decoration."[19] But, observes Perez-Gomez, the sciences fail to address the most important and real issues of human behavior, although modern man nonetheless operates under the "illusion of the infinite power of reason" and is therefore bereft of his "capacity for wonder."[20]

Perez-Gomez, like Tafuri and even like stylistic Post Modernists, comments upon the sterile and dehumanizing character of the modern city and its vacuous architecture. But Perez-Gomez also indicts the two major contemporary schools of thought for asserting the separation of structure and meaning. Capitalist formalism denies culturally based meanings and instead promotes architecture as elitist manipulation, while Marxism defines architecture as a craft resulting from typological analyses devoid of personal expression.

The one bright spot in the last two hundred years has been theoretical projects, such as those of Piranesi, which gave expression to a higly personal vision but which also criticized the dominance of scientific thought and the loss of poetry. Indeed, for Perez-Gomez, the way out is disarmingly simple: contemporary architecture must seek a "new metaphysical justitication in the human world . . . the reconciliatory mission of the architect is poetic."[21] He concludes with the observation that "while construction as a technological process is prosaic — deriving directly from a mathematical equation, a functional diagram, or a rule of formal combinations — architecture is poetic, necessarily an abstract order but in itself a metaphor emerging from a vision of the world and Being."[22]

Perez-Gomez and Tafuri represent two of the most important and perceptive architectural theorists today, but they are hardly the first to detect this loss of meaning, or even to declare the death of architecture. In some respects their conclusions echo those of Victor Hugo when he argued that since the Renaissance, architecture has irredeemably yielded its communicative role to the written word.[23] Tafuri and Perez-Gomez, then, articulate unspoken perceptions that have underlain architectural discourse for some time.

Despite obvious differences in their theories and their intellectual sources, their conclusions — that is, the consequences for the concerned practitioner — turn out to

---

18. *Ibid.*, p. 4.
19. *Ibid.*, p. 11.
20. *Ibid.*, p. 6.
21. *Ibid.*, p. 325.
22. *Ibid.*, p. 326.
23. Victor Hugo, *Notre Dame de Paris*, translated by Jessie Haynes (New York, 1955, Paris, 1932).

be parallel. Both confront the loss of meaning in architecture and the marginalization of the profession, in a sense, by retreating from engagement. Thwarted by the modern conditions of production, architecture for Tafuri must return to pure formalism, uselessness, and succumb to its own emptiness. For the architect who does build, each structure can only be a blank gesture of despair, a monument to the "pastness" of architecture and to its futility in the modern world. For Perez-Gomez, on the other hand, the architect can recover meaning only through a retreat into a private world of "personal expression and reference to the totality."[24] And indeed, he asserts that it is in "theoretical projects, rather than in buildings, that symbolic intentionality has been best embodied after the Industrial Revolution."[25] Although Perez-Gomez carefully avoids advocating that the architect draw rather than build, the conclusion is almost inescapable, and Libeskind and his Cranbrook students indeed draw it.[26] The reification of abstract personal visions occurs not in structures but on paper and in books, which for them is the only possible architecture. It is as if, having lost the redemptive promise so integral to the utopian aspects of the Modern Movement, and having been cast adrift from secure cultural values in the post Enlightenment world, architecture has lost everything. For the architect who wants to construct, the news is disquieting.

One cannot avoid detecting a certain nostalgia in the comments of both Tafuri and Perez-Gomez, although it is a far more considered one than what appears in Stylistic Post Modernism: a nostalgia for an earlier time when an architecture rich with maening was intimately bound to cultural values and institutions. Both Tafuri and Perez-Gomez correctly identify major changes in architectural practice since the Industrial Revolution, but I wonder whether the current crisis is itself as much one of perception as anything else. Distance obscures details, and so it is with history. So little of the constructions of the past millenia remain for us to examine that it is impossible to gain a sense of the building production of past ages, and what little does remain largely consists of the most symbol-laden public or private (often commemorative) structures. Although houses, barns, and chicken coops carried a symbolic change in a world dominated by *mythos,* it hardly matched the weight of symbolism embodied in public or religious structures. Likewise, a solitary Medieval or Renaissance house (even a palazzo for the wealthy) rarely expressed broad cultural and religious values with the same richness, complexity, and power as a cathedral or a town hall. The point is simply that perhaps Tafuri and Perez-Gomez demand a symbolic weight of structures incapable of supporting it, and certainly not on a mass basis. At the same time, they refuse to accept what may be painful but true: The "banal box" skyscraper of a bank, an oil company, a communications company or a multinational conglomerate may, for the future archeologist, express the values of our society quite well: production, profit, and waste.

The best and most interesting architects — Aldo Rossi, Peter Eisenman — have found a way out of the dilemmas outlined by Tafuri and Perez-Gomez without succumbing to formalism, refusal to build, or mindless games of style. Rossi has have lost the "sense of wonder" which Perez-Gomez correctly identifies as crucial for an architect. Rossi's *Scientific Autobiography* in fact is a sustained account of his *meraviglia,* and his architecture apportions symbolic meaning where it belongs: more in the

---

24.   Perez-Gomez, *op cit.*, p. 325.
25.   *Ibid.*, p. 324.
26.   Daniel Libeskind, *Between Zero and Infinity* (New York, 1981); *Chamber Works* (London, 1983).

cemetery, the school, the monument, less in other constructions.[27] And the symbolism is rooted specifically in his culture and his sense of wonder at the world. Rossi manages to accomplish this despite a full recognition of the current "crisis."[28] A younger generation of architects seems to pursue rather different but equally valid tectonic realizations of personal vision: Steven Holl, Mario Botta, Batey/Mack, Stirling and Wolford, Agrest and Gandelsonas.

Peter Eisenman, on the other hand, is consumed by an apocalyptic vision of the post-Holocaust, post-atomic bomb world. Intellectually indebted to Foucault, Derrida and post-struturalists, Eisenman argues that post fifteenth century architecture — including modernism — operated under the influence of three fictions: representation (a billboard for a message), reason (a rational source for design), and history (a mirror for the *Zeitgeist*). Ensnared in a wider crisis of value, architecture ended up bereft of legitimacy. So far, Eisenman concurs with Perez-Gomez's assessment, but he cannot accept a refusal to build as an answer. A 'not-classical' architecture, in Eisenman's view, attempts only "to be a representation of itself, of its own values and internal experience."[29] Elsewhere he describes this "negative of the classical" as the idea of decomposition, "which becomes in a particular building, such as Giuseppe Terragni's Giuliani Frigerio apartments, a series of fragments."[30] Eisenman successfully implemented his understanding of contemporary architecture in his design for the Visual Arts Center at The Ohio State University (1983). A series of fragments — traces of the past and current context — which hover between significance and arbitrariness renders a structure at once rooted in a specific sense of place, but also engaged with the "loss of center" which Eisenman so keenly perceives in the contemporary world.[31]

Despite vast qualitative differences, in some respects stylistic and theoretical Post Modernism are quite similar. They share a nostalgia for architecture's ability to represent, to have meaning. Stylistic Post-Modernists paper over the loss with representational kitsch derived from earlier times; theoretical Post Modernists either reject building in favor of drawing, attempt to embody the loss in construction, or retreat to a formalist architecture of "uselessness." It is as if, having ushered representation out, theoretical Post Modernists sneak it in again through the back door: the absence of external validation becomes the source of new representation, whether in drawings or buildings. In each case, representation remains the key element.

Both Post Modernisms likewise selectively misread history. Except for Tafuri, they reduce Modern Movement architecture to style: functionalism, the machine aesthetic, and so forth. To read their analyses, one would never know that for many European Modernists, architectural style was the handmaiden of political and social programs. Indeed, notably absent from both versions is any sense of political, ecological, or social responsibility, let alone utopian hopes. Both also tend to dismiss the efforts of architects who attempt to address these more pragmatic concerns. One Libeskind disciple sniffs at those who want to discuss the future prospects for architecture: "There's no point in talking with you until you've read Heidegger." There is a danger that disciples of theoretical Post Modernism — who typically lack the broad vision of their mentors

27. Aldo Rossi, *Scientific Autobiography* (Cambridge, MA, 1982).

28. See Rossi's introduction to Libeskind, "Semplicemente un percorso," in Libeskind, *Chamber Works, op. cit.*, pp. 13-15.

29. Peter Eisenman, "A non-classical Architecture: The End of the Beginning, the End of the End," *Perspecta 21*, forthcoming.

30. Peter Eisenman, "The Futility of Objects: Decomposition and the Processes of Difference," *Harvard Architecture Review* 3 (1984), pp. 65-81.

31. See Kurt Foster's essay in *The Visual Arts Center at Ohio State University* (New York, 1984).

— will attempt to tyrannize with their theories in a manner parallel to that exercised by the disciples of scientific rigor and rationality in the eighteenth and nineteenth centuries. Frank Lloyd Wright long ago observed that disciples tended to bastardize their master's work, an observation which still holds.[32]

A related problem concerns the recent trend in architectural theory to raid contemporary philosophical and literary theories: during the 1970s linguistics and semiotics were in vogue, today post-structuralism dominates. The impetus toward scientific rigor which Perez-Gomez identified has been supplanted by an attempt to endow architecture with an intellectually rigorous metaphysical content parallel to that found in philosophical and literary criticism. It is difficult to explain why this happens, but architects and critics who perceive themselves as members of an intellectual community seem to find architecture validated only by reference to theories current in other disciplines. The influence seems not to run the other way, either: literary critics and philosophers do not avail themselves of constructs derived from architectural theory. Architectural texts fashioned in this manner are often tortured or incomprehensible, partly because the authors sometimes fail to understand the models, but also because the distinctive subject matter of architecture does not lend itself to such Procrustean beds. The less comfortable the fit between architecture and the borrowed finery of another discipline, the more unreadable and obscure the relevant texts: but instead of dooming them to failure, incomprehensibility seems to guarantee their success until a new fad emerges, usually to be picked up with a lag-time of five to ten years after its original appearance. Insights derived from other disciplines may usefully serve as springboards for creative activity or for theoretical analysis, to be sure, or they might serve as private intellectual exercises. But the more or less rigorous imposition of rigid systems from literary theory means that often the most important issues are not even addressed, that architecture's unique character remains unexamined.

Those who engage in such enterprises seem to ignore that architecture's impact upon our daily lives, even upon our intellect, differs quite substantially from the impact of literature, for example — and we are unlikely to learn much about the nature of that impact by forcing the models of literary theory and criticism upon architecture. Even the poetic content of the greatest architecture resists explanation or codification by reference to these theories, and the designs of someone like John Hejduk, for example, are hardly enhanced, let alone explained, by the mystification which seems endemic to the current fads in architectural theory. Such enterprises, though perhaps more erudite than those of stylistic Post-Modernism, seem equally compensatory and evasive.

While the arrogance of early Modernists about the prospect of fabricating a brave new world through architecture exploded with World War II, for many architects this signals neither a refusal to build nor total capitulation to the cycle of production and consumption. For them, architecture may involve representation, but it also has many other aspects. Architecture, building, construction: they shape our environment and embody our relationship with the world. Some architects are more concerned about the way this occurs. Like Tafuri and Rossi, Jaquelin Robertson identifies the city as the locus of investigation, and like Socrates, he advocates engagement.[33] If America does

32. Frank Lloyd Wright, *Genius and the Mobocracy* (New York, 1949).

33. Jacquelin T. Robertson, "In Search of an American Urban Order, Part I: The Nagasaki Syndrome," *Modulus 16, The University of Virginia Architecture Review* (1984), 2-15; Aldo Rossi, *The Architecture of the City* (Cambridge, MA, 1981), translated by Diane Ghirardo and Joan Ockman. Of course, Robertson is neither the first nor the only one to argue such a position: among those who

not alter its processes of city building, we will be condemned to a world of Mexico Citys. Propelled by greed and laziness, building campaigns since 1945 have violated ecological laws that hold this fragile system together. Architects cannot singlehandedly save the world, but as Robertson argues, they can operate in their arena of competence with a sensitive awareness of larger concerns; they can help build more healthful cities.

Time and human efforts quelled the ecsatic utopian aspirations of early Modernists: perhaps the limited, sober position articulated by Robertson constitutes another, more modest post Modernism. It argues for architects to take seriously the well-being of the cities: it comes as a surprise that Marxist critics such as Tafuri encourage abandoning any attempt to improve the city. One current example of positive action involves architects from Texas A & M University, Rice University, and the University of Houston working to save Allen Parkway Village, a low-cost housing project, and the adjacent poor but historic Black district, the Fourth Ward, from the wreckers. The enterprise will not save the world, but it might spare one community, and it might stall the savaging of Houston in one small area. Nothing could be further removed from stylistic Post Modernism, nothing could be less glamorous, less fashionable. As Victor Hugo observed, however, "Fashion has committed more crimes than revolution."[34]

have argued along similar lines are Lewis Mumford, in many books; Jane Jacobs, *The Death and Life of Great American Cities* (New York, 1961); Peter Blake, *Form Follows Fiasco: Why Modern Architecture Hasn't Worked* (Boston, 1974).

34.   Hugo, *Notre Dame de Paris, op. cit.*, 68.

CRITICAL THEORY AND THE
CULTURE INDUSTRIES: A REASSESMENT

by Douglas Kellner

The theory of the culture indistry is central to critical theory and has had a major often unacknowledged impact on C. Wright Mills, Dwight Macdonald, George Gerbner, Alvin Gouldner, and others. Although the Institute didn't really develop the theory of the culture industries until after the emigration to the U.S., it can be traced back to Adorno's early 1930s writings on music, which stress the commodity character of popular music and its reifying effects.[1] From the mid-1930s to the 1950s, there was a

1.   See "Zur gesellschaftlichen Lage der Musik," *Zeitschrift fur Sozialforschung*, Vol. 1, No. 1-2 and 3 (1932), translated in *Telos* 35 (Spring 1978); "Uber den Fetischcharakter in der Musik und die Regression des Hörens," *Zeitschrift fur Sozialforschung*, Vo. VII, No. 3 (1938); and "On Popular Music," *Studies in Philosophy and Social Science*, Vo. IX, No. 1 (1941). Max Horkheimer spoke of the "entertainment industry" in several 1930s articles, and analyzed the differences between "authentic art" and "mass culture"in "Art and Mass Culture," *Studies in Philosophy and Social Science,* Vol. IX, No. 2 (1941). Leo Lowenthal, who earlier had carried out a study of popular magazine biographies in Germany, analyzed images of success in American magazines, noting a shift from "heroes of production" to "heroes of consumption," in which the "stars" of the culture industry played a major role. See *Literature, Popular Culture and Society* (Englewood Cliffs, N.J., 1961) and the special issue of *Telos* 45 (Fall 1980) dedicated to Lowenthal's work. A 1941 issue, in English, of *Studies in Philosophy and Social Science* (Vol. IX, No. 1) was devoted to mass communications and advanced the notion of "critical research" which combined "theoretical thinking with empirical analysis."

proliferation of mass communications and culture and the rise of the consumer society, the advent to cultural power of the commerical broadcasting systems, Roosevelt's remarkable use of radio for political persuasion, and the ever-growing popularity of cinema.[2] During the 1940s, Adorno and Horkheimer saw in California how business interests dominated mass culture. Lowenthal, Marcuse and others, who were then working in Washington for the Office of War Information and intelligence services, were able to observe government use of mass communications as instruments of political propaganda. Critical theorists thus came to see the "culture industries" as a central feature of advanced capitalism.

The culture industry is crucial to Adorno's and Horkheimer's *Dialectic of Enlightenment*.[3] The rationalization of leisure and culture it brought about was seen as parallel to the rationalization of labor and the work place, and constituted an advanced stage of the process through which the domination of nature turned toward domination of human beings. This analysis helped to explain why revolutions did not take place in major capitalist countries[4] and provided a rebuttal to Brecht's and Benjamin's positive evaluation of the new forces of mass communications — especially radio and film.[5] Adorno and Horkheimer thus argued that the culture industries inhibit the development of class consciousness and provide a powerful instrument of social control. Whereas fascism destroyed civil society, the culture industries turned isolated individuals into passive spectators.

But Adorno and Horkheimer assigned mass communications and culture too large a role in social control, and underestimated the workplace, the family, religion, schooling, the state, business, etc. as mechanisms of socialization. They claimed that "The need which might resist central control has already been suppressed by the control of the individual consciousness," and described the culture industry as "absolute master," part of an "iron system" that imposed a "ruthless unity" on culture, politics, and everyday life.[6] This thesis of the absolute manipulative power of the media presupposes that individuals constantly fall prey to mass deception and that people are completely controlled by the culture industry and the social system of which it is a part. Such a view of human nature is dubious and denies the relative autonomy of consciousness. It leads to a politics of resignation and despair and cannot account for struggles against advanced capitalism, nor for the "legitimation crisis" that is undermining ideological consensus and social integration.[7]

Like every theoretical conception, the notion of the culture industry was a product of its historical period. The experience of fascism obviously shaped the critical theorists' view of the cultural apparatus and the eclipse of political economy.[8] Subsequently, during the war, the political use and control of the media, coupled with capitalist control of the entertainment industries, provided the historical roots of the Institute's

2. See William Dieterle, "Hollywood and the European Crisis" in *Studies, op. cit.*, pp. 96ff.

3. T.W. Adorno and Max Horkheimer, *Dialectic of Enlightenment* (New York, 1972).

4. See Helmut Dubiel, *Wissenschaftsorganisation und politische Erfahrung* (Frankfurt, 1978).

5. See Walter Benjamin, *Illuminations* (New York, 1969); and Bertolt Brecht, *Gesammelte Schriften*, Vol. 18 (Frankfurt, 1967), translated as "Radio as a Means of Communication," in *Screen*, Vol. 20, Nos. 3/4 (Winter 1979/80), pp. 24-28. The theory of the culture industry can also be seen as an application of Lukács' theory of reification to mass communications and culture to show how these phenomena prevent the development of class consciousness.

6. Adorno and Horkheimer, *op. cit.*, p. 121, 124, 127.

7. Jürgen Habermas, *Legitimation Crisis* (Boston, 1975).

8. On critical theory and fascism, see *Wirtschaft, Recht und Staat im Nationalsozialismus*, edited by Helmut Dubiel and Alfons Sollner (Frankfurt, 1981). For studies of fascist culture and politics, see *New German Critique* 11 (Spring 1977).

analysis. This analysis accurately described the post-World War II Cold War situation when the media were enlisted in the anti-communist crusade and subject to tight control.[9]

The theory of the culture industry was developed just before the introduction of television, whose importance Adorno and Horkheimer anticipated.[10] Interest in mass communications was growing, and a new discipline was emerging to study its social functions. Research into mass communications in the U.S. was largely inaugurated by the Institute for Social Research, then located at Columbia University, and by Paul Lazarsfeld and his associates in the "Radio Research Project" and later the "Bureau of Applied Social Research" at Princeton and then Columbia University.[11] In 1938, Lazarsfeld invited Adorno to head the music section of his Radio Research Project. Although collaboration between Adorno and Lazarsfeld was not particularly success-ful, Horkheimer asked Lazarsfeld to collaborate in their *Studies in Philosophy and Social Science* issue on mass communications.[12] Lazarsfeld's contribution drew the distinc-tion between "administrative research" which "is carried through in the service of some kind of administrative agency of public or private character" contrasted to "criti-cal research" which requires that "prior and in addition to whatever special purpose is to be served, the general role of our media of communication in the present social sys-tem should be studied."[13] This is, of course, the conception of critical theory, and Lazarsfeld admits it. Thus, this collaboration of Lazarsfeld and his associates with Horkheimer and his group launched critical research into mass communication and culture.[14]

9.   On the control of U.S. cultural and communications industries during the Cold War, see Stefan Kanfer, *A Journal of the Plague Years* (New York, 1973); John Henry Faulk, *Fear on Trial* (reprinted; Austin, 1984); and Russell E. Shain, "Hollywood's Cold War," *Journal of Popular Film*, Vol. 3, Nr. 4 (Spring 1974).

10.   Theodor W. Adorno, "How to Look at Television," *The Quarterly of Film, Radio, and Tele-vision,* Vol. VIII (Spring 1954); republished as "Television and the Patterns of Mass Culture" in *Mass Culture*, edited by Bernard Rosenberg and David Manning White (Glencoe, Ill., 1957). Interestingly, Adorno and Horkheimer also anticipated in the early 1940s that television would become the most powerful part of the culture industry: "Television aims at a synthesis of radio and film . . . its consequences will be quite enormous and promise to intensify the impoverish-ment of aesthetic matter so drastically, that by tomorrow the thinly veiled identity of all industrial culture products can come triumphantly out into the open, derisively fulfilling the Wagnerian dream of the *Gesamtkünstwerk* — the fusion of all the arts in one work," *Dialectic of Enlightenment, op. cit.*, p. 124.

11.   On the relation between Lazarsfeld, Adorno, and the Institute, see the memoirs by Paul Lazarsfeld, "An Episode in the History of Social Research: A Memoir" and Theodor W. Adorno "Scientific Experiences of a European Scholar in America," both in *The European Migration*, edited by Donald Fleming and Bernard Bailyn (Cambridge, Mass., 1969), and David E. Morrison, "Kultur and Culture: The Case of Theodor W. Adorno and Paul F. Lazarsfeld," *Social Research*, Vol. 45, No. 2 (Summer 1978). Lazarsfeld published over fifty books and many articles that helped to found the new discipline of communications research. For a provocative critique of Lazarsfeld's paradigm, see Todd Gitlin, "Media Sociology: The Dominant Paradigm," *Theory and Society*, Vo. 6, No. 2 (1978), pp. 205-253. Although Gitlin presents an excellent critique of Lararsfeld's paradigm, he tends to neglect the critical elements of Lazarsfeld's work and fails to point out that an alternative critical paradigm was present alongside Lazarsfeld's in the work of the Institute. For appraisals of Lazarsfeld's influence on communications research see the *Journal of Communication, Ferment in the Field*, Vol. 33, Nr. 3 (Summer 1983).

12.   Max Horkheimer in *Studies in Philosophy and Social Science*, Vo. IX, No. 1 (1941), p. 1.

13.   Paul F. Lazarsfeld, "Remarks on Administrative and Critical Research," *op. cit.*, pp. 8-9.

14.   After the war, Lazarsfeld tried to secure the integration of the Institute into the Sociology Department of Columbia University, and although an offer was made, Horkheimer declined, deciding instead to return to Frankfurt. See Martin Jay, *The Dialectical Imagination* (Boston, 1973), p. 201.

Lazarsfeld became the central figure in communications research and although he was more oriented toward quantitative research and the critical theorists were more attracted to theoretical work, both groups saw the benefits of combining these orientations. Yet, while there were critical moments in some of Lazarsfeld's work, for the most part, his research and publications established the paradigms of administrative research[15] which tended to downplay the direct manipulative effects of the mass media.[16]

At that time, C. Wright Mills directed the research for Lazarsfeld's group in their study of public opinion in Decatur, Illinois, during the 1940s. In 1950 Mills followed Lazarsfeld's position that "in the last analysis, it is people talking with people, more than people listening to, or reading, or looking at, the mass media that really causes opinions to change."[17] But in his *White Collar* (1951), Mills stressed the crucial role of the mass media in shaping individual behavior and in inducing conformity to middle class values.[18] Mills also analyzed the banalization of politics in the media through which "the mass media plug for ruling political symbols and personalities" and in *The Power Elite*, he focused on the manipulative role of media in shaping public opinion and strengthening the power of the dominant elites.[19] Like critical theory, here Mills focuses on *manipulation*. He eventually paid explicit homage to the Institute for Social Research in 1954 when he described the dominant types of social research as those of the Scientists (quantitative empiricists), the Grand Theorists (structural-functionalists like Talcott Parsons), and genuine Socialists. As for the last ones Mills wrote: "I know of no better way to become acquainted with this endeavor in a high form of modern expression than to read the periodical, *Studies in Philosophy and Social Sciences*, published by the Institute of Social Research. Unfortunately, it is available only in the morgues of university libraries, and to the great loss of American social studies, several of the Institute's leading members, among them Max Horkheimer and Theodor Adorno, have returned to Germany. That there is now *no* periodical that bears comparison with this one testifies to the ascendency of the Higher Statisticians and the Grand Theorists

---

15. Although most of Lazarsfeld's research can be categorized as "administrative," his writings are full of critical remarks on media industries. See Lazarsfeld's collection of essays *Qualitative Analysis* (Boston, 1972).

16. In a study of the 1940 Presidential election, *The People's Choice* (New York, 1944), Lazarsfeld and his colleagues attempted to discover how the mass media determined political attitudes and voting behavior. They discovered that people claimed that they were more influenced by "opinion makers" in small political discussions than by the mass media. This led Lazarsfeld and his colleagues to construct a "two-step flow" model of mass communications effects. The guiding hypothesis was that influence and information "often flows from the radio and print to the opinion leaders and from these to the less active sections of the population." The paradigm held that "personal influence" was more significant than direct media effects in forming public opinion and that the influence of the mass media was thus not as great as was previously believed. The "two-step flow" hypothesis guided much communications research in the 1940s and 1950s. See Paul Lazarsfeld and Elihu Katz, *Personal Influence* (New York, 1955) and Gitlin, *op. cit.*

17. C. Wright Mills, "Mass Media and Public Opinion," collected in *Power, Politics, and People* (New York, 1963), p. 590.

18. C. Wright Mills, *White Collar* (New York, 1951), p. 333.

19. C. Wright Mills, *The Power Elite* (New York, 1956). In an analysis that anticipated Habermas' theory in *Structural Changes in the Public Sphere*, Mills discusses the shift from a social order consisting of "communities, of publics," in which individuals participated in political and social debate and action to a "mass society" characterized by the "transformation of public into mass" (298ff.). The impact of the mass media is crucial in this "great transformation" for it shifts "the ratio of givers of opinion to the receivers" in favor of small groups of elites, who control, or have access to, the mass media. Moreover, the mass media engage in one-way communication that does not allow feedback, thus obliterating another feature of a democratic public sphere.

over the Sociologists."[20]

Other critical theorists like Fromm, Marcuse and Habermas also attributed a fundamental role to mass culture and communications. Fromm's first book in the U.S., *Escape From Freedom* (1941), applied the culture industry model to a critique of advertising, mass culture, and political manipulation. He called attention to how mass communications dull capacity for critical thinking and contribute to the decline of the individual.[21] These themes were further developed in *The Sane Society* (1955) where he criticized passive, manipulated leisure activity from the perspective of the theory of the culture industry.

Marcuse was also very influential in propagating the critical theory model of mass culture and communications. In *Eros and Civilization*, he described the process through which sexual and aggressive instincts are tamed and channelled into socially necessary, but unpleasant, labor.[22] Like other critical theorists, Marcuse stressed the manipulation of both consciousness and instincts in inducing the individual to conform. Following the Institute model of socialization, he noted the decline of the family as the dominant agent of socialization and the rise of the mass media. He continued to stress the manipulative character of mass communication and culture in *One-Dimensional Man* as "new forms of social control" which engender "false needs" and "one-dimensional" thought and behavior necessary for the smooth reproduction of advanced capitalism.

In his first major work in 1962, Habermas analyzed the rise of the culture industries and decline of the *public sphere*,[23] and in his later works he further developed this concept which mediated between the state and civil society.[24] Habermas' account of the disintegration of the bourgeois public sphere and the classical critical theory model of the culture-industry overlap. Both posit contemporary mass media as instruments of manipulation in the hands of the state and giant corporations, and both posit an increasingly privatized, passive, and manipulated audience that is the object of social control.

These analyses of the culture industries have led many U.S. social theorists to pay close attention to the role of mass communications and culture. Thus, Riesman, for example, dedicated a book to Fromm, who was also his analyst, and Adorno is reputed to have claimed that Riesman popularized his ideas.[25] And Gouldner has stated: "My relation to the first generation of the Frankfurt School, for and with whom I worked while they were in exile in the U.S., has been a lasting, if hybridized influence."[26]

20.   C. Wright Mills, "IBM Plus Reality Plus Humanism = Sociology," in *Power, Politics, and People, op. cit.*, p. 572.

21.   Erich Fromm, *Escape From Freedom* (New York, 1941), p. 128ff. This book helped introduce critical theory to the U.S. See Dwight Macdonald's review in *Common Sense*, Vol. 11 (Jan. 1942), p. 29.

22.   Herbert Marcuse, *Eros and Civilization* (Boston: 1955).

23.   Jürgen Habermas, *Strukturwandel der Offentlichkeit* (Neuwied and Berlin, 1962).

24.   Jürgen Habermas, *Theorie des kommunkativen Handelns* (Frankfurt 1981), translated by Thomas McCarthy (Boston, 1983). For critiques of Habermas' theory of the public sphere, see Oskar Negt, "Mass Media: Tools of Domination or Instruments of Liberation?", translated in *New German Critique* 14 (Spring 1978), pp. 61-82.

25.   Riesman dedicated *Abundance for What? and Other Essays* (Garden City, N.Y., 1964) to Fromm. On Adorno's perception of the unacknowledged impact of critical theory on Riesman's work, Martin Jay writes: "An attempt in 1955 to get him to contribute to a book on David Riesman's *The Lonely Crowd* produced a negative response because he considered Riesman a popularizer of his and Horkheimer's work." Based on a letter from Adorno to Lowenthal, Sept. 22, 1955 and cited in "The Frankfurt School in Exile," *Perspectives in American History* VI (1972), p. 368.

26.   Alvin W. Gouldner, *The Dialectic of Ideology and Technology* (New York, 1976), p. 22.

While Lazarsfeld's model became the "dominant paradigm" in mainstream communications theory, there have been also some critical approaches. Adorno's 1954 article "How to Look At Television" focused on the standardization, predictibility, and repetitiveness of television conventions and stereotypes. In the transition to the administered society, mass culture devalued the inwardness and internal psychological conflicts prevalent in older cultural forms, and instead encouraged conformity, other-directedness, and extroversion; the culture industries aided in this process by eliminating suspense and unresolvable conflicts, and by making fun of "introverts" while celebrating the happy conformity of well-adjusted, or resigned, character types. The constant repetition of the same values and messages assumed an increasingly authoritarian ring operating in a way similar to "psychoanalysis in reverse."

Some television critics adopted the critical theory model. Gerbner, who helped Adorno with the research in his television article and later became head of the Annenberg School of Communications, called television "the central cultural arm of American society."[27] In his view, television had supplanted religion as the chief producer of dominant cultural myths and symbols. His approach combined Lazarsfeld's quantative methods with Adorno's cultural critique; like both, he and his school focused on the social roles and functions of television. Yet, their approach is closer to critical theory since they were more interested in analyzing the dominant images and messages and in ascertaining the central social functions than in measuring more specific and localized effects.

Although their model of society and the media is similar to critical theory, other critics such as Barnouw, Smythe and Schiller have adopted a much more empirical and historical approach. They tend to focus on the political economy of the communication industry rather than on its cultural forms, messages, or general effects on audience socio-psychology. Thus, Smythe has objected to the overemphasis on ideology and culture in the focus of the Frankfurt school[28] and Schiller has analysed the media both as instruments of cultural imperialism and of social control.[29] Similarly, Barnouw documents how corporate control of the broadcasting industry from the beginning structured the system of communications and made it a powerful vehicle of social control in the hands of a political-economic elite.[30]

On the whole, critical communications research has taken a more historical, empirical, and economic direction in contrast to the theoretical and philosophical emphasis of critical theory. Thus, the impact of the culture industry theory on communications research is often indirect. Debates over "popular culture," on the other hand, can be more directly traced back to critical theory.

Whereas Horkheimer and Marcuse never really analyzed mass culture, Adorno and Lowenthal developed both global theories of mass culture and carried out detailed studies. Their work influenced the first major anthology on *Mass Culture* (1957). This anthology contained articles by Adorno, Lowenthal, Kracauer, and Lazarsfeld, as well as many other studies influenced by the critical theory model. One of the editors,

27.   George Gerbner and Larry Gross, "Living with Television," *Journal of Communication*, Vol. 26, No. 2 (Spring 1976). In the original 1954 publication of his article on television, Adorno thanks Gerbner for his help.

28.   Dallas Smythe, "An Analysis of Television Programs," *Scientific American*, Vol. 184, No. 6 (June 1951), and his later articles collected in *Dependency Road: Communications, Capitalism, Consciosness, and Canada* (Norwood, N.J., 1981).

29.   Herbert Schiller, *Mass Communications and American Empire* (Boston, 1971); *The Mind Managers* (Boston, 1973); and *Communication and Cultural Domination* (White Plains, N.Y., 1976).

30.   Erik Barnouw, *Tube of Plenty* (New York, 1975) and *The Sponsor* (New York, 1977).

Rosenberg, attacked mass culture in terms reminiscent of Adorno and Horkheimer, while the other editor, White, defended it as the culture of the people appropriate to a democratic society. Lowenthal's own essay in *Mass Culture* contrasted mass culture with "genuine art" and attacked modern social science's approach to culture and communication as an "applied asceticism."[31]

Macdonald's influential journal *Politics* published frequent criticisms of mass culture by C. Wright Mills, Paul Goodman, and others. In fact, Macdonald's own approach to "popular culture," outlined in the first issue of the journal, is remarkably similar to the culture industry theory. He distinguished between "folk art" which was "hitherto the culture of the mass of common people" which is shaped by the people themselves and satisfies their own needs; "high culture" that is "chronicled in textbooks"; and *"popular culture"* which "is imposed from above."[32]

Against these critiques of mass culture, Shils attacked its critics as elitist radicals who had no sympathy for the tastes of the masses. He signaled out Macdonald and Horkheimer and his circle as "marxian socialists" leading the onslaught against mass culture. According to him, disappointed Marxian hopes led these radicals to turn with a fury against mass culture which they blamed for seducing the proletariat away from its revolutionary vocation. These "European anti-American intellectuals" were full of unjustified contempt for the common people and understand neither the culture, people, or society that they so vehemently criticize. Their picture of the victims of mass culture had its parallel, Shils claims, in the German romantic, elitist, and Marxian attacks on industrialism. All the criticisms, Shils confidently maintains, are fuelled by "the frustrated attachment to an impossible ideal of human perfection, and a distaste for one's own society and for human beings as they are."[33]

Critical theory claimed throughout that the uncritical celebration of mass culture promoted an uncritical, conformist attitude toward the established society. Theory could help break the hold of mass culture by de-naturalizing it. During the 1960s and 1970s there was a renewed interest in critical theory as well as criticisms of the Institute's theory of mass culture. Thus, for example, Enzensberger stressed the similarity of critical theory's analysis with conservative criticisms of mass culture and condemned them for their cultural elitism.[34]

While the theory of the culture industry contains a compelling vision of the media and of popular culture as manipulative instruments of social control, it has serious limitations. In general, classical critical theory texts on mass communication and culture lack adequate historical analysis, are superficial in their treatment of the political economy of the media, and do not provide an adequate model of cultural interpretation. Although critical theory accurately described the communications and culture industries during the era in which the theory was formulated, it lacks specific historical analysis that would clearly root the conception of the culture industries within a particular socio-historical conjuncture. Instead, Adorno's and Horkheimer's conception of culture industries is quite ahistorical, perhaps reflecting "Adorno's secret hostility

---

31.   Leo Lowenthal, "Historical Perspectives of Popular Culture," in *Literature, Popular Culture, and Society, op. cit.*, p. 52.

32.   Dwight Macdonald, "A Note on Popular Culture," in *Politics,* Vol. 1, No. 1 (1944), pp. 20ff.

33.   Edward Shils, "Daydreams and Nightmares: Reflections on the Criticism of Mass Culture," *Sewanee Review,* Vol. XLV, No. 4 (Autumn 1957), pp. 596-606.

34.   See Alan Swingwood, *The Myth of Mass Culture* (London, 1977; Diane Waldman, "Critical Theory and Film," *New German Critique* 12 (Fall 1977); and Hans Magnus Enzensberger, "Constituents Toward a Theory of the Media" in *The Consciousness Industry* (New York, 1974).

toward history."[35] It indiscriminately generalizes from Nazi Germany and New Deal America without focusing on the specific historical features that produced various types of culture industries in different capitalist countries. Hence, a new critical theory of culture and mass communication must achieve more historical specificity.

When conditions changed in the 1960s, the application of classical critical theory became problematic. The growing centrality of capitalist markets — theorized by the Institute as the power of capital to control increasing domains of life — contributed to both the differentiations and internal contradictions of media content and forms. Moreover, the social struggles from the 1960s to the present were increasingly acted out through the media which became much more contradictory, complex, and controversial. Indeed, in the 1960s an entire generation, socialized through the culture industries, rebelled against middle class society. Was the rebellion fueled in part by rebellious forms of popular music, film images of James Dean, Marlon Brando and other film rebel heroes, media images of beatniks and bohemia, as well as by the advertisements for sex, drugs, student rebellion, and the counterculture which the culture industries broadcast in the 1960s as they sought to capture an audience by addressing the issues and symbols of the day? It is conceivable that attempts to de-legitimize student rebellion and the counterculture may have surreptitiously advertised it.

The key point is that the model of the culture industry cannot account for these events. The media mediate social conflict and negotiate social change. Thus they reflect, express, and articulate social reality in a mediated fashion. Since the terms of media mediation — social reality — enter into media discourse, the culture industries must draw upon an often nasty and conflictual reality in order to gain an audience and credibility. In these ways, the culture industries may deflate or undermine the ideological illusions of their own products and however unwittingly engage in social critique and ideological subversion.

Whereas the culture industries were once instruments of ideological conformity and cultural homogenization, they are now increasingly theaters for social conflict and instruments of cultural diversity. This is in part due to the diversifications of media markets which in desperate pursuit of profitability target audiences on the margins. These new audiences may be different from the amorphous and undifferentiated "mass" that continues to be the center of mass society, but which is ever more surrounded by marginal groups and differences threatening the breakup of social homogenization and integration. Though the culture industries may provide something for everyone so that everyone will stay in their place, cultural differentiation may still have unintended and radicalizing effects by opening the spaces for alternatives. These developments require a more subtle critical theory which analyzes, evaluates, and discriminates between the products and social functions of the new media (such as cable TV and home video recorders) and the changing content of mainstream media.

Today there is really no natural center of the media society and no one, unitary, homogeneous ideology or way of life broadcast. Whereas there are few radical alternatives which enter into the culture industry spectacles, there is enough novelty and contradiction to splinter the ideological hegemony which was once the fragile accomplishment of the culture industry, and a critical theory today must attend to this phenomenon. Indeed, new technologies and communications media require new theories of culture and communications. Whereas, the Institute theory of the culture industry describing the dominant communications media as instruments of mani-

---

35.   Hans Mayer, cited in Andreas Huyssen, "Introduction to Adorno," *New German Critique* 6 (Fall 1975), p. 3.

pulation and social control was relatively accurate when broadcast and national print media were tightly controlled by the state and capitalist class, it is not clear that the culture industry model continues to be applicable when new communications technologies like cable and public access television, satellite and direct broadcasting systems, personal computers and decentralized users networks, print media of all ideological tendencies and special interests, and new interactive technologies (CB radios, call-in television and radio shows, video recorders and cameras, etc.) are appearing. Whereas capital and the state continue, for the most part, to control these technologies and to use them for profitability and social control, the technologies also contain possibilities for interaction that can be used against the interests of the dominant elites.

Moreover, as a method of cultural interpretation and criticism, the culture industry model is deeply flawed. Rather than seeing artifacts of popular culture as simple expressions of hegemonic ideology and ruling class interests, it is more useful to see popular entertainment as a complex product that contains contradictory moments of desire, as well as displacement and repression, articulations of hopes and fears, dreams and nightmares, ideological celebrations of the status quo and utopian transcendence, moments of rebellion and its attempted containment.[36] Recent studies of popular culture also perceive how social conflicts enter into works of popular entertainment and see culture as a contested terrain rather than a field of one-dimensional manipulation and illusion.[37]

The classical critical theory approach to cultural interpretation, especially Adorno's work, is for the most part denunciatory, attacking the ideology and retrogressive effects of radio, popular music, films, television, etc. In this sense, the model of cultural interpretation and criticism is remarkably similar to crude Marxian critique of ideology which restricts cultural analysis to denunciation of ideology. Part of the problem is that for Adorno and Horkheimer, the artifacts of the culture industry were simply beneath contempt. In *Minima Moralia*, Adorno writes: "Every visit to the cinema leaves me, against all my vigilance, stupider and worse."[38] Such disdain is unable, however, to understand what gratifications popular culture actually provide and what needs it serves, in however distorted a fashion. This attitude also leads Adorno, Horkheimer, and Marcuse to neglect analyzing specific films, television programs or artifacts of popular culture since they presume in advance that such artifacts are simply a debased form of culture.

But while popular music may, as Adorno argued, exhibit features of commodification, reification, and standardization which may in turn have retrogressive effects on consciousness, such a theoretical optic cannot account adequately for the genesis and popularity of popular music. Since music is the most non-representational of all arts, it can more directly express emotions of pain, rage, joy, rebellion, sexuality, etc. Moreover, the production of popular music was often carried out by oppressed groups, like blacks or hispanics, or by working class whites or marginalized youth. Much popular music thus articulates rebellion against standardization, conformity, oppression, etc., however much this oppositional articulation is contained in standard musical forms. Moreover, the forms of reception of popular music have frequently been dances and festivities in a context of transgression of propriety through drinking, making love,

36.   See Fredric Jameson, "Reification and Utopia in Mass Culture," *Social Text* 1 (Winter 1979), pp. 130-148.

37.   See Peter Biskind, *Seeing is Believing: How I Stopped Worrying and Came to Love the Fifties* (New York, 1983).

38.   Theodor W. Adorno, *Minima Moralia* (London: 1974), p. 25.

wildly dancing, communally singing, etc. Ragtime, jazz, bop, swing, and rock have been more at home in the brothel, dance-hall, or bedroom than His Master's Voice in the living room. Though punk and hard rock can provide appropriate background for young fascists and rednecks, it can also provide the social cement for a culture of political mobilization — as the Rock Against Racism and *Rock gegen Rechts* concerts in England and Germany proved. And music like reggae can be as bound up with a sub-culture of protest as much as with the commodification of culture for profitability and harmless catharis.

The problem with the critical theory model is that it often substitutes denunciation and dismissal for careful analysis and discriminate critique. For example, the initially feeble critical response of the German Left to the U.S. television series *Holocaust* shows the limitations of the critical theory model. Many German leftists initially attacked the series merely by attacking its "commodity form," its being a debased example of U.S. television, and its "bourgeois ideology" without considering the possibility that popular television may have progressive effects.[39] A more adequate analysis would have to discuss the series' ability to elicit critical historical remembrance, its critical and graphic portrayal of the horrors of fascism, its implicit celebration of armed resistance to fascist tyranny, and its ability to foster identification with the victims of fascist horror — as well as its ideological limitations and contradictory effects.[40] No doubt the series could be passively consumed, serving to help reinforce the passive spectator of media spectacles, but, in fact, it elicited a spirited discussion of fascism and the holocaust in both Europe and the U.S. And when such a series is seen together in a group which discusses what is being protrayed, or if it is part of classroom activity for young people who have little concrete sense of fascism and its insane persecution of Jews, then such television programs might have critical uses. Obviously, *Holocaust* has serious limitations and omissions, but a critical theory approach that sees nothing but ideology and media manipulation in culture industry productions fails to produce a multi-dimensional critical perspective that can analyze the full range of messages and cultural effects in the artifacts of popular culture.

Likewise, analyses of contemporary Hollywood films should not simply limit themselves to denouncing bourgeois ideologies and escapist functions. Even conservative films often provide insight into dominant ideologies and sometimes unwittingly provide images of social conflict and opposition. Recent studies of Hollywood films show how this medium of commercial culture can provide a conflict of representations between competing social ideologies over the last several decades. Particularly, from around 1967 to the present, a variety of competing ideological standpoints have appeared in mainstream film. Consequently, there is no one monolithic, dominant ideology which the culture industries promote, and indeed the conflicting ideologies in contemporary culture industry artifacts point to continuing and intensifying social conflict within capitalist societies.

The classical critical theory model of the culture industry therefore fails both to emphasize the importance of analyzing possible oppositional, subversive, utopian and emancipatory moments in popular culture as well as failing to provide theories of oppositional and emancipatory uses of the media and cultural practices. There is

39.   See the discussions of the left reception and other debates over the effects of *Holocaust* in the articles in *New German Critique* 19 (Winter 1980) and *Telos* 42 (Winter 1979-80).

40.   See Andreas Huyssen, "The Politics of Identification" and Siegfried Zielinski, "History as Entertainment and Provocation" in *New German Critique* 19 for readings of *Holocaust* that go beyond the sort of one-dimensional denunication of artifacts of popular culture practiced by some devotees of critical theory.

neither a strategy for cultural revolution as is found in Brecht, Benjamin, and Enzensberger, nor is there a media politics to overcome the harmful effects that Adorno and Horkheimer describe. Indeed, a radical media politics should replace the pessimistic denunciation found in classical critical theory. Part of the problem is that Adorno and other critical theorists rigidly juxtapose their concepts of "authentic art" — modelled on masters of the avant garde like Schonberg, Kafka, and Beckett — against mass culture and denounce mass culture for failing to have the qualities which they find in their preferred aesthetic models. But the very distinction between "high culture" and "popular culture" has come under attack, and it seems perverse to expect products of the culture industries to have the qualities of works of previous "high culture" or the avant-garde.

Instead of juxtaposing a supposedly debased "popular culture" against supposedly emancipatory "authentic art," critical theory today should take the artifacts of the culture industries as seriously as critical theorists and other elite critics take so-called "high culture." That is, critical theory today should engage in much more detailed and probing studies of mass communications and culture. Although classical critical theory provides indispensable theoretical tools to analyze the ways in which the culture industries serve the interests of capitalism, what is needed today is the development of new critical theories of culture and communications which also articulate contradictions within these areas, and between the media, economy, and state. Such are some of the challenges facing those of us who wish to carry on the tradition of critical theory in a different theoretical and historical context.

KELLNER'S CRITICAL THEORY:
A REASSESSMENT

by Moishe Gonzales

Frustrated radicals who have managed, over the last 20 years of chaotic growth and revolutionary restructuring of higher education, to translate their "revolutionary rhetoric" only into tenured academic positions, tend to have an ambivalent relation to critical theory. On the one hand, they are irresistibly attracted to it. In a sophisticated scholarly fashion especially appropriate to their new professional status, critical theory addresses all those troublesome cultural questions that were becoming increasingly urgent but which traditional brands of Marxism could not readily tackle through standard materialist approaches. But, on the other hand, they were never able to digest critical theory's discouraging political implications which, for all practical purposes, effectively undermined most radical conventional wisdom and assumptions — assumptions that even such critical theorists as Adorno and Marcuse could not always do without. The one-dimensional or totally administered society analyzed by critical theory simply could not be seen headed toward any kind of classless utopia, thus reducing most radical projects to futile exercises in speculative idealism. If the culture industry did in fact successfully freeze the social consciousness of atomized and fragmented individuals, thus preventing the process of reification from proceeding to its logical revolutionary explosion so elegantly deduced by Lukács, then radicals had few political options other than to slide, like most of their conformist peers, further into middle class, middle age, and an expanding middle waist.

Obviously, recognition of such a predicament is not conducive to a healthy radical self-image. So critical theory in general — and the analysis of the culture industry in particular — had to be modified to fit better into the radical ideology of *de facto* conformist academics, whose professional future, however, was predicated on the indefinite lingering of allegedly irresolvable social conflicts and contradictions. While deemed appropriate for the 1940s and '50s, critical theory's account of the culture industry had to be judged obsolete for the '80s, even though, if anything, the role of the media had become even more pervasive and manipulative than before.

So far so good. After all, a bit of ideological agit-prop to legitimate one's own tenuous professional status is part and parcel of the New Class' version of the American way of life. In the same way that the doctor needs sick patients and the bureaucrat needs helpless dependent clients, so the academic radical needs constantly intensifying social conflicts to analyze, to elaborate, and, in extreme proto-Leninist cases, even to attempt to resolve. What is problematic and annoying in self-apologies such as Kellner's, consequently, is not so much their self-serving character so much as the theoretical sloppiness evident in their construction.

Consider the structure of his analysis. Allegedly, critical theory "denies the relative autonomy of consciousness;" leads to resignation and despair; "cannot account for struggles against advanced capitalism" or for "the legitimation crisis that is undermining ideological consensus and social integration;" "lacks historical analysis;" provides "a superficial treatment of the political economy of the media;" and "has no adequate model of cultural interpretation." For Kellner, on the other hand, the media tend to reflect social reality and thus depict social conflicts and contradictions; this very role, he suggests, may have been responsible for the 1960s, when the media had to integrate outsiders in the desperate competitive search for new audiences. In addition, he claims that new techological developments "contain new possibilities for interaction that can be used against the interests of the dominant elite." Popular music remains a main avenue for social protest in Kellner's world, and for him, the impact of the TV miniseries *Holocaust* and its emancipatory possibilities is sufficient proof of his notion that the media no longer advocate any "monopolistic ideology" but portray how "conflicting ideologies in contemporary culture industry artifacts point to continuing and intensifying social conflict."

It is important to analyze these claims in detail, not out of deference to the compelling force of Kellner's argument (he offers none, other than a string of groundless ideological statements for which he offers no evidence or substantiation), but because so many of the remaining aging radicals mothballed in archaic academic institutions persist in advocating at least some of them.

Apparently Kellner finds it too pedestrian to say forthrightly what he means — i.e., that people are probably not as dumb as critical theorists supposed. He has to mystify this simple claim by deploying miserable Althusserianisms such as "the relative autonomy of consciousness." It may be impressive, but unfortunately it is also irrelevant. Critical theory never held that people were dumb, only that the culture industry systematically cretinized them by keeping them from attaining an adequate understanding of their own predicament. While this realization may lead Kellner to resignation and despair, it did not depress Adorno, Marcuse or Lowenthal a hell of a lot. If anything, they managed to establish quite a reputation as *bon vivants*, living, to use

Lukács' invidious description, in the Grand Hotel on the edge of the abyss. While the precise distance from the sweeping veranda to the precipice may be debated, there has never been any question about the Grand Hotel. Marcuse's love for whiskey and good cigars was as well known as Adorno's roving eye.

What bothers Kellner most, though, is that the theory of the culture industry implies a relatively pacified populace just like one finds anywhere in America or Western Europe. He would much prefer that there be "struggles against advanced capitalism," which presumably critical theory would be helpless to account for. But what struggles is he talking about? In the name of what? Socialism or communism? If there is any consensus in the U.S. today it is that the welfare state, that pitiful capitalist version of socialism, is dead — even in the mangled form introduced by the New Deal. If there are any struggles, they are *entirely* about redistribution. The logic of the system, although rotten as ever, is no longer subject to question.

The real tragedy of the overwhelming success of the culture industry is precisely that it has managed so well to make unthinkable any hint that qualitative alternatives may exist. Thus, Kellner must be daydreaming when he trots out that old chestnut about "the legitimation crisis that is undermining ideological consensus and social integration." Perhaps Habermas can be excused for recycling this dubious Weberian notion in the immediate aftermath of 1968, when the student and the anti-war movements had briefly challenged the system. But there's no excuse for Kellner hauling it out today. The irony of Habermas' analysis is that, of the four crises he describes in the book of that title, legitimation is the only one that definitely does not obtain now. Interestingly, this is because Habermas, like Kellner, cannot really deal with the troublesome implications of alienation or the cretinizing effects of the culture industry, so he ends up postulating a kind of ideal individuality that exists only in introductory economics texts. Whereas a strong case can be made for a rationality crisis, a motivational crisis, and even an economic one, it is impossible to argue that there exists in the U.S. today any legitimation crisis.

Kellner's other charges — that critical theory's analysis of the culture industry lacks historical specificity, an adequate account of the political economy of the media, and an appropriate model of cultural interpretation — are even more absurd. Of course, the account best describes the 1930s and 1940s. Things are changed today. But this does not mean the original account was wrong. Rather, the effects of the culture industry have altered the earlier situation. In the 1930s and 1940s the main objective was the homogenization of consciousness to rationalize distribution in keeping with what could profitably be produced by new, capital-intensive mass technologies. Once that was accomplished, the objective had to be refocused. New needs for new commodities had to be created to retain the economy of scarcity needed to legitimate the performance principle and ultimately capitalism itself. To do so, it became necessary to go beyond the 1950s stereotypes and reintroduce a minimal negativity that had been entirely eliminated before. The media did open up, but only to better manipulate the over-homogenized consciousness. Otherness, particularity and difference were reintroduced, but only to help sell still more junk in a society already saturated with it.

It is not clear what political economy of the media Kellner thinks critical theory ought to have provided. But in a situation where television is pretty well controlled by three major networks, where newspaper ownership is increasingly concentrated in the hands of a couple of chains and where what is printed in even the independently owned papers is determined largely by what runs over the AP or UPI wires, where

Hollywood is controlled just as tightly, and where the book publishing industry is increasingly centralized, one wonders what more political economy is necessary to understand the logic of the media. The importance of advertising has not declined and its main objective — profitability — has not changed. So what was wrong with the old analysis? Kellner conveniently forgets all discussions of monopoly capital during the past half century and, with a straight face, writes about a situation in which the media, "in desperate pursuit of profitability," set aside their ideological priorities and unwittingly depict objective social conflicts and contradictions. In so doing, they allegedly contribute a possible radicalization of their viewers and readers. This, presumably, is the kind of more sophisticated political economy of the media that he is calling for: a simplistic return to a crude Marxist analysis of a long-gone competitive capitalism privileging economics in a silly base-superstructure model.

The covert recycling of a crude brand of orthodox Marxism is not limited to political economy. Things deteriorate further when Kellner broaches questions of epistemology and of aesthetic theory. The up-to-date theory of the media he calls for to go beyond the analysis of the culture industry turns out to presuppose the long discredited theory of reflection, a late-Lukácsian defense of realism, and a neo-romantic aesthetics of folk culture. In language not all that different from what the old Lukács used to defend the bourgeois realism of, e.g., Balzac, Kellner thinks that the media "reflect, expose, and articulate social reality" so that they must "draw upon an often nasty and conflictual reality" and, consequently, "unwittingly engage in social critique and ideological subversion." This is not the place to re-enact epistemological battles won decades ago against the Soviet state-sponsored idiocies of *Materialism and Empirio-criticism* or to take seriously Kellner's version of "socialist realism." The media do engage in social critique, but only, at best, to facilitate the further rationalization of advanced capitalism by eliminating social anachronisms or lingering dysfunctional features, such as racism, sexism and any kind of discrimination that resists the collective homogenization that is already, for the most part, fairly well accomplished. Far from subverting anything other than obsolete traditional remnants, this social critique is one of the most powerful legitimating forces at work, positing advanced capitalism, *as it is*, as the best of all possible emancipatory and democratic social systems.

It is embarassing to find that, as an example of the kind of analysis he is proposing, Kellner discusses the TV miniseries *Holocaust* as conducive to "critical uses" in demystifying fascism, anti-Semitism, and much of usually repressed recent history. Marooned in the land of J.R. Ewing and LBJ in the intellectual Alamo of the University of Texas, it is probably unfair to expect Kellner to be up to date on the aftermath of the German reception of *Holocaust*. But as participants in the drawn-out discussions in *Aesthetik und Kommunikation* and *New German Critique* have finally come to admit, the extraordinary success of *Holocaust* is now widely recognized to have been inextricably bound up with the resurgence of German nationalism, efforts to conveniently close a shameful chapter of Germany's recent past, and a general ideological maneuver having little to do with emancipation or social subversion. If anything, *Holocaust* may turn out to be the most ideologically *affirmative* media event in Germany in the last couple of decades.

And so it goes. What should be fairly clear by now, however, is that, far from carrying out the tradition of critical theory, Kellner is merely reverting to a peculiarly raw brand of Marxism, thought to be buried long before the advent of the Cold War. With "followers" like Kellner, critical theory will never need detractors.

Studies in Contemporary German Social Thought
edited by Thomas McCarthy

Philosophical Apprenticeships
Hans-Georg Gadamer
translated by Robert R. Sullivan

Perhaps more than anyone else, Hans-Georg Gadamer is the doyen of German philosophy and the recognized chief theorist of hermeneutics. These autobiographical reflections offer an enjoyable tour not only of his own intellectual development, but of the rich and fruitful collaboration of minds during an exciting period in German cultural history. Along the way Gadamer traces his "philosophical apprenticeships" with such important contemporary thinkers as Paul Natorp, Max Scheler, Martin Heidegger, Rudolf Bultmann, Gerhard Kruger, Richard Kroner, Hans Lipps, Karl Reinhardt, and Karl Jaspers.
208 pp. $17.50

Understanding and Explanation
A Transcendental-Pragmatic Perspective

Karl-Otto Apel
translated by Georgia Warnke

Karl-Otto Apel, as much as any German theorist, bridges the gulf between Anglo-American and continental thought in both the style and content of his work. The present book stands between the two shores and illuminates both, while it also clarifies the explanation versus understanding debate that is particularly important in the philosophy of the social sciences.
320 pp. $25.00

Available in paperback
Against Epistemology: A Metacritique
Studies in Husserl and the Phenomenological Antinomies

Theodor W. Adorno
translated by Willis Domingo
248 pp. $8.95

The MIT Press
28 Carleton Street, Cambridge, MA 02142

James Sloan Allen, *The Romance of Commerce and Culture: Capitalism, Modernism, and the Chicago-Aspen Crusade for Cultural Reform.* (Chicago: University of Chicago Press, 1983).

Serge Guilbaut, *How New York Stole the Idea of Modern Art: Abstract Expressionism, Freedom and the Cold War*, trans. Arthur Goldhammer. (Chicago: University of Chicago Press, 1983).

Looking back in the late fifties on the rise of New York's postwar avant-garde, Clement Greenberg remarked that "some day it will have to be told how 'anti-Stalinism,' which started out more or less as 'Trotskyism,' turned into art for art's sake, and thereby cleared the way, heroically, for what was to come."[1] It was a good point, and one that Greenberg himself had largely neglected in his own accounts of American Modernism. The story of how New York Intellectuals and Abstract Expressionists came to the defense of artistic vanguardism from a common past of Marxist commitments, and of how that defense ended in the fifties with a celebration of American cultural freedom, certainly had to be told. And since Greenberg first suggested the topic, we have listened as both historians and members of the New York avant-garde have taken us on the long march through the manifestoes that concludes with *Partisan Review*'s 1952 symposium on "Our Country and Our Culture." After reading two new books on American Modernism by Serge Guilbaut and James Sloan Allen, the question must be asked: do we need to hear this story again?

Although both books examine the changing relationship between avant-garde culture and capitalist society, their titles indicate the authors' different emphases. Guilbaut wants to explain how "New York" — i.e., American business and foreign policy — "*stole*" the "adversary" culture of Modernism. His is a history of theft and betrayal. What Greenberg, Irving Sandler, and others have described as "heroic" in the so-called "triumph of American painting," Guilbaut sees as simply another episode in the ascendancy of American military and economic power after 1945. Eschewing the "idealist notion" that the success of Abstract Expressionism as an aesthetic movement and media event was inevitable, Guilbaut promises a materialist, even a "revisionist" account of that movement, much as revisionist historians have rewritten the history of American diplomacy. Allen lacks Guilbaut's passion. In fact, he is not sure whether there is any issue of power involved in the "romance of commerce and culture" that ended in such a profitable, well-publicized marriage. Allen humbly informs his readers that his book "wears no ideological badge." His history may be read either as a tale of "how capitalism and high culture ended their age-old antagonism in a pattern of alliances beneficial to both sides" or as a study of "how capitalism gained hegemony over high culture by turning artists and intellectuals into its agents, thereby robbing them of their ability to criticize or pose alternatives to the kingdom of consumer culture." Did Modernists simply join the Great Barbecue of Cold War America or were they served up as the main course? It doesn't matter, apparently; just help yourself to a plate and get on line. The absorption of "adversary" Modernism into the mainstream of bourgeois culture — the de-clawing of the avant-garde — is an old favorite, and there are plenty of anecdotes and stories for everyone.

The problem with this kind of history is not just that it tells us what we already knew

---

1.   Clement Greenberg, "The Late Thirties in New York," in Greenberg, *Art and Culture* (Boston: Beacon Press, 1961), p. 230.

(many radical artists and intellectuals of the thirties subsequently gave up Marxism and social realism for liberalism and cultural Modernism, avant-garde culture no longer shocks anyone, let alone capitalists, etc.), but also that it conceives of the politics of culture strictly in terms of the political pronouncements of artists and critics. Guilbaut's book is the most egregious example of this tendency in cultural history in recent memory. Those familiar with the work of Peter Fuller, Eva Cockcroft, Max Kozloff, and other New Left-inspired historians of the New York School will discover little that is new in Guilbaut's discussion of the de-Marxification of the Abstract Expressionists and their impressment into the service of the United States during the ideological Cold War of the fifties. What will hopefully startle a reader who knows this earlier body of criticism is Guilbaut's eagerness to rehash the history of this period in American art without even *one* sustained analysis of any painting or sculpure.

Guilbaut is too intent on drawing parallels between Abstract Expressionist concepts of artistic freedom and risk and the Cold War liberalism of Arthur Schlesinger's *The Vital Center* to bother with any aspects of the New York School's work. At least five pages of Guilbaut's book are devoted to the Marshall Plan and its repercussions — five pages that rely heavily on the writings of revisionist diplomatic historians. No single painting receives comparable treatment. Dwight Macdonald's career as a cultural critic also comes under close scrutiny, as do the writings of other New York radicals en route from Trotskyism to what Guilabut dogmatically considers apoliticism. Here he borrows from James Gilbert's *Writers and Partisans*, a landmark study of literary radicalism that is quoted so frequently that Guilbaut must surely have tested the limits of the copyright laws. Whatever else this kind of approach might be, it most certainly is not a "materialist" history of American art, since the real, material practice of painting and the products of that practice are completely ignored. Instead, Guilbaut's book is a history of the ideas of writers and critics who surrounded the Abstract Expressionists set against the backdrop of an unfolding Cold War. Guilbaut complains that purely formalist analyses of the American avant-garde "ultimately obscure what was alive, real, and contradictory in the works of the artists themselves." I agree, but I don't recommend Guilbaut as an authority on the vitality of works he never mentions.

Even as a history of well-known ideas, *How New York Stole the Idea of Modern Art* is fundamentally flawed. Despite his criticism of Greenberg's formalist art theory, Guilbaut essentially agrees that the intellectual trajectory of the avant-garde consisted of a political regression from anti-Stalinist Marxism to an embrace of art for art's sake. Guilbaut understands the incorporation of Modernism into the Cold War consensus solely in terms of the depoliticization of its leading figures, and he therefore follows Greenberg's typology of avant-garde development. "Radical intellectuals, unable to situate themselves in contemporary political events or even to interpret those events in a satisfactory way, deserted politics altogether."

By making the desertion of politics the central theme of his study, Guilbaut misses the key assumptions that continued to motivate avant-garde artists and critics even as they gave up Marxism. The belief that industrial technology necessitated a dramatic change in the nature of artistic production, the insistence that a "vanguard" culture must break completely with common sense and "kitsch," and the facile identification of artistic development with a progressive view of history: these were the chief theoretical underpinnings of American Modernism in this century, regardless of the formal political allegiances of particular painters and intellectuals. Such ideas united the social realism of the thirties with the abstraction of the forties and fifties, undermining the simple chronology of manifestoes that Guilbaut uses to structure his narrative. The political issues at stake in a serious examination of these notions do not fit neatly into the categories of the conventional political left, which has not yet freed itself from many of the same assumptions. Cultural politics that resist classification along a left-to-right spectrum, or which do not lend themselves to the history of manifestoes and organizations, are apparently not the stuff of materialist art history. Like the paintings of the Abstract Expressionists, they do not figure in Guilbaut's story.

Nor do radical ideas that challenge the cliches of cultural fronts and party platforms. Guilbaut finds only "pessimism on the left" in the efforts of Dwight Macdonald, Barnett Newman, Clyfford Still, and others to escape the either-or politics of the Cold War. When Macdonald wrote in 1947 that, "on the world scale, politics is a desert without hope," he never meant that an intellectual should turn away from politics to the contemplation of his or her own existential anxiety, as Guilbaut claims. Likewise, the New York School artists did not abandon social, political, and ethical concerns when they rejected the manipulation of art by socialist realism and New Deal cultural nationalism. Rather, they believed that a new radical critique of industrial life required the reconstitution of the subject through the renewal of moral and artistic realms of experience. Anyone who compares this intellectual position to that of Ayn Rand's *The Fountainhead*, as Guilbaut does in one incredible footnote, is not be be trusted as an interpreter of post war radicalism. The writings and artwork that form the major legacy of forties radicalism question the very equation of political commitment with large-scale organization, mass mobilization, and party propaganda that Guilbaut assumes to be the only alternative to apathy and acquiescence. Guilbaut's condemnation of leftist "pessimism" after the second World War and his easy assimilation of any move away from Marxism to the liberalism of Schlesinger or the libertarianism of Rand have less to do with the avant-garde's retreat from politics than with the theoretical poverty of Guilbaut's own politics. Were there really reasons to be cheerful in 1947 or 1948? Even if there were, what would that have meant for radical artists and writers? More manifestoes and ritual denunciations of capitalism?

Guilbaut cannot conceive of any explanation for the exhaustion of the avant-garde other than his simple-minded notion of "theft" because his analysis remains trapped in categories that have only rhetorical significance. According to those categories, Modernism is by definition an "adversary" culture that could only be reconciled to the social and political status quo by outside pressures. "The artistic avant-garde followed the same course as American government policy," he writes at one point, as if the Modernists themselves had no independent role in the creation of a new American cultural identity. When Guilbaut describes advertisements that appeared in the *Partisan Review* in 1948, which used engravings by Jackson Pollock and Adolph Gottlieb to sell homes in a luxury development in Tarrytown, New York, he implies that the final humiliation of the avant-garde was complete. Nowhere does he consider that there might have been a dynamic intrinsic to Modernism that attracted the attention of advertisers, or that modern art itself had any claim to power of its own, which would explain the eagerness of Washington policymakers and suburban executives to acquire the furnishings of Bohemian sophistication. No, for Guilbaut, Modernism had to be "stolen," enslaved, and forced to do the bidding of its new masters.

One of the virtues of Allen's book is that it suggests an alternative reading of "the romance of commerce and culture," one that Allen himself never fully explores and that Guilbaut — with his tired theme of capitalist control of "adversary" Modernism — could never imagine. In describing the career of Walter Paepcke, the president of the Container Corporation of America who enlisted the aid of Modernist artists, university presidents, philosophers, and advertisers in his grandiose mission of culture reform, Allen has uncovered the reasons for the convergence of Modernism and consumer culture in the twentieth century. Instead of reciting the old antagonisms between the avant-garde and mass culture, Allen has begun to probe the ideas and styles that bound them together.

The most interesting section of Allen's book focuses on Paepcke's unceasing efforts to introduce European Modernism into American advertising and industrial design. During the 1920s, advertisers and public relations firms had begun to turn to psychoanalysis and other theories of personality for clues to the workings of the consumer's mind. Turn-of-the-century revelations in psychology and social thought had uncovered the unconscious impulses lurking below the calm exterior of the rational Economic Man, and exponents of mass consumption were quick to see in such findings the means of tapping previously-unknown wants and desires in the buying public. European Modernist styles, with their appeal to a fractured consciousness and their evocation of an emotional-intuitive realm beyond the senses, seemed equally promising to advertisers. Moreover, the Modernists' ever-shifting succession of movements and manifestoes upheld an ideal of novelty and constant change that exactly paralleled that of the mass production industries. One advertising magazine told its executive readers that Modernist style "change the fashions overnight . . . , writes a damning 'out of date' on yesterday's favorite . . . , and by boldly challenging the imagination, opens new avenues to the interest of the buying public — avenues which keen merchandisers are following apace."

During the 1930s, Paepcke and CCA art director Egbert Jacobson led the way among American industrialists in pioneering the use of Modernist graphic design in advertising and packaging. Looking for a clean, bold "corporate image," Paepcke and Jacobson began hiring European artists like A.M. Cassandre, Fernand Leger, Man Ray, and others to design CCA advertisements. Paepcke often admitted that he did not fully understand the avant-garde work he commissioned for CCA ads, but he reminded one skeptic, "it stopped you, and you remembered it — that's all I ask." His success led other corporations to follow suit, and soon Paepcke was moving beyond advertising to a vision of a full-scale renovation of American culture. That project brought him into contact with László Moholy-Nagy, whom Paepcke invited to revive the Bauhaus at Chicago's Association of Arts and Industry in 1937. From that year until Moholy's death in 1946, the two men worked together to bring the lessons of Bauhaus design to American industry. Along the way, Paepcke enlisted the aid of Walter Gropius, who saw in the American businessman the very union of culture and practice he and Moholy had strived for at the Bauhaus. "You represent for me," he wrote Paepcke, "the rare exception of a man in power and leadership who seriously tries to fuse business with cultural progress." For Moholy, the opportunity to work alongside Paepcke made possible the fulfillment of his dream of transforming the fine artist into an "art engineer," whose work would be as practical as that of a research scientist. The bourgeois division of art and production had been overcome — or so it seemed to Moholy and Gropius — thanks to the support of the indisputably bourgeois Paepcke.

Unfortunately, Allen does not make enough of the material he has uncovered. As he pursues Paepcke's career, he loses the main thread of his story of the mutual development of American Modernism and consumer capitalism, turning instead to Paepcke's involvement with a host of other cultural projects. Of these, Paepcke's participation with Mortimer J. Adler and Robert M. Hutchins in promoting the University of Chicago's "Great Books" program was probably the most influential, but this aspect of Paepcke's vision of cultural reform had little to do with Modernism. In fact, as Adler,

Hutchins, and Paepcke first "sold" Great Books to the American public in the early forties, and then "sold" Goethe to Americans at the Goethe Bicentennial Festival in Aspen in 1949, they moved closer and closer to the middlebrow humanism of Archibald Macleish and Van Wyck Brooks than to anything resembling the avant-garde. Like Macleish and Brooks, Paepcke and his associates believed that liberalism had to shed its abstract rationalism in order to survive in an age of totalitarian ideologies. Goethe symbolized the liberal creed or "faith" that America required in the postwar era, and to publicize that creed Paepcke subsidized a humanistic carnival show that brought José Ortega y Gasset, Thornton Wilder, Giuseppe Borgese, Albert Schweitzer, and other intellectuals to Aspen. In between lectures on the fate of the West, the assorted luminaries schmoozed with Gary Cooper and other Aspen locals, gave interviews to gossip columnists, and revelled in the high spirits and thin air of the Aspen summer. The spectacular success of the festival — perhaps the first major intellectual media event in the United States — encouraged Paepcke to found the Aspen Institute for Humanistic Studies and the International Design Conference in Aspen. Not surprisingly, all the hype and attention transformed Aspen from a sleepy former mining town to a fashionable vacation spot for the wealthy. Paepcke was appalled by what his public relations campaign for the city had produced: not the Athens of the Rockies, but something closer to Sodom and Gomorrah with ski lifts.

Allen is too quick to subsume all of these incidents under the rubric of the alliance of Modernism and capitalism, and his unwillingness to confront the political implications of that alliance weakens those sections of his book that really do touch upon that subject. But his story does bring up a number of fascinating new issues for future historians of American Modernism. Rather than retrace the "theft" of the avant-garde, historians would do better to look at evidence like that of the relation between Moholy and Paepcke, which indicates that modern industrialists and artists shared many ideas about culture, personality, and social change in an age of advanced technology. Moholy's last book, *Vision in Motion*, outlined a theory of cultural leadership that reverberates throughout much of the literature of modern liberalism and Modernist art. Hoping to "translate Utopia into action," Moholy proposed "an international cultural working assembly . . . composed of outstanding scientists, sociologists, artists, writers, musicians, technicians and craftsmen" to "investigate the roots of our intellectual and emotional heritage" and restructure every aspect of modern life. This ideal of a techno-cultural vanguard, responsible for everything from government and city planning to industry and art, comes up again and again in the modern American imagination, whether in the writings of Edward Bellamy, Elton Mayo, and the contemporary neo-liberals on industrial relations or in the many Modernist reformulations of avant-gardism. Moholy's very notion of "art engineers" highlights the link between the avant-garde and advanced capitalism, namely the "mechanical functionalism" that Albrecht Wellmer has traced to the origins of the Modernist movement.[2] Once Modernists gave up on the arts-and-crafts movement's campaign to reconcile art and labor through the reinvigoration of craft and the destruction of the factory system, they plunged into the dubious project of trying to unify "the functions of the artist, technician, and merchant . . . at a higher level of differentiation."[3] But, as Moholy's partnership with Paepcke demonstrates, the hope of transcending the industrial division of culture and labor within the confines of factory production was doomed to failure. An art that lends an aesthetic aura to industrial goods, and that upholds industrial

---

2. Albrecht Wellmer, "Art and Industrial Production," *Telos* 57 (Fall 1983), p. 55.
3. *Ibid.*, p. 53.

specialization as a cultural ideal, in no way establishes an "adversary" culture within modern capitalist society. In fact, just the opposite is true. As Jacques Ellul has noted, "art has become one of the major functions of the integration of man into the technological complex."[4]

At the same time, modern art has largely failed to live up to its major theorists' dreams of a culture uncontaminated by kitsch and mass comsumption. As Thomas Crow has argued in an important essay on Modernism and mass culture, the historical relation between these two currents of modern culture has always been one of uneasy coexistence. At its best (in Dada, Surrealism, and Abstract Expressionism), Modernist art referred to the iconography and media of advertising in order to heighten the tensions between fine art and mass culture, thereby exposing the false pretensions of both genres. On the other hand, the Western avant-garde has also largely envisioned a future reunion of art and everyday life on the terrain of urban leisure and consumption, which has undercut its insights into the tensions and affinities between "high" and "low" cultures. In an argument that echoes the Marxist criticism of Meyer Schapiro and Malcom Cowley in the 1930s, Crow concludes that "functionally, the avant-garde serves as a kind of research and development arm of the culture industry: it searches out areas of social practice not yet completely available to efficient manipulation and makes them discreet and visible."[5] The Modernist flight from the ascetic "iron cage" of nineteenth-century capitalism was not that far removed from the emerging consumerist offer of a life of ease and spiritual wholeness beyond the travails of work and power. As more than one cynic has observed, yesterday's Bohemia has become today's Club Med.

A new appreciation of the connections between Modernism and consumer culture would move current discussions beyond simple ideas of capitalist "theft" of the avant-garde and of the thorough manipulation of the public psyche by "captains of consciousness." Increasingly, the work of cultural historians turns up evidence of major emotional and psychological upheaval in turn-of-the-century American society. The dramatic social and political transformations associated with industrialization went hand-in-hand with what can only be considered a massive crisis of faith among Americans. As the old culture of family, religion, and region crumbled under the weight of outside pressures and its own contradictions, the traditional notion of the self as an autonomous, finely-crafted "character" gave way to a loose, shifting sense of "personality." While the older character ideal of the nineteenth-century bourgeoisie revered the acquisition of culture as a means of self-discipline and spiritual training, the new cult of personality looked to personal charm, affability, and a superficial familiarity with a fleeting body of information as the means to success and popularity in an interdependent, bureaucratic world. For Americans hungry for some larger meaning to life, a consumer culture offering both intense experience and psychic well-being looked very attractive. The irony, of course, was that self-realization through

---

4.   Cited in Serge Guilbaut, "The Relevance of Modernism," in Benjamin H.D. Buchloh, et al., eds., *Modernism and Modernity: The Vancouver Conference Papers* (Halifax: Press of the Nova Scotia College of Art and Design), p. xii.

5.   Thomas Crow, "Modernism and Mass Culture in the Visual Arts," in Buchloh, et al., eds. *Modernism and Modernity, op. cit.*, p. 253. This collection also includes papers by Henri Lefebvre, T.J. Clark, and Greenberg, among others, as well as some interesting exchanges between Greenberg, Clark, and Guilbaut on Abstract Expressionism, Modernism and art criticism. Crow's analysis of the relation between the avant-garde and mass culture is reminiscent of that of Meyer Schapiro, "The Nature of Abstract Art," in Shapiro, *Modern Art: 19th and 20th Centuries* (New York: Braziller, 1978), pp. 185-211, and of Malcolm Cowley, *Exile's Return* (New York: Viking Press, 1956).

consumption identified the self with external agencies of influence and control.[6]

Is it too much to suggest that the appeal of Modernism, particularly that of its image of an aestheticized daily life, had similar roots? If not, then the place to look for the union of commerce and culture would not be the postwar period, when industrialists and foreign policy advisors studied up on the avant-garde, but the very beginnings of Modernism and mass culture in the late nineteenth century. Just as both movements rejected a craft-based culture for industrial technology, so too did Modernists and theorists of a post-scarcity society imagine a new selfhood composed of evanescent experiences, dreams, and submerged desires. This is not to say that the two movements always agreed in their visions of a new self, or even to suggest that they may not at times have produced competing images of self-realization and personal fulfillment. Nineteenth-century workers and capitalists interpreted ideals of autonomy and character in very different ways. There is no reason to assume that the modern culture of personality has been any less contentious. But attention to the common denominators in the Modernist and consumerist revolts against the separation of culture and daily life should at the very least put an end to fairy tales about the heroic battle of the "adversary" culture against conniving bourgeois phillistines.

The myth of that battle has occupied the spare time of the intellectual left for much too long. Not only has it been proven inaccurate, it has also grown downright boring. Does anyone other than the editors of the *New Criterion* really think that the success of the American avant-garde was unrelated to developments in politics and social life? Is there anyone outside the offices of the *Village Voice* who still believes that the Modernist vanguard and its "post-modern" epigoni represent a fundamental challenge to consumer capitalism? While the left rehearses the old struggle to preserve the "adversary" tradition from the encroachment of commercialization, the artists, writers, and students educated in that tradition are themselves engaging in some pretty sophisticated commercial ventures, forcing the poor and other culturally-backward tenants out of desirable urban neighborhoods. Along with the galleries, lofts, and studios, the adversarial gentry are bringing bank machines, boutiques, and chic restaurants into Bohemia. Soon they will be joined by their more successful siblings, the young professionals who delight in urban entertainments and the freedom provided by a two-hours' drive to their parents' home in the suburbs. The critique of the capture of oppositional culture explains everything but what is important in the relation between Modernism and advanced capitalism. Now that Modernism as a way of life has become indistinguishable from the culture of consumption, will the intellectual left live off its memories of a once-pure avant-garde, at least until it too receives an eviction notice? Hopefully not. Once its critics and historians give up the false struggle of vanguards and kitsch, they may yet ask significant questions about our country and our culture.

Casey Blake

---

6. See Warren Susman, " 'Personality' and the Making of Twentieth-Century Culture," in John Higham and Paul K. Conkin, eds. *New Directions in American Intellectual History* (Baltimore: Johns Hopkins University Press, 1979), pp. 212-26; Jackson Lears, *No Place of Grace: Antimodernism and the Transformation of American Culture, 1880-1920* (New York: Pantheon, 1981); and Richard W. Fox and Jackson Lears, eds., *The Culture of Consumption: Critical Essays in American History 1880-1980* (New York: Pantheon, 1983), particularly Lears's "From Salvation to Self-Realization: Advertising and the Therapeutic Roots of the Consumer Culture, 1880-1930," pp. 1-38.

Edward Shils, *Tradition,* Chicago, 1981. University of Chicago Press, (Chicago, 1981) 330pp. + viii, $20.00.

Josef Haym Yerushalmi, *Zakhor: Jewish History and Jewish Memory.* Seattle and London, 1982. University of Washington Press, (Seattle, 1982) 144pp + xvii, $17.50.

One of the common grounds of neo-conservatism and an increasingly important current in leftist thought has been their shared doubts about the ideologies of progress and modernization These doubts have recently taken the form of a defense of tradition against the total insemination of the spirit of capitalism. In the face of the insatiable lust of modernization, one turns not to the self-conscious, playful impotence of modernists and post-modernists, but rather to the powerful "grip of the past" on communities and families. The forms in which the past is preserved over time should show us the sacred limits that bourgeois capitalism and state socialism are out to mystify with the opiate of development. If we only look back to the heart or haven of our modern, routinized world, we might find that we already possess one of the key defenses against the inhumanity of progress. Beneath the appearance of incessant change should lie the roots of essential continuity, which nourish our ongoing beliefs and practices.

Both Shils' and Yerushalmi's books attempt to understand the presence of the past in contemporary life. Both are concerned with how we make meaning and direction out of our past, as well as with how our past infuses the present with an aura of signification. Both studies raise some central questions about the role of modern historical consciousness in regard to tradition, and about the function of this consciousness in regard to the preservation and deepening of memory.

Shils' book is an effort to understand as well as to cultivate the wellsprings of continuity which inform our daily lives. He begins by showing how "post-Enlightenment scholarship" has been "insensitive" to traditionality, and goes on to give a detailed account of how objects and practices endure, and why traditions change over time. His goal is to show "what difference tradition makes in human life," and to argue that we must protect that difference from rationalization and routinization, the dark sides of historical progress.

The problem for Shils, however, is that rationalization and routinization are also traditions.[1] Both of these networks of beliefs and practices thrive, though, by denying their own traditionality while destroying aspects of what Shils calls "substantive" traditions. Once Shils starts to discuss this competition of traditions, however, his criteria for evaluating what is preserved and destroyed over time become vague.[2] He fails to make clear why his favorite survivors from the past are more "deep" or "substantive" than others, and he is ready to dismiss in a cavalier fashion efforts to recover certain traditions that do not immediately excite his anti-secular proclivities.[3]

The vagueness of Shils' criteria for evaluating traditions stems from his basic faith

---

1.   I have discussed this theme briefly in "Opening a Dialogue between Cultural Conservatism and Modernism," *Democracy*, III:4 (Fall 1984).

2.   Distinctions among substantive, deep and derivative traditions, as well as between tradition and fashion, are made throughout the book and discussed explicitly on pages 21f., 221f., and 305.

3.   The slur against women's studies and black studies is of particular interest insofar as both of these disciplines are deeply concerned with cultivating tradition: "Such novelties as 'black studies,' 'women's studies' . . . have become relatively common in colleges and universities without a reputation for intellectual achievement to maintain, or they occur in those parts of superior universities which teh more demanding parts of the university have never taken seriously" (p. 183). Evidently, the traditions with which black studies and women's studies are concerned are not deep or substantive enough for Shils.

that the existence of something is evidence that that something was needed or necessary. For Shils, traditions exist because they serve human needs, and "the fact that a practice or belief has persisted for an extended period of time is an argument for its retention" (p. 328). Of course, the author probably does not want us to muster up feelings of sacred awe for some of the most brutal and oppressive of human practices simply because they may have been around for a long time. By failing, however, to give any content to his notion of "human needs," and by completely ignoring the question of whether they should all be treated equally, Shils would escape the problem of choosing among competing traditions. In fact, he merely avoids the responsibility of justifying his own choices and evaluations.

The appeal of Shils' book evidently comes from his animosity towards the ideology of progress combined with his willingness to affirm an alternative to this ideology. That is, Shils does not merely criticize modernizers from a reactionary position *vis-à-vis* technological and social change. Rather, he spends most of his book on those forces — that can be described as popular — which act as inhibitors of these changes. Thus, his work has connections with those branches of the social sciences that have focused on the vitality of popular culture, and which have stressed that this vitality has been one of the major forces of resistance to political centralization and the development of capitalism.

Shils' book evidences once again that the appeal by intellectuals to the virtuous forces of popular culture is at best politically ambiguous, and can often be intellectually dubious. The discursive appeal to traditions must be made on the basis of a critical historical perspective, and can never be made on the basis of tradition itself. That is, unless one is participating *in* a tradition and developing its significance from the inside, one is left in a critical position *vis-à-vis* (often competing) traditions. The problem then becomes how to understand (dismiss, make propaganda for) a tradition or group of traditions in relation to others. This problem cannot be avoided by talking about tradition *as such*, as Shils ably demonstrates in his marked — but unsupported — preference for some traditions over others.

Shils' functionalist presupposition leads him to say that "this book about tradition is evidence of the need for tradition" (p. vii). It seems, instead, that this book evidences the need for understanding the ways in which we choose from what is left to us from the past in order to give sense and direction to the present. One of the chief tasks of historical consciousness has been to discursively legitimate some of these choices, or, at least, to apprehend the ways in which people have tried to do so. That is, to tell a story in which these choices make sense, have meaning and direction. The call for piety that concludes *Tradition* is yet another technique for avoiding and obscuring this task.

The role of historical consciousness as a vehicle for the discursive legitimation of traditions has often led it into an antagonistic relation with the forces of traditionality. In *Zakhor: Jewish History and Jewish Memory*, Yerushalmi provocatively discusses this antagonism as one of the major themes of post-biblical Jewish history. Yerushalmi is painting with a large brush in this collection of his four 1980 Stroum Lectures at the University of Washington. He has much to say, and little time in which to say it. But the non-specialist in Jewish history benefits from this form, insofar as it allows the author to raise questions that are central both to the immediate concerns of the historiography of Judaism, and the wider problems involved in the connection between tradition and history.

Yerushalmi shows that in post-biblical Jewish society and culture, up until the 19th century, the writing of history had little or no importance, with the exception of the period just following the expulsion of the Jews from Spain in 1492. This is not to say that the Jews were not concerned with history; on the contrary, he shows that an intense attachment to the past was a crucial part of everyday life and regular ritual (including the law and celebrations). History, however, was not the "vessel" in which memory was contained. Or, rather, the history that was crucial to Jewish life was fully articulated through halakhah (jurisprudence), philosophy and Kabbalah. The only event that had to be added to that history was its final closing time: the coming of the Messiah. Historiography was unimportant as a way of making sense of the past because it was disconnected from the final redemption to come in the future.

The flowering of historiography in the 16th century is for Yerushalmi the exception that proves the rule. That is, the historians, like Azariah de'Rossi, broke little new ground in their methodologies, and left a legacy that would be taken up by no one. When faced with the destruction of Europe's most powerful Jewish community, the historians' tools for making sense of suffering in the world seemed weak in comparison with the metahistorical cosmology offered by Lurianic Kabbalah.[4] In their attempt to make meaning out of memory, the historians were all but impotent to preserve a vision of a significant future connected to the horribly difficult present and the glorious past of biblical times. For the successful completion of this task, metahistorical myths (the themes of exile and redemption are most important for Yerushalmi) were much more powerful.

This distinction between metahistorical myth and historiography is, of course, too neat. All historical visions — even those that have the greatest scientific pretensions — have important metahistorical components.[5] That said, we can, and do, distinguish between historical and mystical visions, if only on the basis of the respective importance of immanence and transcendence to each of them.[6] In any case, it is clear that Jews did distinguish between these two ways of making sense of the past, despite the fact that there may be no significant epistemological difference between them. Although Judaism can be regarded as an intensely historical religion (insofar as it places paramount importance on actions in this world), Yerushalmi shows that historiography played little or no role for Jews trying to make sense of their past after the biblical age and before the 19th century. Although he does not talk in any detail about the various mystical movements during this long period, it is clear that they had a much more important role in Jewish communities than did any school of historians.

As an historian, then, Yerushalmi uncovers the "at best . . . ancillary role" that historiography played among the Jews before the 19th century. In his final lecture he discusses the problems that arise with the growth of Jewish historiography during the last 200 years; the ways in which history is used as ideology in the wake of emancipation. Emancipation brings with it a new kind of crisis for the Jews: not a crisis — for the moment — of physical survival, but a crisis of memory. Jewish historiography, then, begins at a time of communal disintegration and doubt: "The modern effort to reconstruct the Jewish past begins at a time that witnesses a sharp break in the continuity of Jewish living and hence also an ever-growing decay of Jewish group memory.

---

4.   Yerushalmi does not mean to suggest that historiography and Lurianic Kabbalah were in conscious competition with each other, but that by juxtaposing these movements we can learn something about 16th-century Jewish mentality.

5.   Hayden White's work has been important for showing the ways in which historiography depends on metahistorical structures. See his *Metahistory: The Historical Imagination in 19th Century Europe* (Baltimore, 1973).

6.   See Scholem's distinction between the allegorical and the symbolic in *Major Trends in Jewish Mysticism* (New York, 1954), p. 28ff.

In this sense, if for no other, history becomes what it had never been before — the faith of fallen Jews. For the first time history, not a sacred text, becomes the arbiter of Judaism. Virtuall all 19th-century Jewish ideologies, from Reform to Zionism, would feel a need to appeal to history for validation. Predictably, 'history' yielded the most varied conclusions to the appellants" (p. 86).

Although the response of Jewish historiography to this crisis of memory has been and continues to be great, Yerushalmi is not sanguine about its results. The weakness of historiography as a guardian of memory is revealed by the rejection of all of diaspora history by important components of Israeli society, as well as by the turn to mysticism and simple forgetting by Jews everywhere. The appeal to history has evidently not provided a new faith; as Yerushalmi puts it, the historian has not healed "the wounds of memory," he is only the pathologist who explores them (p. 94).

The phrase "wounds of memory," which Yerushalmi borrows from Eugen Rosenstock-Huessy, recalls Hegel's discussion of the "wounds of Sprit;" wounds, it will be remembered, which "heal and leave no scars behind."[7] For Hegel, the wounds left no scars because they were re-collected by the philosopher, and in this re-collection they were redeemed by their being understood as a part of the development of history as reason. Philosophy made painful memory into the triumph of Spirit, but since there were "no scars left behind," it may be more accurate to say that philosophy negated, even repressed, memory. Re-collection was an essential component of philosophy, but in the completion of history announced by philosophy, the meaning and direction of memory were left behind.

The juxtaposition of Hegel and Yerushalmi in this regard is instructive, insofar as the latter seems ready to acknowledge that the historian cannot replace the philosopher to heal the "wounds of memory." He points out that, "Jewish memory cannot be 'healed' unless the group itself finds healing, unless its wholeness is restored or rejuvenated" (p. 94). Here he is in one sense close to the spirit of Hegel, who also knew that wholeness was not the product of philosophy, but of action in the world that was made sense of by philosophy. The important difference between their two perspectives is that Yerushalmi does not see the possibility for a new wholeness in his own time, whereas Hegel was quite sure that *the* final wholeness had been achieved.

Of course, few, if any, people look to historiography to create a new wholeness. Although many turn to their personal histories in order to "pull themselves together," professional historiography does not typically see itself in this therapeutic vein. Indeed, so much of theoretically minded or self-conscious historiography finds its *raison d'être* in demystification or critical analysis, that it seems fair to say that the writing of history — insofar as it has any practical effect at all — would inhibit the realization of any new form of wholeness, or at least would make it more difficult for us to take our present forms of life as constituting this wholeness.

Are we to conclude, then, that history has no role to play in sustaining the life of a community or nation? If so, it would seem that my earlier comments on Shils' avoidance of history were misguided. That is, I pointed out that Shils' discussion of tradition seemed to be informed by his own prejudices rather than by a sense of history. The implication of this was that an analysis of the role of tradition in modern life would benefit form a historical perspective that would enable us to evaluate the function and significance of a tradition over time. Without such a perspective, we are unable to legitimate discursively our preferences or antipathies for particular practices and beliefs from the past; and, we might add now, we can be put at the mercy of those

---

7. G.W.F. Hegel, *The Phenomenology of Mind*, trans. A.V. Miller (Oxford, 1977), p. 407.

who would like to legitimate through other means particular practices and beliefs as traditional in order to benefit their own private interests.

Yerushalmi's discussion of the role of historiography in relation to Jewish memory reveals the darker side of our own call for a sense of history discursively to legitimate tradition(s). When a traditional way of life is in need of "discursive legitimation," it is no longer traditional in any simple sense of the word. If a tradition is a belief or practice that "goes without saying," then any attempt to justify it through speech or writing will change the very nature of the belief or practice. In other words, a sense of history becomes important only at the moment when group memory is no longer providing the continuity essential to community life. This would not be an occasion for regret or pessimism if historiography were able to compensate for the disintegration of communal memory. The "modern dilemma" that Yerushalmi ends with, however, is that modern historiography, by its very nature, is unable to fulfill that role. As he says: "Nothing has replaced the coherence and meaning with which a powerful messianic faith once imbued both Jewish past and future. Perhaps nothing else can. Indeed, there is a growing skepticism as to whether Jewish history can yield itself to any organizing principle that will command general assent." Historiography will not provide this organizing principle, and it certainly will not develop for us any new traditions or resurrect in usable form any old ones. Does historical consciousness, then, offer us any protection from or critical understanding of the march of modernization?

It does offer this "protection" *through* a critical understanding. That is, in the modern world we have been confronted with an "organizing principle that commands general assent," and it is the ideology of progress and modernization. Historiography, which originally had a crucial role in formulating this ideology, how has assumed the important task of exposing its weaknesses and dangers. If for the Jews, emancipation coincided with a general (but certainly not universal) disintegration of messianic faith, it also was paralleled by the increasingly important faith in personal and social progress in this world. This faith became an important "organizing principle" for individual, family and community life. More generally, the idea of progress and development has become a central tradition with its own rituals and sacred beliefs.

To do so, of course, still leaves us with the problem discussed above: how do we choose between (or simply evaluate) competing forms of traditionality? It seems that what I have been calling the "historical consciousness" merely leaves us with this problem, rather than giving us a solution to it. No such solution, however, *could* be given because the problem is not one of consciousness. That is, the "choice" between forms of traditionality is a problem of politics, or public life, and not a problem to be solved merely through discursive means. We may come to understand facets of traditionality through discussion and analysis, but prior to this discussion is our participation in or rejection of the traditions which we *must* confront in the present.

We can say, then, that historical consciousness is parasitic on tradition. The appeal to tradition without this critical consciousness is blind, but an appeal only to this consciousness is empty. Historiography, Yerushalmi teaches us, cannot create the bonds of community by reinvigorating memory, but it can help us conceive and care for the possibilities for "a time when men and women think differently than we, be it in the future or the past" (p. 103). This ability is not a substitute for a messianic belief, nor is it the key for rebuilding a meaningful community life. It is, however, essential for us if we are to preserve a past and a future we can live with without having to flee from the present we must live in.

Michael S. Roth

Christopher Lasch, *The Minimal Self: Psychic Survival in Troubled Times* (New York: Norton, 1984).

Few works of social criticism about contemporary America have elicited so much response as *The Culture of Narcissism.* There Christopher Lasch argued that the traditional American emphasis on individualism has degenerated into a narcissistic preoccupation with the self. He explained this transformation by pointing to the psychological consequences resulting from changes in the nature of production, consumption, and socialization. Of particular importance was the shift from handicraft to factory modes of production and the subsequent takeover of workers' knowledge by a managerial elite. Rarely encouraged to be self-sufficient, today's individual is asked to rely too often on professional experts, who provide certified answers for every aspect of life — a process which unwittingly duplicates the conditions of infancy in which we are all dependent on the adult world.

One of Lasch's difficulties in *The Culture of Narcissism* was his failure to clarify the nature of his allegiances, so that it was tempting to believe that he glorified the autonomous, rational man of the previous era whose desire for independent mastery of the world often resulted in a denial of feelings, particularly dependency needs. In *The Minimal Self,* Lasch is much more careful in his use of psychoanalytic theory and indicates that he upholds neither "the illusion of self-sufficiency" or "a radical denial of selfhood that tries to restore the illusion of absolute unity with nature" (p. 20). His new book is a response to critics of *The Culture of Narcissism* and, at the same time, develops some of his earlier ideas.

In assessing the American national character, Lasch emphasizes the degree to which a survival mentality has taken hold. He speaks of the aim of preserving a minimal narcissistic emotional equilibrium in the face of a sense of impending disaster. The instability of the economy and the resulting social dislocation, the deterioration of the environment, the ever present nuclear threat, as well as a sense of political powerlessness have made it difficult for many people to feel secure in planning for the future. Instead, they have become much too apathetic, emotionally disengaged, and inclined to live for the moment.

If Lasch overestimates the extent of this phenomenon, his analysis of its consequences is illuminating.[1] For Lasch, the numbing repetition of this motif no longer serves to alarm but has become a strategy for enduring the uneasiness of the present as well as a foreboding future. In addition, the widespread use of the language of survival makes it difficult to discriminate among the various dangers; it "emasculates the idea of crisis and leaves us indifferent to appeals founded on the claim that some sort of emergency commands our attention" (p. 64). Lasch is particularly concerned with the unwillingness to examine those dangers which actually threaten human existence. Instead, everyday difficulties have come to assume unwarranted importance, perhaps, because people feel so powerless in dealing with larger issues.

Lasch discusses at great length the tendency to employ metaphors that refer to Nazi

---

1. Lasch, however, does not explore works reaching conclusions that differ significantly from his own. The composite portrait of the American people in these works tends to describe a populace that is far less desperate than he has suggested. See Joseph Veroff, Elizabeth Douvan, and Richard A Kulka, *The Inner American: A Self-Portrait from 1957-1976* (New York: Basic Books, 1981); and Daniel Yankelovich, *New Rules: Searching for Self-Fulfillment in a World Turned Upside Down* (New York: Random House, 1981).

genocide as a means of speaking about forms of victimization for which the language of mere survival is inappropriate. Not only do victims of oppression draw on this imagery, but many of us "conduct ourselves as if we lived in 'impossible circumstances,' . . . in the 'extreme and immutable environment' of the prison or the concentration camp" (p. 95). Moreover, the sense of being a victim does not necessarily lead to resisting unjust authority. Indeed, it often contributes to feelings of helplessness that "can also destroy the capacity for resistance by destroying the sense of personal responsibility" (p. 77). If there is a sober realism in America that is correctly suspicious of the romantic rebel, there is also a debilitating mood of resignation in the face of "the onslaughts of everyday life" (p. 95). People have come to concentrate on the demands of the moment, hoping for minimal personal success. They often shield themselves by taking the stance "of a detached, bemused, ironic observer" (p. 96), if they are not content with assuming a variety of roles, none of which command allegiance.

Lasch also notes the decline of the capacity to sacrifice, still another example of the survivor mentality whose only imperative is to remain alive. However appropriate it may be as part of a set of convictions about the necessity for nuclear disarmament, this is not an ethic which carries moral conviction or humane intention in other contexts: "the demands of daily survival absorb energies that might once have gone into a collaborative assault on the common dangers confronting humanity" (p. 82). Here, he speaks disparagingly of those who have come to believe that, with sufficient preparation, even a nuclear holocaust can be endured. This preparation often entails a commitment to emotional disengagement and a relinquishment of one's personal history. Thus, the primary "injunction" is "to prepare for the worst" and to search for salvation "in old-time religion, in mystical traditions imported from the East, in a revival of nineteenth-century technology and nineteenth-century individualism, in a repudiation of individualism, or in space travel" (p. 86). Neither this kind of "doomsday mentality" nor the widespread compulsion "to take refuge in the immediate" (pp. 93, 92) is a realistic response. Ironically, those who survived the holocaust now view their struggle in the camps not so much in terms of mere survival, but as an attempt to retain their humanity. They sought meaning in survival, unlike many Americans today who are simply concerned about staying alive.

Utilizing a psychoanalytic framework, Lasch sees the concern with "psychic survival" as a manifestation of the tendency of the "minimal self" "either to remake the world in its own image or to merge into its environment in blissful union" (p. 19). He claims that certain features of American society encourage a regressive solution to the problem of separation. For Lasch the feeling of loss which occurs as the child differentiates itself from the primary caretaking figures is the central issue of human development. The accompanying experience of helplessness and inferiority, as well as the fear of desertion, inevitably give rise to a desire to reinstate the earlier condition of intrauterine contentment in which the child experienced both the illusion of narcissistic self-sufficiency as well as a real sense of union with the world. Unlike Freud who saw psychological activity as "overdetermined" by an interlocking array of constitutional, intrapsychic, and social factors, Lasch confines his understanding of selfhood to the critical interplay of the desire for oneness and separation. Moreover, Lasch accepts too readily the universal affect of those needs and does not question whether they may have been in part socially and historically contingent.

Lasch, however, does describe how the tension between these needs is exacerbated by the current social climate. Thus, as in his previous work he criticizes family life for being overly egalitarian and permissive. In addition, he laments the absence of the father from the home and the resulting over-reliance on the mother whose continual presence is often experienced as suffocating — particularly when inspired by professionals' advice. If not the mother, then outside agencies are increasingly caring for the young who are then exposed "to new forms of manipulation, sexual seduction, and outright sexual exploitation" (p. 186). Regardless of who takes care of the child, fantasies of sexual and generational interchangeability as well as the possibility for instantaneous sexual satisfaction are advanced, all of which perpetuate in the child a feeling of omnipotence — itself a defensive strategy to deny the anxiety resulting from separation.[2]

Fantasies of omnipotence are also encouraged by mass culture which has weakened the distinction between illusion and reality in its obsession with images of instant success, pleasure, and power. The media have become a tool for domination, "a one-way system of management and communication" (p. 26), that has dire consequences. For example, advertising has fostered styles of consumption that discourage "initiative and self-reliance" and promote infantile helplessness, "dependence, passivity, and a spectatorial state of mind both at work and at play" (p 17). In this context, Lasch speaks of the emergence of "a new kind of self-consciousness" (p. 29) that festers under the gaze of others. In contrast to those who equate consumerism with hedonism, Lasch speaks of the "uneasiness and chronic anxiety" (p. 28n.) that result when one feels continually scrutinized by others. Thus, the current fascination with "protean" forms of personal identity is but a symptom of the fact that the individual now comprehends the world "largely through insubstantial images and symbols that seem to refer not so much to a palpable, solid, and durable reality as to his inner psychic life, itself experienced not as an abiding sense of self but as reflections glimpsed in the mirror of his surroundings" (p. 34).

But it is not just the perception of the self that is altered. The individual's sense of the external world has also been affected. One is encouraged to view objects as an "extension or projection of the self" (p. 30). The "boundaries between the self and its surroundings" (p. 19) have become blurred especially because of the over-reliance upon technology which has made even the simplest task odious to perform, if it can be done a little more easily with the aid of a mechanical device.[3] Whatever the nature of the objects, they quickly become woven into one's fantasies insofar as they "gratify or thwart" (p. 30) one's immediate desires — an infantile state of mind conducive to an economy rooted in consumption. Caught up in a fantastic environment of disposable objects, many people not only feel powerless, but also lack a sense of durability which is a necessary defense against the intense anxiety associated with the early process of separation.

This inability to deal with the "creative tension between separation and union, individuation and dependence" (p. 177) is also reflected in the cultural realm, particularly in art and literature. Here too a "passive" attitude prevails as painters and

2.   Lasch's discussion of child care is much too harsh. Though he accurately describes the victimization of some children, he has a limited sense of the increased sensitivity to the problems of the young which has resulted from the dissemination of psychological knowledge. See Lloyd de Mause, "The Evolution of Childhood," *History of Childhood Quarterly* 1 (1974), pp. 503-606.

3.   Though Lasch is too quick in claiming that there is "no connection" between "technological progress" and "material or social progress," he is sensitive to the "incalculable" "long term effects" that may result from "short-term modifications of nature" (p. 42). Moreover, he is concerned about the fact that there is little control over which devices are available on the market — a condition which contributes to a sense of passivity, as it adds to the monopolization of power and wealth of those intent upon eliminating "older technologies even when the old ones remain demonstrably more efficient for many purposes" (p. 43).

novelists confine themselves to "an immersion in the ordinary, a deliberate efface-
ment of the artist's personality, a rejection of clarifying contexts that show relationships among objects or events . . ." (p. 132) Overwhelmed by a sense of helplessness in
an indifferent or hostile world where many events defy understanding, the artist no
longer simply retreats within but goes to an even more drastic extreme of minimizing
the significance of interiority. For example, Lasch notices that contemporary fiction is
populated with figures who try to anesthetize themselves against the harshness of the
environment, their relations with others, and their own internal conflicts. Thus, he is
distressed with the fact that the self is often viewed as nothing more than a useful fiction, a composite of various attempts to find meaning in the flux of inner or outer
experience. Moreover since the basic constituents of personal identity (words and
images) have come to be employed by the media as "instruments of surveillance and
control" (p. 136), some novelists and painters engage in a "deliberate depersonaliza-
tion of the work of art, the elimination of the artist himself or at least a drastic reduction
of his role as an interpreter of experience" (p. 143).

   Given this sense of being overwhelmed by the world, it is not surprising that the self
can also be perceived "as something programmed by outside forces" (p. 164). Thus
novelists such as Pyncheon portray characters engaged in a ruthless quest for meaning
"in which the search for patterns and connections turns back on itself in tightening
solipsistic circles" (p. 155). If this kind of search may prevent disintegration, it is fueled
by the desire to maintain order and control, however paranoid, in a world riddled with
uncertainty. Even the literature of social exposure fails because the earlier concern
with social injustice, especially "the misuse of the power vested in persons of authority," has given way to an obsession "with the indignities suffered by the victims" (p.
160). According to Lasch, it is difficult to identify with the oppressed because their
experience becomes intelligible primarily to those drawn from the same group whose
connection to outsiders is rarely clarified.

   Lasch's sensitivity to the problem of victimization is central to his political stance.
He believes that "psychoanalytic terminology now provides a more reliable guide to
the political landscape than outmoded distinctions between left and right" (p. 198).
Lasch utilizes an "ideal typology" to describe "the geography of cultural politics" (p.
198) which has prevailed in America since approximately 1960. There is the "party of
the superego" (p. 200), mainly neoconservatives, such as Trilling, Rieff and Bell, who
believe that authority must be restored because of the collapse of moral inhibitions
and the rise of permissiveness.[4] At best, they advocate the internalization of morality
and not the reimposition of external sanctions. To achieve this end, there should be
"moral and religious instruction, collective rituals, and a deeply implanted though not
uncritical respect for tradition" (p. 201).

   The problem with this position is that today "a commanding moral presence" is
barely discernible, given our "rapidly changing and unpredictable world, a world of
downward mobility, social upheaval and chronic economic, political, and military
crisis" (p. 204). If Lasch does not elaborate on the way authority has become delegiti-
mated because of abuses and corruption, he does indicate that "those who uphold law
and morality find themselves unable to maintain order or to hold out the rewards formerly associated with observance of social rules" (p. 204). In addition, these neocon-

---

   4.   See Lionel Trilling, *Beyond Culture* (New York: Viking, 1965), and *Sincerity and Authenticity*
(Cambridge: Harvard University Press, 1972); Philip Rieff, *The Triumph of the Therapeutic: Uses of
Faith after Freud* (New York: Harper and Row, 1966), and *Fellow-Teachers* (New York: Harper and
Row, 1973); and Daniel Bell, *The Cultural Contradictions of Capitalism* (New York: Basic Books,
1976).

servatives tend to overestimate the attributes of the superego, especially the use of fear to suppress feelings of rage. The process of self-censorship relies on primitive aggressive energy to allow for acts of suppression which can result in further "resentment and insubordination" (p. 203).

Unlike "the party of the superego" which values "custom, prejudice, and patriarchal constraints," "the party of the ego" consists primarily of liberal humanists, such as Parsons, Weinstein and Platt, who are convinced that the rational faculty must be strengthened in such a way as to provide "moral enlightenment" (pp. 205-6, 198) about the options available in a pluralistic society.[5] Like their nineteenth-century forebears who were opposed to vindictive retribution and championed the "salutary effects" of "remedial" punishment, they are preoccupied with the importance of "moral striving and spiritual self-help" (pp. 206, 210). Here Lasch lumps together in a much too facile manner therapeutic traditions derived from quite diverse sources. Thus he states that Adler, Jung, Sullivan, Skinner, Hartmann, and Rogers offer under the guise of therapy a secularized version of nineteenth-century liberal theology which "stressed the possibility of achieving rational control over the self and its environment" (p. 211). Lasch does distinguish between "game therapies" and "growth therapies," though both "present themselves as 'humanistic' solutions to the problems not just of unhappy individuals but of industrial society in general" (pp. 211-12). In the former, the "ghost of Adler" is recognizable because of the emphasis on manipulating the interpersonal world in a meaningful manner. In the latter, there is the "shadowy presence of Jung" who stressed the importance of transforming the individual's inner world with the hope of furthering emotional and intellectual growth. Lasch believes that both forms of therapy "advance their own version of behavior modification . . . in the hope of making the client self-directing" (p. 213). But he is especially critical of behaviorists for weakening even the possibility of becoming self-directing, given the Skinnerian belief in the importance of "the skillful manipulation of social rewards by a scientific elite" (p. 217).

Even within the orthodox psychoanalytic tradition there are those, mainly the ego psychologists, who also tend to idealize the ego by underscoring its "capacity for masterful, creative action . . ." (p. 219). Like Hartmann, who was preoccupied with the problem of adaptation, they do not do justice to the manner in which unconscious conflict is to some extent involved in all activities, including basic forms of perception and thought. Instead, they stress the human capacity for problem solving and ignore its darker dimensions, particularly its instinctual origins and "ideological compulsions" (p. 221). According to Lasch, like the behaviorists, they promote "a technical conception of rationality" which is minimally self-reflexive and therefore may buttress unwittingly "the illusion of infantile omnipotence" (pp. 221n, 222).

There is, finally, though Lasch does not name it as such (perhaps because of his awareness of its complexity), the party of the id which was spawned in the sixties by the new left: the cultural revolutionaries opposed to industrialism and large-scale bureaucracies who promoted new forms of community with fewer restrictions than in the past. For Lasch, despite "the anti-intellectualism, the infantile insurgency, and the taste for destruction so often associated" with this kind of "cultural politics," it "addresses issues ignored by the dominant political tradition: the limits of reason; the

---

5.   See Talcott Parson, *Social Structure and Personality* (New York: Free Press, 1964); and Fred Weinstein and Gerald Platt, *The Wish to Be Free: Society, Psyche, and Value Change* (Berkeley and Los Angeles: University of California Press, 1969). Lasch also indicates that this position appeals "to democratic socialists and even to many revolutionary socialists" (p. 199).

unconscious origins of the desire for domination; the embodiment of this desire in industrial technology . . ." (p. 227).

In "Freudian feminism," which challenges the destructiveness of reason, Lasch finds a promising theoretical perspective, although not one without difficulties.[6] Committed to a conception of adulthood which values dependence and connection to others as much as autonomy and individuation, theorists such as Benjamin, Chodorow, and Dinnerstein flounder "as soon as the qualities associated respectively with the ego ideal and the superego are assigned a gender so that feminine 'mutuality' and 'relatedness' can be played off against the 'radically autonomous' masculine sense of self" (p. 245).[7] Though he agrees that we must learn to balance gracefully the desire for separateness and the need for connection, Lasch is also convinced that to identify the desire for union with others as "feminine mutuality" is to obscure "its universality and the illusions of 'radical autonomy' to which it also gives rise, in women as well as in men" (p. 245). In addition, Lasch is concerned about the tendency of some feminists to luxuriate in the narcissistic features of dependency which they view as an antidote to "masculine" autonomy and the use of instrumental reason. Both the urge for oneness and separation, if carried to an extreme, lead respectively to self-annihilation and self-sufficiency: "opposite aspects of the same archaic experience of oneness with the world" (p. 20)[8]

To avoid regressive solutions to the problems posed by the continual interplay of the basic needs for separation and dependence, Lasch calls for "the creation of cultural objects, 'transitional objects,' that simultaneously restore a sense of connection" (p. 246) to the environment while allowing people to express the need for autonomous mastery of the world.[9] In criticizing the work of some feminists because of their heavy

---

6.   Lasch finds the work of Herbert Marcuse and Norman O. Brown equally interesting but not as useful. He is very critical of Marcuse's commitment in *Eros and Civilization* to "the triumph of polymorphous perversity" which "depends on its antithesis: instrumental rationality carried to the point of total regimentation" (p. 234). Though he likes *Life Against Death* because of Brown's appreciation of the sense of "urgency" created by the "instinctual demands" of the child who can barely tolerate the inevitable dissatisfaction that accompanies the early process of separation from the mother, he is opposed to his "reduction of culture to a massive conspiracy against human nature and happiness" (pp. 235, 240).

7.   See Jessica Benjamin, "Authority and the Family Revisited: Or, a World without Fathers," *New German Critique*, 13 (Autumn 1978), 35-57; Nancy Chodorow, *The Reproduction of Mothering: Psychoanalysis and the Sociology of Gender* (Berkeley: University of California Press, 1978); and Dorothy Dinnerstein, *The Mermaid and the Minotaur: Sexual Arrangements and the Human Malaise* (New York: Harper and Row, 1976).

8.   In speaking of the extreme urge toward self-sufficiency in relation to the "archaic experience of oneness with the world," Lasch is referring to the condition of primary narcissism when the infant does not yet perceive the mother as having a separate existence. The child "mistakes dependence on the mother who satisfies his own needs as soon as they arise, with his own omnipotence." See *The Culture of Narcissism: American Life in an Age of Diminishing Expectations* (New York: Norton, 1978), p. 36. It is in this context that Lasch is concerned about the fact that many feminists do not comprehend the significance of technology which "itself originates — insofar as we can trace it to its psychological roots — in the attempt to restore narcissistic illusions of omnipotence" (p. 19). For Lasch, "The technological project of achieving independence from nature embodies the solipsistic side of narcissism, just as the desire for a mystical union with nature embodies its symbiotic and self-obliterating side" (p. 246).

9.   Here Lasch draws upon the work of D.W. Winnicott who describes the child's entry into the adult world as a process involving, in part, the creation of "transitional objects," artifacts (such as a teddy bear) which simultaneously provide a symbolic connection to the mother but at the same time take on an independent, and therefore more realistic, meaning. As Lasch notes, the child eventually "outgrows the need for transitional objects, but only because the 'transitional phenomena have become diffused, have become spread out over the whole intermediate territory between inner psychic reality and the external world as perceived by two persons in com-

commitment to the values of dependence and connection to others, Lasch does not do justice to their acknowledgement of the importance of both autonomy and separateness. Nevertheless, he is correct in pointing out that much of what passes as a feminist appropriation of psychoanalytic theory consists of a sanitizied reading of Freud. In their preoccupation with transforming the world, particularly gender relations, many "Freudian feminists" tend to forget that all gratification which takes place in a cultural context is, in part, compensatory: i.e., a sublimation of extremely primitive desires. According to Lasch, there is always the reminder "of the sense of division and loss" (p. 274n.) that permeates human experience.

It is this condition that many feminists tend to overlook, as do other advocates "of a cultural revolution" who "hold up narcissism as the cure for a disease that springs from the same source. They recommend a narcissistic symbiosis with nature as the cure for technological solipsism, itself narcissistic in its origin" (pp. 247-48). In doing this, they conceive "of 'feminine' virtues as the remedy for environmental devastation, imperialism, and war" (p. 248). Here, too, Lasch laments the failure to acknowledge the importance of values associated with autonomy and individuation, particularly as they are embodied in the attempt to actively engage the world, though he shares the counter-culture's larger political and economic concerns. Their critique overlooks the "important need to restore the intermediate world of practical activity, which binds man to nature in the capacity of a loving caretaker and cultivator, not in a symbiotic union that simply denies the reality of man's separation from nature" (p. 256).

For Lasch, it is imperative that we remain committed to the exercise of practical reason as opposed to "mysticism, spirituality, or the power of 'personhood' " (p. 253), the inflated rhetoric of so much popular work. He speaks of the necessity to resurrect a concern with the "means" utilized to pursue a given set of ends. In this context, he criticizes the tendency to overvalue technique and thus to lose a commitment "to standards of excellence designed to extend human capacities for self-understanding and self-mastery" (p. 155). Lasch hopes that in the future both work and politics may be viewed not merely as means to increase material and personal satisfaction, but as intrinsically valuable in the formation of character.

Moreover, given the American obsession with personal well being, he is concerned that ideas about morality have become so relativized as to be minimally binding. In speaking of the necessity to reawaken an interest in ethics and public life, Lasch is extremely critical of the industrial expansion in the latter part of the nineteenth century which has undermined "local institutions of self-government," weakened "the party system," and discouraged "popular initiative" (p. 41). The modern industrial system has also invaded the cultural and personal spheres, so that here too there is "a loss of autonomy and popular control, a tendency to confuse self-determination with the exercise of consumer choices, a growing ascendance of elites, the replacement of practical skills with organized expertise" (p. 42). Thus he criticizes those who claim that not only the process of modernization but also challenges to vested authority over the last two centuries have resulted in a democratization of American society. For Lasch, what we have today is "a shift to a manipulative, therapeutic, 'pluralistic,' and 'nonjudgmental' style of social discipline that originated . . . with the rise of a professional and managerial class in the early years of the twentieth century and then spread from the industrial corporation . . . into the political realm as a whole" (p. 46).

---

mon, that is to say, over the whole cultural field' " (p. 194). Here Lasch quotes from Winnicott. See *Playing and Reality* (Harmandsworth , England: Penguin Books, 1974), p. 5.

Given these developments, authority is no longer rooted in a set of moral principles tested and refined over time but has become based upon a codification of psychiatric norms.

Just as these norms are defined by an administrative elite, so too in the larger political realm rules and regulations as well as their implementation are the province of a few "experts" who believe that the economy and foreign affairs cannot be left to the ignorant public. Thus Lasch challenges the shibboleth that America is a true democracy. He notes that the voting process is badly tarnished since the public is essentially handed candidates who are often indistinguishable from one another, if they do not represent a limited range of possible choices. In addition, polling procedures and other devices that presumably exist simply to gauge public opinion manipulate it as well by creating norms and excluding unpopular ideas.

With this broad attack on American society, it is not surprising that Lasch hopes for a radical social transformation. Throughout *The Minimal Self,* his political allegiances tend to echo his work in the past. He has stated that "The solution to our social problems lies in a completion of the democratic movement inaugurated in the eighteenth century, not in a retreat to a pre-democratic way of life. Socialism, notwithstanding the horrors committed in its name, still represents the legitimate heir of liberal democracy."[10] Today, the nucleus of change resides in the various movements that address the issues of nuclear disarmament, ecological imbalance, the growth of consumerism and high technology, as well as "the 'masculine' psychology of conquest and competitive enterprise" (p. 18).

In his commitment to democratic socialism, Lasch aligns himself with those who embrace the rational ego, the valuable remnant of the "Western, Judeo-Christian tradition of individualism (as opposed to the tradition of acquisitive individualism, which parodies and subverts it)" (p. 258). But in doing so, he dissociates himself from those who refuse to acknowledge sufficiently "man's divided nature" (p. 258). In speaking of the necessity for a major social transformation, Lasch remains cognizant of the ambiguous status of the ego ideal which "calls attention to the links between the highest and lowest forms of mental life, between the most exalted aspirations for spiritual transcendence and the earliest illusions of omnipotence and self-sufficiency" (p. 179). Always acknowledging his commitment to an orthodox psychoanalytic perspective with its emphasis on the power and intricacy of desire, Lasch believes that the need to engage in any activity, however noble and generous, is also in part a reflection of the wish to reinstate the world of infancy in which the experience of merger gives rise to feelings of grandiosity and symbiotic bliss. It is only under social conditions which encourage the recognition that we are forever caught up in the conflict between the inconsolable longing for perfect union with others and the equally powerful desire to become self-sufficient and omnipotent that it will be possible to create a humane society.

Robert Ehrlich

---

10.   "Politics and Social Theory: A Reply to the Critics," *Salmagundi,* 46 (Fall 1979), p. 199.

Alain Touraine *et al., Solidarity: The Analysis of a Social Movement: Poland
1980-1.* Translated from the French by David Denby (Cambridge:
Cambridge University Press, 1983) 203 pp.

Solidarity is a complex theoretical and historical investigation of one of the most
dynamic social movements in post-World War II Europe. For some time now, Touraine
has attempted to develop a comprehensive theory of social movements. In *Solidarity*,
he and fellow researchers François Dubet, Michel Wieviorka, and Jan Strzelecki,
apply the theories of action, movement and sociological intervention elaborated in *The
Voice and The Eye*[1] to the situation in Poland 1980-1. *Solidarity* is one of many attempts by
Touraine to combine a comprehensive theory of social change and action with the history of a contemporary social movement.[2] Here Touraine *et al.* attempt to explain "the
nature, internal workings and the evolution of Solidarity." (p. 2) Unlike many journalistic
accounts,[3] this interpretation does not lend itself to cold-war polemics at the expense
of understanding the Polish events. The movement is described as simultaneously
national, trade-union, and democratic. A major innovation is the integration of these
three aspects. Concerning the 'internal workings' of the union, the book has little to
add. The research teams seem to have spent much of their time in "sociological inter-
ventions." Thus, much of the book is drawn from sessions between sociologists and
militants to the neglect of first-hand observation of the union and its militants in
action. Finally, on the question of Solidarity's evolution, Touraine *et al.* trace the movement through three distinct phases. Yet, despite the fact that they have produced a rich
account, its accuracy remains to be determined.

Society, for Touraine, is a combination of action and class relations.[4] Action is
defined in terms of the behavior of the actors guided by cultural practices, and is predicated on the unequal access to the production of those practices. The theory postulates three forms of social relations: "organizations and their relations to authority;
political decisions and the processes leading to them; and class relations and the
mechanisms of exclusion and elimination." It has been pointed out that Touraine
defines all action in terms of social movements and all social classes in terms of action.[5]
Recently, he has attempted to distinguish between social movements and social

---

1.   *The Voice and the Eye* (Cambridge: Cambridge University Press, 1981).

2.   The following are the most important empirical studies conducted by Touraine and his
research team: *Le Mouvement Ouvrier* (Paris: Fayard, 1984); *Le pays contre l'Etat* (Paris: Le Seuil, 1981);
La prophetie antinucleaire (Paris: Le Seuil, 1980); and *Lutte etudiante* (Paris: Le Seuil, 1978). An over-
view of these studies and an assessment of the method was the subject of a conference held in Paris
in 1979 and recently edited by Alain Touraine, *Mouvements Sociaux D'aujourd'Hui* (Paris: Les
Editions Ouvrieres, 1982).

3.   See Daniel Singer, *The Road to Gdansk* (New York: Monthly Review Press, 1982); Denis Mac
Shane, *Solidarity, Poland's Independent Trade Union* (London: Spokesman, 1981); Neil Ascherson *The
Polish August* (New York: Viking, 1982); Oliver MacDonald, "The Polish Vortex," *New Left Review*,
139 (1983), pp. 5-48; Stan Persky, *At the Lenin Shipyard* (Vancouver: New Star, 1981); William
Robinson, ed. *August 1980, The Strikes in Poland* (Munich: Radio Free Europe Research, 1980);
John Taylor, *Five Months with Solidarity* (London: Wildwood House, 1981); and Jean Yves Postel *The
Summer Before the Frost* (London: Pluto Press, 1982).

4.   For critical analysis of Touraine's social theory, see Charles Lemert's insightful discussion
in *French Sociology* (New York: Columbia University Press, 1981) and the caustic review by William
Gamson of *The Voice and the Eye* in the *American Journal of Sociology,* 1983. See also Jean Cohen, "Be-
tween Crisis Management and Social Movements," *Telos* 52 (Summer, 1982); Klaus Eder. "A New
Social Movement," *Telos* 52 (Summer, 1982); and Ferenc Feher and Agnes Heller. "From Red to
Green," *Telos* 59 (Spring 1984).

5.   Cohen, *op. cit.,* p. 30-1.

classes.[6] Classes are defined in terms of a "situation" whereas a social movement is understood as a class subject. This, however, does not avoid an obvious reduction to action. In order to escape this pitfall Touraine, would need to produce a convincing set of identity conditions for a class subject.

The system of historical action is the centerpiece of Touraine's theoretical construct and he has developed a periodization of society based on "historicity." As Feher and Heller have pointed out, this concept has been derived from Castoriadis's notion of the "imaginary institution."[7] Historicity is the threefold combination of systems of knowledge, an accumulation process, and a cultural matrix. Every society is the product of a social conflict over the control of historicity. Eder has shown that Touraine is attempting to adapt the Parson/Smelser model of four functions by locating production on top and consumption at the bottom.[8] The functionalists assume that a belief held by a mass constituency determines collective action. In this theory belief is employed to explain everything from a food riot to a social revolution. The variation in intensity of belief corresponds to the forms of collective behavior. Functionalists do not recognize that social movements are more than just aggregate behavior. They can also be historical actors which redefine the parameters of a social system. In contrast with the functionalists, Touraine's cultural model "determines the action system, and articulates the material processes of reproduction in consumption, distribution, organization of production, and production as a collective activity."[9] It follows that a society with a cultural composition dominated by distribution will generate very different struggles and with different goals, than a society with a cultural composition based on production. This is an important difference. As Alberoni[10] has pointed out, Touraine incorporates conflict into a multifaceted conception of social movements in contrast with the functional classification of "aggressive movements" as distinct phenomena. For Touraine, conflict is an embodiment of every social movement, and society is a creation of social movements.

Touraine's theory has several shortcomings. While he tries to transcend the structuralist/functionalist model, he too reduces all action to a final determination by belief. Like the functionalists, Touraine is left without objective criteria for determining truth. The difference lies in the relative stakes the two theories attribute to the outcome of conflict. Moreover, Eder has shown that Touraine's revamped "hierarchy of economic function" is unable to account for historical time. Touraine's model presupposes an evolutionary theory which has yet to be assessed in terms of competing theories of historical development. The theory of historicity presupposes two class actors, a dominant and a subaltern class. Class is not defined in terms of production relations or life chances, but in terms of levels of social organization. However, he does not attempt to account for the causal processes on the level of the social organization

---

6.   Alain Touraine. "Social Movements: Special Area or Central Problem in Scoiological Analysis," *Thesis Eleven* no. 9, (July 1984), pp. 5-15.

7.   Feher and Heller, *op. cit.,* p. 35. The term historicity is dropped in *Solidarity,* but the object of struggle is characterized as . . . "the social definition of historicity" characterized as . . . "the general orientations of a society and a social system for controlling the use of the main resources, cultural and in particular economic" (p. 7).

8.   Eder, *op. cit.,* p. 12. Jeffrey Alexander in *Theoretical Logic in Sociology, Part IV* (California: University of California Press, 1983) points out that . . . "Alain Touraine has incorporated much of Parsonian functionalism, as a counterweight to Marxism . . . " (p. 4).

9.   Eder, *op. cit.,* p. 13.

10.   Francesco Alberoni. *Movement and Institution* (New York: Columbia University Press, 1984), p. 28.

which manifest themselves in the individual behavior of agents. In contrast with Touraine's methodological collectivism other theorests, like Roemer, integrate individual agents into class theory.[11] They account for agents' choices based on their specific social conditions and objectives. This bears resemblance to life-chance theories of class but is not so narrowly economistic. Roemer assumes that social relations are best understood in terms of choices available to an agent. Only within these structures can the agent identify choices, measure available alternatives and correspondingly adopt a line of action. Social relations are not understood in terms of unbounded choices, but as a set of complex human events over time. Like Touraine's concept of social relations, Roemer's theory attempts to account for the conditions under which agents struggle to generate a new set of social relations, i.e., historicity in Touraine's terms.

Touraine claims that a social movement is defined in terms of the participants' abilities to both identify opponents and define the stakes of the conflict. The framework requires a methodology which permits the sociologist privileged access to the theoretical object of analysis, i.e., the social movement. Thus, in *The Voice and the Eye,* the sociologist's function is seen both as meant to record the actions of an intervention group and to facilitate its development.

Touraine and a team of Franco-Polish sociologists designed their research of Solidarity on the principles of sociological intervention. Between April and November 1981, six worker-militant groups were formed in Gdansk, Katowice, Warsaw, Szczcin, Wroclaw, and Lodz. Each group included eight to ten worker-militants and, in most cases, four representatives of the research team. These groups were selected and brought together by the Polish members of the research team. Group meetings were held for several days and, in some instances, divided into two time periods with a several month lapse between sessions. Touraine argues that the regulative role of the researcher is to attempt to unearth the specific roles of the militants in the group. To do so, he has developed a three-stage process. The first stage entails the establishment of intervention groups to initiate a dialogue between worker-militants and the select group of interlocutors. In "Solidarity" the interlocutors were drawn from lay church intellectuals, Solidarity advisors with dissident backgrounds, state officials and party functionaries. This stage is a major part of the process of understanding the actions of the group. In the second stage, two researchers designated "agitator" and "secretary" encourage the group to analyze the conditions and meanings of their actions. The third stage requires the agitator to develop hypotheses, and present them to the group explaining the highest possible meaning of their actions. A "conversion" occurs if there is a group action which is the result of the acceptance of an interpretation advanced by the agitator. The final phase of sociological intervention is "permanent sociology." This is a process whereby the results of the conversion are discussed by the researcher and the group in order to apprehend the social movement's potential to translate the analysis into a coherent program of social action.

The intervention method is predicated on the ability of the group members to establish a consensus. Touraine claims that the militant group, by accepting the sociologist's hypotheses of the situation, will result in a new level of learning in the group and of the social conflict. Moreover, a hypothesis is acceptable if and only if it provides the conditions for the renewed action of the group. Touraine asserts that a true proposition will be obvious because a false proposition, if accepted, will promote

11.   John Roemer. *A General Theory of Exploitation and Class* (Cambridge: Harvard University Press, 1984).

conditions of instability and incoherence among group members. This argument assumes the unity of a group in order to determine the truth content of a proposition. To the extent a group is not unified, a true proposition could conceivably divide the group and, correspondingly, a false proposition might unify it. Thus, on the basis of Touraine's dubious claim for the unity of "Solidarity," one can challenge the sociological conclusions his researchers drew from these sessions. The teleological aspects of this argument are hard to overlook. To the extent that the unity relation holds, it only applies to propositions which describe the group. Touraine seems to be making the following argument. A proposition is true if and only if it does not disrupt the unity of the group. This argument ignores structure and any independent method of verification outside the group's self-image. Moreover, the fact that a group accepts a hypothesis might depend more on the agitator creating coercive conditions, than on free group dialogue, where the proposition is debated.

While Touraine is interested in developing a unified theory of action, there is a disturbing split in his definition. On the level of macro-social phenomena he defines action in terms of strategic maneuver. However, the concept of action as employed in sociological intervention is restricted to a set of speech acts. It is unusual that a research methodology designed for the study of social movements should focus on the cognitive aspects of belief formation of group members, at the expense of other courses of action by the social movement in its struggle. The postulating of the equivalence of the beliefs of sample groups, whose criterion of assembly were not justified, with the collective of millions of people is a ladder-of-abstraction problem that would warrant at least another hefty volume.

The primary goal of sociological intervention is to determine the meaning actors attribute to their actions. Touraine's account of ideology fails to confront the issue of relativism. While suggesting that the researcher avoids the problem through active mediation, i.e., identification with the highest goals of the social movement, this does not show why these goals are more true than any other set of beliefs. Touraine's approach fails to confront the issue because it cannot determine the complex meaning beneath social relations.

Touraine's research program also ignores the conditions under which the groups were formed. Touraine et al. tells us little about the length of association between the group members, nor do they provide sufficient detail on differences in occupational position, previous political sympathy or involvement. Moreover, we lack a firm understanding of the social researcher's criteria for selection of the group. Touraine's procedure is difficult to assess because the intervention groups were not uniformly operationalized. The examination of the social groups is the most important link in Touraine's understanding of the action of a social movement. However, Touraine does not show how the actions at the micro-level intersect with those at a macro-level. In particular, concepts employed in conversation with group members are presented in such a way that the reader must assume that they hook up with complex social structures. It is unclear that the specific objects identified by the militants and the researchers are sufficiently complex or specific to approximate the variety of social phenomena under analysis.

Also, the authors fail to show how the structure of communication in the group presupposes different levels of abstraction, which might be perceived as necessary to produce the author's intended analysis. In addition, we would have expected Touraine et al. to explore the subject's moral attitudes.[12] In the case of Solidarity, it is essential to

12.   See, James Fishkin. Beyond Subjective Morality (New Haven: Yale University Press, 1984);

provide an account of the normative framework on the basis of which the agents acted. Specifically, the moral grounds for action required an understanding of objective social conditions and with it an understanding of notions like human dignity, freedom from exploitation, and national sovereignty.

Touraine *et al.* argue that Solidarity evolved through three pahses. By this they do not mean ". . . to imply that a different type of movement replaces the original one: the idea is rather that the same movement passes from one phase to another . . . but retaining its status as a social movement simultaneously trade-unionist, democratic and national in character." (p. 97) The first phase, emerged with the ratification of the agreements between the Inter-factory Strike Committee in Gdansk, Szczecin, and Jastrzebie-Zdroj (Silesia) in August-September 1980 and lasted approximately until the Bydgoszcz crisis.[13] This was the period when the union established itself as an organization, swelled in membership, and secured formal recognition from the courts. In this phase, it became ". . . more and more clearly identified with the whole of Polish society by virtue of the size of its membership and its capacity for uniting the democratic and national aspirations of the population around the theme of free trade unions." (p. 84)

The second phase was a response to Bydgoszcz that avoided the direct confrontation with the regime yet still presented a new challenge to authorites. It was dominated by the issue of workers' self-management. In this phase, ". . . the movement, feeling direct threat of foreign intervention . . . , and seeing the economic crisis going from bad to worse, tried to consolidate its gains, seeking through institutional reform to find some ground for compromise with the party, which was weakened but was attempting to change and said that it recognized the rights of free trade unions." (p. 134) During this time there were numberous high level meetings between the union and the government over how to implement the Gdansk accord.

The third phase began in late summer or early fall 1981. Touraine *et al.* characterize it in this way: "The aims are now manifestly political: freedom of information, and especially normal access to television for Solidarity; open nominations in the local elections scheduled for February 1982; creation of a second chamber with the *Sejm,* made up of the representatives of social and economic groups; creation of a social council for the national economy, a group of specialists with considerable powers of initiative; and, ultimately, free elections to Parliament." (p. 98) During this time there was considerably more political tension in the movement, especially between elements of the left democratic opposition (KOR and supporters) and various strongly nationalist currents. This was also the time when the party went into eclipse. It began to disintegrate both ideologically and organizationally. In this period the army first stepped in, on a limited basis, to replace or supplement the state bureaucracy in running the country. The security forces became more prone to stage provocations and

---

Julian Henriques *et al., Changing the Subject* (New York: Methuen, 1984); and especially, Elliott Turiel. *The Development of Social Knowledge* (Cambridge: Cambridge University Press, 1983).

13.   After being invited to a local council meeting in Bydgoszcz in March 1981, Solidarity leaders and local peasant activists were barred from speaking by procedural manipulation. When they tried to continue the session and present their greivances, the local security forces proceeded to beat them up. This led to a series of multi-issue negotiations between the state and Solidarity which threatened a general strike if these did not reach a settlement. Negotiations yielded an ambiguous compromise on a number of issues and the union's leadership voted at the last minute to cancel the general strike. This brought an outcry from a significant minority of militants reaching up the National Coordination Committee. The union's press spokesman, Karol Modzelewski resigned, and Vice-chairman of the Committee, Andrzej Gwiazda, published an open letter in which he critized Walesa.

certain hardline groups openly called for the suppression of the "counterrevolution," while trying to use political anti-semitism as a mobilization tool. Solidarity became very defensive in this period, due to the dangerous political atmosphere and the imminent collapse of the food distribution system.

In characterizing Solidarity as a self-limiting movement, Touraine *et al.* examine the constraints posed by the threat of Soviet intervention and the straightjacket of economic crisis. In practice this meant not being able to fully dismantle Soviet barriers to national sovereignty or push structural reform while accounting for its economic impact. The persistance of these limits obviously affected the evolution of the movement.

The problem with such an approach is that the movement's evolution is understood as primarily caused by its own agency in terms of self-imposed limits. What is lacking is a notion of the Polish state with which the movement evolves. The notion of the state presented by Touraine *et al.* is confusing. Despite their contention that theories of totalitarianism are ". . . of only limited use in understanding present events in Poland " (p. 15) they insist on labelling the state as totalitarian throughout the book.

They also introduce two other theories of the state. One is the comparative historical analysis of Ferenc Fejto. In this theory, tension between eternal coercion and the desire for national autonomy, leads to a cyclical repetition of uprising, state concessions and state repression. The theory is based on induction from a small number of cases. It is reminiscent of Crane Brinton's *The Anatomy of Revolution* in that it tends to strip historical events of their specificity and context in order to force them into the general pattern of comparative historical development. Touraine *et al.* also introduce the modernization theory of Jan Szczepanski and Alexander Matejko, which lies within the American political science school of economic and political development. The criticisms of this approach are far too numerous and well known to be listed here. Yet, one must ask what this approach is doing in this book, uncritically adopted by sociologists who are interested in the challanging of historicity by class agents.

Finally, Touraine *et al.* find neither of these theories sufficient in itself. Yet, each explains a component of the struggle — Fejto, national struggle, and Szczepanski and Matejko, the problems of industrial society (pp. 18-9). These two approaches, uncritically assimilated and not suitably integrated with each other, do not constitute an adequate theory of the state. The state mostly appears as a set of perceived limits, rather than as an agent that evolves in relation to the movement. This presents problems in the analysis of the evolution of the movement. Thus, in terms of the evolution from phase one to phase two, the perception of danger (or perhaps, simply the danger) of Soviet intervention, caused the movement to shift away from the national level of action directly, and instead to seek a path combining the trade union and democratic levels. At this point the union took a step towards expanding its realm of action by advocating worker's self-management. This was both a matter of economic reform (re-rationalization of production by self-managing, self-financing enterprises on a market) and political reform (undermining the *nomenklatura* principle of personnel selection in the enterprise). If successful, such a reform would have caused an evolution in the Polish state, both in the domain of its bureaucratic central control and the predominant principle of economic organization.

Furthermore, Touraine *et al.* fail to spell out clearly that this strategy was an attempt to change the rules of the game of state-movement interaction. It is, if the assessment of the developments by Touraine *et al.* is correct, a shying away from direct national action when faced by threat of intervention, while simultaneously, in its intent to re-rationalize production to change the crisis ridden state of the economy, to give the union leeway of action, or in the terms of Touraine *et al.* — to push back the economic limit. In effect, the movement was trying to limit the state's domain by bringing about an economic reform and thus extending its possible courses of action by changing the agent with which it was in conflict, the Polish state.

Touraine *et al.,* do not convince the reader that the self-management issue was the dominant level of action occupying the movement at this time. The issue seems to have strongly committed partisans only in Warsaw, not the other cities that figure prominently in the book. It is important to remember that the *siec*[14] (network) was quite small and just beginning in the spring of 1981. However, Touraine *et al.,* do acknowledge that self-management did not have the mobilization capacity that Solidarity had during the first phase on the issue of trade union independence. (p. 98) Its proposals, still only broad principles and not detailed plans, were not common wisdom until the Solidarity Congress in the autumn, which marks the starting point of the third phase. Another omission is that the National Coordinating Committee of Solidarity, in the spring, seemed to be concentrating on a series of issues concerned with the aftermath of the Bydgoszcz crisis and negotiating the full implementation of the Gdansk accords.

The lack of a fuller notion of the Polish state presents a problem to the analysis of evolution from the second to the third phase. This third phase is seen by Touraine *et al.* as a defensive turn inward. If this is the case, then greater attention should have been spent on the state's resistance to the self-management thrust during the second phase. The state fought tenaciously to derail this action, in particular over the selection of a new general manager for LOT[15] (the Polish national airline), and in maintaining its perogative in management selection and numerous aspects of production, during the negotiations concerning the enabling legislation for self-management which finally passed the Polish *Sejm* (Diet) in late September 1981. The State's defense of its power and perogatives, as a political agent that delayed and watered down structural reform proposals that would have weakened it, should have been worked into the analysis of the movement's evolution to the third stage. The path of evolution is simplified to an unfortunate extent when the state is perceived as "limits," not as a key sub-system which engages in struggle and has a major impact.

Finally, with respect to the state's suppression of the movement, Touraine *et al.,* fail to adequately emphasize the state's internal developments. In particular, questions regarding who held power, with whose support, and which state resources were mobilized, are crucial. Is it possible to ignore the constant struggle for power within the party and the consequence this had for Solidarity? In this case, the replacement of

---

14.   *Siec* — In March 1981, self-management committees on the enterprise voluntarily formed the "Network of Large Scale Enterprises" on the initiative of activists from the Lenin Shipyards in Gdansk and Rzeszow public services. With time, the number of enterprises grew (to 14,000) and its experience and proposals were definitive in the framing the economic program "Solidarity and Self-management." *Labor Focus on Eastern Europe,* (Jean-Yves Postel, "Solidarity and Self-Management" 5:3-5 (1982) and Committee in Support of Solidarity, *Bulletin Solidarnosc* 2 (New York, 1982).

15.   In June-July 1981, the employees of LOT and the Ministry of Transport disagreed over the procedure to replace the retiring general manager. The employee's council eventually elected a replacement which the Ministry refused to recognize. Despite the threat of a general strike of the airline, the Ministry's nominee, an air force general, assumed the position.

Kania by General Jaruzelski is not carefully integrated into the analysis. The replacement of a First Party Secretary perceived as either too weak or conciliatory, and whose support came from the increasingly enfeebled compromise wing of the party, by a tough-minded general who controlled the armed forces, is too significant to be glanced over.

The most unique and controversial aspect of the interpretation of Touraine *et al.* is the unity of the three component elements of the movement's action — the trade union, the democratic and the national. The difficulty of assessing whether this claim is valid, is complicated by the ambiguity of what they mean by "unity." Employed in one sense, the less demanding of the two, one ". . . must show that all the different tendencies which are present in Solidarity at different times and different places make up a coherent whole defined as all the possible different combinations of the action's component elements" (p. 173) — national and democratic, trade union and national, trade union and democratic. There is ample evidence presented in the book to substantiate that Solidarity conforms to these conditions of unity. All that is necessary is to demonstrate that there was at least one tendency of each combination anytime in the movement's existence. Touraine *et al.* do this — the workers' control tendency is trade union and democratic; the defensive populism tendency is trade union and national, and the political democracy tendency is a democratic and national.

Another sense of "unity," the far more demanding of the two, is the following: "If just one of the elements disappears or becomes separated from the others, the movement will disintegrate and its capacity for action will collapse." (p. 173) In this sense of unity, the component elements of action are so interpenetrated, so near identity in what they address, that the disappearance or separation of one would cause the collapse of the ensemble of the three, destroying the *raison d'etre* of the total social movement.

What makes this ambiguous is that if the movement is unified in the first sense, it is logically possible for it to be syncretic (defined *a contrario* to unified) with respect to the second sense. What would it mean if the movement was unified in sense one and syncretic in sense two? Could the movement have been unified in sense one and yet collapse because one of its component elements disappeared or separated at a latter stage? With respect to sense one of "unity," the phrase "at different times and different places" makes the definition so broad that it is almost impossible to argue against it.

However, with respect to sense two, the unity-in-action sense, the thesis is very hard to maintain. Testing for, or setting a good criterion for when "disintegration of the movement" occurs or when "capacity for action collapses" is a very tricky business. This becomes more of a problem under conditions where the state monopoly of the means of coercion and official political power is good cause for all democratic forces to maintain solidarity and organizational unity. Furthermore, there are some reservations about the "unity in action" thesis with respect to the third phase that bear expression.[16]

Before doing so, a summary of the book's description of this phase is in order. The major historical event of this period is the Solidarity Congress, held in two sessions in September-October 1981. Touraine *et al.* accurately describe the outcome of these meetings as "the politicization of the movement." (p. 140) They see this in the

16.   For a very different interpretation of this period, specifically that the movement was disintegrating, see Jadqiga Staniskis. *Poland: The Self-Limiting Revolution* (Princeton: Princeton University Press, 1984), Chapter 2.

demands for self-management and the threat to hold a referendum on the issue if the party did not meet them,[17] the call for free elections to the *Sehm* and Regional Councils, and the "Message to All Workers of Eastern Europe."

The Congress was also marked by a fierce debate on the question of internal democracy, which marked a gap within Solidarity between those who favored step-by-step negotiations with the state (thus stronger centralism) and those who were pushing for more direct action (thus less centralized control over local political initiative). Touraine *et al.* suggest this is only the development of a gap between the base and the leadership of the movement, not the development of a split (p. 143). Yet, when and how does a "gap" turn into a "split?"

In its third phase, the movement entered into some very dangerous situations. Proceeding from the first phase, a social movement which confined its political component to securing the conditions for its existence, through the intermediate stage of self-management during phase two, phase three became more of a movement for the implementation of the "programme for the liberation of society" by the turn to the explicitly political.[18] Yet, at the same time, the movement had run up against its limits. The events of the Solidarity Congress were rightly described by Touraine *et al.* as an expression of the movement's highest goals and aspirations. However, with its call for free elections to state positions and its threats to hold referenda, Solidarity had verbally shifted toward rupture. At the same time, it could not take action because it was constrained by the limits.

Thus, the movement accepted the *Sejm* draft on self-management although it was less than it demanded. Despite Solidarity's call for free elections, it was unwilling to threaten to dismantle the power of the party in the state by running a slate of candidates, because it was not just the Polish state that would respond. There was no other significant organized political force prepared to step into the fore and run slates of candidates. The movement was in a very difficult situation. Confronted by the limits constituted by the system, the movement had symbolically broken them by expressing its desire for freedom. Yet, it did not pursue this desire beyond the symbolic level, because such a course of action meant real rupture with the state. It had come to a point where it did not (or could not) act on its highest values and aspirations. This may well be a dilemma for *any* movement which has some limits and causes which coincide (in the case of Solidarity — Soviet domination and economic crisis).

The events on the local level at this time were, as well, very chaotic and confused. Touraine *et al.* provide extremely valuable descriptions of the state of local branches of Solidarity in the six cities that they studied. In Gdansk, the political and trade union elements began to separate out, marking the beginning of ". . . a slow process of disintegration." In Katowice, the union remained integrated around its sense of working class community and the idea of workers' control. Yet, there was some debate over whether this was best pursued by a political program or revolutionary workers' councils (pp. 176-7).

---

17.   This was averted by the passing of enabling legislation by the *Sejm* in the period between the two halves of the Solidarity Congress.

18.   Touraine *et al.* do not see the social movement and the program for the liberation of society as mutually independent. Rather, they are " . . . two distinct sides of Solidarity's action, each with its respective supporters within the movement." (p. 56) The concern of the first group is with the movement itself while the second concentrates on the changes that must be made in the system. The first group tended to be suspicious of political action, while the latter concerned themselves with freedoms and sought to direct the union's actions along political lines to realize them.

In the autumn of 1981, in Lodz and Wroclaw, Touraine *et al.* found the movement in a defensive state, favoring working class and national identities. The democratic element of action tended to disappear, and the groups usually favored one of the two elements alone. In these cities the capacity for action disintegrated. In Szczecin, the movement perceived the situation as hopeless, and unified all three elements by a nostalgia for the first phase. The group was marked by pessimism due, in part, to the gap between its ". . . hopes and a social crisis whose dramatic consequences they foresaw." In the Warsaw group, the elements of action remained unified by self-management in its phase two form (pp. 177-8).

Thus, the question, "does Solidarity look like a unified movement in sense two?" must finally be asked. The broad picture is that of a movement which is having trouble acting on its major public pronouncements. Within the local branches, widely differing concepts of the movement and its action are evident (except in Lodz and Wroclaw, where the capacity to act had collapsed). Does the action fit together anymore on a macro-level? Is it this disparity between stated goals and aspirations and possible actions, the lack of a focus of action, that causes this disarray on the local level? Can we state that these disparate branches constitute a unity any longer, or are they on the verge of disintegration and collapse of their capacity for action?

These and other questions could have been answered, if it had not been for the declaration of martial law. Yet, the evidence that Touraine *et al.* present concerning the third phase is not convincing regarding the question of whether or not the movement was maintaining its unity of action (sense two) throughout this period. We do not wish to argue that it was not in a process of inevitable disintegration during this phase, yet Touraine *et al.* present only inconclusive evidence on unity of action in phase three. Therefore, we cannot preclude the possibility that the disintegration of the movement was in process or that it was a syncretism held together by special circumstances (e.g., a voluntaristic notion of mutual solidarity between actors under coercive conditions learned through the experiences of the strike waves of the 1970s).[19] It is, of course equally possible that the movement could have summoned the strength and character that it had displayed on so many occasions to stem the tendencies toward disintegration had it not been for Jaruzelski's *coup d'etat.*

Michael Bernhard
Joseph McCahery

---

19.   For instance, Jacek Kuron stated at one point: "At this stage solidarity is more important than demands. If the authorities were to concede the demands and then, soon afterwards dismiss the workers' leaders from their jobs, they could easily go back on their promises as they have done in the past." See "Not to Lure the Wolves Out of the Woods: An Interview with Jacek Kuron." *Telos* 47 (Summer, 1981), p. 97.